Fodor's

E X P L O R I N G

ITALY

FODOR'S TRAVEL PUBLICATIONS, INC.

NEW YORK • TORONTO • LONDON • SYDNEY • AUCKLAND

Copyright © 1996 by The Automobile Association.
Maps copyright © 1996 by The Automobile Association.

Published in the United States by Fodor's Travel Publications, Inc.
Published in the United Kingdom by A.A. Publishing.

Fodor's and Fodor's Exploring Guides are registered trademarks of Fodor's Travel Publications, Inc.

ISBN 0-679-03010-7
Second Edition

Fodor's Exploring Italy

Author: **Tim Jepson**
Series Adviser: **Ingrid Morgan**
Joint Series Editor: **Susi Bailey**
Cartography: **The Automobile Association**
Cover Design: **Louise Fili, Fabrizio La Rocca**
Front Cover Silhouette: **Kevin Galvin**

Special Sales

MANUFACTURED IN ITALY
10 9 8 7 6 5 4 3 2

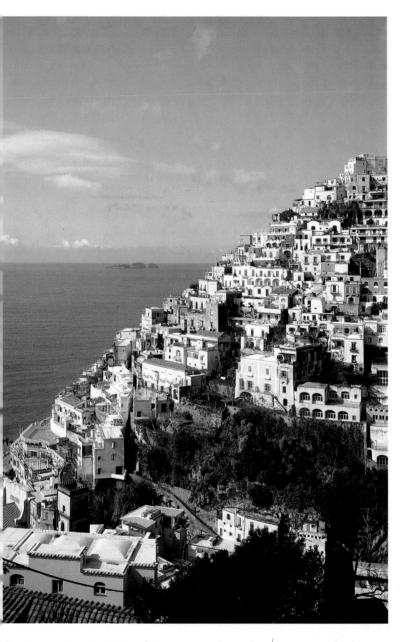

Positano, on the Amalfi Coast, Campania

Tim Jepson is the author of *Exploring Rome, Umbria—The Green Heart of Italy, Wild Italy, The Rough Guide to Tuscany and Umbria* and *Fodor's Italy by Train*. He has contributed to *The Rough Guide to Italy* and *Fodor's Italy*. Until 1989 he was the Rome correspondent for the London *Sunday Telegraph,* and he has also worked for the Italian section of the B.B.C. (British Broadcasting Corporation) World Service.

How to use this book

This book is divided into five main sections:

❏ Section 1: *Italy Is*

Discusses aspects of life and living today, from politics to the family.

❏ Section 2: *Italy Was*

Places the country in its historical context and explores those past events whose influences are felt to this day. This section also discusses important periods in Italian art.

❏ Section 3: *A to Z Section*

Is broken down into regional chapters, and covers places to visit, including walks and drives. Within this section fall the Focus-on articles, which consider a variety of subjects in greater detail.

❏ Section 4: *Travel Facts*

Contains the strictly practical information vital for a successful trip.

❏ Section 5:
Hotels and Restaurants

Recommended establishments throughout Italy.

How to use the star rating system
Most of the places described in this book have been given a separate rating:

▶▶▶ **Do not miss**

▶▶ **Highly recommended**

▶ **Worth seeing**

Not essential to see

Map references
To make the location of a particular place easier to find, every main entry in this book has a map reference to the right of its name. This includes a number, followed by a letter, followed by another number, such as 176B3. The first number (176) refers to the page on which the map can be found. The letter (B) and the second number (3) pinpoint the square in which the place is located. The maps on the inside front cover and inside back cover are referred to as IFC and IBC, respectively.

Contents

ALBEROBELLO
BARI (ITALY)
Nº 33925

6

This quick-reference guide highlights the features of the book you will use most often: the maps; the introductory features; the Focus-on articles; the walks and the drives.

Quick reference

Piazza Navona, Rome

Beppe Severgnini
Beppe Severgnini is 38 and was born in Crema, a small town in northern Italy. In 1981 after a law degree at Pavia University, he began a career in journalism and has worked for *Il Giornale, The Economist* and BBC Radio. Currently he is writing for *Il Corriere della Sera*. He is the author of four books, most recently *Un Italiano in America*.

My Italy

by Beppe Severgnini

Italians care more about what is beautiful than what is fair. They only obey the rules that they have privately decided are just and useful. They do not possess the two qualities—discipline and self-restraint—that help to bring about the perfect democracy. But they are hard working, resilient and resourceful, true masters of the art of *l'arrangiarsi* (in English: to manage, to get along), which has been for centuries a defense against the arrogance and the incompetence of those who set the rules.

Italians are realists to the point of cynicism, and have a sense of humor (you need a sense of humor when half of the people you voted for in 1992 are under investigation for corruption a year later).

Italians are passionately loyal to their friends and families. *La famiglia*, a concept that extends to distant relatives, is still the key to understanding modern Italy. Your family can help support you when you are sick and old. The family becomes, in other words, employment agency, bank and insurance company, shelter, hospital and old people's home. No bad thing, if you think about it.

I am prepared to say that my country, with all its problems, is sound at heart. We Italians are prone to being knocked out, but strong enough to bounce back, quite capable of getting ourselves into the most appalling mess—you can witness this every day, as soon as you open a newspaper—but smart enough to try and get out of it. Let's hope that, once again, we succeed. Wish us luck.

Aridea Fezzi Price
Aridea Fezzi Price was born in Italy, studied at the *Liceo Classico* in Milan and later in Paris, where she read literature and history at the *Institut Catholique*. She then lived for a while in Montreal with her Canadian husband. Now back in Europe she lives in London, Milan and Venice. She is a literary journalist and writer.

My Italy

by Aridea Fezzi Price

I am a Lombard, born in Cremona, a town with a stupendous medieval center on the River Po, and brought up in Milan. But the deep South speaks to my soul more than the arresting beauties of Venice, Florence and Rome. I love the chaos of Naples, where people are indeed tricky but have an amusing and warm sense of humor unknown in the North, the beautiful, misunderstood land of Calabria, the poor and dignified land of Basilicata, and Apulia with its magnificent romanesque churches and castles and delicious cooking. Above all I love Sicily, with its austere people, and its amazing cultural heritage.

What never ceases to surprise me about Italy is its immense variety. This peninsula, with its large, small and tiny islands, which before unification had a rich history of independent states and often enlightened rulers, offers the inquisitive traveler, Italian or foreign, an extraordinary diversity of experience.

My Italy is a splendid mosaic of cultures that are reflected not only in our inexhaustible wealth of art and architecture, in the variety of our cooking and in the unbeatable wisdom of the simple people. Yet it is a mosaic that can glitter only in its entirety, for only in its complexity can it explain our turbulent politics and our invincible love for life.

ITALY IS

"We have made Italy," said Cavour, founding father of the Italian state, "now we must make Italians." Some 130 years later, how many Italians, from the German-speaking burghers of Alto Adige to the blue-eyed Sicilians of Norman descent (unless united behind their soccer team), still feel bound by the idea of a single nation?

Stereotypes Everybody has a picture of the typical Italian: philandering Latin lover; son-smothering *mama*; pasta-bloated patriarch; louche Mafia Godfather; black-clad widow; deranged driver; sensuous sex siren (*à la* Sophia Loren). Picking national stereotypes is always a dangerous game, but in Italy it is especially fraught with pitfalls. The country was unified only 130 years ago, having been divided for centuries, a historical legacy that has produced countless regional variations of character. For every Italian who conforms to a stereotype, there is another who proves the exception to the rule.

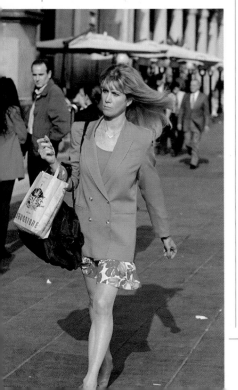

❑ "And don't, let me beg you, go with that awful idea that Italy's only a museum of antiquities and art. Love and understand the Italians, for the people are more marvelous than the land." E. M. Forster, British Novelist. ❑

Region by region The cool arrogance of the Florentines, for example, is at odds with the fierce honor of the Sicilians; the mild-mannered Venetians are a world away from the more abrasive Romans; and the dignified reserve of the Piedmontese contrasts with the mannered efficiency of the Milanese. Italians stand by their regions, proclaiming themselves Tuscans first and foremost, or Sicilians, Sardinians, Umbrians, Calabrians... Others are divided from compatriots by language and cultural tradition (German in Alto Adige, Slovene in Friuli, French in Piedmont, Greek and Albanian in Sicily and Calabria).

Characteristics Despite these contrasts we instinctively recognize Italians, not only from the way they look (fashion is a common denominator in Italy) but also from their outlook on life, whether a pragmatic aptitude for survival—born of constant political upheavals and foreign invasions—or a natural spontaneity and sensual self-indulgence in anything from food and friends to family and soccer. We admire their apparent free spirit while lamenting their occasional inefficiency—and wonder why, when most nations have something to teach, Italians seem to have much more.

The family

For all the Italians' intrinsic differences there is no doubt the family—though diminishing in size and losing its hierarchical rigidity—is still a major influence in the mainstream of Italian life. Mother and son are its pivotal members, children its sentimental axis, and marriage and death its dynastic climaxes.

History The family, with its ties of loyalty and obligation, is as much a metaphorical as a literal force, binding Italians to nearest and dearest rather than neighbor and nation. Its roots lie in Italy's agricultural past (when survival demanded cooperation), firmly grounded in Catholicism's teachings, and reinforced by times when it became essential to preserve family (or family-like) groups —either in the wake of emigration or in the face of outside interference.

Economic necessity Demography and social change are weakening family ties—witness Italy's drug problem and the numbers of old people living alone. Divorce and abortion are now readily available, and attitudes have been modified by the student and feminist movements of the last 20 years (less so in the more traditional south). Yet children often continue to live at home into their thirties—unable to move away to

study (there are few scholarships) and unable (or unwilling) to buy their first home alone. At least 65 percent of working Italians, moreover, are dependent on a family economy, a structure that still strongly binds extended families.

Mother and child *Mammismo*—the attachment of Italian men to their mothers—is as strong as ever. Christ, runs the old joke, was an Italian, brought up at home for 30 years in the belief that his mother was a virgin and he was the son of God. Psychologists say the search for a woman that replicates the mother's selfless devotion is the key to the Italian family, resulting in the south's elevation of virginity as the ultimate of feminine virtue, the male's constant philandering (and eventual return to the nest) and the matriarchal structure that, for all men's sexual braggadocio, leaves women the rulers of the Italian roost.

11

The Church

The Catholic Church has been bound up with Italian life for almost 2,000 years. Although now in apparent decline and no longer obsessed with political power, it still plays a part in national affairs and impinges —however subtly—on many aspects of day to day life.

Decline In many respects Italy is no longer a Catholic country. Although 97 percent of Italians are baptized, only around 10 percent regularly attend Mass. Divorce, abortion and birth control are freely available, and the Church's political influence is now almost negligible.

Christian focus At the same time, Italy qualifies as one of the holiest spots on earth, not only for its saints, shrines and churches (and myriad religious festivals) but also because it contains the Vatican. Attitudes towards the latter are ambivalent. On one hand it was Italy's only real unifying force after the fall of the Roman Empire, yet on the other it opposed political unification, only reluctantly

Religiosity on sale

relinquishing the Papal States in 1870. It is remembered as a poor ruler, bleeding regions dry and giving little in return—still a source of anti-clerical feeling in much of Italy.

Structure It is important to differentiate between the Vatican and the Catholic Church. The Vatican (with the pope at its head) rules 850 million Catholics worldwide (including those

in Italy), while the Italian Church is ruled by a cardinal and the Italian Episcopal Council (composed of 29 bishops). Overseeing all is the pope— *Il Papa* in Italian, from the Greek *pappas*, "father" (Pope John Paul II, elected in 1978, is the 263rd such spiritual successor to St. Peter). Pontiffs enjoyed political power until 1870, when they retired to the Vatican, only emerging in 1929 after Mussolini's Lateran Treaty (which formalized Church and State relations and created the independent Vatican territory). Once all 10 major posts in the Curia, or church government, were held by Italians: now only one or two are native incumbents, a measure of the degree to which Catholicism's power base has shifted away from Italy.

Pagan inheritance Italy's holy heritage goes back to ancient Rome's taste for myth, superstition and pagan observance. Wandering Rome's Forum you might have sampled dozens of recipes for salvation— Mithraism, Judaism, Christianity, Manichaeism, the worship of Isis, Osiris and Atargatis, even oddities like the cult of the goddess Cybele, whose priests were expected to indulge in ritual self-castration.

The burial of apostles Peter and Paul in Rome put Christianity firmly on the Italian map. Unable to shake off the pagan trappings of its antecedents, it merely incorporated them. Old festivals were given new names—December's *Saturnalia* became Christmas, Isis' day of the dead became November's All Souls' —and churches were raised all over Italy from the ruins of old temples. Incense, candles, holy water, even marriage rites were all adapted from various Roman ceremonies.

Eating is one of Italy's greatest pleasures. Its cuisine—fed by the natural bounty of land and sea—ranks among the world's greatest, and if the applause for its wines is less resounding, there are still good wines that perfectly match the simple genius of the cooking.

A culinary voyage around Italy is a pleasant surprise. There are many specialties unique to each region—and even if you stick to the classics, pizza or *spaghetti bolognese* taste better in their places of origin.

Restaurants The appearance of a restaurant has little to do with the quality of food offered. *Ristorante, osteria* and *trattoria* are now fairly interchangeable terms; a *tavola calda* or *pizzeria* is more humble (though the food can still be excellent). Nowhere do you have to wade through the entire menu (*la lista*)—Italians themselves often stick to a plate of pasta and salad; nor should you overlook bars and markets as sources of cheap snacks. Avoid fixed-price tourist menus—always a false economy.

Meals More expensive hotels may offer you the breakfast (*prima colazione*) you eat at home, but Italians tend to start the day with sweet croissants (*una brioche* or *un cornetto*) and coffee (*espresso* or *cappuccino* and *caffè latte*). In Sicily or German-speaking Alto-Adige, breakfast might include wine, salami, and grilled cheeses.

Lunch (*pranzo*) is no longer the extended and overblown occasion of days gone by. Save the big meal until evening and stick to something light—a picnic or bar snack with rolls (*panini*) and sandwiches (*tramezzini*). In bars

pay first for what you want at the cash register (*cassa*) and take your receipt (*lo scontrino*) to the counter, where a L200 tip slapped on the bar works wonders with the staff.

Full-scale meals start with *antipasto* (an *hors d'oeuvre*), followed by the *primo piatto* (first course), which may be soup, pasta or rice, and then by the main meat or fish dish (the *secondo*). Vegetables (*contorni*) or salad (*insalata*) follow separately and the meal is rounded off with cheese (*formaggio*), fruit (*frutta*) and/or a dessert (*dolce*).

Washing it down Italy produces more wine than any other country. The D.O.C. classification system is no real indicator of quality; ask instead for local wines (*vini locali*) or house wines (*vini della casa*), and treat yourself to more famous varieties in the appropriate regions—notably Piedmont (*Barolo* and *Barbaresco*) and Tuscany (*Chianti, Brunello* or *Vino Nobile*). Happily, standards are rising among small, independent producers (notably in Umbria, Trentino–Alto Adige and the Veneto).

Try firewaters like *grappa* at least once, as well as aperitifs (Cinzano, Campari and Cynar) and liqueurs like *amaro* (a bitter digestif), *amaretto* (a sweet almond-based drink) and the aniseed-flavored *sambuca*.

13

Turnout at Italian elections is higher than anywhere else in Europe, yet for all this apparent enthusiasm most Italians treat politics with the resignation or weary disdain it largely deserves. Only recently have corruption scandals and a crumbling of the old order challenged indifference to the system and made political progress a real possibility.

The system Italy has been a republic since a referendum in 1946, overseen by a largely symbolic president (who occupies Rome's Palazzo Chigi), and underpinned by a decision-making lower house, the Chamber of Deputies. Housed in Rome's Palazzo Montecitorio, this has around 630 deputies, of whom about 30 are ministers. Nearby lies the upper house (Palazzo Madama), comprised of 315 senators, made up of six representatives from each Italian region plus various lifelong senators, appointed for their service to the state (such as ex-presidents of the Republic).

Local government Italy's 21 regions (*regione*) also enjoy a large measure of self-government, some—usually those in "problem" or multiethnic areas—being semi-autonomous (notably Sicily, Sardinia, Trentino–Alto Adige and the Valle d'Aosta). Each region is divided into provinces (*provincia*), and each province is then further divided into a series of local councils (*comune*).

Publicity material for the Leghe

Democracy The Italian postwar political system rose from the ruins of Fascist dictatorship—with all the democratic frailties and insecurities that implies. Despite its many faults it has been behind (if not always directly responsible for) the transformation of Italy from an agricultural backwater to one of the world's leading industrial nations. Its institutions, if now looking increasingly moribund, were framed to prevent a throwback to Mussolini and seemed initially to match the country's particular needs.

Voting Voting is written into the Italian constitution as a "civic duty," being seen after the war as an act in support of the very idea of democracy. Failure to vote can in theory be marked on a citizen's criminal record. A complicated system of proportional representation led to the series of coalition governments whose corruption finally brought about their own downfall (see opposite page). In August 1993, parliament voted in an electoral reform bill, whereby 75 percent of both upper and lower houses are elected by a first-past-the-post system, the remaining 25 percent by proportional representation.

Italians also occasionally vote in referendums, held when 500,000 or more signatures are collected on an issue, a democratic device that decided such crucial issues as divorce and abortion in the 1970s and electoral reform in 1993.

A crooked waltz For all the 50 or so postwar governments in Italy elected under the old voting system, ultimate control remained all but unchanged, power and position being shared out around the coalitions in a gentle waltz of slowly changing partners.

The largest party, the broadly center-right *Democrazia Cristiana* (Christian Democrats), commandeered the four- or five-party coalitions, sharing the spoils of government with the Socialists (P.S.I.), Republicans (P.R.I.), Liberals (P.L.I.) and Social Democrats (P.S.D.)—and keeping out the popular Communists (now renamed *Partito Democratico*

❏ "And what is the prize eventually to be won? The rebirth of democracy. The glorious prospect of being able one day to choose their rulers from a list of powerful men, most of whose corruptions are already known and accepted with weary resignation."—Norman Lewis with the Allies in Italy in 1944. ❏

---

della Sinistra, Democratic Party of the Left). None of these parties has survived untainted by corruption, which has crept in largely under the cover of *clientelismo*—the hidden links, votes for favors, kickbacks and the like that have characterized Italian political life since Machiavelli, but which recently seem to have become too much even for the long-suffering Italians.

In 1993 politicians agonized over the formation of a new electoral system

Present and future Italian politics are currently undergoing a sea change. Scandal after scandal has revealed the breadth and depth of corruption, with the highest in the land, in politics and industry, under investigation for bribery, misappropriation of billions of lire—even murder. Such was the disgust with politicians that in April 1993 the President asked the respected governor of the Bank of Italy to form a government. Carlo Azeglio Ciampi was the first non-parliamentarian prime minister of Italy this century. New parties are springing up, notably the *Leghe* (Leagues), northern coalitions in favor of a federal Italy (see page 16), and *La Rete* (The Network), a southern-based party directed against political collusion with the Mafia. Further signs of public disenchantment with the old parties were seen in June 1993, when local elections brought large gains to the *Leghe* and the P.D.S. (former Communists), mainly at the expense of the Christian Democrats and Socialists. However, new parties have sprung up before, such as the Radicals and Greens in the 1970s, and there is some doubt—especially given Italian bureaucracy's Byzantine obduracy—whether the present upheavals really mark the death throes of old-style Italian politics.

Geography and history have always handicapped southern Italy—which starts somewhere between Rome and Naples—leaving it not only considerably poorer than the north but also the victim of an unholy trinity comprised of prejudice, corruption, and organized crime.

Problems Some of the south's problems will never go away. Little can be done to alter Italy's shape, which leaves the region far from markets, thus crippling industrial initiative; nor to alter the south's harsh climate, which leaves agriculture hamstrung; nor to change its geology, which offers nothing by way of energy sources or raw materials. Nor, it appears, can much be done to tackle the Mafia, whose tentacles strangle legitimate enterprise and discourage long-term investment.

Calabrian women

Potential for change Others of the south's problems can perhaps be resolved, principally those that are rooted in the autocratic Spanish regimes (from 1559) that stifled the south for centuries—corruption, poor education, crumbling infrastructure and latent feudal hierarchies. Money has been thrown at the region for decades, every so often hitting its targets—notably in eradicating malaria and in building new roads—but more often than not falling into the pockets of Mafia barons.

Emigration The south has known two great periods of emigration: the first to the United States at the turn of the century, the second to the industrial heartlands of the north (Milan, Turin and Venice), where cheap southern labor fueled the economic boom of the 1950s and '60s. While boom has hardly turned to bust—they say Italy without the south would be Europe's richest country—southerners are now resented by some with a virulence which amounts to racism.

New bigotry Northerners have always looked with mock horror on the south. In the wake of recent political disillusionment, however attitudes have taken a more ugly turn. Graffiti warns *terroni* (peasants) to go home (or worse), and there has been growing support for the *Leghe* (Leagues), increasingly popular political parties who—angered at what they see as the north subsidising the south—argue for a more federal, even partitioned, Italy. This is unlikely to happen, but the longing—130 years after unification—is a symptom of some greater malaise in the Italian soul.

Symbol of the prosperous north

Italy has long hummed with a babel of dialects descended from Greek, Latin, and the languages introduced by foreign invaders over the centuries. Regional differences still define Italian character, but the advent of mass media is gradually eroding the country's linguistic diversity.

History Italian draws the bulk of its vocabulary from Latin, and is still the closest of the Romance languages to its Roman roots. It has evolved in its present form from the educated language of Tuscany, primarily because this was the regional dialect used by great medieval writers such as Dante, Petrarch and Boccaccio. Even today an Italian saying describes how "Tuscans polish the air around them," and the best Italian is said to be *la lingua toscana in bocca romana* (a Tuscan tongue in a Roman mouth).

Usage For all its occasional verbosity, Italian is one of the world's most beautiful languages, its musical cadences more seductive to the heart than the mind. Its particular spell was well captured by Charles V, the Holy Roman Emperor, in the famous observation that he spoke Spanish with God, French to his courtiers, German with his horse, and Italian to women. He might have added that Italian is one of the best languages for displays of anger and passion.

Dialects Italy's particular shape, its remote mountain enclaves and its past have all fostered an estimated 1,500 different dialects. In fact, it is estimated only two percent of Italians

are unable to speak some form of dialect. Some even speak a different language, notably in the Valle d'Aosta (French), Friuli (Slovene) and Alto-Adige (German). The Venetian dialect has words of Spanish and Portuguese origin (a legacy of its seafaring tradition). Lombardy's has German imports (having been ruled by Austria), while Piedmont's is heavily laced with French. Spanish and French crop up in Neapolitan, while a bastardized Greek and

Albanian is spoken in parts of Calabria. Sicily boasts a sprinkling of Arabic, French and Spanish; so does Sardinia, which has its own language, Sardo (as well as a Catalan enclave in Alghero). And small pockets of *Ladino* (Ladin) are still spoken in certain remote Alpine valleys. In as little as a generation, however, with the leveling influence of television, Italy may find itself speaking a standard Italian, its dialects no more than quaint memories.

Movies are among Italy's major contribution to mainstream 20th-century culture. They not only influenced a generation of postwar moviemakers, but also defined a very particular image of Italy with movies like *La Dolce Vita* and stars such as Sophia Loren , Marcello Mastroianni and Isabella Rossellini.

Epics and escapism Italian movie-making launched itself in Turin with blockbusting silent movies like Enrico Guazzoni's *Quo Vadis?* (1913), before moving to Rome—to take advantage of its climate and ready-made locations—where lack of funds and its head-on encounter with Fascism saw it crash to near oblivion in the 1930s. Movies made under Fascist auspices were usually ideologically approved propaganda or the so-called *telefoni bianchi*, named after the white telephone that always appeared in the heroine's bedroom—symbol of the exotic Hollywood fairytale for Italians who had never owned a telephone, and much less a white one.

Neorealism Rome's great studios, Cinecittà, were opened by Mussolini in 1938 with the words "cinema is our greatest weapon." Cinecittà became Italian cinema's spiritual home, inhabited after the war by a generation of young moviemakers whose new-found freedom produced the revolutionary genre known as Neorealism (which greatly influenced American *films noirs* and the French New Wave of the

1960s). Its earliest exponents were Luchino Visconti (*Ossessione*, 1942) and Roberto Rossellini, whose *Roma, Città Aperta* (1945), with its real locations, visceral style, jerky camerawork and almost documentary footage, prepared the ground for classics in the same genre such as Vittorio de Sica's *Ladri di Biciclette* (*Bicycle Thieves*, 1949).

To the present day Tastes changed during the boom years of the 1950s and 1960s, when the Neorealists' mantle was taken up by Federico Fellini, Francesco Rosi and Michelangelo Antonioni (though Pier Paolo Pasolini continued to chronicle the new underbelly of Italian urban life in movies like *Accatone* and *Una Vita Violenta*). Fellini's distinctive view is seen in *La Strada* (1954), *La Dolce Vita* (1960) and *Otto e Mezzo* (*8½*, 1963). Antonioni is perhaps best known for *Blow-Up* (1966), an English-language movie. Later moviemakers such as Bertolucci (*The Last Emperor, Last Tango in Paris*) and the Taviani brothers (*Good Morning Babylon*) also filmed in English. Cinecittà's reputation, meanwhile, grew fat on American epics like *Ben Hur* and *Cleopatra*, before television and rising costs reduced it to peddling "spaghetti westerns," soft porn and money-making potboilers. Of recent hits, perhaps the most familiar to foreign audiences is Giuseppe Tornatore's *Cinema Paradiso*, set in Sicily, though old-timers like Bertolucci are still making movies.

Top: Roma, Città Aperta
Left: Ossessione

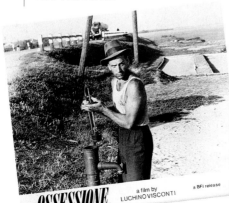

OSSESSIONE
a film by LUCHINO VISCONTI   a BFI release

Italy's archeological record goes back over half a million years to early Stone Age hunters. Generations came and went, leaving few traces of their passing, until the advent of the Greeks and Etruscans, who brought Italy into the light of history. Soon a great civilization was born.

Prehistory The first modern human remains found in Italy date from pale-olithic times around 20,000 BC. More advanced cultures made their appearance between 3000 and 1800 BC, notably the Ligurians (who settled modern-day Liguria), the Siculi (Lazio and southern Italy) and the Sards (who developed a pastoral culture in Sardinia). They were followed by migratory peoples, principally the Picini and Messapians, who crossed the Adriatic from the Balkans, as well as the Veneti, Latins and Umbrii, who moved down the peninsula from the north.

Phoenicians and Carthaginians By 800 BC the Phoenicians had drifted along the African coast and estab-lished colonies in Sicily and Sardinia (introducing an alphabet into Italy for the first time). One of their leading African cities, Carthage, eventually became a power in its own right, establishing footholds in southern Italy, Sicily and Sardinia at about the same time as Greek and Etruscan influence emerged elsewhere.

Greeks The first Greek colonies on Italian soil were established around 735 BC in Sicily, eventually develop-ing into a network of independent cities all over southern Italy known as Magna Graecia (Greater Greece). Despite internecine wars and con-flicts with the Carthaginians (in Sicily) and the Etruscans (in Campania), the colonies immeasurably enriched Italy's indigenous cultures in the realms of art and architecture. In agriculture, they introduced two great staples—the vine and the olive.

Etruscans The Etruscans occupied much of present-day Lazio and Tuscany, in an area roughly bounded by the Arno and Tiber rivers (though they occasionally expanded beyond these borders). Where they came from is one of history's great myster-ies, but they were probably a mixture of indigenous and foreign peoples, who became linked by a common language. They assimilated neighbor-ing tribes (like the Ligurians and Umbrians) to forge a loose political (and religious) affiliation based on a 12-city confederation. Like the Greeks, they were culturally, techno-logically and agriculturally advanced, though militarily they were to prove no match for the Romans, who by about 350 BC had all but defeated their leading cities.

Engraving depicting a Phoenician merchant fleet

The rise of Rome

After obscure beginnings Rome conquered its Greek and Etruscan neighbors, its sophisticated republican structure evolving through periods of social disorder into an empire that endured almost a thousand years and whose limits touched almost every corner of the known world.

Beginnings According to legend, Romulus founded Rome in 753 BC However, the city's earliest archeological remains date from around 1200 BC (though it may be 2,000 years older). By 900 BC Rome formed the border between the Etruscan and Latin spheres of influence, possibly ruled until around 600 BC by the Tarquins, an Etruscan royal dynasty.

The Republic The Etruscan kings were ousted by the Romans in 509 BC and replaced by a Republic (*res publica*), where in theory the "people were kings." In practice the city was riven by disputes between the plebeians (the lower classes) and the patricians (the military and political elite). The plebeians were partly placated by the tribune (494 BC), a magistracy that looked after their interests, and an uneasy consensus allowed Rome to expand, first into Etruscan and Samnite territory, and then into Greek-dominated southern Italy.

Right: Julius Caesar
Below: The Roman Forum

The Punic Wars Rome's expansion inevitably brought it into conflict with Carthage. The struggle for supremacy took the shape of three protracted campaigns—the Punic Wars—the first of which (264–241 BC) saw Rome seize control of Sicily, Corsica and Sardinia. In the second (218–202 BC), Carthage dispatched Hannibal and his army—elephants and all—across the Alps to inflict defeats on Rome at Cannae and Trasimeno. Scipio Africanus at last defeated Hannibal at Zama in 202 BC. The Third Punic War (149–146 BC) left Rome master of the Mediterranean and territories as far flung as Jerusalem and Asia Minor.

Julius Caesar In Rome the city's internal divisions simmered on. Popular revolt exploded in the Social Wars (90–88 BC), bringing about an increasingly authoritarian response from the Senate. The general Sulla was installed to restore order, followed by Pompey, who with two other leading figures—Crassus and Julius Caesar—formed the First Triumvirate (60 BC).

The Roman Empire

Julius Caesar became dictator of Rome, but it was his grandnephew and adopted son and heir, Octavius, who first assumed the title of emperor (as Augustus). He ushered in a period of reforms, public works and military consolidation that saw Rome emerge as the cultural, religious and political center of the known world.

The Ides of March Caesar's military prowess eventually made him pre-eminent, a dictatorial position he used to heal the scars of a century's civil strife. Institutions were reformed, and new temples and civic buildings blossomed. Jealousy mounted, however, and in 44 BC, on 15 March (the Ides), he was assassinated.

Assassination of Julius Caesar

The age of Augustus The Second Triumvirate—Lepidus, Mark Antony and Octavius—was then formed. Designed to wage war on Caesar's assassins, it soon became a battle-ground for control of the empire. Antony compromised his chances by dallying with Cleopatra, leaving the field clear for Octavius, who sealed his position with victory at the Battle of Actium in 31 BC. He took the title of *princeps* in 27 BC, changing his name to Augustus Caesar. The Augustan Age was to mark the high point of the Roman civilization.

The Emperors Few subsequent emperors were as successful as Augustus (27 BC–AD 14), but the immense spoils accruing from the empire masked their more grotesque deficiencies. Three of the more decadent incumbents were—Tiberius (14–37), Claudius (41–54) and Nero (54–68)—followed in turn by the Flavians (Vespasian, and his sons Titus and Domitian), under whom the Empire enjoyed a period of relative peace and prosperity. This golden age continued under the Antonines, the great military emperors Trajan (98–117), Hadrian (117–138) and Marcus Aurelius (161–180).

Decline and fall After Aurelius' death, revolts broke out against the Roman yoke across the empire; emperors came and went with increasing rapidity; cultural life stagnated; and political, military and economic institutions teetered on the brink of collapse. Diocletian divided the empire in two (East and West), and the empire briefly stabilized under Constantine, whose Edict of Milan (313) allowed Christians freedom of worship. In time the capital of the Western Empire was moved to Ravenna (with Constantinople the capital in the East).

The Mausoleum of Augustus, Rome

The Dark Ages

Neither the Dark Ages nor the various waves of barbarians who swarmed into Italy after the fall of the Roman Empire were as black as they are usually painted. Today, however, little evidence remains of the Goths, Franks and Lombards who dominated the peninsula for more than three centuries.

Barbarians Raids by "barbarians" (the word meant outsiders, or foreigners) had preoccupied Rome for centuries, but as the empire floundered they became more organized, and the empire did less to withstand them. When Rome itself was sacked in 410 by Alaric the Goth, a tremor was felt around the civilized world. Subsequent incursions came to a head in 476, when Odoacer the Goth displaced the last Western Emperor, Romulus Augustulus. In 493 Theodoric, another Goth, seized Ravenna, and with it control of the old empire's western territories.

Byzantines Constantinople— modern Istanbul—prospered as the capital of the Eastern Empire (Byzantium), and to a large extent escaped the turmoil that marked the demise of its western counterpart. Between 536 and 552 its emperor, Justinian, retook large areas of Italy (through his famous general Belisarius), in the so-called Gothic Wars. As a result, Byzantine influence dominated parts of the country for centuries. At the same time the Church took advantage of uncertain political times to assert an increasing influence on Italian affairs.

Lombards and Franks Territorial gaps left by the Byzantines were partly filled by the Lombards (568–774), a race from the north, who established three duchies in Italy centered on Pavia, Cividale and Spoleto. They were later joined by the Franks, a Christian race from Gaul, whose loyalties were divided between two rival factions—the

Carolingian and Merovingian dynasties. Pepin the Short, a Carolingian, resolved the division in 754 by appealing to Pope Stephen III, who sanctioned his rule by anointing him with holy oil (a symbolic gesture of immeasurable consequence). In return, Pepin and his son, Charlemagne, defeated the Lombards (774), handing over large areas of conquered territory to the papacy. These papal states became the source of the papacy's temporal power. On Christmas Day in 800 Charlemagne was crowned "Emperor of the Romans" by Pope Leo III, an act which forged enduring links between the popes and northern-based emperors and guaranteed centuries of conflict.

23

Charlemagne, Holy Roman Emperor

The centuries following Charlemagne's death saw a struggle for ascendancy between the papacy and the Holy Roman Empire. With the popes claiming the right to crown emperors, and the emperors the right to sanction popes, opposed camps began to emerge across Italy—the Guelphs (papal supporters) and Ghibellines (imperial supporters).

Rival powers The Frankish empire disintegrated, but the office of emperor stayed intact—though emperors increasingly remained in their northern power bases, entering Italy only intermittently in attempts to assert imperial authority. While the fortunes of empire and papacy waxed and waned, there were rarely periods when they were not at one another's throats.

Tit for tat The most famous encounter came in 1076, when Emperor Henry IV rejected Pope Gregory VII and his proposals for radical political reforms. Gregory in turn excommunicated Henry, thus—in theory—freeing faithful catholics from imperial allegiance. Although this squabble was resolved diplomatically, others were to be more violent, notably the rampaging campaigns of Frederick I (Barbarossa) against northern Italian cities from his base in Germany in 1155. Papal

fortunes hit rock bottom in the 14th century with the move of the Church's capital from Rome to Avignon, followed by the Great Schism, when three rival popes vied for recognition.

Arabs and Normans While northern Italy swayed between pope and emperor, events in southern Italy followed a more orderly path. The Saracens (Arabs) invaded Sicily in 827 and assumed control for two centuries. Elsewhere the Byzantines held sway until supplanted by the Normans (11th century), who arrived in the region as mercenaries. They carved out a kingdom (including Sicily) under Robert Guiscard and his successors Roger I and Roger II.

Anjou and Aragon The marriage of a Norman princess and Emperor Henry VI brought the south within the imperial orbit. Unfortunately the Norman kingdom had been legitimized by the papacy, thus creating the same power struggle that dogged papal and imperial relations in the north. Italian-born emperor Frederick II briefly dominated the south in defiance of the papacy, but his heirs were defeated by Charles of Anjou (1265), brother of the French king, who received Naples and Sicily as a "gift" from a grateful papacy. The Anjous (Angevins) ruled most of the south for two centuries, except for Sicily, which they forfeited to Spain (Peter III of Aragon) after the uprising known as the "Sicilian Vespers" in 1282. In 1442 Alfonso V of Aragon was named heir to the last of the Angevins, and the south was united under Spanish control until the 18th century.

GREGORIVS·VII·PAPA·SAONENSIS

The city states

City states have been a constant feature in Italian history, but they reached their zenith during the 14th century—when 400 of them stretched across the north of the country—riding high on increased trade and the relative decline of papal and imperial authority.

Climate for change Rivalry between pope and emperor left a power vacuum in which cities could evolve independently. This was especially true after 1300, when few emperors could combine control of Italy with their dynastic obligations in northern Europe. For the papacy's part, after a dispute with Philip of France, it fell under French domination, and in 1307, hopelessly compromised and subordinate, moved to Avignon under the protection of the French kings (The Great Schism).

Meanwhile, the maritime republics (Amalfi, Pisa, Genoa, and Venice) and cities which stood on trade routes (Bologna, Milan, Verona, and Florence) grew rich on commerce.

The Comune Many cities initially developed a quasi-democratic structure known as the *comune*, a ruling council consisting of merchants, guildsmen and minor nobility. As cities prospered, they acquired magnificent *palazzi* and cathedrals. This was the period of Dante (1265–1321), Petrarch (1304–74) and Boccaccio (1313–75), all pillars of Italy's literary tradition, and of the first stirrings of artistic change heralding the Renaissance.

The Signoria As cities fought one another, or were fractured by internal power struggles, they increasingly abandoned the *comune* and looked to one man (*signore*) to cut through the muddle. Despotic rule followed, usually under a powerful noble, merchant or *condottiere* (a mercenary employed by the cities to fight on their behalf). Thus rose the Visconti (Milan), Gonzaga (Mantua), Este (Ferrara), Montefeltro (Urbino), Medici (Florence) and many other powerful families.

An agreement in 1455 between Italy's major powers—Milan, Florence, Venice, Naples and the papal states—cemented a period of calm that lasted until the death of Lorenzo de' Medici in 1492. Thereafter Italy became a pawn in the hands of foreign players—first France and Spain, then Austria.

France France entered the equation in 1494 when the Duke of Milan, after a quarrel with the Neapolitan king, invited Charles VIII of France to conquer the Kingdom of Naples. Charles for his part claimed the throne on the basis that his Anjou ancestor formerly ruled Naples and southern Italy (see page 24). He captured the kingdom easily, but stayed only three months, after which it was regained for Spain by Ferdinand II of Aragon. A later French king, François I, took Milan in 1515, basing his claim on a marriage between a Visconti (former rulers of Milan) and the French royal family.

Napoleon in all his glory

Spain Spain joined France in the scramble for territory in Italy in the person of Charles V (1500–58), Holy Roman Emperor and Habsburg heir to the Austrian and Spanish thrones. His troops ransacked Rome in 1527, and defeated the French at Pavia (1526) and Naples (1529). The Treaty of Cateau-Cambrésis (1559) ratified Spanish rule over Sicily, Sardinia, southern Italy, Milan and parts of Tuscany for 150 years. France held other pockets, leaving only Venice and the papal states independent of foreign powers. It was against this background that the great religious movements of the Reformation and Counter-Reformation were played out.

Austria and Napoleon Spain's stranglehold slackened following the War of the Spanish Succession, which saw Lombardy, Mantua, Naples and Sardinia pass by treaty to the Austrians (1713). Machinations later in the 18th century saw further realignments (Lorraine took Tuscany, Piedmont was ruled by the Savoys, and in 1734 the Spanish Bourbons took southern Italy). Austria meanwhile remained in control of the north under Maria Theresa (1740–80) and her son Joseph II (1780–92).

All changed with Napoleon's Italian campaigns in 1796 and 1800. He succeeded in conquering the Italian peninsula, establishing a republic. Though it was short-lived, it reduced papal power, reformed feudal hierarchies, and—perhaps most importantly—suggested the potential for a single Italian state. The Vienna Settlement (1815) restored Austrian control, but over the next 50 years did little to halt the momentum of the unification movement.

Three obstacles lay in the path of a unified Italy—Austria (who ruled northern Italy), the papacy (rulers of central Italy) and the Spanish (rulers of Sicily and the south). Although unification was ultimately engineered by Italian patriots, it was only made possible by conflict and collusion between foreign powers.

Leading players Unification's Italian protagonists were Giuseppe Mazzini (1805–72), a political agitator, and Giuseppe Garibaldi (1807–82), an inspired military leader. Both favored linking royal and republican efforts towards unification, the former spearheaded by Count Camillo Cavour (1810–61), prime minister of Piedmont, an independent kingdom ruled by the Savoys. Externally, Napoleon III of France was motivated by concerns for French Catholics and the survival of the papacy. Britain favored the end of Spanish (Bourbon) domination in southern Italy, and Austria was opposed to unification at the expense of its position in northern Italy.

Garibaldi, military genius of unification

The 1859 campaigns In 1859 Cavour engineered an alliance with Napoleon III against the Austrians, joining the French armies to those of Piedmont (under the Savoy king, Vittore Emanuele II). The Austrians were defeated at Magenta and Solferino, after which Napoleon III—to Cavour's frustration—signed an armistice with them. Meanwhile, revolts elsewhere had gathered a momentum of their own, with uprisings in Tuscany and Emilia, both of which were annexed by Piedmont (along with Lombardy, won at Solferino).

Unification In 1860 the job of unification was only half complete. To finish it, Garibaldi left Genoa with 1,000 volunteers (the *Mille*) to overthrow the Bourbons in the name of Vittore Emanuele II. Sicily and Naples fell within four months, the papal states surrendered to Cavour, and the Kingdom of Italy was proclaimed in February 1861. The Austrians were removed from Venice and the Veneto in 1866 (defeated following an alliance with Prussia), and Rome and the papacy were taken in 1870 after the withdrawal of the French garrison (precipitated by the fall of Napoleon III, defeated by Prussia that year in Sedan).

The 1848 Republics Revolutionary unrest swept over all of Europe in 1848. In Italy, it sparked off a war against Austria in Lombardy (under Carlo Alberto, the Savoy king), and the restoration of Venice's Republic of San Marco (again in defiance of the Austrians). In Rome, the pope fled from rioting and Mazzini established the Roman Republic (Garibaldi organized the city's defenses). The republics were short-lived. Austria crushed the northern uprisings and French troops relieved Rome, restoring the *status quo* of a year earlier.

Italy entered both world wars in the hope of territorial gain—after piecemeal colonial expansion in Eritrea, Libya and Abyssinia. Success in 1918 bred only debt and disappointment, and gave rise to Fascism, while failure in 1943—ironically—laid the foundations of progress and the country's present prosperity.

World War I At the start of the Great War, Italy was neutral, but by 1915 had joined the Allied cause, lured by promises of colonial rewards and the chance of gaining the partly Italian-speaking regions around Trento and Trieste. Its ill-prepared army lost several bitterly fought battles, notably at Caporetto in 1917, before a last-ditch victory at Vittorio Veneto. Although denied certain territories, Italy's gains at the peace conference included (present-day) Trentino-Alto Adige and Friuli-Venezia-Giulia, though at a high cost: national assets fell by 26 percent, and 40 percent of the 5½ million Italians who fought were killed or wounded.

Fascism Italy's government was unable to deal with the social and economic chaos unleashed by the war, creating a power vacuum quickly filled by Benito Mussolini, whose high-sounding promises pandered to the panic-stricken middle and upper classes. A threatened general strike in 1922 provided the excuse for his "March on Rome," after which—fearful of civil war—the king handed power to Mussolini (who had an intimidating mob presence on the streets, but still only a tiny showing in parliament itself). By 1925 Italy was ruled by a dictatorship, held together with bluster and brute force, and bolstered by imperial adventures in north Africa.

World War II After a hesitant start, Mussolini took Italy to war in June 1940, emboldened by Hitler's success and eager to share in the spoils of victory. After successes in the Adriatic, he suffered defeats in Greece, heavy casualties in Russia and the loss of Sicily (August 1943), all of which led to his downfall and an armistice with the Allies. The Nazis assumed control, installed Mussolini as the head of a puppet republic, and confronted the Allies—and a force of 450,000 partisans—as they inched up the Italian peninsula to liberate Rome on June 4, 1944. Mussolini's end came in April 1945, when he was shot and strung up in Milan's Piazzale Loreto.

Fêting the triumphant Mussolini

Italy's progress since World War II has been remarkable, developing in less than a generation from an agricultural backwater to one of the world's leading industrial nations. In its wake, however, the transformation has brought social tensions, terrorism and the inexorable rise of organized crime.

The Fifties A referendum in June 1946 voted narrowly (54–46) to replace Italy's monarchy with a republic. With the help of Marshall Aid from the United States, the hardships of the immediate postwar years gave way to an economic boom bolstered by cheap, compliant labor and most Italians' thirst for the world of cars, televisions and material well-being. This was the era of *la dolce vita*, Sophia Loren, baby Fiats, and mass migrations from the south to the industrialized cities of the north. In 1957 the Treaty of Rome was signed, and Italy became a founding member of the European Community.

The Sixties The boom tailed off somewhat in the 1960s, and the orthodoxy of past governments (dominated by the center-right Christian Democrats) gave way to coalitions in which the left demanded a voice. Inflation soared, and social tensions surfaced, the bitter fruit of Italy's sudden wrench from traditional ways of life. Unrest culminated in the *autunno caldo* (hot fall) of 1969, when strikes and student demonstrations crippled the country.

The Seventies Matters became worse in the next decade, when at times it appeared Italy was on the brink of disintegration. Right- and left-wing terrorism was rife, culminating in 1978 with the kidnap and murder of Aldo Moro, a former prime minister, by the *Brigate Rosse* (Red Brigades). These were the so-called *anni di piombo* (years of lead), named after the period's weight of bullets, but also evocative of the gloomy and apocalyptic mood of the times.

The Eighties and Nineties By about 1985 the economy steadied and terrorism was all but defeated. Italy continued to prosper (at least in the north) despite its upheavals and political scandals, progress occurring despite rather than because of its institutions. Today, however, after almost 50 years of corrupt government, the country seems to be approaching the millennium with a heartfelt desire for institutional reforms. If it succeeds, and the problems of the Mafia and the south are addressed, Italy may finally solve this century's problems in time for the next century.

Rome, April 1968: student protests were brutally put down by riot police

Italy's artistic heyday may not have been the Renaissance, but the centuries when Greek, Etruscan and Roman artists and sculptors produced their classical masterpieces. These still lie scattered across the country's museums and archeological sites.

Greek influences Greek art came to Italy with the colonies of Magna Graecia around 800 BC (see page 231), making its mark on much of southern Italy and influencing the Etruscan and Roman cultures that followed for more than a millennium. Particularly influential were the temple architecture of Sicily and southern Italy (Paestum provides supreme examples), and the semicircular Greek theaters, fine examples of which survive in Taormina and Siracusa. Hellenistic painting, in contrast, has almost vanished, though its influence permeates the tomb paintings and decorated vases of Etruscan culture. Sculpture was immensely significant, and Greek bronzes and ceramics also served as models for Italian craftsmen.

Etruscan art While borrowing from Greek models, Etruscan art retained a distinct character, its often earthy naturalism in marked contrast to the idealized strivings of Greek artists. Tomb paintings survive in Tarquinia and Chiusi, mixtures of visionary, realistic and superstitious tableaux, testimony to the Etruscans' vivacious and outward-looking culture. Bronze and terracotta, rather than marble, were favored for sculpture (perhaps because the materials were readily available), producing beautiful and sophisticated pieces, many of which are now on display in Rome's Vatican and Villa Giulia museums. Little is known of Etruscan architecture, though it probably made use of the arch and vault, forms later adopted by the Romans.

The Romans Roman art's debt to Greece and Etruria was immeasurable, from the use of mosaics and Etruscan sarcophaghus reliefs to the masterpieces of Roman sculpture copied from Greek originals. The derivative nature of Roman sculpture in no way detracts from its often sublime execution, but for originality one must look to Roman architecture (and engineering) with innovations such as the basilica, triumphal arch, and commemorative column. There are Greek borrowings in the Colosseum and Pantheon, and in villas, palaces and baths, but all are unmistakably Roman. Wall paintings, widespread in their day, but surviving mainly as fragments uncovered at Pompeii and Herculaneum, also showed a Hellenistic bent.

Etruscan vessels of exquisite workmanship

The stylized Madonnas and mosaic tradition of Byzantium look stilted today, but they were to influence Italian art until at least the 13th century. Together with aspects of Roman art and architecture, they formed the backbone of Christianity's earliest artistic tradition.

Old forms, new themes Christianity presented art with new themes and iconography, and was to be its chief inspiration until the Renaissance. In its earliest incarnations Christian art remained wedded to the prevailing tastes of the day: sculptures graced a few sarcophagi; paintings, except in a handful of catacombs, were rare—though it may be that early Christian artifacts have been lost. Church architecture aped the forms of Roman aisled basilicas, often relying for decoration on mosaics, the most prominent medium of early Christian art. Early mosaics—those of Rome's 4th-century Santa Costanza, for example—followed classical Roman models, but most quickly adopted the more highly colored attributes of Byzantine models.

Byzantium Byzantine art was a hybrid of classical and oriental influences, introduced by Justinian, emperor of the eastern half of the Roman Empire, when he invaded parts of Italy in the 6th century (see page 23). It was distinguished by abstraction, gold backgrounds and a profusion of ornamental motifs, usually seen in the form of mosaics. Notable examples are found in Ravenna (Byzantium's Italian capital), Rome (Santa Maria Maggiore and elsewhere), Milan (Sant'Ambrogio) and Aquileia (the Basilica). Not only did Byzantium's artistic influence spread over a wide area, it also proved remarkably durable, and Byzantine-influenced craftsmen were still producing mosaics in the 12th century (principally in Palermo's Cappella Palatina, the cathedrals of Cefalù and Monreale, and—most famously—in Venice's Basilica di San Marco, the apotheosis of Byzantine art, architecture, and decoration).

Byzantine painting Byzantium's influence pervades three images that dominated Italian painting until the 14th century: portraits of saints; the iconic Madonna and Child; and

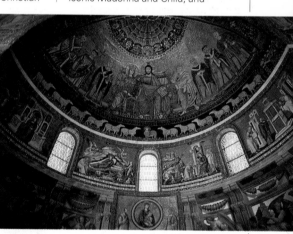

Santa Maria in Trastevere, Rome

Christus Triumphans, a large painted crucifix of Christ. All were distinguished by a mystical or reverential tone and stiff, formalized figures, with little attempt at verisimilitude. Byzantium is also ever-present in an often overlooked but vital artifact of the Dark Ages—the illustrated monastic manuscripts that carried art's banner for centuries.

Apart from beautiful mosaics and illustrated manuscripts, Italy's most conspicuous artistic flowering, as the country emerged from the Dark Ages, was primarily in the Romanesque churches and then in the Gothic palaces and cathedrals that accompanied the growth of independent city states.

32

Romanesque Romanesque architecture emerged during the 11th century, fostered by the upsurge of church building in the emerging city states. Northern European (Lombard) and Italianate influences combined to produce a style distinguished by simplicity, round arches, and thick-walled buildings with cross vaults or exposed beam ceilings. Churches often had a basilical plan, with a raised choir and correspondingly sunken crypt.

Decoration was simple, usually confined to the apse or main portal, but often extended to separate campaniles and baptisteries.

The style emerges all over Italy, particularly in Lombardy (Modena, Parma and Cremona),

Milan cathedral, northern Italian Gothic at its finest

around Pisa (Lucca and Pistoia), in Sicily (Cefalù, Palermo and Monreale) and in Apulia, where Arab, Byzantine and Norman elements combined to create the hybrid known as Apulian-Romanesque (Bari, Ruvo, Trani, Troia and elsewhere). Masterpieces of Romanesque sculpture include the reliefs of Wiligelmus in Modena, Antelami's work in Parma, the doors of San Zeno (Verona) and the works of the Pisanos across central Italy.

Gothic Where Romanesque architecture was robust and earthbound, the Gothic, which originated in 13th-century France, was light and airy. Its emphasis was on verticality, its staples the pointed arch, rose windows, stained glass, rib vaulting and flying buttresses. In Italy, Milan's Duomo, with its pinnacles and soaring lines, best shows the genre in all its characteristic glory.

Elsewhere, a lesser version of the Gothic appeared, its grandeur suited to the desire of cities to make conspicuous displays of their new prosperity. It distinguished the civic palaces (*palazzi pubblici*) of Siena (the Palazzo Pubblico), Florence (Palazzo Vecchio) and Venice, whose Palazzo Ducale captures Italian Gothic at its most dazzling. The style also emerged in the great cathedrals of central Italy, notably Pisa, Siena, Florence, and in the Basilica di San Francesco in Assisi (1228), an early Gothic masterpiece.

During the Gothic period the Renaissance was prefigured by a handful of artists and sculptors who cast off the conventions of Byzantine art to sow the seeds of artistic renewal. It was also at this time that regional schools began to develop a style that, while working on familiar lines, breathed new life into old traditions.

Sculptors Nicola Pisano (*c.* 1220–84) was the first of a trio of 13th-century artists whose marriage of Gothic and classical ideas was a harbinger of things to come. His graceful, sinuous style can be seen in four outstanding works—Fontana Maggiore (Perugia), Arca di San Domenico (Bologna) and pulpits in Pisa (the Baptistery) and Siena (the Duomo). Pisano's pupil and assistant, Arnolfo di Cambio (*c.* 1245–1310), disseminated his influence in works scattered all over central Italy, though the influence of Pisano's son, Giovanni Pisano (*c.* 1248–1314), whose figurative skill was revolutionary, was of still more resounding significance.

Painters Glimmerings of a new artistic dawn began with men like Pietro Cavallini (active 1273–1308), who began to explore the possibilities of fresco. After working in Rome (Santa Maria in Trastevere), he moved to the Basilica di San Francesco in Assisi, where he was joined first by Cimabue (*c.* 1240–1302), whom

Vasari dubbed the "father of Italian painting," and then by Giotto di Bondone (1266–1337), a seminal figure in the development of Italian art. Giotto introduced emotion, natural settings and narrative detail into his paintings (fresco cycles in Assisi and Padua in particular) that broke decisively with the stilted and stylized strictures of Byzantine art.

33

Above: Nicola Pisano's Fontana Maggiore in Perugia.
Left: detail from Siena cathedral

Siena While Giotto preached innovation in Assisi's Basilica, the artists of Siena were reinterpreting the Byzantine tradition, forging the most dynamic of the schools of painting that sprang up across central Italy during the 13th and 14th centuries. Glorious swathes of color and gold backgrounds dominated its early masterpieces, exemplified by the works of Duccio di Buoninsegna (*c.* 1255–1318). These features were later wedded to the courtly and beautifully detailed style enshrined in the paintings of Simone Martini (*c.* 1284–1344) and Pietro Lorenzetti (active 1306–45).

A serendipitous mixture of social, artistic and intellectual ferment gave rise to the *Rinascimento* (Renaissance), which spread from Florence over the course of 125 years to become one of the greatest periods in the history of western art.

What and why Several closely related factors helped bring about the Renaissance—the "rebirth" of art and science. Humanist scholarship freed art of its devotional obligations and rediscovered Greek and Roman texts, from which it was a short step to a revival of the classical ideal in art. Where conservative Church patronage had previously stifled innovation, lay patrons like the Medici provided the financial wherewithal for voyages of artistic discovery. Free-thinking Florence, a prosperous and cosmopolitan city, provided an atmosphere in which creativity could flourish, attracting ever more artists as its reputation snowballed. And as more artists arrived, the exchange of ideas and atmosphere of innovation intensified (particularly in crucial areas such as the study of anatomy and perspective).

Florence Three artists in three key disciplines ushered in the Florentine Renaissance. Filippo Brunelleschi (1377–1446) triumphed as an architect, not only creating a

dome for the city's cathedral, but also clarifying ideals of design and advancing the new science of perspective. The sculptor Donatello (1386–1466) produced staggeringly innovative work, returning the nude to the mainstream of artistic expression. And in painting Masaccio (1401–28)—together with Masolino da Panicale—pioneered techniques of perspective that dazzled contemporaries. An army of hallowed names followed—Paolo Uccello, Fra Angelico, Filippo Lippi, Benozzo Gozzoli, Luca della Robbia, Verrocchio, Ghirlandaio and Sandro Botticelli (not to mention architects like Michelozzo, Sangallo and Leon Battisti Alberti).

Outside Florence Florence did not have a monopoly on Renaissance talent. Piero della Francesca, from the Tuscan town of Sansepolcro, produced singular works that combined ethereal beauty with compositional precision. In Cortona, his pupil Luca Signorelli painted influential work distinguished by striking nudes. The Marches claimed Venetian-bred Carlo Crivelli, while neighboring Umbria had Perugino, responsible for melancholy, soft-edged devotional paintings (sometimes executed in tandem with another Umbrian, Pinturicchio). Siena's masters included sculptor Jacopo della Quercia and

Ghirlandaio's Adoration *in Florence's Santa Trinita*

The Raphael Rooms in the Vatican Museum in Rome contain some superb frescos

painters Sassetta and Giovanni di Paolo. Elsewhere, other artists of genius included Mantegna (Mantua), Correggio (Parma), Lorenzo Lotto (Lombardy), Tura (Ferrara), Melozzo da Forlì (Forlì), Pisanello (Verona) and Antonello da Messina (Sicily).

High Renaissance Much as three innovators tower over the Renaissance's formative years, so a trio of artistic geniuses dominate its maturity—the so-called High Renaissance—a period that begins at the turn of the 16th century with the painting of Leonardo da Vinci's *Last Supper* (in Milan). The end of Florence's artistic primacy was marked by Michelangelo (1475–1564), who left his Medici patrons to work in Rome, where papal patronage was the spur for the frescos of the Sistine Chapel—perhaps the supreme achievement of western art. Another consummate genius lured to Rome was Raphael, born in Urbino, apprenticed to Perugino, and responsible for such masterpieces as the Vatican's *Stanze di Raffaello* (Raphael Rooms). Paragons of High Renaissance architecture included Bramante, Baldassare Peruzzi, Sangallo the Younger, Sansovino and the great Andrea Palladio (1508–80).

Mannerism Following the Sack of Rome by the troops of Emperor Charles V in 1527, Renaissance self-confidence gave way to the self-conscious and disquieting world of Mannerism, a genre—part-inspired by Raphael and Michelangelo—that put art above nature, valued style above substance, and flouted the conventions of scale, color and composition. Its leading lights were Pontormo, Bronzino, Rosso Fiorentino, Benvenuto Cellini, Andrea del Sarto, Domenico Beccafumi (from Siena), Parmigianino (from Parma) and the sculptor Giambologna.

Venice Venice charted a course of its own during the Renaissance, its artists more concerned with color and atmosphere than the Florentine preoccupations with line and composition. Early on, the Vivarini family of artists (Antonio, Bartolomeo and Alvise) emphasized the city's debt to Byzantine art and the opulent courtly style known as "International Gothic." Another dynasty, the Bellinis, Giovanni Bellini in particular, marked the city's Renaissance heyday (together with Carpaccio). Venetian painting reached renewed heights during the High Renaissance with painters like Titian, Tintoretto, Paolo Veronese and Giorgione—the last as mysterious in his way as Piero della Francesca.

Born in Rome, and nurtured by papal largesse, baroque—the artistic expression of Counter-Reformation optimism—may have been named after the irregularly shaped pearls known in Italian as *perle baroche*. In the words of Luigi Barzini, it "came to be used metaphorically to describe anything pointlessly complicated, otiose, capricious and eccentric."

Architecture Baroque's first star, Carlo Maderno (1556–1629), responsible for the façade of St. Peter's, was soon outshone by the two giants of the period—Gianlorenzo Bernini (1598–1680) and Francesco Borromini (1599–1667). Bernini transformed the face of Rome, infusing everything—from fountains to St. Peter's monumental piazza—with his exuberant *joie de vivre*. Borromini, his bitter rival, was more tortured and introspective (he eventually committed suicide) but proved the more innovative—even more eccentric—architect. Lacking Bernini's sculptural skill, he was famous instead for his sophisticated geometry and exotic combinations of shapes (best seen in Rome's Sant'Ivo, San Carlo and Sant'Agnese).

Sculpture In sculpture Bernini knew no rivals, his genius apparent from an early age in such works as *Apollo and Daphne* and the *David* in Rome's Galleria Borghese (Italy's first important sculptures since Michelangelo's final works). His masterpiece, *The Ecstasy of St. Teresa* (in Rome's Santa Maria della Vittoria) captures fully the period's emphasis on emotion and stylized drama, his own

Bernini's St. Teresa, *pierced by the arrow of divine love*

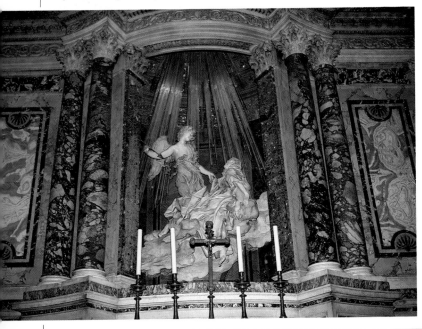

The powerful David *of Bernini in the Galleria Borghese*

Painting The baroque spawned two broad schools of painting, the first dominated by Caravaggio (1573–1610), whose vividly realistic works displayed virtuoso effects of light and shade (*chiaroscuro*), the second championed by the Carracci family (Ludovico, Annibale and Agostino), whose works signaled a return to the clarity of classical models. Ornate and illusionist ceiling frescos were also a feature of the age, and in Pietro da Cortona (1596–1669) they found their chief exponent, best known for work in Rome's Palazzo Barberini (other masters of the art included Bernini's protégé G. B. Gaulli and Andrea Pozzo). Naples proved a hotbed of baroque endeavor, producing artists such as Luca Giordano, Salvator Rosa and Artemesia Gentileschi, one of Italy's finest woman painters.

passion for illusion and sensuality, and—above all—the intense spirituality of Teresa's ecstatic vision of God. Alessandro Algardi challenged Bernini briefly, but the period's other principal players operated outside Rome—in Turin (Guarini and Juvarra), in Lecce (Zimbalo) and in Catania, Noto and Ragusa in Sicily.

St. Peter's Rome. Above: the baldacchino; *below: the piazza*

The last three centuries of Italy's artistic history are often written off as a sad anti-climax, yet Italian artists produced two new styles—neoclassicism and Futurism—and excelled in another (rococo). Today, Italian artists still manage to make Italy one of Europe's leading centers of fashion and design.

38

The 18th century Art and architecture reacted in different ways to the baroque. While architecture turned away from its excesses to find refuge in neoclassicism, a return to the most basic of classical principles (notably in Rome), painting turned to the still more florid and opulent world of rococo, a sensually obsessed style born in France that in Italy found its greatest expression in Venice. Though stripped of its political pre-eminence the city was still a wealthy, even decadent retreat, capable of producing and patronizing artists such as Sebastiano Ricci, the great Giovanni Battista Tiepolo (1696–1770), and three leading landscapists, Francesco Guardi, Bernardo Bellotto and Canaletto (1697–1768). Neoclassicism's more restrained outlook found its way into painting, but was more marked in sculpture, as in the erotic works of Antonio Canova (1757–1822).

The 19th century Neoclassicism continued its architectural march in the 19th century, but in painting it was largely outflanked by the Europe-wide Romantic movement, whose Italian trendsetter was Francesco Hayez (1791–1882)—almost the country's only notable artist for several decades. The middle of the century saw the emergence of the *Macchiaioli* (from the Italian *macchia*—spot or stain), a group of painters whose use of color marked a reaction against the polish of neoclassicism and shared the modern outlook of the French Impressionists (leading artists included Lega, Fattori and Signorini). All were overshadowed by Amedeo Modigliani (1884–1920), the best known of Italy's more recent artists (though most of his life was spent in Paris).

The 20th century Art nouveau took a glittering hold in Italy, where it was known as *Lo Stile Liberty*; examples can still be seen in the galleries of Milan and the turn-of-the-century interiors of cafés in Turin, Trieste and elsewhere. In painting, Futurism—which was founded by Italians in Paris (in 1909)—aimed to capture and glorify the dynamism of the new mechanical age, its style pioneered by Umberto Boccioni (1882–1916), and developed by Gino Severini and Giacomo Balla. Elements of Futurism, fused with Cubist ideas, are found in the Surrealist works of Italy's last big "name" in painting, Giorgio de Chirico (1888–1978).

de Chirico's The Melancholy of Departure

ROME

The Trevi Fountain

Essentials

Rome (Roma) We expect a lot of Rome—seat of empire, mother of civilization, *caput mundi* (head of the world). It is the city of the Caesars, of romance, the city of *la dolce vita* and languorous sunny days, the city of endless art, of churches and museums, of fountain-splashed piazzas and majestic monuments to its golden age of empire. Sadly, it is also the city of uncontrollable traffic, the city of frenetic noise and confusion, the city of wanton crowds, obstinate bureaucracy and groaning inefficiency. Its 20th-century face is not a pretty one, and to get under its rumpled skin requires an oblique approach to sightseeing.

Seeing the city Head-on confrontation with Rome, however energetically you join the fray, always leaves you dispirited and defeated. Plan ahead, therefore, don't attempt too much, don't tackle its streets in the heat of the afternoon. Avoid the temptation to join the trudge around the famous sights. Avoid St. Peter's and the

Sistine Chapel; forget the Colosseum and the Pantheon, at least in the beginning. Reflect instead over a quiet *cappuccino* in Campo dei Fiori, the city's loveliest square. Forgo the Spanish Steps' aimless mob and climb to the Pincio Gardens for a view over the rooftops to St. Peter's. Thus initiated you can prepare for the assault on the Vatican museums, or the stroll around the Forum; you can face the traffic and the chaos—and perhaps in time even come to enjoy them as dynamic aspects of a city that is struggling, as it has for centuries, to incorporate the present into its eternal past.

Layers of history Rome belongs to no single historical period. Its sights and quarters are a lavish medley of ancient, medieval, Renaissance, and modern buildings, making it difficult to define areas, or to plan your sightseeing around a single epoch. In the earliest days Rome gathered around seven famous hills—the Aventino, Capitolino, Esquilino, Caelio, Palatino, Quirinale and Viminale. Later, Augustus created several *rioni*, a series of wards like Paris' *arrondissements*. Neither of these divisions, however, adequately defines the present city.

Areas of the city Piazza Venezia is now Rome's hub, a junction of streets that strike off to the four points of the compass. The *centro storico* (Historical Center) is not, confusingly, the Forum and the ancient heart of Rome, but a warren of streets that made up the city's core from the Middle Ages to the last century. Contained between the Tiber and Via del Corso, it divides into a medieval quarter (north of Corso Vittorio Emanuele II) centered around Piazza Navona and the Pantheon—and a Renaissance district (south of Corso Vittorio Emanuele II), centered around Via Giulia and Piazza Farnese. The latter contains the Ghetto, one of the city's most captivating areas (the streets east of Via Arenula). Across the river is **Trastevere** ("across the Tiber"). Once Rome's 19th-century slum— and still seedy in places—it is now generally a charming area, especially good for aimless wandering, restaurants, and evening entertainment. To its north lies **Vatican City**, centered around St. Peter's, an independent state under papal control. Nearby stretch the leafy residential districts of Prati and Parioli.

Romulus and Remus This is the myth about Rome that everyone knows. It begins in the old Latin capital *Alba Longa*, where Amulius usurped the throne of his brother Numitor. To avoid rival claims Amulius forced Numitor's only daughter, Rhea Silvia, to become a vestal virgin. A visit from the god Mars left her pregnant with Romulus and Remus. Amulius cast the twins adrift in a basket, but the gods steered them safely to the Palatine, where a she-wolf cared for the pair until they were found by a shepherd. Told of their destiny by Mars they founded Rome in 753 BC. The brothers could not agree whether to name the city *Rema* or *Roma*—but Romulus started building his walls regardless. Incensed, Remus jumped over them and was killed by his brother.

Weekend's itinerary

Saturday
Breakfast in Campo dei Fiori (walk: Ghetto–Isola Tiberina–Piazza Bocca della Verità–Campidoglio). *Morning*: Campidoglio, Forum, Colosseum, San Clemente (San Giovanni in Laterano). Lunch (walk: Colle Oppio–Foro Traiano–Fontana di Trevi). *Afternoon*: Fontana di Trevi, Santa Maria sopra Minerva, Pantheon, Piazza Navona (walk: Via dei Coronari–Via Governo Vecchio/shopping: Via Condotti, Via del Corso). *Evening*: Walk/bus to Trastevere (Santa Maria in Trastevere, Santa Cecilia). Dinner in Trastevere.

Sunday
Breakfast in Piazza Navona (walk to Castel Sant'Angelo). *Morning*: (Castel Sant'Angelo), St. Peter's, Vatican Museums. *Afternoon*: (Walk: to Piazza del Popolo). Pincio, Piazza di Spagna.

43

Etruscan bronze of a she-wolf in the Capitoline Museum. The human twins were added later.

Colonna Traiano
Trajan's Column was built in AD 113 to celebrate Trajan's victories over the Dacians (tribes from present-day Romania). Its great spiraling frieze contains 2,500 figures and 18 huge drums of Greek marble. The reliefs have provided a wealth of information about Roman arms and modes of warfare.

Vestal Virgins
Vestal Virgins were the guardians of Rome's sacred flame. They were chosen, before they reached the age of 14, from Rome's leading patrician families. Up to 30 years were spent in service, after which they could retire on a state pension. The only man allowed in their temple was the Pontifex Maximus, or high priest. His title— "Greatest Bridge Builder"— was adopted by the popes, hence the abbreviation *Pont Max* on many papal buildings.

Roman Monuments

▶▶   **Ara Pacis Augustae**   *40E3*
Via di Ripetta
The "Altar of Peace" was raised by the Senate in 13–9 BC to commemorate the victories of the Emperor Augustus. Its superb reliefs include mythological scenes and episodes from the altar's ceremonial consecration.

▶▶   **Arco di Costantino**
         (Arch of Constantine)   *41A6*
Piazza del Colosseo
The largest and best preserved of Rome's ancient arches was raised to honor the victory of the Emperor Constantine over Maxentius in AD 312. Many of its reliefs were taken from earlier monuments, partly for practical reasons, and partly to link the Emperor's regime to the glories of the past. The battle scenes, for example, show Trajan at war with the Dacians.

▶▶▶   **Castel Sant'Angelo (see page 46)**   *40E1*

▶▶   **Catacombe (Catacombs)**   *41A6*
Rome has over 480 miles of catacombs, the underground tombs of pagans and early Christians. The best are the **Catacombe di San Callisto** (*Via Appia Antica*) with 170,000 graves; others are the nearby **Catacombe di San Sebastiano,** and those of Domitilla and Priscilla.

▶▶▶   **Colosseo (Colosseum) (see page 50)**   *41A6*

▶▶   **Fori Imperiali**   *41B5*
Via dei Fori Imperiali
The five imperial fora were built by successive emperors after the Foro Romano and Palatino became too small. The best are the Foro di Augusto and Foro Traiano. The latter contains the great **Colonna Traiano**▶▶▶ (Trajan's Column) and the **Mercati Traianei**▶ (Trajan's Market).

▶▶▶   **Foro Romano (Roman Forum)**   *41A5*
The old heart of the Roman empire is crowded with the jumbled ruins of temples, basilicas and other buildings spanning 1,100 years—a wonderfully evocative place to wander in. Be sure to see the **triumphal arches**▶▶ of **Tito** and **Settimio Severo**, the mighty **Basilica di Massenzio**▶▶▶, and the **Tempio di Vesta**▶▶▶ (Temple of the Vestal Virgins).

▶▶▶   **Palatino**   *41A5*
Via dei Fori Imperiali-Via di San Gregorio Magno
The Palatine hill was the first of the famous seven hills to be inhabited. In time it became the favored residential district of Rome's elite, including emperors. Most buildings are now badly ruined, or buried under the beautiful 16th-century **Orti Farnesiani**▶▶ (the Farnese Gardens).

▶▶▶   **Pantheon**   *40C3*
Piazza della Rotonda
This, the grandest monument of Roman antiquity, built by Hadrian in AD 128, became a Christian church in 609 (one

reason for its remarkable state of preservation). The immense cupola was the largest free-standing dome in the world until as late as 1960.

► **Teatro di Marcello** 41B4

Via del Teatro di Marcello

When Augustus built this theater in 11 BC it must have been as impressive as the Colosseum—which it closely resembled. Used as a fortress in the Middle Ages, it now stands bizarrely over-built with medieval houses.

► **Terme di Caracalla** 41A6

Via delle Terme di Caracalla

The Baths of Caracalla (AD 206) were not as large as the Baths of Diocletian (remains of which you can see around Piazza della Repubblica), but they were more luxurious and are far better preserved. They could accommodate 2,000 bathers, and many thousands more in the complex of sports and leisure facilities nearby.

►► **Via Appia Antica** 41A6

Via Appia Antica

Rome's "Queen of Roads" was built in 312 BC and connected the city with Capua and Brindisi in southern Italy. Today it still has many of its original cobbles (see below), and is lined by ancient tombs and catacombs. Much of the route is delightful to drive down or wander along—a little piece of countryside only a stone's throw from the city.

The classical splendor of the Pantheon

Coffee and ice cream
Immediately off the Pantheon's Piazza della Rotonda is **La Tazza d'Oro** (Via degli Orfani 84), generally considered to sell Rome's best cup of coffee. One minute's walk north is the **Gelateria della Palma** (Via della Maddalena 20), known for its 100-plus flavors of ice cream.

The Ghetto
The area west of the Teatro di Marcello is the old Jewish Ghetto (created in 1555). The area contains some of the city's quietest and nicest backstreets. Wander here during siesta or in the early evening. A good stroll is from Campo dei Fiori along Via Giubbonari and Via Portico d'Ottaviano to explore the picturesque streets of the Ghetto. Be sure, too, to see Bernini's delightful Fontana delle Tartarughe (Fountain of the Tortoises) in Piazza Mattei.

The cobbled surface of the 2,300-year-old Via Appia Antica

Elegance and force: the Ponte Sant' Angelo leading to the Castel Sant'Angelo

Paolina Borghese
Numerous myths attach to Canova's erotic statue of Paolina Borghese, doubtless because of the knowing sensuality of its subject —bare-breasted, hips half-draped in veils and a pose of haughty yet come-hither languor. Paolina was as slyly seductive in life as in art, and caused a lot of gossip with her jewels, her clothes, her long line of lovers, the servants she used as footstools and the black attendant who carried her from the bath.

Museums & Galleries

►►► Castel Sant'Angelo 40E1
Lungotevere Castello
Built as the tomb of the Emperor Hadrian (AD 139), the great circular bulwarks of the Castel Sant'Angelo have been used over the centuries as prison, barracks, papal fortress, and now a museum, interesting both for its precious works of art and the labyrinth of imperial tombs, state rooms, and endless nooks and crannies that honeycomb the interior.

►► Galleria Nazionale d'Arte Antica-Palazzo Barberini 41E6
Via delle Quattro Fontane 13
This is Rome's foremost art gallery, most famous for Raphael's *La Fornarina*, but also home to paintings by old masters including Fra Angelico, Perugino, Filippo Lippi, Tintoretto, Holbein and El Greco. The sumptuous gallery's rooms are attractions in their own right, notably the tremendous **Gran Salone►►►**, dominated by Pietro da Cortona's exuberant ceiling frescos.

►►► Galleria Borghese 41E5
Villa Borghese-Via Pinciana
Only the Vatican offers a grander art collection than the Galleria Borghese. Its many highlights include Canova's *Paolina Borghese* and outstanding masterpieces by Bernini: *David, Apollo and Daphne*, and *The Rape of Prosperine*. On the upper floor (closed for restoration), the paintings include Raphael's masterly *Deposition* and fine works by Caravaggio and Pinturicchio.

►►► Musei Capitolini (Capitoline Museums) 41B5
Piazza del Campidoglio
Two museums face one another across Piazza del Campidoglio. **Palazzo Nuovo►►►** contains many masterpieces of classical sculpture, principally the *Dying Gaul*, *Capitoline Venus* and *Amor and Psyche*. Sculptures in the

Palazzo dei Conservatori▶▶ across the way include the *Spinario*, the *Esquiline Venus* and the *Capitoline Wolf*. Upstairs, the **Pinacoteca Capitolina▶▶** has fine paintings by, among others, Caravaggio, Van Dyck, and Titian.

▶▶▶ **Musei Vaticani** (see pages 48–49)   *40D1*

▶▶ **Museo Nazionale Romano**   *41D6*

Piazza dei Cinquecento-Piazza della Repubblica (due to move to Palazzo Massimo)

This museum incorporates part of the Terme di Diocleziano, the largest baths built in ancient Rome. The museum's vast collection includes numerous classical artifacts, most notably the **Ludovisi throne**, part of a 5th-century BC Greek altar.

▶▶ **Palazzo-Galleria Doria Pamphili**   *41C4*

Via del Corso-Piazza del Collegio Romano 1a

With over 1,000 rooms, this is one of Rome's largest palaces. Only part is open to the public, four large galleries crammed with paintings that include works by Titian, Raphael and Caravaggio. Its most famous canvas is a portrait of *Innocent X* by Velázquez. Worthwhile guided tours offer glimpses of the palace's other private apartments. (The gallery is open only Tuesday and Friday to Sunday 10AM–1PM.)

▶▶▶ **Villa Giulia (Museo Nazionale Etrusco)**   *41E5*

Viale delle Belle Arti

This museum holds the world's most exhaustive collection of Etruscan art and artifacts. The villa in which it is housed is an attraction in its own right. Highlights include the *Sarcofago degli Sposi* (Sarcophagus of the Married Couple); the giant terracotta statues of *Apollo and Hercules*; the many urns and vases; and a panoply of jewelry, household utensils and other objects.

Museo di Palazzo Venezia
This modern museum occupies the second floor of the Palazzo Venezia (Via del Plebiscito). It houses splendid Italian, German and Flemish tapestries, and a miscellaneous collection of medieval art, sculptures, ceramics, jewelry and other artifacts.

Stroll
Walk from Piazza Navona to the Pantheon by way of the church of San Luigi dei Francesi, Piazza Sant'Eustachio and the church of Sant'Ivo alla Sapienza.

Inside the Galleria Borghese. Much of its collection was accumulated by Cardinal Scipione Borghese.

Vatican City is an independent sovereign state in the heart of Rome. Although it has museums which are open to the public, most of the 106-acre principality hides behind high walls and is out of bounds to all but a privileged few.

The Swiss Guard
The Vatican's 90-strong army is designed to protect the papal person. Recruited from Switzerland's four Catholic cantons, the guards must be aged between 19 and 25, be at least 5ft. 7in. tall, and remain unmarried during their tours of duty. Their striped uniforms, designed by Michelangelo, bear the medieval colors of the Medici popes (red, yellow, and blue).

48

Vatican City About 200 people live and work in the world's smallest state (only 30 of them women); 800 "foreigners" commute in daily. The state is ruled by Europe's only absolute monarch, Pope John Paul II, and has its own judicial system, stores, bank, currency, post office, garages —even its own radio station and daily newspaper (the *Osservatore Romano*). Its official language is Latin.

Musei Vaticani (Vatican Museums) The museums, the largest in the world, include the Sistine Chapel, the Raphael Rooms and at least a dozen self-contained museums. The most important is the **Museo Pio-Clementino**, housing some of the greatest works of classical sculpture. The finest are in the Cortile Ottagono: the *Apollo Belvedere* and the incredible *Laocoön* group. The **Museo Gregoriano-Etrusco** contains some of Italy's best Etruscan artifacts, notably the *Mars of Todi* and *Head of Athene*. The **Pinocoteca** has Rome's greatest paintings, with works by Giotto, Fra Angelico, Filippo Lippi, Leonardo, and Raphael.

The **Cappella di Nicolò V** contains sublime frescos by Fra Angelico. Five dark rooms with outstanding frescos by Pinturicchio (1492–5) form the **Appartamento Borgia**. The **Museo Gregoriano Profano** is a museum of pagan art, mainly classical sculpture, while the **Museo Missionario Etnologico** has a fascinating collection of artifacts brought together from missionary expeditions all over the world.

Raphael Rooms (Stanze di Raffaello) Raphael's frescos, commissioned by Julius II in 1503, are one of the masterpieces of the Renaissance. The **Stanza della Segnatura** (Room II) is the most celebrated and was the first to be painted. Its four main frescos are allegories of Theology, Philosophy, Poetry, and Justice. The **Sala dell'Incendio** (Room I) was the last to be executed, by which time Leo X was pope. Raphael celebrated Leo's papal namesakes, painting the *Coronation of Charlemagne* (performed by Leo III); the *Oath of Leo III*; the *Battle of Ostia* (where Leo IV showed mercy to the defeated Saracens); and the *Fire in the Borgo*, where Leo IV (actually a portrait of Leo X) extinguishes a fire by making the sign of the Cross. Room III's frescos describe episodes where Divine Providence has intervened to defend the Christian faith, notably Leo I (again Leo X in disguise) *Repulsing Attila the Hun*.

Cappella Sistina (Sistine Chapel) Michelangelo's frescos in the Sistine Chapel are the pinnacle of European artistic achievement. The 1,116 square yard-ceiling (1508) took four years to complete, the artist lying recumbent most of the time to paint. The newly restored frescos divide into nine sections, arranged chronologically. The first describe five

A Fra Angelico in the Vatican Museum

Side walls
The Sistine Chapel's side walls are often overlooked. These were painted in 1481–3 by leading artists such as Perugino, Botticelli, Pinturicchio, Piero di Cosimo, Ghirlandaio, and Luca Signorelli. Many are collaborations. Panels on the left as you face the altar show scenes from the life of Christ, on the right scenes from the life of Moses.

key events from the Book of Genesis: *The Separation of Light and Darkness*; *The Creation of the Heavens*; *The Separation of Land and Sea*; *The Creation of Adam*; and *The Creation of Eve*. After them come: *The Fall and Expulsion from Paradise*; *The Sacrifice of Noah*; *The Flood;* and *The Drunkenness of Noah*. The *Last Judgment* on the rear wall was painted 20 years later, and shows Christ in the center with the damned sinking to the right, the saved rising heavenward on the left. Around Him are the Virgin and saints.

Papal audiences
To join the 7,000 or so at papal audiences each Wednesday, apply for a ticket from the Prefettura della Casa Pontifica (through the bronze doors in the right-hand colonnade of Piazza San Pietro, open Monday and Tuesday 9–11).

49

The Colosseum

The most magnificent of Rome's ancient monuments was started by the Emperor Vespasian in AD 72 and was completed seven years later by his son, Titus. The Colosseum was inaugurated (in the taste of the times) with a gala in which no fewer than 5,000 animals were slaughtered in one afternoon, followed by over 100 days of continuous games and other entertainment.

A trendsetter
An architectural and engineering marvel, the Colosseum's arena has provided the model for large stadia ever since. Over 50,000 spectators could leave their seats within minutes through the 76 numbered exits or *vomitoria*. On the upper levels, a huge movable sailcloth (*velarium*) could be winched into place to shade spectators from the sun.

On stage Contrary to myth, the stage was probably not used to kill Christians. It was, however, used for a variety of violent and decadent gladiatorial games (the Romans took the idea of gladiators from the Samnites and Etruscans, who used them originally to train soldiers for battle).

Men, women—even dwarfs—fought each other (and animals) to keep the crowds entertained. The arena could also be flooded to stage mock sea battles. Audiences often exercised the power of life and death. They could reply to a fighter's appeal for mercy (raising a finger on the left hand) with a waving of handkerchiefs (a reprieve), or with the notorious thumbs-down. Survivors, if they were criminals, often had their throats cut anyway.

Days of ruin The games were finally outlawed in AD 438. Fires and earthquakes then began to take their toll on the arena. The clamps holding the massive travertine blocks were removed in AD 662–4, leaving the distinctive holes that punctuate the exterior today. Over the Middle Ages huge amounts of stone were pillaged to build the city's churches and palaces. Preservation only began in 1744 when the area was consecrated and a cross erected in memory of murdered Christians.

Below stage in the Colosseum

Churches

▶ **Gesù**　　　　　　　*41C4*

Piazza del Gesù

The Gesù is the principal church of the Jesuits. Initiated by the movement's founder, Ignatius Loyola, it was designed by Vignola and Giacomo della Porta. Both its plan and façade (1575) were to be imitated in later churches all over Europe. The overwhelmingly rich interior has works of art by Bernini, Pozzo, and Pietro da Cortona.

▶ **Sant'Andrea al Quirinale**　　　*41D6*

Via del Quirinale

Sant'Andrea is a baroque jewel. It was designed by Bernini and was one of his favorite churches. Many of its ideas were unique at the time (1658–71), notably the two-columned portico and stretched-oval floor plan. The aristocratically elegant decoration largely relates to the martyrdom of Sant'Andrea (St. Andrew).

▶ **San Carlino (San Carlo alle Quattro Fontane)**　　　*41D6*

Via del Quirinale

Bernini's great rival, Borromini, designed San Carlino (1634–8). It is another baroque masterpiece, but expresses the idiom in a completely different style from that of neighboring Sant'Andrea. The interior is crammed with details, shapes and symbols, all bound with precise geometrical patterns. The same inspired use of space is found in the cloisters, also by Borromini.

Santa Cecilia
Cecilia—*coeli lilia* (The Lily of Heaven)—was martyred around 303. The executioner's three axe blows—all he was allowed under Roman law—failed to remove her head. She survived for several days, converting many to the faith before dying of her wounds (Maderno's statue of her clearly shows the three sword cuts). Cecilia is the patron saint of music, having reputedly invented the organ ("to enlarge her prayer"), and sung during her execution.

▶▶ **Santa Cecilia in Trastevere**　　　*41A3*

Piazza di Santa Cecilia

Santa Cecilia dates largely from 824, but the interior was disastrously remodeled between 1725 and 1823. Its gardens and 12th-century portico are still enchanting. The apse contains 9th-century **mosaics** and an altar canopy by Arnolfo di Cambio (*c.* 1293). There is a fine statue of St. Cecilia by Stefano Maderno (1600). The cloister has fresco fragments of Pietro Cavallini's important *Last Judgment* (1293).

▶▶▶ **San Clemente**　　　　　*41B6*

Via di San Giovanni in Laterano

San Clemente comprises three distinct levels. The present church has the city's finest medieval interior (1130), with superb 12th-century mosaics, pulpits and frescos by Masolino da Panicale (*c.* 1428). The lower 8th-century church has faded (but important) early frescos. Below it lie the ruins of a Mithraic temple.

Santa Cecilia in Trastevere

▶▶▶ **San Giovanni in Laterano**　　　*41B6*

Piazza di San Giovanni in Laterano

San Giovanni (not St. Peter's) is Rome's cathedral church. It was founded by Constantine in 313, and although much has now been restored, it still remains immensely impressive. The **cloisters▶▶▶** with their Cosmati marblework are one of Rome's loveliest spots. The much-copied octagonal **Baptistery▶▶▶**, adapted from 5th-century Roman baths, is the earliest in Christendom. The church was damaged by a terrorist bomb in 1993.

Bocca della Verità
The "Mouth of Truth" is a weatherbeaten stone face once used by the Romans as a drain cover. According to tradition, anyone suspected of lying would have their hand forced into the gaping mouth (*bocca*). If they were lying the mouth would clamp shut, severing their fingers. A priest supposedly hid behind the stone to chop the hands of those known to be lying. Oaths and business deals were sworn and settled here.

▶▶▶ San Luigi dei Francesi 41D3
Piazza di San Luigi dei Francesi
The French church of Rome (1589) has a single great treasure, a chapel containing three paintings by Caravaggio (5th chapel on the left). All three deal with events from the *Life of St. Matthew*, showing the painter's earthy realism and *chiaroscuro* techniques to virtuoso effect.

▶▶ Santa Maria in Aracoeli 41B5
Piazza del Campidoglio
This church occupies Rome's Holy of Holies—the crown of the Capitoline Hill that once housed the city's first *Arx* (Citadel) and Temple of Juno Moneta. Founded in the 6th century, or possibly earlier, the church has a dazzling interior with ancient columns, chandeliers, and a quite magnificent wooden ceiling. Its main treasures are Pinturicchio's frescos on the *Life of San Bernardino* (first chapel in the right-hand aisle) and, until it was stolen, the *Santo Bambino*, a miracle-working statue carved from an olive tree in Gethsemane.

Nightlife outside Santa Maria in Trastevere

Bernini's Elephant
Piazza della Minerva's famous statue of an elephant with a small Egyptian obelisk on its back was designed by Bernini for Pope Alexander VII. The inscription states that it takes the massive strength of the elephant to sustain the weight of true wisdom.

▶▶ Santa Maria in Cosmedin 41A4
Piazza Bocca della Verità
Though it lacks great treasures, few Roman churches are as beautiful as Santa Maria in Cosmedin, one of the handful of medieval buildings in the city to have escaped the baroque. The portico contains the famous *Bocca della Verità* (see panel), while the sublime interior boasts a lovely pavement, pulpits and choir screens, faded patches of fresco and an 8th-century mosaic.

▶▶▶ Santa Maria Maggiore 41B6
Piazza di Santa Maria Maggiore
Rome's finest early Christian basilica, 5th-century Santa Maria is the largest and most important of the city's 80 churches dedicated to the Virgin. The interior is magnificent, graced with 40 ancient columns and mosaics from the 5th and 13th centuries. The Paolina and Sistina chapels are also outstanding.

▶▶ Santa Maria sopra Minerva 41C4

Piazza della Minerva

Rome's only Gothic church lies behind the Pantheon, built over (*sopra*) the ruins of a temple dedicated to Minerva. It contains many fine works of art. Filippino Lippi left frescos in the Cappella Carafa, and there is a statue of *The Redeemer* by Michelangelo to the left of the altar. St. Catherine of Siena, the Medici popes Leo X and Clement VII, and the painter Fra Angelico are buried in the church.

▶▶▶ Santa Maria del Popolo 40E4

Piazza del Popolo

Bramante and Bernini designed much of this church, which contains superlative frescos by Pinturicchio and two masterpieces by Caravaggio. The **Cappella Chigi▶▶▶**, commissioned by a Sienese banker, was designed and executed by Raphael. The choir boasts a pair of tombs by Andrea Sansovino.

▶▶ Santa Maria in Trastevere 40A2

Piazza di Santa Maria in Trastevere

This church provides the backdrop to Trastevere's liveliest piazza. At night its mosaic-covered façade (12th-century) is beautifully floodlit. Inside the solemn interior are more mosaics, the work of Pietro Cavallini (1290) and earlier Byzantine craftsmen. The ancient columns are from the Terme di Caracalla.

▶▶▶ San Pietro (St Peter's) (see page 55) 40D1

▶▶ San Pietro in Vincoli 41B6

Piazza San Pietro in Vincoli

The chains (*vincoli*) are the links that bound St. Peter in Jerusalem, and to which were later added those that shackled him in Rome's Mamertine prison. Both sets of chains, miraculously fused together, can be seen below the high altar. The church is renowned, however, for Michelangelo's monumental statue of Moses (1503–13), considered one of the sculptor's greatest works.

The sumptuous interior of Santa Maria Maggiore

Nero's Tomb

Santa Maria del Popolo was supposedly built on the site of Nero's tomb in 1099. The Virgin appeared to Pope Paschal II and ordered him to chop down a great walnut tree that had grown from the grave. Paschal obliged, then built a chapel. The Emperor's ghost reputedly wandered the area, making for the pyramid tomb that contained the remains of his wife. Today it is the stylish *Rosati* café, a fashionable spot now haunted by the city's artists and literati.

Stroll

From Piazza Santa Maria in Trastevere wend through the streets to the south and climb the Gianicolo hill for views over the city.

Piazzas: Barberini and Colonna
Piazza Barberini has two Bernini fountains, both commissioned by the Barberini—the Fontana del Tritone and Fontana delle Api. Piazza Colonna takes its name from the Colonna di Marco Aurelio (AD 196), a column raised to celebrate Aurelius' military campaigns in northern Europe.

Of wedding cake and tortoises
Piazza Venezia is a vast square near the heart of Rome, dominated by the Monumento Vittorio Emanuele II (known to Romans today as the "wedding cake" or "typewriter"). Piazza Sant'Ignazio is noted for its architectural harmony, while Piazza Mattei harbors Bernini's touching Fontana delle Tartarughe (Fountain of the Tortoises).

Stendhal's syndrome
Beware of trying to see too much in Rome. There is a passage in Stendhal's *Journal* where he alludes to the symptoms brought on by an excess of culture: "If the foreigner who enters St. Peter's tries to see everything, he will develop a furious headache, and presently satiety and pain will render him incapable of any pleasure."

Piazzas and Fountains

▶▶▶　Fontana di Trevi　40D5
Piazza Fontana di Trevi
Rome's most famous fountain lives up to expectations as it foams dramatically from a whole wall of the Palazzo Poli. Its central figure, Neptune, is flanked by figures representing a calm and stormy sea. The tradition is to throw a coin into the fountain if you wish to return to Rome. It is one of the city's main meeting places.

▶▶▶　Piazza Campo dei Fiori　40C2
This lovely square is as picturesque as any in Italy, with its colorful street market, crammed with stalls selling flowers, fish, and mounds of fruit and vegetables. Take time to sit out at one of the cafés and enjoy the streetlife.

▶▶▶　Piazza Navona　40C3
Rome's social center is Piazza Navona, an exhilarating spot thronged with life and edged with elegant ocher *palazzi* and outdoor cafés. Its contours match exactly the outlines of the Emperor Domitian's *circo* (stadium), built to hold games and horse races in AD 86. It was transformed in 1644 by Pope Innocent X. Bernini designed two of its fountains, the **Fontana dei Quattro Fiumi** (Fountain of the Rivers), and the **Fontana del Moro**.

▶▶▶　Piazza di Spagna　41E4
At the heart of Rome's best shopping area, and backed by the famous **Spanish Steps▶▶▶**, this colorful square rivals Piazza Navona and the Fontana di Trevi as the city's most popular meeting place. It is named after the palace of the Spanish ambassador to the Vatican. The **Museo di Keats-Shelley** is here, together with the eccentric **Fontana della Barcaccia▶**.

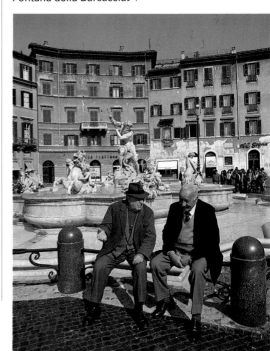

Piazza Navona: the heart of Rome

St. Peter's (San Pietro)

The most famous church in Christendom and Catholicism's most important point of pilgrimage, St. Peter's sees visitors from all over the world, drawn to the spot where St. Peter was buried after his crucifixion in AD 64 or 67. Few remain unimpressed by the basilica's size and spiritual significance, though many perhaps come away disappointed by its chill interior and—for a church of such fame—its surprising lack of great art.

The first St. Peter's was built in 326 by Pope Sylvester I with the backing of the Emperor Constantine. It was to survive until 1452, when Pope Nicholas V and then Julius II began to consider plans for a new basilica.

The new church Designs were drawn up by Bramante, then Antonio da Sangallo. Michelangelo, aged 72, was asked to correct mistakes, which he did by removing much of Sangallo's work and redesigning the dome. Carlo Maderno (1605) made more additions, and in 1637 Bernini was called in to act as the interior's chief architect.

Highlights Inside, the overall impression is of size, with little of real artistic merit among the gloomy tombs, heavy marble and welter of baroque decoration. The exceptions are Michelangelo's *Pietà* (1499) behind glass at the beginning of the right aisle and Bernini's colossal bronze *baldacchino* (altar canopy) in the crossing. See also the two finest tombs, della Porta's for Paul III and Bernini's influential tomb of Urban VIII. They lie at the rear of the apse, flanking Bernini's *Cathedra Pietri*, designed to encase a chair reputedly used by St. Peter to preach to the Romans.

Climb the dome for breathtaking views, and visit the piazza's tourist office to organize a trip to the crypt, where early Christian tombs possibly include St. Peter's.

Piazza San Pietro, Bernini's great square framing St. Peter's

Entrances
The church's grand portico contains the famous Porta Santa (Holy Door), opened only every 25 years (on the right), and the main bronze doors (1433), one of the few treasures salvaged from the first basilica.

Walk **Three walks through Rome's piazzas to the Spanish Steps**

For routes see map on pages 40–1

Trastevere Start from Piazza Santa Maria in Trastevere and take Vicolo delle Cinque to explore the quarter's pretty backstreets. Return to the piazza and follow Via della Lungaretta to Piazza Piscinula. Cross to the Isola Tiberina to wander the island's promenades and see the church of San Bartolomeo. Head south for the Roman temples and church of **Santa Maria in Cosmedin** (page 52) in Piazza Bocca della Verità. Cross back to Trastevere and wind through the backstreets to **Santa Cecilia in Trastevere** (page 51). Return to Santa Maria in Trastevere.

Piazza Navona–Castel Sant'Angelo
See the church of Sant'Agnese in Agone and Piazza Navona's fountains and walk to Piazza **Campo dei Fiori** (page 54). Stroll through Piazza Farnese (with detours to Palazzo Spada and Santa Maria dell'Orazione

e Morte) and then follow Via Giulia before cutting up to the Chiesa Nuova (worth a look for frescos by Pietro da Cortona). Next door see Borromini's idiosyncratic façade for the Oratorio dei Filippini and his clocktower in Piazza dell'Orologio. Walk to Via dei Coronari and across the Ponte Sant'Angelo to **Castel Sant'Angelo** (page 46).

Piazza Navona–Piazza di Spagna
Walk to the **Pantheon** (page 44) via **San Luigi dei Francesi** (Caravaggio frescos see page 52). Then see **Santa Maria sopra Minerva** (page 53) and Sant'Ignazio (for Andrea Pozzo's ceiling frescos) *en route* for Piazza Colonna and the Colonna di Marco Aurelio. Head for the **Fontana di Trevi** (page 54) and stroll through the grid of shopping streets around Via dei Condotti towards **Piazza di Spagna** (for the Spanish Steps see page 54).

Accommodations

Where to look Rome has the range of accommodations you can expect of any great city, from squalid *pensioni* to palatial luxury hotels. The best part to stay in is around Piazza Navona, although it is an area with relatively few hotels. More establishments cluster around Piazza del Popolo and Piazza di Spagna, both pretty and reasonably central but a notch below the top hotels on Via Veneto and the area south of the Villa Borghese. The station hotels (on Via Magenta, Via Amendola, Via Principe Amadeo) are a cheap last resort. More pleasant *pensioni* are dotted around the outlying areas of Prati and Borgo (near the Vatican).

Prices and booking Rome lacks charming hotels in the mid-range. The best in this bracket are booked up months in advance, so aim to reserve well ahead during the city's peak season (Easter to mid-October). Even off season (when reservations are still recommended), prices in Rome are high, and you often get less for your money than elsewhere. Anywhere with a garage, though, is worth its weight in gold. It usually pays to take meals in restaurants, rather than choosing full or half-pension. Watch out for breakfast and air-conditioning supplements, and remember that prices vary even within a hotel —so ask to see a variety of rooms.

Tourist offices
Avoid the con artists and the long lines at the station's tourist office if you need help finding accommodations. Try instead to use the booths at Fiumicino airport (tel: 06/6501 0255); at the Roma-Nord service station on the A1; the Roma-Sud Frascati service area on the A2; or the E.P.T. office at Via Parigi 5, near Piazza della Repubblica (tel: 06/487 1270).

Guided tours
The best guided tours of the city are offered by C.I.T. and American Express. Both offer a variety of (bus) itineraries, most of which last around three hours.

Rome's Grand Hotel lives up to its name

Noise and appearance Rome is one of Europe's noisiest cities, and you will never entirely escape the cacophony. Many hotels have double-glazed windows, but unless they are also air-conditioned you will need the windows open in summer. You can reduce the problem by avoiding Termini and the main thoroughfares in favor of back-streets or hotels near the parks. Also ask for a room either away from the front of the hotel or facing onto a central courtyard. Finally, when choosing a hotel do not judge by the exterior, as many a crumbling façade conceals a sumptuous interior.

Food and drink

Wine

Rome's local wine is the amber-colored bianco of the Castelli Romani. Frascati is the most famous version, though most varieties are fairly similar. Good wine bars to try include *Cul-de-Sac*, Piazza del Pasquino 73; the intimate *Enoteca Piccola*, Via del Governo Vecchio 75; and the relaxed *Enoteca Cavour*, Via Cavour 313. Also visit the *Enoteca Isabelli*, Via della Croce 76, a lovely shop where you can buy or drink wine.

Cafés and coffee

Rome's best cups of coffee are to be had at *La Tazza d'Oro*, Via degli Orfani 84 and *Sant'Eustachio*, Piazza Sant'Eustachio 82. Other famous bars include the 18th-century *Caffè Greco*, Via dei Condotti 86, a Roman institution; *Bernasconi*, Largo di Torre Argentina 1; *Columbia*, Piazza Navona 88; the trendy *Bar della Pace*, Via della Pace 5 (off Piazza Navona); and two bars on Piazza del Popolo—*Canova* and *Rosati*.

Sidewalk dining in Rome

What to eat Few things—perhaps only cars, soccer and families—come between Romans and a good meal. Eating out is all the nightlife many of them need, and a summer evening's meal *al fresco* can be one of Rome's most memorable experiences. The city's specialties may not always be appetizing—things like tripe, brains, salt cod, veal (often inhumanely raised) and offal—but more common Italian staples can be found in most restaurants. Favorite pasta dishes include *bucatini all'amatriciana*, *spaghetti alla carbonara*, *fettucine*, *gnocchi* and *penne all'arrabiata*. *Stracciatella* is the classic soup, a clear broth with egg, pasta, and cheese. The best known main course is *saltimbocca alla romana* (veal with ham and sage cooked in wine and butter). Grilled meats—lamb and beef—are also common. Purple Roman artichokes are renowned, as are asparagus and leaf vegetables like spinach and rocket (*rucola* or *rughetta*). The best desserts are simple treats like ice cream or mixed fruit salad (*macedonia*).

Where to eat Trastevere and the streets around Piazza Navona contain many restaurants, though few areas are without their quiet neighborhood *trattorie* and pizzerias. It is often in these places, away from tourist areas, that you will enjoy your best (and most reasonably priced) meals. Rome has more than its share of deceptively chic restaurants where the food and the prices are equally appalling. At the other extreme, do not overlook bars as a source of cheap snacks, and bear in mind that Rome now has many fast-food outlets (there are branches of McDonald's in Piazza di Spagna and Piazza della Repubblica). Tourist menus are as cheap as elsewhere, but the standard of food they offer is perhaps as low as anywhere in Italy.

The tradition of making lunch (*pranzo*) the main meal of the day is slowly dying out—though you can still indulge heavily between 1 and 3PM. In the evenings Romans eat dinner (*cena*) from around 8PM, a little earlier in pizzerias, a little later (and longer) in summer.

Shopping

Fruit stall in Rome's Campo dei Fiori

Shopping districts Though not a shopping city to compare with London, Paris or New York, Rome still has much to satisfy the wealthy or discerning shopper. It's best known for luxury goods—its silks, leather, jewelry, shoes, and accessories are of the highest quality. The most exclusive stores cluster in the grid of streets around Via dei Condotti and Piazza di Spagna. Less expensive streets include Via del Corso, Via Nazionale and Via del Tritone, Via Cola di Rienzo and the areas around Campo dei Fiori and the Fontana di Trevi.

Markets Rome's most attractive food and vegetable market is in Piazza Campo dei Fiori. Piazza Vittorio Emanuele, however, is the city's main market, selling food and all kinds of general goods. Via Andrea Doria is another large market (north of the Vatican Museums). Porta Portese is the city's most famous flea market (Sunday only), but there are few bargains and the crowds are overwhelming (be on special guard against pickpockets). Via Sannio next to San Giovanni in Laterano has a smaller junk and second-hand clothes market on Saturday.

Leather goods Shoe stores almost outnumber food shops in Rome. For quality look on and around Via dei Condotti; for low prices try Via Nazionale. Leather shops are similarly numerous. **Beltrami** (Via Condotti 18–19) and **Valextra** (Via del Babuino) have high-quality selections. For gloves you need to visit only **Sergio di Cori** (Piazza di Spagna 53 and Via Nazionale 183). For socks, tights and stockings try **Calza e Calze** (Via della Croce 78).

Department stores La Rinascente is Rome's grandest department store (with branches at Piazza Colonna and Piazza Fiume). **Coin** at Piazzale Appio is best for clothes and kitchenware (five minutes from San Giovanni in Laterano). **Standa** at Via del Corso 148 and elsewhere is cheap and popular; while **UPIM** in Via del Tritone, Piazza Santa Maria Maggiore and elsewhere has a full range of medium-quality goods at good prices.

Antiques
Antique shops with breathtaking pieces and prices to match concentrate on Via del Babuino and Via Monserrato. Via Giulia's stores specialize in furniture: those on Via dei Coronari offer items a touch below Via Babuino in cost and quality.

China, fabrics and linen
For china try *Ginori*, Via Cola di Rienzo 223 and Via del Tritone 177, or the 100-year-old *Cavatorta*, Via Veneto 159. For silks and fabrics visit *Bises* (Via del Gesù 63 and 91), *Meconi* (Via Cola di Rienzo 305) or *Galtrucco* (Via del Tritone 18–23). *Frette* (Piazza di Spagna 11) is famed for its household linens.

Nightlife

Rome's *dolce vita* days are all but over, and nightlife for many Romans means a meal out or relaxing in a sidewalk café (though there are plenty of more active nightspots if you want them). Cultural entertainment is what you would expect of a capital city, though movies and theater hold relatively few rewards for non Italian speakers.

Concerts and recitals The **Accademia di Santa Cecilia** stages concerts by its own and visiting orchestras at Via della Conciliazione 4 (box office Via dei Greci 18, tel: 06/6880 1044). The **Accademia Filarmonica** (tel: 06/320 1752) holds a major recital series at the Teatro Olimpico, Piazza Gentile da Fabriano 17 (tel: 06/323 4890). The **Oratorio del Gonfalone** stages baroque and chamber recitals at Via del Gonfalone 32A (tel: 06/4770 4664 or 687 5952). A wealth of classical music can also be heard free of charge throughout the year in Rome's churches.

Music clubs Jazz and Latin music clubs are especially popular in Rome. Latin music features heavily at **Caffè Caruso** (Via Monte Testaccio 36), jazz at **St. Louis**, Via del Cardello 13a. **Yes! Brazil** is also great fun (Via San Francesco a Ripa 103). The best overall spot is **Big Mama** (Vicolo San Francesco a Ripa 18), with both jazz and blues; **Caffè Latino** (Via Monte Testaccio 96) and **Alexanderplatz** (Via Ostia 9) are also popular. Most places offer light meals as well as drinks and music.

Beer and bars Sitting at cafés until the small hours is a feature of Rome's summer nightlife. **Bar della Pace** (Via della Pace 5) is perhaps the most popular, the more exclusive **Hemingway** the most trendy (Piazza delle Coppelle 10). Pubs and beer halls (*birrerie*) are also well-patronized. Try the **Fiddler's Elbow** (Via dell'Ormata 43, near Santa Maria Maggiore); **Tempera**, Via San Marcello 19 (behind Piazza Venezia); or Trastevere's buzzing **La Scala**, Piazza della Scala.

Discos and Nightclubs Discos and clubs are subject to sudden changes of fashion (and ownership), so consult *Trovaroma* for the places of the moment. Admission is often expensive and dressing up *de rigueur*. Longer-established places include **Piper** (Via Tagliamento 9) and **Black Out** (Via Saturnia18), both of which attract a young crowd. **Gilda** (Via Mario de'Fiori 97) and **L'Alibi** (Via Monte Testaccio 44–57) are celebrity spots.

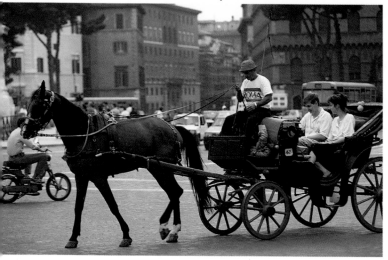

Buses Rome's orange buses are run by A.T.A.C. Most services start from Piazza dei Cinquecento in front of the main station (Stazione Termini). You must buy tickets before boarding, at shops with an A.T.A.C. sticker or at the green A.T.A.C. booths at major stops. Tickets are valid for any number of journeys during 90 minutes. You can get a day pass or a weekly tourist ticket (B.I.G.) (also valid on the *metro*). Remember to board buses at the back and leave at the center. Cancel tickets in the small machine near the rear doors. There is a patchy night service (*notturno*) on main routes.

Metro Rome's subway (*la metropolitana*) is fast and easy to use, but it has only two lines. **Line A** connects Ottaviano (north of the Vatican) to Flaminia (for Piazza del Popolo and the Villa Borghese), Piazza di Spagna (Spanish Steps), Piazza Barberini (for the Galleria Barberini), Termini, Vittorio Emanuele and beyond. **Line B** is useful for Piramide (Protestant Cemetery), Circo Massimo (the Aventino and Santa Sabina), Colosseo (Colosseum), Cavour (the Roman Forum) and Termini. Direct trains to Fiumicino airport leave from Termini railroad station. Tickets are obtainable from booths at the main stations, otherwise from machines (exact change essential).

Taxis It is hard to hail Rome's yellow cabs on the street. Most gather at taxi ranks or can be called by phone (tel: 3875, 3570, 4994 or 8433). Useful ranks are at Piazza Venezia, Termini, Piazza San Silvestro, and Piazza Sonnino (Trastevere). Use only metered yellow cabs ensure the meter is running. Supplements are charged for phoning for a taxi: after 10PM; on Sundays; and for each piece of luggage.

Bicycles Despite Rome's traffic, bike rental outlets are springing up all over the city. There are concessions in Via del Corso, Piazza Navona, Viale del Bambino (Pincio), Piazza San Silvestro, Largo Argentina and near the Piazza di Spagna and Piazza del Popolo (Flaminia) metro stops.

Yet another way to see Rome

61

Trains and stations
Most trains arrive and leave from Stazione Termini, Piazza dei Cinquecento (usually called "Termini"). Lines for tickets are long, especially on Friday evening and Saturday morning. Afternoons are the quietest times, but if you are buying a ticket in advance be sure to specify the day you wish to travel. International tickets, ferries, reservations and couchettes (sleeping compartments) are all dealt with by separate booths. Only a few trains use Tiburtina, Ostiense or Trastevere stations.

Useful bus routes
No. 27 Termini–Via Cavour–Roman Forum–Colosseum; No. 64 Termini–Via Nazionale–Piazza Venezia–Piazza Navona–St. Peter's; No. 81 Colosseum–St. Peter's/Vatican Museums (Piazza del Risorgimento).

THE NORTHWEST

Tourist information
Aosta: Piazza E Chanoux 8
(tel: 0165/236 627).
Asti: Piazza Alfieri 34 (tel:
0141/530 357 or 582 007).
Levanto (Cinqueterre):
Piazza Colombo 12 (tel:
0187/807 175).
Genoa: Via Roma II (tel:
010/541 541).
Turin: Via Roma 226 (tel:
011/535 181); Porta Nuova
Station (tel: 011/531 327).

Scenic drives
(*Piedmont*) SS21
Cuneo–Vinadio–Argentera;
Cuneo–Valdieri–Parco
Naturale dell'Argentera;
Turin–Lanzo Torinese–Val
Grande–Val di Ala; SS460
Turin–Locana–Ceresole
Reale; (*Valle d'Aosta*) SS26
Pont-St.-Martin–Aosta; SS
505 Pont-St.-Martin–Val di
Gressoney; SS506 St.
Vincent–Val d'Ayas;
(*Liguria*) SS530 La
Spezia–Portovenere;
La Spezia–Lerici–
Montemarcello.

The Northwest The regions of Piemonte (Piedmont), Valle d'Aosta and Liguria have riches to offer every kind of visitor, with a combination of mountain scenery, beaches, and fine food.

Piemonte Cradled by the Alps on three sides, Piedmont—*piede dei monti*, or "foot of the mountain"— is a region of mountains, vineyard-covered hills, crumbling castles and half-forgotten villages. Scenery is the main attraction for most visitors, principally the upland enclaves of Monviso, Gran Paradiso, and the Alpi Marittime. In the west, France's proximity colors culture, cuisine and language. At the same time, Piedmont produces such Italian staples as Fiat cars, vermouth and, that mainstay of Italian restaurants, breadsticks (*grissini*).

Torino (Turin), Piedmont's capital, is a refined, baroque city made prosperous by industry. North are the mountains of the Valle d'Aosta and south the rippling hills and vineyards around Asti and Alba, home of great wines like Barolo and Barbaresco.

Valle d'Aosta One of Italy's smallest regions, the Valle d'Aosta contains some of the country's most spectacular scenery. Its links with France were reinforced by the opening of the Mont Blanc tunnel in 1965, and increased trade has brought prosperity, along with busy roads and some light industry.

A journey through the Valle d'Aosta, the valley which scythes through the region and gives it its name, provides a fine introduction to the area's mountains and fairytale castles. Its focus, Aosta, offers Roman remains and a splendid cathedral. Almost any of the smaller nearby valleys offers wonderful views, stone-housed hamlets, Alpine meadows and ice-clear streams. The Val d'Ayas and Val di Gressoney are outstanding, but probably the most rewarding is the Val di Cogne, if only because it leads to Italy's premier national park, the Parco Nazionale del Gran Paradiso.

Maritime Liguria With Genoa (Italy's largest port) as its capital and Christopher Columbus as its most famous son, Liguria is naturally a region dominated by all things maritime. Its beautiful coastline—the so-called Italian Riviera—divides into the Riviera di Ponente (west of Genoa) and the Riviera di Levante (east). Both are sheltered by the Ligurian and Maritime Alps, mountain walls which guarantee mild winters and a long growing season —resulting in the region's nickname of *Riviera dei Fiori* (Riviera of Flowers).

If you have time for only one sojourn on the coast head for the Cinqueterre, five tiny fishing villages wedged into the cliffs and mountains on the Riviera di Levante. If your itinerary is more leisurely, amble down the entire coast from Ventimiglia, stopping at Alassio, for its broad beach, or San Remo for its mixture of old world charm and tacky modernism. Drive inland to explore the hills, dotted with attractive, little-known villages, and visit the coast's most famous hilltowns, pricey Portofino and Portovenere. Spend time in Genoa, a salty and industrialized port, of interest principally for its old quarter and collection of modest galleries.

▶ **Alba** 62B3

Austere and medieval Alba is renowned above all for its food and wine: wine in the form of Barolo and Barbaresco (both red), and food in the form of truffles (*tartufi*), culled from the oak woods of the surrounding hills (see page 174). After sampling the town's food shops head for **San Lorenzo▶**, the old cathedral, containing a finely carved and inlaid choir. Another church, **San Giovanni▶** contains the town's most prized painting, the *Madonna delle Grazie* by Barnaba da Modena (1377).

▶ **Aosta** 62D2

Capital of the Valle d'Aosta, relaxed and largely French-speaking Aosta is a sedate and historic town whose lightly industrial fringe is redeemed by a tremendous mountainous backdrop. Its **Cattedrale▶** is worth a look for its choir stalls and small museum housing a magnificent early 5th-century ivory diptych. The finest church, however, is **Sant'Orso▶▶** renowned for its 11th-century crypt and the wonderfully carved columns of its cloister (1133). Also outstanding are the town's Roman remains.

▶▶ **Asti** 62C3

One-time rival to Milan, Asti is well worth a visit, and deserves to be known for more than Asti Spumante, its famous (if unsophisticated) sparkling wine. Most of its best monuments—towers, palaces and churches—are on or near the main street, Corso Vittorio Alfieri. The Gothic Duomo (1309–54) has a checkered façade of red and white stone, but is less interesting than the church of **San Pietro in Consavia▶**, whose little circular baptistery dates from around the 12th century. Look, too, at **San Secondo▶**, a looming Gothic church with numerous frescos, the most noted a polyptych by Gandolfino d'Asti.

You could make an excursion to Albugnano, to see the **Abbazia di Vezzolano▶▶**, the finest Romanesque building in Piedmont (13 miles from Asti). Reputedly founded by Charlemagne, it has a remarkable 12th-century façade, magnificent carved rood screen and lovely cloister.

Sant'Orso church below the snow-capped mountains of the Valle d'Aosta

The wines of Piedmont
Piedmont produces some of Italy's most famous wines, from its noble, tannic reds, Barolo and Barbaresco, to semi-sweet and sparkling whites like Asti Spumante and Moscato d'Asti. Other outstanding reds include Gattinara, Ghemme, Lessona, Barbera and Dolcetto d'Alba. Whites are less renowned, though Gavi is fashionable (if sometimes bland) and Arneis has a rising reputation.

Bagna cauda
Meaning literally a "hot bath," *bagna cauda* is a type of Piedmontese fondue, a spicy dip made by simmering together a mixture of butter, olive oil, garlic, white truffle, anchovies, and cream. It is a common wintertime dish all over the region.

66

Vernazza's pretty fishing harbor

▶▶   **Cinqueterre**   63A5

The Cinqueterre (Five Lands) are five tiny seafront villages strung along one of the most dramatic stretches of the Ligurian coast. Each is a picturesque jumble of pastel-colored houses gathered around a small fishing harbor (though tourists these days heavily outnumber fishermen). Above the huddle of houses, mountains covered in woods and lush vegetation provide a beautiful backdrop. Savage cliffs tumble to the sea on all sides, cut by terraces of vines and olives that date back thousands of years. Well-marked and panoramic paths follow the coast and crisscross the hinterland.

Access to the region for centuries was possible only by sea, and even today some of the villages have no road links to the outside world. Boats connect them all, and this is a fine way of seeing the coast. The train, however, is the most practical way of moving from village to village. Any one of the villages makes a fine place to stop, though most people base themselves in **Levanto**, a town just to the north with plenty of hotels and services—as well as a fair amount of charm in its own right.

The villages Each of the villages has its own attractions, and if you get tired of one, it is only a few minutes by rail to the next. From north to south you will find: **Monterosso**, the largest and perhaps least charming of the five, but with the biggest beach and most hotels; **Vernazza,** a tangle of tiny streets, alleys and arcades; **Corniglia**—the smallest—sitting high above the sea, but with a long, if pebbly beach; **Manarola,** the jewel in the crown, clustered behind a sickle of sand and hemmed in by precipitous mountains, with charming, steep cobbled streets and a harbor that is a rustic picture of bobbing fishing boats and seamen mending nets in the sun; and **Riomaggiore,** which also sits behind a sliver of sand, and has a more generous range of rooms than most of the villages.

Pesto
Liguria's best known culinary specialty, pesto, was created around Genoa, but is now eaten the world over. It is made from basil, olive oil, garlic, parmesan, and pine nuts, all ground in a mortar and pestle (hence its name). The Ligurians claim that only the region's special, smooth basil and highly prized olive oil are good enough for the real thing.

► **Genova (Genoa)**   *63B4*

Italy's premier maritime city, Genoa receives relatively little attention from visitors, most of whom are put off by its lack of famous sights and by the grim suburbs which spread in a confused sprawl over the surrounding hills. Away from the vibrant—and sometimes sordid—waterfront, however, the *centro storico* (historic center) is a medley of teeming streets, some best avoided after dark, but all a joy to explore. Public elevators and railways transport you around the city's confusing multitude of levels.

The proud city One of Italy's four great medieval maritime republics, Genoa in the 14th century claimed territories stretching from North Africa to Syria and the Black Sea. It became Europe's most densely populated city, nicknamed La Superba, "The Proud," by the poet Petrarch.

Genoa's medieval trading prowess brought it great wealth, much of which went to build the imposing patrician palaces lining **Via Garibaldi**►►, one of Italy's most impressive streets. Most of the palaces are now offices or grand shops, but two house important art galleries: the **Palazzo Bianco**►► contains works mainly by Genovese masters, with additional pieces by Veronese, Pontormo and Filippino Lippi, plus an outstanding medley of Dutch and Flemish paintings. The **Palazzo Rosso**►► offers canvases by Caravaggio, Dürer and Van Dyck, among others, and the masterpiece of Genoa's own Bernardo Strozzi, *La Cuoca*.

Other museums to hunt out are the **Museo Chiossone**►, home to Italy's foremost collection of oriental art, and the **Galleria Nazionale di Palazzo Spinola**►, crammed with furniture, sculpture and Renaissance paintings.

San Lorenzo►► is the city's cathedral, fronted by a fine black-and-white-striped façade. Inside, the Museo del Tesoro contains a collection of the gold and silverware for which medieval Genoa was renowned. Close by, head for **Piazza San Matteo**►► an outstanding ensemble of medieval buildings.

Christopher Columbus
Columbus spent his childhood in Genoa, in the ivy-clad *palazzo* in Piazza Dante (close to Porta Soprana). For centuries, however, scholars have sought to prove he was born elsewhere. Several towns in Liguria claim him, as does Piacenza in Emilia-Romagna. Some historians say he was a Jewish convert of Spanish origin, forced by religious persecution to flee to Liguria. A 17th-century English manuscript claims he was English, while the Corsican town of Calvi is sure he was born there. Other theories have him as Swiss (Geneva), French or the Levantine corsair, Giorgio Bissipat. In the *Mayorazgo* (a will made in Seville in 1498), however, Columbus himself wrote that he was "born in Genoa."

67

THE NORTHWEST

Cable cars
If you want views of the mountains without having to work for them, several ski lifts and cable cars operate during the summer. One of the most convenient is the telecabina from Cogne, which climbs to Montseuc (6,930ft.) just a half mile south of the town. A couple of little paths from its upper station offer easy strolls in the woods, or to the upper summit of Montseuc (7,699ft.).

▶▶ **Parco Nazionale del Gran Paradiso** 62D2

Italy's first ever national park is also its most spectacular. Ranged around the Gran Paradiso massif (13,401 feet)—the only mountain over 13,200 feet solely in Italy—the park started life as a hunting reserve for the Savoys in the 19th century. In 1919 the family donated the area to the state, thus helping to preserve not only the area's stupendous scenery, but also the ibex, a type of wild goat, for which the park is now best known. Snow-capped mountains, vast glaciers, verdant valleys, and deep-green forests lie within easy reach of drivers and walkers alike.

Three valleys push into the park from the Valle d'Aosta—the Val di Rhêmes, Val Savarenche and Val di Cogne. Roads run up each one, offering superlative views and many opportunities for walks into the mountains. The best approach overall, though, is via the Val di Cogne, and its main center, **Cogne**▶▶, just half an hour from Aosta. A pleasing little winter and summer resort, it has plenty of places to stay and makes a perfect base for exploring the whole of the park. It is a particularly good launching pad for walks. For details of the best hike see "Walking," pages 70–1.

Rocky wilderness in Gran Paradiso National Park

Just south of the village is the hamlet of **Valnontey**, a little too swamped by visitors for its own good, but home to the Giardino Alpino, a botanical garden that contains examples of much of the park's outstanding alpine flora. Come in June to see the flowers at their best, and if at all possible try a few walks up to mountain meadows to see them in their natural habitat. The same walks will almost certainly reward you with sightings of ibex (the park's herd totals around 4,500), as well as the more numerous chamois (a goat-like antelope) and a range of smaller fauna and alpine birds.

▶ **Riviera di Levante** 63A4

The Riviera di Levante is the less developed and more spectacular half of the Italian Riviera. Like the Riviera di Ponente, however, it is a region where you have to choose carefully if you want to avoid overpriced or over-popular resorts. Almost any town will suffice, though, if all you want is racy nightlife and noisy beachlife.

Portofino's colorful waterfront, setting for Italy's high society on vacation

A general tour by car or train gives you marvelous glimpses of turquoise sea, tiny fishing villages, and a romantic medley of cliffs and mountains. Pine forests plunge to pebbly beaches, interspersed with luxuriant and herb-scented swaths of *maquis*. The best section is the Cinqueterre (see page 66).

Moving east from Genoa, however, the first stop is Camogli▶, little changed since Charles Dickens described it as the "saltiest, roughest, most piratical little place." Clustered around a pleasant harbor, it is quieter than many spots on the coast, full of steep streets, brightly painted houses, and dozens of *al fresco* restaurants. Beyond lies Rapallo▶, once a fashionable Edwardian resort, now rather spoiled by modern building and the crush of summer tourists. People come to enjoy its mild climate, beaches with long promenades, and its many cultural events.

From Rapallo or nearby Santa Margherita Ligure you can reach Portofino▶▶▶, one of Italy's most beautiful but also most exclusive seafront villages. The country's rich and famous treat this as their personal playground, with the inevitable result that prices are high and the atmosphere exclusive. Nevertheless, the village's sheer prettiness makes it well worth a day trip. Escape the crowds by walking to the Castello di San Giorgio and the little church of San Giorgio just beyond.

Farther round the coast Sestri Levante▶ has one of the area's better beaches, the Baia di Silenzio, edged around one of the town's two large bays. Portovenere▶▶ is almost as pretty as Portofino, but not as expensive. It has plenty of restaurants and bars, a ruined fortress and a beautiful sanctuary believed to stand on the site of a temple to Venus. Italians in the know go to Lerici▶, an attractive and unpretentious resort with sheltered beaches and an imposing 13th-century Pisan castle.

Parco Naturale di Monte di Portofino
Most of the Portofino promontory is protected as a *parco naturale*, designed to preserve one of the few unspoiled stretches of the Italian Riviera. The hills are cloaked in *macchia* (like the French *maquis*), a thick vegetation of aleppo and maritime pines, and a fragrant undergrowth of herbs, juniper, heathers and cistus. Tranquil paths crisscross the park's hilly interior. Boat trips from Portofino and Camogli offer views on to the often dramatic coastline.

The Golfo dei Poeti
The area around Lerici has been praised for its beauty for centuries, never more enthusiastically than by Byron and Shelley, the two poets after whom the area —the Golfo dei Poeti—was named. In one noted incident, Byron swam from Portovenere across the Gulf to visit Shelley in San Terenzo, a quaint fishing village across the bay from Lerici. It was here in 1822 that Shelley started the fateful voyage to Livorno that ended in shipwreck and his death by drowning.

Northwest Italy offers some of the country's best walking, from the spectacular high Alps of the Gran Paradiso National Park to the coastal cliffs of the Cinqueterre and Portofino peninsula.

La Morra and Le Langhe
The lovely hilly countryside around Alba is known as Le Langhe, a region swathed in vineyards and dotted with castles and hilltop villages. La Morra is one of the finest, enjoying all-embracing views (hence its nickname, the *Belvedere delle Langhe*). It also boasts a wine museum and a series of walks following designated wine routes. Each path is color coded according to its destination and takes you past vineyards, wine cellars and rustic inns where you can sample the local vintages.

Explore the Italian countryside on foot

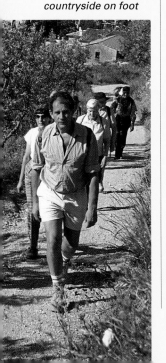

Hiking is not always easy in Italy. The Alps, however, benefit from well-marked trails and a range of up-to-date and readily available maps. This also applies to less well-known areas, foremost of which are the scarcely explored mountains of the Parco Naturale dell'Argentera in southwest Piedmont. Walking possibilities are endless throughout the Alpine areas of Piedmont and Valle d'Aosta. Below are a few of the finest to get you started.

Parco Nazionale del Gran Paradiso To explore this park buy the Kompass 1:50,000 map *Gran Paradiso-Valle d'Aosta* (No 86) or I.G.C. *Parco Nazionale del Gran Paradiso* (No. 3). The most popular walk in the area starts from Valnontey south of Cogne. From the village (5,497 feet) take trail 106/36 to the *Rifugio Vittorio Sella* (8,527 feet). The path climbs through pine forests, with grand views of the surrounding mountains and glaciers, as well as excellent opportunities of seeing ibex and chamois. At the *rifugio* take trail 39 south towards Lago di Lauson (8,764 feet) and follow it to the *Rifugio Sella Herbetet* and the head of the valley. Then walk down the valley on trail 33 back to Valnontey. Allow a full day for the walk, and try to avoid August and summer weekends, when the route is extremely popular.

Parco Naturale dell'Argentera This walk starts from Terme di Valdieri, a hamlet at the heart of the park (20 miles south west of Cuneo in southern Piedmont). Use the I.G.C. 1:50,000 map *Alpi Marittime e Liguri* (No. 8). Pick up the N8 trail which strikes west up the Valle di Valasco from immediately south of Terme di Valdieri (4,514 feet). Follow the well-made mule track to the upper part of the valley which flattens out into one of the most beautiful upland meadows in the Alps (5,817 feet). At the small Savoy hunting lodge, the ruined *Casa di Caccia*, take the trail over the river and follow the main path into the mountains to the Lago di Valscura (7,504 feet). Then descend via trails N22, N20 and N18 to the *Casa di Caccia* and thus back to Terme di Valdieri. Allow a full day for the walk.

Parco Naturale del Monte di Portofino All sorts of marked walks, long and short, are possible on the Portofino promontory. The most popular depart from Portofino itself, whose tourist office has several maps and guides covering many local hikes. The neatest circuit, a marked trail, leaves the village and climbs to San Sebastiano (630 feet), continuing to Monte delle Bocche (1,702 feet) before dropping down to the little fishing village of San Fruttuoso. Here you can either take one of the regular boats back to Portofino, or walk back along a quite magnificent coastal path via Punta Carega and the Val

Ruffinale. You should allow four hours to follow the complete circuit from Portofino.

Cinqueterre Numerous paths have been marked and mapped around the Cinqueterre villages and their mountainous hinterland. Maps and details are available from all local tourist offices, and the Italian Alpine Club (C.A.I.), produce their own 1:40,000 *Carta dei Sentieri delle Cinque Terre*, available in local bookshops. Trains linking all the villages mean you can easily return to base without having to retrace your steps. The most obvious walks link the coastal villages, traversing breathtaking scenery, often by means of precipitous terraces or thousands of tiny steps cut into rocks. Any stretch between two villages has its rewards, though it is also worth exploring the mountains to the rear, where paths run along the entire summit ridge (linked by transverse trails to the coast).

The Castello di Verres lies in the Valle d'Aosta, northeast of the Parco Nazionale del Gran Paradiso

San Remo's flower market
Every morning except Sunday, at around 6:30, traders gather in San Remo's Corso Garibaldi for one of Europe's largest flower markets. Over 20,000 tons of roses, carnations, mimosa, and other flowers change hands here every year.

A scenic train journey
The railroad from Ventimiglia to Limone Piemonte is one of Italy's most scenic, passing through French territory as it climbs from the coast into the heart of the Alpi Marittime. An engineering marvel, the line was badly damaged in World War II and only reopened as late as 1979. Around ten trains daily ply the route. The journey takes 70 minutes.

The palms of Bordighera
Bordighera has the unique privilege of supplying the Vatican with palms during Easter week, a tradition said to go back to 1586, and the raising of the Egyptian obelisk in front of St. Peter's, Rome. The supporting ropes threatened to break, but a sailor from Bordighera shouted "Water on the ropes," despite an order that the watchers should stay silent on pain of death. The pope, Sixtus V, awarded the village the palm concession in gratitude. Sadly, the story is probably a tall one.

► **Riviera di Ponente** 62A3

The Italian Riviera's western portion stretches from Ventimiglia on the French border to Genoa. For the most part it is an unbroken chain of popular beach resorts, all far cheaper and more down-to-earth than their neighbors across the border.

Ventimiglia has a passable old quarter, but remains essentially a border town, crammed with dreary hotels, garages and duty-free shops. **Bordighera**►► beyond is more refined, one of the first resorts to attract well-heeled British and European visitors in the 19th century. The beach is good and the historic center still boasts several medieval monuments.

San Remo► was once the Nice of the Italian Riviera, its mild climate, gardens and genteel charm the magnet for the cream of European aristocracy. These days its appeal combines ritz with kitsch, though the old town (La Pigna), flower market and palm-lined promenades are all worth an hour's exploration. The cable car up Monte Bignone also makes a good excursion, offering views on clear days as far as Cannes.

Diano Marina and Laiguelia are both functional, family-oriented resorts, overshadowed by **Alassio**►, a large, affluent and lively town with the best beach in Liguria (more than 2 miles of fine sand).

Albenga►only has a pebbly foreshore, but its old town is the most historically rewarding on the Riviera. Its chief draws are the 5th-century baptistery—Liguria's most important early Christian building—the cathedral, the Museo Igauno, the intimate Piazza dei Leoni and the Palazzo Peloso-Cipolla, which contains finds from a Roman galley sunk nearby in the 1st century BC.

Finale Ligure► is among the Riviera's most pleasant spots, less crowded than Alassio. There is an interesting old-town area (Finalborgo) 1 mile inland. Little **Noli**► is a picturesque resort-cum-fishing village, with a good beach and interesting Romanesque church, San Paragorio. Savona, the last town before Genoa, is a heavily industrialized seaport.

Elegant San Remo's palm-fringed harbor

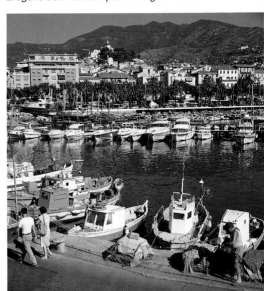

The Hanbury Gardens

The Hanbury Gardens (Giardino Hanbury) lie near the village of Mortola Inferiore, 4 miles from Ventimiglia. Founded in 1867 by Sir Thomas Hanbury, a wealthy English tea merchant, they were acquired by the Italian state in 1960. They are now ranked as some of the most important gardens in Italy.

The Ligurian coastline has one of the mildest winter climates in the country. Flowers of all varieties flourish here even in February, a natural bounty that has been turned to commercial advantage by the region's market gardeners. All down the coast you see checkered fields of brightly colored blooms, or row upon row of cavernous greenhouses.

At Mortola, Sir Thomas Hanbury took advantage of the region's benign climate to produce Italy's largest botanical gardens, planting out over 5,000 species of plants and flowers from all corners of the globe. Many were exotic specimens from Africa and Asia, carefully acclimatized to grow alongside the staples of Mediterranean and Alpine flora. The palms together with succulents and cacti are particularly outstanding. These days the garden is past its prime, over three-quarters of the species having been lost over the years (restoration work, however, is currently in hand). Nonetheless it still remains worth visiting, particularly if you come armed with a picnic.

At the gardens' center is an extravagant Islamic-style mausoleum, Sir Thomas Hanbury's eccentric final resting place. From here the gardens fan out on steep terraces, a clever piece of design that constantly unfolds new vistas as you walk from level to level.

The gardens' partial ruin in places only adds to their atmospheric appeal, creating overgrown nooks and hidden corners among the more formal settings. The terraces fall away to the sea in a mixture of unkept arbors and riotous pergolas, occasionally revealing an artificial grotto or crumbling fountain.

The gardens are open daily from 10AM to 6PM (until 4PM off season): admission charges are high.

The Hanbury Gardens are one of Italy's finest, their mild climate making them worth a visit throughout the whole year

THE NORTHWEST

62C2

Old world cafés

Turin is famous for its elegant *fin-de-siècle* cafés and coffeehouses. The best known include *Caffè Torino*, Piazza San Carlo 204; *Caffè San Carlo*, under the arcades of Piazza San Carlo (across the street from *Stratta*, the city's top chocolate shop); the wonderfully intimate *Mulussano* in Piazza San Carlo; and *Baratti e Milano*, just off Piazza Castello in the gallery leading to Via Po.

Basilica di Superga

On September 6, 1706, King Vittorio Amedeo II climbed a hill outside Turin to survey the positions of the French and Spanish armies that had been besieging the city for four months. Looking down, he promised to build a basilica in honor of the Virgin if she came to the city's rescue. Turin was duly spared and the pledge fulfilled in the shape of the Basilica di Superga, one of Italy's most striking baroque buildings.

▶▶ **Torino (Turin)**

Piedmont's capital is a mixture of industrial hinterland—the domain of Fiat and Lancia—and a gracious city center of gardens, arcades, and boulevards. A quiet university town during the Middle Ages, it acquired a French flavor it has never entirely lost when the Savoys moved from Chambéry to establish their capital here in 1574.

The two main sights gather under one roof in Piazza San Carlo's Palazzo dell'Accademia delle Scienze: the **Museo Egizio**▶▶, generally considered the most important museum of Egyptian antiquities outside Egypt, and the **Galleria Sabauda**▶▶, an outstanding art gallery built around the Savoys' family collection. Nearby, visit the **Museo Nazionale del Risorgimento**▶, for more background on Turin's pivotal role in Italian unification.

A little to the north lies the traffic-choked Piazza Castello, home to a trio of easily seen sights. Most prominent is the **Palazzo Reale**▶, a Savoy royal palace crammed with gaudily decorated state apartments (guided tours), of less interest than the gardens to the rear, the Giardino Reale. Across the piazza stands the **Palazzo Madama**▶▶, fronted by a fine baroque façade. Inside is the Museo Civico dell'Arte Antica, an eclectic collection of glassware, ceramics, jewelry and paintings. On the square's north side the **Armeria Reale**▶ offers one of the world's greatest collections of arms and armor. The **Duomo**▶▶▶ off Piazza Castello is best known for the Turin Shroud (see opposite page). For an overall view, and if you have the requisite energy, climb the **Mole Antonelliana**▶▶, the towering 19th-century folly (once the world's highest building) that can be seen from all over the city.

Turin, capital of Piedmont: cityscape

The Turin Shroud

Turin's cathedral contains one of the most famous—and most controversial—relics in Christendom: the *Sindone*, or Holy Shroud, the cloth reputedly used to wrap Christ after His crucifixion.

The Turin Shroud is a four-yard length of linen, unremarkable except for the fact that it contains an imprint of what the faithful claim is an image of the crucified Christ. It first made its appearance around the middle of the 15th century, when it was presented to Ludovico of Savoy in Chambéry. In 1578 it was brought to Turin by another member of the Savoy family, Duke Emanuele Filiberto.

It is only in the last few years that the Church has allowed rigorous scientific study of the shroud. The results have been double-edged. On the one hand three separate university teams—in Italy, Britain and the United States—have concluded, as a result of Carbon 14 dating, that the cloth is a forgery dating from between 1260 and 1390. On the other, they are unable to explain how the shroud's image, which is like a photographic negative, could have been created.

Housing the Shroud The *Sindone* is only brought out of hiding on very special occasions. The original is kept in the Cappella della Sacra Sindone, locked securely away in a silver casket, which in turn is hidden in an iron box, a marble coffer and a heavy urn on the chapel's main altar. Although Filiberto intended to build a new church to house the relic, his successors commissioned first Amedeo di Castellamonte and then the more gifted Guarino Guarini (1624–83) to design a chapel within the cathedral.

One of the baroque school's leading lights, Guarini has monuments built to his designs in places as far afield as Lisbon, Paris and Prague. The chapel in Turin, however, is perhaps his masterpiece; a consummate piece of baroque-mannerist frippery, notable for the exuberant excess of its unusual cupola.

The shroud's image
A photographic replica of the shroud on display in the cathedral shows the face of a bearded man, complete with a crown of thorns, as well as front and rear images of a body displaying spear wounds, the marks left by a thonged whip and bruises compatible with carrying a cross.

75

The face of Christ?

Drive The Valle d'Aosta

See map on pages 62–3.

A spectacular drive through one of Italy's major Alpine valleys, full of castles, old stone villages and Europe's highest mountains, Mont Blanc, the Matterhorn and Monte Rosa.

Note: although this drive follows the valley floor, be sure to explore the minor roads that strike off into scenic side valleys along the way—Val di Gressoney, Val d'Ayas, Valtournenche and Val di Cogne.

Pont-St.-Martin, gateway to the valley, is a fine old village, surrounded by vineyards and known for its 1st-century BC Roman bridge. Bard offers the first of the valley's castles, most of which were built by the Challant family who ruled the region for seven centuries. The stark fortress at Verres comes into view soon after, perhaps less interesting than the castle at Issogne▶, a plain affair from the outside, but inside completely full of fascinating apartments and period furnishings.

St.-Vincent is a fashionable spa with one of Italy's largest casinos. Further west, **Fenis▶▶** is the one castle to visit if you visit no other, a fairytale fortress of towers and turrets, its court, chapel and loggias covered in 14th-century frescos.

Fairytale Fenis Castle

Aosta is the region's focus (page 65), an interesting town in its own right and a base for trips to the **Parco Nazionale del Gran Paradiso** (page 68) and **Valle del Gran San Bernardo** (page 77). Beyond it, castles come thick and fast, with particularly fine ones at Sarre, St.-Pierre and Avise—all pretty villages.

Round off a drive by taking the renowned cable car ride over Mont Blanc, the **Funivia del Monte Bianco▶▶▶**, which starts from La Palud, a hamlet 2 miles north of the resort town of Courmayeur. There are three stages; you can ride to 10,960 feet at Punta Helbronner, press on over the Géant Glacier, or cross right over the mountain to Chamonix over the French border.

Farming in the Valle d'Aosta

►► Val d'Ayas 62D2

The Val d'Ayas is one of the prettiest of the valleys that branch off the Valle d'Aosta: broad, heavily wooded and crowned by the colossal peaks of Monte Rosa and the Matterhorn (Cervino in Italian). Champoluc is the chief resort, departure point for mountain hikes and the cable car to Testa Grigia (11,000 feet), one of the most spectacular vantage points in the Alps. Brusson to the south is a base for easier walks, the best being the trail to the coronet of mountain lakes below Punta Valfredda (3hr 30min).

► Valle del Gran San Bernardo 62D2

Easily seen from Aosta (see page 65), this valley is best known for its pass and famous St. Bernard dogs (see panel). Along its entire length, however, it is a scenic delight, well worth traveling for the ride alone. For still grander scenery, take the tortuous mountain road east of the valley into the wild reaches of the Valpelline.

► Val di Gressoney 62D3

So perfect an alpine valley it is almost a cliché, the Val di Gressoney is a vision of emerald-green meadows, snow-capped peaks, shimmering glaciers and geranium-hung wooden houses. Its inhabitants, the Walser, speak an obscure German dialect, having migrated here from the Swiss Valais in the 12th century. The main centers, Gressoney-St.-Jean and trendier Gressoney-La-Trinité, offer plenty of hiking and skiing opportunities.

► Valle di Susa 62C1

The Valle di Susa lacks the drama of smaller alpine valleys, and is spoiled in places by light industry and its busy road and rail links. It has, however, one or two highlights, notably the dramatic abbey of **Sacra di San Michele►►►**, just west of the pretty lakeside village of Avigliana. **Susa►** features a scattering of Roman remains and several ancient churches. Close by, roads lead into glorious scenery, particularly around the nature reserves of Salbertrand and Orsiera-Rocciavré.

Bridge leading to the St. Bernard Tunnel

The St. Bernard Pass
The 8,148ft. pass has long been one of the Alps' most important routes, used by Roman legions, Celts, Charlemagne and Napoleon. Today, its chief attraction is the Hospice of St. Bernard, founded in 1050. It is just in Switzerland, so take your passport. Part of the monks' vocation involved ministering to weary and snowbound travelers, helped by a uniquely robust type of dog. The souvenir shacks are stuffed with china, plastic and fluffy versions of the famous brandy-carrying St. Bernard dog.

LOMBARDY & EMILIA-ROMAGNA

78

Tourist information
Bellagio: (Lake Como)
Piazza della Chiesa 14 (tel:
031/950 204).
Bergamo: Viale Papa
Giovanni XXIII 106 (tel:
035/242 2226).
Bologna: Via Marconi 45
(tel: 051/238 660).
Como: Piazza Cavour 17
(tel: 031/262 091).
Mantova: Piazza A
Mantegna 6 (tel: 0376/328
253).
Malcesine (Lake Garda):
Via Capitanato del Porto 1
(tel: 045/740 0555).
Milano: Via Marconi 1 (tel:
02/809 662); Stazione
Centrale (tel: 02/669 0432).
Parma: Piazza Duomo 5
(tel: 0521/233 959).
Pavia: Via Fabio Filzi 2 (tel:
0382/22 156).
Ravenna: Via Salara 8 (tel:
0544/35 404).
Stresa: (Lake Maggiore)
Via Principe Tomaso 70
(tel: 0323/30 150).

Lombardy and Emilia-Romagna Italy's richest regions are a perfect balance of city and countryside. Lombardy is divided between the plains of the Po and the mountains of the high Alps (Emilia-Romagna is mainly plain). Two cities lie at their heart: Milan, Italy's fashion and finance capital; and Bologna, ancient seat of learning and gastronomic star. Elsewhere, scattered small cities combine medieval centers with industrial hinterlands. Immense agricultural riches spring from the plains, creating, sadly, unlovely landscapes. If it's fine scenery you want, head for the Italian Lakes, a dozen or more lakes that fill the great Alpine valleys north of Milan.

Milan Italy's capital by rights is Rome, but these days it could as easily be Milan (Milano), a major industrial center, and a flourishing hotbed of fashion, design, and high technology. Visitors often find its modern face less appealing than more obviously historic cities like Venice and Florence, yet the city's sights include a grand cathedral, the world-class Brera art gallery—and Leonardo da Vinci's *Last Supper*. The city also makes a good touring base: the lakes and mountains are surprisingly close, and fascinating towns like Bergamo and Pavia—with its magnificent abbey—are less than an hour away.

The Italian Lakes Celebrated for centuries for their great natural beauty, the lakes these days are slightly sullied by people and pollution, but for the most part they remain a romantic medley of mountains, forests, lakeside villas, and mild-weathered resorts. The big three—Como, Garda and Maggiore—are well known; slightly less frequented are Iseo and Orta. The latter, in particular, is still largely unspoiled by crowds and commercialism. Como takes most of the scenic plaudits, and Maggiore is a must, if only to visit the Isole Borromee (Borromean Islands).

You need a car to do the lakes justice (though trains offer firsthand views of them all save Garda). Try to avoid July and August, and weekends in particular, when Lombardy's cities empty northwards towards the region.

Bellagio, the jewel of Lake Como

Ideally, make base camp near a lake, then take boat trips to its other towns—by far the best way to see the scenery. Stresa is the best overall center on Lake Maggiore; Como the best on Lake Como; and Malcesine the first choice on Garda. All these places are popular, of course, and smaller villages are always worth checking out. If in doubt, head north, away from the spots easily reached from Milan.

Cities Northern Italy's plains offer next to nothing in the way of scenery. Their tedium is relieved only by some of Italy's finest medium-sized cities, places that most people pass by as they rush to Florence or Venice. Lombardy's are perhaps the least known, and as a result can make surprisingly peaceful spots to while away a couple of days. Mantova is the best, a perfect medieval city in a strange, lagoon-circled setting. Cremona is a little too provincial, but attracts attention as the birthplace of the great violin-maker Stradivari. Bologna and Parma are the big draws in Emilia-Romagna, prosperous cities renowned for their cuisine and wide range of medieval monuments.

Rice and risotto It comes as a surprise to many people to see the vast paddy fields that spread over large areas of Piedmont and Lombardy. Rice—and not pasta—is the mainstay of the Milanese diet (the area is Europe's largest rice producer). No one knows when or why cultivation started, though the theory is that the grain spread from Asia to Egypt and was then brought by Arabs to Sicily. The classic recipe for risotto uses rice fried with butter and onions, then cooked with stock, marrow and saffron (butter and parmesan are added before serving). Other versions include *Certosa*, with crayfish (invented by Carthusian monks); *Monza*, with sausage; *Comasco*, using perch; *Lomellina*, with frogs; and *alla pilota*, from Mantova, with salami.

Scenic railroads
Europe's highest and most spectacular railroad, the "Red Train," runs from Tirano (near Sondrio) to St. Moritz. Special tourist trains operate in summer, carrying observation cars for better views of the peaks and glaciers of the Bernina Alps. Almost equally spectacular is the two-hour run through the mountains from Domodossola to Locarno.

Scenic drives
SS 229 Lago d'Orta; SS 337 Domodossola–Santa Maria Maggiore–Locarno; SS 659 Domodossola–Crodo–Formazza; (*Lake Como*) SS 340/SS 583 Como–Gravedona–Bellano–Lecco–Bellagio–Como; SS 38/SS 39 Sondrio–Aprica–Edolo; (*Stelvio National Park*) SS 300 Bormio–Santa Caterina–Ponte di Legno: (*Adamello Regional Park*) SS 345 Breno–Collio–Iseo.

The Colleoni chapel, Bergamo

Donizetti
Gaetano Donizetti, master of *bel canto*, the style of virtuoso aria that characterized his operas, was born in Bergamo in 1797. Around 60 operas and 51 years later he also died there, riddled with syphilis and certifiably insane.

Eating and epithets
Bologna has many nicknames: *La Dotta* (The Learned), after the university; *La Turrita* (The Turreted), after its towers; and *La Grassa* (The Fat), after a cuisine widely considered Italy's finest. Besides *bolognese* sauce (or *ragù*), specialties include baloney (Bologna) sausage; *mortadella* (a kind of Italian cold cut); *tortellini*; and *tagliatelle*, reputedly invented for the wedding feast of Lucrezia Borgia and the Duke of Ferrara. The long, straw-colored strands of pasta were said to have been inspired by the bride's flowing locks.

▶▶ **Bergamo** 78D2

Bergamo is in two parts: an old hill town, Bergamo Alta, and the more modern Bergamo Bassa. Most of the sights cluster in Bergamo Alta's Piazza Vecchia and the adjoining Piazza del Duomo. The French writer Stendhal thought the Piazza Vecchia "the most beautiful place on earth ... the prettiest I have ever seen." Gracious medieval buildings fill both squares, notably the Romanesque church of **Santa Maria Maggiore▶▶**, its riotously over-decorated interior distinguished by a magnificent wooden choir. Flanking the church is the even more impressive **Cappella Colleoni▶▶▶**, designed in 1476 for the Venetian *condottiere* Bartolomeo Colleoni by G. A. Amadeo (also responsible for Pavia's Certosa, see page 91). Its ceiling frescos, by Tiepolo, depict the life of John the Baptist. Nearby, see also the **Baptistery▶**, and climb to the **Cittadella▶** for fine views over the town.

Walk towards Bergamo Bassa on Via Pignolo to take in the **Accademia Carrara▶▶▶**, one of northern Italy's most important—and least-known—art galleries. Many of the greatest Italian masters are represented (Botticelli, Titian, Raphael), as well as other European "greats."

▶▶▶ **Bologna** 79B4

Capital of Emilia-Romagna, wealthy Bologna is known for its cuisine, its left-leaning politics, Italy's oldest university, and its mellow-bricked palaces and porticoes. It centers around Piazza Maggiore and Piazza del Nettuno, home to Giambologna's 1556 Fontana del Nettuno, the medieval Palazzo Comunale and **San Petronio▶▶▶**, one of Italy's greatest Gothic churches (note its portal in particular, by the Sienese sculptor Jacopo della Quercia). The nearby **Museo Archeologico▶** has a wide-ranging collection, best seen in conjunction with the **Archiginnasio▶▶**, part of the city's original medieval university.

No trip to the city is complete without climbing the leaning Torre degli Asinelli, but leave time also for the **Pinacoteca Nazionale▶▶**, with its important collection including Raphael's famous *Ecstasy of St. Cecilia*; **San Giacomo Maggiore▶▶** for its Bentivoglio chapel; the Gothic church of San Francesco; Santo Stefano, a group of ancient churches; and the art-crammed **San Domenico▶▶▶**, with the Arca di San Domenico, the saint's sarcophagus, bearing sculpted decoration by Nicola Pisano and Michelangelo.

▶ **Brescia** 78D3

Lombardy's second city is disappointing, its historic center tarnished by hideous Fascist architecture, its sights scattered around chill modern streets. **Piazza della Loggia▶** has a delicately festooned Loggia, a palace designed in part by Palladio and Sansovino (1492–1570). The nearby Piazza del Duomo has two cathedrals, one drab, the other—the **Rotonda▶**—a more interesting 12th-century affair. Via dei Musei contains several Roman remains, the excellent **Museo Romano▶** and the Museo dell'Età Cristiana, a collection of early church art. The **Pinacoteca Tosio-Martinengo▶▶** offers the works of mainly local artists (plus Raphael, Tiepolo and Tintoretto). But the city's masterpiece—Titian's *Annunciation*—can be seen in the church of **San Nazario▶▶**.

▶   **Como**   78D1

Como, on the shores of Lake Como, is part elegant resort, part industrial town. Parks and bustling cafés line its lakefront promenades, all a stone's throw from the splendid 15th-century Renaissance-Gothic **Duomo▶▶**. Other fragments of old Como include San Fedele (once the town's cathedral), at the heart of the medieval quarter, and the Porta Vittoria, the late 12th-century city gate. Brave the industrial quarter of Como to see **Sant'Abbondio▶▶**, a beautiful 11th-century church, and leave enough time to ride the funicular to hilltop Brunate for views of the lake. When you tire of Como and its lake, you can drive 12 miles west, to **Castiglione Olana▶▶▶** to see the Gothic Collegiata, with its superlative frescos by Giotto's pupil Masolino da Panicale, and his even finer frescos in the Baptistery.

▶▶▶   **Como, Lago di (Lake Como)**   78D2

Edged by plunging mountains, Lake Como is the most dramatic of the Italian lakes. True, its waters are often polluted and its many resorts thronged by British and German tourists, but this said, its lush surroundings, its villas and gardens and the views make a visit essential. The best thing to do is to take a tour of the lake by boat (special passes available at Como allow you to stop off wherever you please). **Bellagio▶▶▶** is by far the most picturesque village (see panel), though Cernobbio, Tremezzo and Menaggio all have their charms.

Bellagio

Lake Como's jewel has been called the prettiest village in Europe. From its promontory, it looks out over both arms of Lake Como, commanding peerless views, and is best approached by boat from either Como or Menaggio. Wander the cobbled streets, almost too quaint for their own good, and visit the gardens of the Villa Melzi and Villa Serbelloni. The apse and capitals of San Giacomo, a 12th-century church, both have some good carvings. From the village you can also visit Varenna, with the Villa Monastero and its lovely garden.

The death of Mussolini

Lake Como's beautiful surroundings were the incongruous setting for the capture and killing of Benito Mussolini by partisans in 1945, when the Fascist leader was attempting to flee to Switzerland. He was caught at a roadblock near Mezzegra (just south of Tremezzo). The partisan leader, Waltger Audasio, tried to shoot Mussolini, but la Duce's mistress Claretta threw herself on the gun, which jammed. Audasio then took his driver's gun and shot Claretta before complying with Mussolini's last request to shoot him in the chest.

Neptune astride his fountain in Bologna

► Cremona 78C2

A quiet provincial town, Cremona is synonymous with violins, and in particular with Antonio Stradivari (1644–1737), the greatest violin maker of all time. Needless to say the town honors its most famous son with a museum, the **Museo Stradivariano►**, complemented by the adjoining Museo Civico, both crammed with violins and miscellaneous memorabilia (as well as displays devoted to Roman Cremona).

Violins apart, Cremona can seem a little stultifying: too quiet to hold your interest for long. The Romanesque **Duomo►►** and medieval **Piazza del Comune►►**, however, are superb, and in the **Torrazzo►►** the town boasts the tallest medieval tower in Italy (369 feet).

► Faenza 79B5

A typical plate from Faenza

You visit Faenza, an otherwise melancholy town, for one thing: the vast **Museo Internazionale delle Ceramiche►►**, one of the most comprehensive ceramic collections in Italy. The town's pottery (faïence-ware), with its characteristic blue and ocher coloring, has been famed throughout Europe for over 500 years. Today it is still produced and sold in numerous workshops. The museum displays not only native ware, but also pottery from many periods and countries—from Roman majolica and Renaissance sculpture to the modern ceramic art of Pablo Picasso, Henri Matisse and Marc Chagall.

84

The violins of Cremona
Cremona's Andrea Amati produced the first modern violin in 1566, handing down his techniques to his son Nicolò, who passed them in turn to his pupils, Antonio Stradivari and Giuseppe Guarneri. Stradivari's career spanned 68 years, during which time he made an estimated 1,200 violins, violas, cellos, harps, guitars, and mandolins. He reputedly kept instruments in his bedroom for a month before completion. In this way, he claimed, his dreams imparted "soul" to his creations.

Between 800 and 1,000 violins annually are still produced in Cremona's 60 workshops (*botteghe liutarie*). Europe's foremost violin-making school, La Bottega, is also here.

►► Ferrara 79B4

In its day, Ferrara—a lovely and unvisited town—could claim one of Europe's most dynamic Renaissance courts. Its driving force was the Este family, a dynasty who ruled and rebuilt the city over several hundred years. Their dynastic seat, the **Castello Estense►** still lords it over the town, worth seeing for its decorated apartments and atmospheric dungeons. Another Este retreat, the **Palazzo Schifanoia►►**, is noteworthy for its Sala dei Mesi, a roomful of fine frescos illustrating the twelve months. Other worthy paintings, including works by Bellini and Mantegna, reside in the gallery of the early Renaissance **Palazzo dei Diamanti►►**. The **Duomo►►** contains a jewel of a museum, the Museo del Duomo, full of precious works of art. Sights apart, it's pleasant simply to walk Ferrara's streets—Via delle Volte and the distinct medieval and planned Renaissance quarters in particular.

►►► Garda, Lago di (Lake Garda) 78D3

Garda is the largest of the Italian Lakes, its landscapes divided between gentle plains in the south and tree-covered hills and mountains in the north. Its most popular spot is **Sirmione►►**, enchanting off-season, tourist-choked in summer. The beautifully situated castle called

Rocca Scaligera▶ is the most memorable sight (great fun to explore). Out of town you should also see the Grotte di Catullo▶, the ruins of a Roman spa scattered over a hillside of ancient olive trees.

Midway up the lake's eastern shore, stop off at **Punta di San Vigilio▶▶**, by common consent the lake's prettiest spot. After enjoying its views and cypress-filled gardens, move on to **Malcesine▶**, one of Garda's more sedate and appealing villages. Like Sirmione, it too has an evocative castle, though more people go for the cable car ride to the 6,600-foot summit of Monte Baldo for its views and wealth of hiking opportunities. It is known as the "Garden of Italy" for its exceptional botanical variety.

Riva del Garda▶ is the lake's best-known resort, a young and lively spot, though its crowds and commercialism weigh against its undoubted prettiness. Nearby, visit the 313-foot waterfall, Cascata del Varone. Moving round to the lake's less ravaged western shore, drive into the hills above Limone sul Garda for a tiny network of scenic roads (via Vesio Pieve and Tignale). Views from the church of Madonna di Monte Castello (near Tignale) are especially good. **Gardone Riviera▶▶** was once the lake's most fashionable resort and still retains much of its erstwhile elegance. Nearby stands the not-to-be-missed Il Vittoriale degli Italiani (see panel). **Salò▶** too, is worth a stop, as it is a nicely situated town with a fine Gothic cathedral.

▶ ▬▬▬ **Iseo, Lago di**   *78D2*

One of the quieter Italian Lakes, Iseo has few sights but shares its neighbors' romantic beauty and mountainous surroundings. The west shore is quieter, served by small resorts like Sarnico, Tavernola and Riva di Solto. **Monte Isola▶▶**, an island in the center of the lake, is known for its panoramic views.

Poetic eccentricity
The extraordinary villa called Il Vittoriale was presented by Mussolini to Gabriele d'Annunzio, larger-than-life poet, soldier, socialite and aristocratic womanizer. The gift was ostensibly in recognition of d'Annunzio's patriotism, but was also designed to keep him quiet (his claim to have eaten dead babies can hardly have helped the Fascist cause). The poet transformed the villa into a kitsch palace, filling it with souvenirs of his military, literary and amatory accomplishments. Furnishings include an embalmed tortoise, a bath surrounded by 200 pieces of bric-à-brac and a World War I biplane.

85

Delightful Sirmione on Lake Garda

The plains of Emilia-Romagna have little to offer the walker, but there are hikes to suit all abilities in Lombardy's Lakes region, the Alpine foothills and mountain fastness of the Stelvio National Park.

Lago di Como On Como's western shore try the walk that starts from the hamlet of Breglia above the lakeshore town of Menaggio. The trail reaches the *Rifugio Menaggio* after about an hour and a quarter and from here several trails lead into higher terrain. The best option (weather allowing), is the path to Monte Bregagno (6,950 feet), a breathtaking viewpoint.

Lago di Garda Monte Baldo on Lake Garda's eastern shore has several easily accessible high-level walks (take the cable car from Malcesine or minor roads into the mountains from the lakeshore). The best of these follows the mountain's main ridge, heading for the *Rifugio Telegrafo* (7,095 feet). To plan this and other local walks use the Kompass map *Lago di Garda-Monte Baldo* (No. 102).

Malcesine's cable car offers an easier way to see the views of Lake Garda

Parco Nazionale dello Stelvio Italy's largest national park has nearly a thousand miles of marked trails. The classic walk for first-time visitors is along the Valle dello Zebrù, a spectacular valley due east of Bormio, a town on the park's western flanks. Immediately to the south, the parallel Valle dei Forni has a great walk to the *Rifugio Branca* from Forni, with magnificent views of the Cevedale glaciers (use Kompass map *Ortles–Cevedale* (No. 72).

Practicalities Walking is best in the Alps from June to September: the season is longer in the Lakes, where snow on low ground melts sooner. Most of the area is well-mapped, the most comprehensive coverage being provided by the 1:50,000 Kompass series. Tabacco maps are better, but cover fewer areas. Both brands are widely available on the spot. Tourist offices often have guides to easier walks, particularly in the Lakes.

▶▶▶ Lago Maggiore (Lake Maggiore) 78D1

You need to pick and choose what you see on Lake Maggiore. Much of the shore is flat and disrupted by factories, the mountains are far away, and the towns crowded. At the same time the villas, lush gardens and vestigial 19th-century elegance of the lake's resorts continue to draw visitors.

Refined **Stresa▶▶**, though busy, is the best center. A cable car runs from the town to Monte Mottarone for stunning views. Pick up boats at Stresa for the **Isole Borromee▶▶▶**, an exquisite archipelago of islands (worth seeing if you see nothing else in the Lakes). Isola Bella's villa and gardens make it the most visited of the group (see panel), but neither **Isola Pescatori▶▶** nor the quieter **Isola Madre▶▶▶** should be missed.

More intimate **Baveno▶** was once patronized by Queen Victoria. **Villa Taranto▶▶** near Verbania is the most famous of all the Lakes' botanical gardens. Resorts further north and on the lake's eastern (Lombardy) shore have little to recommend them other than tranquility. The best are **Cannero Riviera▶**, Ghiffa, Cervo and **Angera▶**.

Right: a palace with a view—Isola Bella
Below: neighboring Borromean island, Isola Pescatori

▶▶▶ Mantova (Mantua) 78C3

Once past Mantova's grim outskirts you can see why Aldous Huxley described it as the most romantic city in the world. Surrounded by lakes (it is sometimes known as *piccola Venezia*—little Venice), the city has an evocative skyline of ancient towers, and an historic center of almost theatrical medieval perfection.

The top sight is the astounding **Palazzo Ducale▶▶▶**, home of the Gonzagas, one of the Renaissance's foremost dynasties. In its day it was the largest palace in Europe. When it was sacked in 1630, 80 carriages were required to remove the two thousand works of art contained in its 500 rooms. Be sure to see the Camera degli Sposi and its Mantegna fresco cycle, the palace's real treasure. The family's summer residence, the **Palazzo Te▶▶** is also more than worth seeing.

Mantua's highlights continue with **Piazza delle Erbe▶▶**, a lovely central square; **Sant'Andrea▶▶**, an overblown Renaissance church; the Rotonda, a half-ruined 11th-century church; and the Torre della Gabbia and Broletto, medieval prison and town hall respectively.

Isola Bella
The most captivating of the Isole Borromee, Isola Bella was no more than a barren rock until the 17th century, when Count Carlo III Borromeo decided to convert it into a garden paradise for his wife, Isabella. The ravishing island is spoiled only by the artificial grottoes, kitsch statues and appallingly decorated villa—described by Robert Southey as "one of the most costly efforts of bad taste in all Italy."

Milan's magnificent Gothic cathedral

Milanese food
Milan's gastronomic specialties include *polenta*, a type of corn-based mush, a staple of northern Italy—trendy today, but overrated. More mouth-watering are breaded cutlets, *cotolette alla milanese*—wiener schnitzel by another name (a legacy of Milan's period under Austro-Hungarian rule). *Risotto alla milanese* is also common, traditionally made with saffron and broth. *Panettone*, a Milanese cake with fruit and raisins, is a Christmas treat now eaten all over Italy.

Local wines
The closest wine zones to the city produce Oltrepò Pavese and San Colombano. From further afield look for Pino and Rosso di Franciacorte; the fine white, Lugana; the reds Groppello, Buttafuoco and Barbacarlo; and the wines from the Valtellina, a high Alpine valley—Grumello, Valgella and Sassella.

▶▶▶ Milano (Milan) 78D2

There is little *dolce vita* in Milan: busy and work-oriented, Italy's capital of fashion and high finance is a slick and businesslike city—and firmly European in outlook (a "southern suburb of Paris," according to some, while Rome is—a "northern suburb of Cairo"). Pollution is a constant plague, and corruption scandals have recently rocked the city's political hierarchy. Modern in appearance as well as outlook, Milan is perhaps less fun to wander in than some cities—though its main sights are as compelling as any in the country.

The finest of these is the **Duomo▶▶▶**, Italy's largest Gothic building, and Europe's third largest church (after St. Peter's and Seville cathedral). The exterior's forest of spires and intricate decoration—a "poem in marble," said Mark Twain—compensates for a disappointing interior. The highlight is a trip to the roof, a magical world of spires and turrets, with views—smog allowing—that extend as far as the Matterhorn.

West of the Duomo, stroll through the **Galleria Vittorio Emanuele**, a Belle Epoque shopping arcade, to reach La Scala, Milan's famous opera house, and then Via Manzoni, one of the city's most fashionable and frenetic streets. Partway up it stands the **Museo Poldi Pezzoli▶▶**, a collection of antiques and paintings, the best of which are in the Salone Dorato (Golden Room). Antonio Pollaiuolo's *Portrait of a Young Woman* is here, one of Italy's most renowned portraits, together with works by Raphael, Mantegna, Botticelli, Giovanni Bellini, and Piero della Francesca.

For the city's single most famous work of art, however, you need to trek across the city to the church of **Santa Maria delle Grazie▶▶▶**. Partly designed by Bramante, the church is a Renaissance tour-de-force, though few people give it more than a passing glance. Most are intent on seeing Leonardo da Vinci's *The Last Supper*, on a wall of Santa Maria's old refectory (see page 90).

The colossal size of the **Castello Sforzesco** makes it the city's principal landmark after the **Duomo▶▶▶**. Built by the Viscontis, Milan's medieval overlords, and enlarged by their successors, the Sforzas, it became the seat of one of Europe's leading courts of the Renaissance period. Now its rambling inner courtyards house two middling art galleries: the **Pinacoteca►►** and **Museo d'Arte Antica►►**. The latter's collection is a mish-mash of sculpture, dominated by Michelangelo's unfinished last work, the *Pietà Rondanini*. The former includes a fresco cycle of scenes from Boccaccio's *Decameron*, a plethora of medieval *objets d'art*, and works by Mantegna, Crivelli, Giovanni Bellini and Filippo Lippi.

Ten minutes away is the **Accademia Brera►►►**, one of Italy's top galleries, and one that is so rich that it probably requires several visits. Among the feast of paintings on display are Mantegna's famous *Cristo Morto* and Veronese's equally well-known *Supper in the House of Simon*. Other treasures include Raphael's *Marriage of the Virgin*, Piero della Francesca's *Pala di Urbino*, Giovanni Bellini's superlative *Pietà*, and works by Caravaggio, Carpaccio, Tintoretto, El Greco, Rembrandt and many more.

For still more art, visit the **Palazzo dell' Ambrosiana►►**, home to a fabulous 17th-century library, but of more general interest for a distinguished art collection that includes Botticelli's *Tondo* and *Madonna del Baldacchino*, Caravaggio's *Fruit Basket* (Italy's first still-life), Giorgione's *Page*; Leonardo's *Portrait of a Musician*; and the cartoon for Raphael's *School of Athens*.

If looking at paintings begins to wear on, you could make for the most eminent of Milan's many churches, **Sant'Ambrogio►►►**, founded in 379 by St. Ambrose, Milan's first bishop and the city's patron saint. Most of the present structure dates from the 11th century. Inside, its chief treasures are a handsome pulpit, one of Italy's finest Romanesque works, the apse's 11th-century mosaic, and the sanctuary's 9th-century gold and jewel-studded ciborium.

Shopping
Milan is tops for high fashion, accessories and luxury goods. The big-name shops cluster in the so-called *Quadrilatero d'Oro* (Golden Quadrangle)—the area defined by Via Monte Napoleone, Via della Spiga, Via Borgo Spesso and Via Sant'Andrea. For more affordable prices you could do worse than visit *La Rinascente* in Piazza del Duomo, Milan's largest and oldest department store—and a city institution. Many of the glass-domed *gallerie* off Galleria Vittorio Emanuele have interesting, high-quality shops.

89

High-class shopping in the Galleria Vittorio Emanuele

The Last Supper

Asked to name the world's most famous paintings, many people would cite first the *Mona Lisa* and then perhaps another of Leonardo da Vinci's masterpieces—*The Last Supper*, painted in the refectory of Milan's Santa Maria delle Grazie.

The search for Judas

The 16th-century art historian Giorgio Vasari tells us that the figure of Judas gave Leonardo great problems in the two years he worked on the painting. He scoured Milan's streets and prisons for models, casting around for someone with a face of sufficient venality. The result, said Vasari, was "the very embodiment of treachery and inhumanity."

The Last Supper
under restoration

Leonardo's vision of the beginning of Christ's agony is one of European art's best known images, yet in person the faded and badly deteriorated surface of *L'Ultima Cena (The Last Supper)* is a sobering sight (Aldous Huxley called it "the saddest painting in the world"). For all its decay, it remains a startling work, capturing the moment Christ announces that He will be betrayed by one of His disciples.

Leonardo chose to apply oil and tempera to a dry surface, rather than the accepted fresco method of painting pigment onto wet plaster. This allowed him greater flexibility of tone and color, but moisture soon began to corrode the painting. Over the centuries the fresco suffered further from clumsy attempts at restoration. At one point, Santa Maria's monks gave up on the project altogether—and whitewashed part of the painting. On another occasion, Napoleonic troops billeted in the refectory used the fresco for target practice. In 1943 a bomb hit the building, destroying everything but *The Last Supper*.

Modern restoration techniques are now attempting to turn back the years. Amazingly, many of the fresco's details are still vivid, gestures and expressions captured in almost photographic detail. Look for the figure of Doubting Thomas and his raised finger; the hangdog profile of Philip, arms folded, fearful that he may be the betrayer; or Peter, partly blocked by Judas hurrying forward with his 30 pieces of silver.

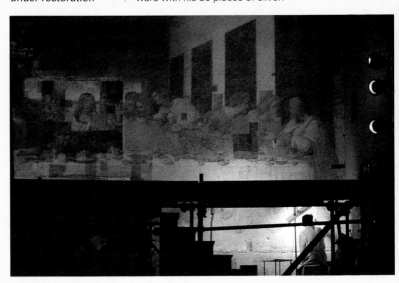

► Modena 79B4

A long-time rival to Bologna, Modena is a northern city in the classic mold: provincial and quietly prosperous, its outskirts industrial, its tight center a medieval delight. Pride of place goes to the **Duomo►►**, a 12th-century Romanesque masterpiece, known for its *tribuna* (rood screen) and a lurching campanile, the **Torre Ghirlandina►**. In the maze of appealing old streets nearby, make a point of visiting the Palazzo dei Musei, home to three museums: the Biblioteca Estense, its prize exhibit the *Bibbio Borso*, a sumptuously decorated medieval Bible; the Museo d'Arte Mediovale e Moderna e Etnologia and the Galleria Estense, a gallery of paintings, many by local Renaissance masters.

►► Orta, Lago di 78D1

Lake Orta's tranquil beauty is the perfect antidote to the commercialism and tainted charms of the larger Italian lakes. Its main center, **Orta-San Giulio►►**, is a peaceful small town, a base for boat trips out to the **Isola San Giulio►►**. This is a dream of an island, its hamlet capital dominated by a brilliant white Romanesque church, the Basilica di San Giulio.

Around the lake the best of the gardens is the **Villa Junker►** near Gozzano. For views walk up the Sacro Monte above Orta San Giulio, or drive to Madonna del Sasso and Quarna perched above the lake's western shore.

►►► Parma 78B3

Italy's most prosperous town, Parma is a monument to good living, with fine food (it is the home of Parma ham and Parmesan cheese), an excellent opera house and a wealth of elegant cafés and exclusive stores. The **Duomo►►►** is one of the country's finest Lombard-Romanesque churches, distinguished by the 16th-century painter Correggio's great fresco of the *Assumption of the Virgin*. Nearby, the 12th-century octagonal **Baptistery►►►** contains some of the most expressive Romanesque sculptures in Italy, a series of reliefs on the exterior and 12 carvings inside depicting the months of the year. Behind the Duomo, **San Giovanni Evangelista►►►** boasts more superlative frescos by Correggio. The Galleria Nazionale, the antiquities museum and the Teatro Farnese are all housed in the vast **Palazzo della Pilotta►►**.

► Pavia 78C1

A day trip from Milan, Pavia—where kings and emperors were crowned in the Middle Ages—has a sleepy collection of medieval streets, with something of interest at every turn. Most of the sights in the city, however, are overshadowed by the nearby **Certosa di Pavia►►►**, one of the most dazzling monasteries in Europe, set in a former hunting ground of the Visconti family and rich in Renaissance and baroque art. Nevertheless, do not miss two outstanding churches; **San Michele►►►** and **San Pietro in Ciel d'Oro►►**, both handsome Romanesque masterpieces. The austere 14th-century **Castello Visconteo►** also houses a trio of modest art and archeology museums.

Ferrari
One of the world's most famous cars is made just outside Modena near the village of Maranello. Enzo Ferrari founded the Ferrari factory in 1945. Today it produces around 2,500 cars a year. Another famous automaker, Maserati, also has a plant near the city.

Your table is ready in Parma's Piazza Garibaldi

The Empress Theodora
The career of Justinian's wife Theodora—featured in the mosaics of San Vitale in Ravenna—would make headlines in today's popular newspapers. Accounts of her life tell of a youth spent as a child prostitute and circus performer, followed by spells as a courtesan and performer in live sex shows. Something of a stir ran around court circles when Justinian picked her as Empress, a ripple of scandal that meant he had to wait until his disapproving mother's death before he could marry. Their reign, by all accounts, was one of rampant corruption.

▶ Piacenza 78C2

Unassuming Piacenza stands in the shadow of better known cities like Parma and Cremona. Few people visit its sleepy medieval center, still laid out on the gridiron pattern of the old Roman colony (the city marked the end of the old Roman road, the *Via Aemilia*). Piazza dei Cavalli, the central square, is dominated by the crenellated **Palazzo del Comune▶▶**, the council chamber of the medieval city. At its center there stand two equestrian statues, frequently lauded as some of Italy's finest baroque sculptures.

▶▶▶ Ravenna 79B5

Most people come to Ravenna expecting only mosaics (see opposite page), and are surprised to find as appealing a small town as any in Italy. True, the mosaics are virtually the only things to see, but the center's tangle of streets are a pleasure to wander. You might also spend a happy hour in **Piazza del Popolo▶**, a square filled with outdoor cafés and noble medieval *palazzi*.

▶ Rimini 149D5

Rimini is nirvana for beach enthusiasts who like their resorts big and brash (none come bigger—this is Europe's largest seaside town). Crammed with Italian families, and German and Scandinavian students, it is known for sun, sea and sex, for dusk-to-dawn nightlife, and for huge, heavily commercialized beaches. Given all this, it remains surprisingly unsleazy—though it is not the place for quiet sunbathing. Smaller resorts in a similar mold run all the way down Italy's Adriatic coast.

Ravenna: Basilica di San Vitale

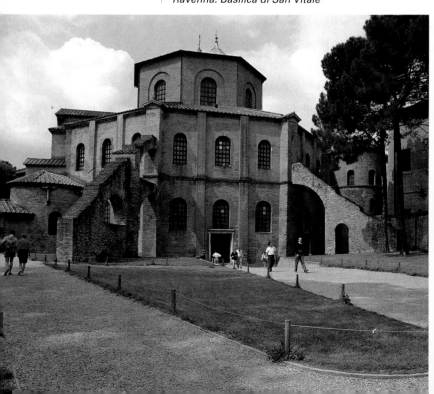

The Mosaics of Ravenna

Ravenna boasts the finest Byzantine mosaics in the world outside Istanbul, a legacy of its role as the capital of the Roman Empire during the 5th century. Its history made it a meeting place of eastern and western artistic trends.

Honorius moved the seat of Empire to Ravenna around AD 403, prompted by Rome's stagnation and by Ravenna's convenient location near *Classis*, the Romans' main port on the Adriatic coast. The city boomed and continued to thrive after the Empire's fall, first under the barbarian leaders Odoacer and Theodoric, and later as a Byzantine vassal ruled by the Emperor Justinian.

The main mosaics Far and away the most breathtaking mosaics—"monuments to unageing intellect," in the words of W. B. Yeats—are to be found in the **Basilica di San Vitale**, a magnificent Byzantine-style church (built in 547) in the city center. Two main strands can be identified in the mosaic panels, the first obviously Byzantine scenes depicting Justinian, Theodora and their court, the second the more classically inspired episodes taken from the Old Testament. Both sets of mosaics date from as early as the 6th century.

Across the grassy piazza outside the church stands the **Mausoleo di Galla Placidia** (see panel), a tiny chapel completely studded with mosaics of ethereal blues and glittering golds —one of the most intimate and most impressive buildings in Italy. The nearby **Museo Nazionale** also boasts many Roman, Byzantine, and early Christian mosaics.

Peacock mosaic in San Vitale

...and the rest The church of **Sant'Apollinare Nuovo** contains two further mosaic cycles. Both show processions, one of virgins and the other of martyrs, both gliding towards the altar against a beautifully evoked background of gold and green-leafed palms. On a smaller scale, the 6th-century **Oratorio di Sant'Andrea** contains mosaics from two eras; one sequence from the building's period as a Roman bathhouse, the other a cycle executed when the building became a Christian baptistery.

Three miles from Ravenna, the church of **Sant' Apollinare in Classe** is about all that survives of ancient *Classis*. Consecrated in 549, its mosaics are as impressive as any in the city, particularly those in the apse of *The Transfiguration of Christ*.

Galla Placidia

Galla Placidia was one of the most remarkable women in ancient Rome's history. Daughter of Theodosius, the father of Emperor Honorius, she was kidnapped when the Goths sacked Rome. Almost immediately she married Ataulfo, one of her kidnappers—who was promptly assassinated. She then sought refuge with her half brother Honorius. Forced to marry Constantius, a Roman general, she contrived to have her husband made joint emperor with Honorius. Widowed again, she had her son, Valentinian III (aged six), made emperor (with herself as Regent). She died and was buried in Rome in AD 450, leaving open the question of who instigated her mausoleum in Ravenna.

E

Canale delle Sacche

Canale

Canale

Sant' Alvise

Madonna dell' Orto

Sant' Alvise

Madonna dell' Orto

Ponte Tre Archi

Rio di San Girolamo

Rio della Sensa

CAMPO GHETTO NUOVO

Canale di Cannaregio

Rio del Battelo

Ponte Guglie

Rio della

RIO TERRÀ FARSETTI

RIO TERRÀ DELLA

C A N N A R E

San Giobbe

GHETTO

RIO TERRÀ SAN LEONARDO

MADDALENA

Misericordia

Mise

D

CAMPO SAN GEREMIA

Palazzo Lábia

San Marcuola

Palazzo Vendramin Calergi

STRADA NOVA

Scalzi

RIO TERRÀ LISTA DI SPAGNA

San Geremia

San Marcuola

C

Stazione Ferroviaria Santa Lucia

PONTE SCALZI

Canal Grande

Riva di Biásio

Fóndaco dei Turchi

San Stae

San Stae

Ca' d'Oro

Ferrovia

San Simeòn Piccolo

Rio Marin

San Giácomo dell'Orio

Palazzo Mocenigo

Ca' Pésaro

Casa Favretto

Ca' d'Oro

Pesche

PONTE DELLA LIBERTÀ

Piazzale Roma

Giardino Papadópoli

CAMPO SAN GIACOMO DELL' ORIO

Palazzo Cornèr della Regina

Rio di San Cassiano

Autorimessa

PIAZZALE ROMA

Piazzale Roma

San Nicolò da Tolentini

Scuola di San Giovanni Evangelista

SAN POLO

SANTA CROCE

Santa Maria Gloriosa dei Frari

CAMPO SAN POLO

PONTE RIAL

San Rocco

Scuola Grande di San Rocco

CAMPO DEI FRARI

San Polo

San Silvestro

Rio Nuovo

San Pantàlon

Rio di San Polo

Canal Grande

B

Rio di Ca' Foscari

San Tomà

Palazzo Cornèr-Spinelli

Palazzo Grimani

Munici

Scuola Grande dei Cármini

CAMPO SANTA MARGHERITA

Sant' Angelo

Palazzo Mocenigo

CAMPO MANIN

San Nicolò dei Mendicoli

Cármini

Ca' Rezzónico

San Samuele

Palazzo Grassi

CAMPO SANT' ANGELO

SAN MARCO

Angelo Raffaele

DORSODURO

CAMPO SAN BARNABA

Ca' Rezzónico

San Samuele

CAMPO SANTO STEFANO

Santo Stefano

CAMPO SAN MAURIZIO

Teatro la Fenice

San Sebastiano

Palazzo Bárbaro

Palazzo Pisani

Pa Ti

FONDAMENTA ZATTERE PONTE LUNGO

Squero di San Trováso

Accademia

PONTE DELL' ACCADEMIA

Santa Maria del Giglio

Gritti

A

San Basilio

Gallerie dell' Accademia

Rio di San Trováso

Collezione Guggenheim

Palazzo Cornèr della Ca' Grande

Palazzo Dario

Salute

Isola della La Giudecca

Canale della

Zàttere

Santa Maria della Salute

Giudecca

FONDAMENTA DELLE ZÀTTERE

1

Il Redentore

2

3

VENÉZIA - SESTIERI

Burano
Murano
Isola di San Michele

PONTE DELLA LIBERTÀ
Canale delle Sacche
Canale delle Navi
Canale delle Fondamente Nuove

Nuova Isola del Tronchetto
CANNAREGIO
Canal Grande
Stazione Ferroviaria Santa Lucia
SANTA CROCE
SAN PÓLO
DORSODURO
SAN MARCO
Isola di San Pietro
CASTELLO

Canale di San Marco

Canale di Fusina
Canale della Giudecca
LA GIUDECCA
Isola di San Giórgio Maggiore
Isola di Sant' Élena

Lido

0 ___ 1 km
0 ___ ½ mile

amente Nuove

Isola di San Michele
Cimitero

0   100   200   300 m
0   100   200   300 yards

Gesuiti (Santa Maria Assunta)
V Fondamente Nuove
Rio dei Gesuiti
FONDAMENTE NUOVE

O

EI
U

Santa Maria dei Mirácoli
Rio dei Mendicanti

Colleoni

Santi Giovanni e Páolo (San Zanipolo)
CAMPO SANTI GIOVANNI E PAOLO

Rio di San Giustina
Celestia

Fadaco dei deschi

CAMPO SANTA MARIA FORMOSA

San Francesco della Vigna

Santa Maria Formosa
salvatore

Palazzo Querini-Stampália e Pinacoteca

Scuola di San Giórgio degli Schiavoni

CASTELLO

San Giórgio dei Grecí

Torre dell' Orológio
atie chie PIAZZA SAN MARCO
Basílica di San Marco
Palazzo Ducale
CAMPO SAN ZACCARIA
San Zaccaria
CAMPO BANDIERA E MORO

Arsenale

apanile rocuratie Nuovo
aseo Correr)
Giardini ex Reali
Prigioni
RIVA DEGLI SCHIAVONI
San Zaccaria
Riva Schiavoni

Santa Maria della Pietà
Rio della Pietà

San Giovanni in Brágora

San Martino

San Biágio

Museo Stórico Navale

an Marco
Ponte dei Sospiri

Arsenale

Bacino di San Marco
a della ogana

Canale di San Marco

San Pietro di Castello

San Giórgio V
San Giórgio Maggiore

Isola di San Giórgio Maggiore

Teatro Verde

4

5

Arriving

Venice's main Marco Polo airport is at Tessera (8 miles away) linked by A.T.V.O. buses (25 minutes) to Piazzale Roma (the end of the causeway joining Venice to the mainland). Treviso airport, 18 miles north of Venice, is the main airport for charter flights. Cars must be parked in the multistory parking garage in Piazzale Roma or the Tronchetto (550 yards away). From here you must walk or take a water bus (*vaporetto*) to the rest of the city.

Essentials

Accademia: Venetian paintings
Basilica di San Marco
Canal Grande
Monumento al Colleoni
Palazzo Ducale
Piazza San Marco
Ponte di Rialto
S.S. Giovanni e Paolo: Tombs of the Doges
Santa Maria Gloriosa dei Frari: Paintings by Titian and Bellini
San Sebastiano: Paintings by Veronese
Scuola Grande di San Rocco: Paintings by Tintoretto
Torcello: Santa Maria Assunta (mosaics)

Venice (Venezia) Not everyone falls in love with Italy's most idiosyncratic city. Its decay can seem sinister, its crowds unendurable, its canals dark and its alleys claustrophobic. Yet there are few people who remain unmoved by it. No matter how you picture the city, be prepared for the reality to be stranger—and probably lovelier—than you imagined. It is no use pretending that you can do justice to its treasury of sights on a short visit. Most of the time it is best simply to wander at random, for Venice is as much a city of atmosphere as of museums and monuments.

A word of warning Visit Venice in the frenetic months of July and August and you risk coming away disappointed. Venice has no real off-season, but during these months the city becomes a travesty (crowds, high prices, packed hotels). Although it sounds like heresy, therefore, give careful thought to taking a room outside Venice—perhaps in Padua, Treviso or Verona—and making several day-trips by train. Leave cars behind—parking is a nightmare and long lines of traffic develop on the causeway from the mainland. Train services are excellent, and link directly to the heart of the city. Follow this advice and it will save you money, hassle, and time.

The city's origins The Venetian lagoon was probably first settled around the time of Christ. More sustained settlement took place during the barbarian invasions (when this little group of islands in the lagoon became a safe haven). By the 6th century a loose confederation of communities had formed, initially under the firm hand of Byzantium (with its rule based in Ravenna), but by 726 under the autonomous control of an elected leader—the Doge. Trading links with the east soon brought great wealth, particularly during the Crusades, and by the 13th century the city owned territories stretching to the Black Sea (a domain "one quarter and one half quarter of the Roman Empire"). These included a sizable mainland empire (present day Veneto and beyond).

Conflict Venice's prestige inevitably led to conflict with the papacy and other leading European powers. The League of Cambrai, formed in 1508, united the major European powers against the city, an alliance the city withstood, but only at the cost of sacked territories and an exhausted treasury. In the east, the Ottoman empire had been an increasing threat since early in the 15th century. Even at sea, Venice faced competition, the opening up of the Americas having tilted world trade away from Venice's traditional eastern markets.

Decadence and decline The Sack of Rome in 1527 left most of Italy except Venice under the control of Charles V. Stranded on the country's periphery, the city declined, its fall hastened by the Turks, who continued to nibble away at its overseas empire. Napoleon demolished the moribund state in 1797, leaving the city to pursue its own decadent devices (casinos, brothels and endless festivities). It passed to the Austrians, who in moving their trade through Trieste, further quashed any hope of Venice's re-emergence. In this century tourism has developed apace (to 20 million visitors a year). The expanding industrial towns of Mestre and Marghera on the mainland have helped reduce the city's population from 180,000 in 1945 to its present level of 70,000.

Orientation Venice has six districts (*sestieri*), hundreds of canals, thousands of streets and *campi* and just one "piazza" (Piazza San Marco). Addresses include the name of the relevant *sestieri* (see map, pages 94–5). The main canal, the Canal Grande, has only three bridges (at the railroad station, the Rialto and the Accademia). Often the best way of finding your way back to Piazza San Marco, the heart of Venice, is by a public canal boat, called a *vaporetto*—so carry a map of the stops and routes.

Tourist information
The main tourist office is at the Casino del Caffè (tel: 041/522 6356), close to Harry's Bar on the waterfront by the Giardinetti Reali (2 minutes' walk from St. Mark's). There are smaller and busier offices at Piazzale Roma (tel: 041/522 7402); Santa Lucia station (tel: 041/719 078); Marco Polo airport (tel: 041/541 6115); and the Tronchetto parking lot. American Express is at San Moisè (tel: 041/520 0844), useful for foreign exchange and a variety of organized guided tours.

Stroll—Riva degli Schiavoni
Running along the waterfront from the Palazzo Ducale, this is one of the most popular strolls in the city. Despite the crowds and occasional commercialism, it still makes an outstanding walk—particularly at sunset.

97

Facing page: Chiesa della Salute. Below: the Canal Grande

Although Venetian painting followed the general currents of Italian art, it always plotted its own distinct course, influenced by ideas from East and West. It was distinguished by an emphasis on color, texture, and the use of light to evoke atmosphere (in contrast to Florence's preoccupations with structure and perspective). The result was an artistic patrimony barely equaled by any city in the world.

Sculpture

Venice differed from central Italy in its lack of indigenous sculptors or sculptural masterpieces (the Colleoni statue—see page 109—is a notable exception and was sculpted by a Florentine, Verrocchio). Instead, the medium tended to be an integral part of larger architectural projects. Its principal exponents were Jacopo Sansovino, the Republic's foremost architect (who came from Rome in 1527), and Alessandro Vittoria, a member of Sansovino's workshop, who dominated Venetian sculpture in the latter part of the 16th century.

Where to see—Giovanni Bellini

The Accademia contains several Madonnas, a series of allegorical panels and a pair of altarpieces by Bellini. Elsewhere in the city the best of his work is to be found in San Zaccaria, San Pietro (Murano), Santa Maria Gloriosa dei Frari, Madonna dell'Orto and San Zanipolo.

Generations have tried—and failed—to find a precise meaning in Giorgione's mysterious painting The Tempest

Byzantine and Gothic Venice's earliest artistic influences came from the east, fostered by the city's close political and commercial links with Byzantium. The greatest evidence of this is the major church, Basilica di San Marco. Byzantine elements continue in the Gothic splendor of the Ca' d'Oro palace, and in the 14th-century paintings of Paolo Veneziano. In time the Orient's influence was married to the Gothic by Lorenzo Veneziano and Michele Giambono.

Early Renaissance painters The Renaissance was slow to take hold in Venice, but the city's artists—with a distinctive use of color—molded Renaissance tenets into a style of painting that was distinctly Venetian.

Some of Venice's most celebrated artists belonged to families that produced generations of painters. The first was the Vivarini family: Antonio (*c.* 1419–80), his brother Bartolomeo (*c.* 1430–91) and son Alvise (*c.* 1445–1505). The most prominent were the Bellinis; father Jacopo (*c.* 1400–70), a pupil of Gentile da Fabriano, and sons

Venetian art

The Miracle of the Cross on San Lorenzo Bridge *by Gentile Bellini, in the Galleria dell'Accademia*

The Istoria
Narrative fresco cycles, or *istorie*, were a distinctive part of the Venetian Renaissance. Although often concerned with lives of the saints, they wove depictions of contemporary Venetian life into their narrative thread. Only three of the ten cycles commissioned between 1475 and 1525 survive: the Accademia has two; Carpaccio's *St. Ursula* and the *Miracles of the Relic of the True Cross* (executed by five artists, including Carpaccio and Gentile Bellini). The third, Carpaccio's *St. George and St. Jerome*, is in the Scuola di San Giorgio degli Schiavoni.

Gentile (*c.* 1429–1507) and Giovanni (*c.* 1430–1516), the latter among the greatest of all the Venetian painters. Gentile is known for his *istoria*, or narrative cycle, (see panel). Another artist involved in the genre was Vittore Carpaccio (*c.* 1465–1526), famous for the color and detail he brought to paintings depicting the Venice of his day.

High Renaissance Two pupils of Giovanni Bellini marked Venice's artistic zenith. Giorgione (1475–1510) is one of art's most mysterious figures. His poetic paintings are as enigmatic as his short life, their strange, unsettling qualities exemplified by *The Tempest* (in the Accademia). Tiziano Vecelli, known as Titian (*c.* 1485–1576), is among the finest painters of any age, and is renowned for a robust style, brilliant color, and technical skill.

Self-portrait by Titian

Initially in thrall to Titian, Tintoretto (1518–94) became his chief competitor. His dynamic paintings were more vivid and concerned with show than Titian's, where the sensuousness is expressive of an event's inner drama. Paolo Veronese (1528–88), by contrast, is less turbulent, his works harmonious blends of warmth, light and color. Both artists worked on huge canvases, often playing visual games—juggling viewpoints and perspective —as they strove for drama and effect.

Baroque and rococo Artistically, the 17th century was a fallow period, dominated by the baroque, a largely Roman preoccupation. In the 18th century, though, Venetian artists adopted rococo, a softer and riper style whose approach emphasized sensuality for its own sake. It was taken up by Sebastiano Ricci, Gian Battista Tiepolo and his son Gian Domenico Tiepolo. They produced brilliant, almost decadent works, their trademark that of so many artists in Venice—dazzling use of color. Venice's artistic last gasp came with Antonio Canal, called Canaletto (1697–1768) and Pietro Longhi (1702–85), both of whom painted often frivolous or idealized portraits of Venice itself.

Where to see—Titian
Despite his long life and prodigious output, Titian is badly represented in his home city (many of his works were stolen by Napoleon and now form the cornerstone of the Louvre's fine collection). In Venice his greatest works are in Santa Maria Gloriosa dei Frari, the Accademia and Santa Maria della Salute.

Basilica di San Marco

A quite literally glittering repository of art and an extravagant mixture of differing architectural styles, the Basilica di San Marco is one of Europe's most exotic cathedrals as well as being Venice's single most famous building.

Four Horses
San Marco's most famous statues, the four gilded bronze horses that stood above the portal, are now kept inside the basilica to protect them from atmospheric pollution (the ones outside today are copies). No one is certain whether the originals are 4th-century BC Hellenistic bronzes, or statues from a Roman triumphal arch cast seven centuries later. They were stolen from Constantinople by the Venetians during the Crusades.

The Pala d'Oro
Made in Constantinople in 976, this gold altar panel is encrusted with 300 sapphires, 300 emeralds, 400 garnets, 15 rubies, 1,300 pearls and countless lesser stones, figures, roundels, and enamel plaques.

Origins The basilica was conceived to house the body of St. Mark, the city's patron saint, stolen from Alexandria by Venetian merchants in 828. Completed in its basic form in 1094, the church was then embellished over nine centuries, creating a unique blend of Islamic, Byzantine and European art and architecture. The decoration is completely overwhelming—so it is best to pick your way through it selectively.

The exterior The most noteworthy details of the exuberantly decorated exterior are the Romanesque carvings of the main portal. In particular, look closely at the central arch's *Months and the Seasons* (1225) and the outer arch's *Trades of Venice*. The mosaics above the doorways (1260) describe the story of St. Mark's abduction and the arrival of his body in the city.

The interior Beyond the vestibule, or narthex, the main body of the basilica is dominated by 13,200 square feet of mosaics—a vast kaleidoscope of color and Biblical anecdote dating mostly from the 12th and 14th centuries. Be sure also to see the Treasury, and its collection of gold and silverware; the rood screen (1394); the 10th-century pulpits; the icon known as the *Madonna di Nicopeia*; and—most important of all—the famous Pala d'Oro (see panel).

Part of the flamboyant façade of San Marco

Churches

All the churches described are outstanding, but if you are short of time the top three are the Basilica di San Marco, Santi Giovanni e Paolo (San Zanipolo) and Santa Maria Gloriosa (I Frari).

▶▶▶ Basilica di San Marco   95B4
Piazza San Marco
Venice's cathedral and finest church is most visitors' first port of call (see opposite page).

▶▶ Campanile di San Marco   95B4
Piazza San Marco
Venice's tallest building rises 326 feet above Piazza San Marco, offering panoramic views over the city, the lagoon and—on clear days—the distant Dolomite mountains. The original tower collapsed in 1902, but was rebuilt over the next ten years. At its base stands the beautifully decorated loggetta▶▶, built 1537–49 by Jacopo Sansovino.

▶▶ Madonna dell'Orto   94D3
Cannaregio
Tintoretto was a parishioner of this little church in the north of the city (and is buried here). Several splendid paintings by him decorate the walls, including *The Presentation of the Virgin* (in the right aisle), and *The Last Judgment* and *The Adoration of the Golden Calf* (both in the chancel). Other major paintings include Cima da Conegliano's *St. John the Baptist.*

▶▶▶ San Giorgio Maggiore   95A4
Isola di San Giorgio Maggiore
This church is one of Palladio's two Venetian masterpieces (the other is Il Redentore). The church occupies its own small island and the views from its courtyard and campanile are some of the most celebrated in the city. The marvelous if austere interior is the setting for two Tintoretto masterpieces, the *Last Supper* and *Shower of Manna* and his *Deposition* is in the Cappella dei Morti (right of the choir).

▶▶ San Giovanni in Bragora   95B5
Campo Bandiera e Moro, Castello
Vivaldi was once the organist in this Gothic church, rebuilt in 1475, whose paintings include the *Baptism of Christ* by Cima da Conegliano, the *Risen Christ* by Alvise Vivarini, and Bartolomeo Vivarini's lovely *Madonna.*

▶▶▶ Santi Giovanni e Paolo (San Zanipolo)   95C4
Campo Santi Giovanni e Paolo, Castello
Venice's largest church (built by the Dominicans in the 14th and 15th centuries) is renowned both for its sheer size and for the tombs of the 25 doges that are buried here. The best are the tombs of Pietro Mocenigo (on the entrance wall) and Michele Morosini (on the right of the chancel). Other outstanding works of art include a polyptych by Giovanni Bellini, *St. Vincent Ferrer,* and an altarpiece, *St. Antony and Supplicants* by Lorenzo Lotto. The ceiling panels of the Cappella Rosario are by Veronese.

The imposing bulk of Santi Giovanni e Paolo (San Zanipolo in the Venetian dialect)

101

A grisly episode
Marcantonio Bragadin was a Venetian general captured, tortured and executed by the Turks in Cyprus in 1571. He was chained to a stake and flayed alive in front of the Pasha. His peeled skin was then stuffed with straw, mounted on a cow, and paraded around the streets. It was then hung from the bowsprit of the admiral's ship for the return voyage to Constantinople. Later the skin was returned to Venice, and is now in San Zanipolo, in the urn next to the first altar of the right aisle. The general's death was avenged at the Battle of Lepanto by Doge Venier, whose bronze statue is also in the church.

Santa Maria Formosa
The church stands close to the Miracoli. *Formosa* means "most beautiful," and refers to an apparition of the Virgin on this site in the 7th century. The present church dates from 1492 (the façades are neo-classical, the campanile baroque). Paintings include a triptych by Bartolomeo Vivarini (1473, 1st chapel right) and Palma Vecchio's fine *St. Barbara and Four Saints* (right transept). Outside is a lively square, with a few cafés and a small vegetable market.

►► Santa Maria Assunta (Gesuiti) 95D4
near the Fondamente Nuove, Cannaregio
Fronted by a soaring façade, and obviously built to impress, this Jesuit church (1714–29) has a quite awe-inspiring interior, its pillars, pulpits and floor draped in what appears to be swaths of green and white damask. All the hangings, however, even down to the tassels and frills, are made from the most delicately carved marble.

►►► Santa Maria Gloriosa dei Frari (I Frari) 94C2
Campo dei Frari, San Polo
Known as I Frari (The Friars) after its Franciscan founders, this cavernous church is a treasury of exceptional paintings and sculpture. Its main glories are three of the greatest paintings in Italian art: Titian's *Assumption of the Virgin* (behind the high altar); his *Madonna di Ca'Pesaro* (second altar of the left aisle); and Giovanni Bellini's sublime *Madonna and Child with Saints* (in the sacristy). Elsewhere the church is loaded with paintings and sculptures that could occupy you for an hour or more. They include works by Donatello, Antonio Canova, Sansovino, Bartolomeo Vivarini, and many more.

►► Santa Maria dei Miracoli 95C4
Campo dei Miracoli, Cannaregio
One of the most exquisite small churches in Venice, the Miracoli is a miniature masterpiece of classical architecture. Elegant and refined in exterior form, its interior contains some of the city's most intricate decorative sculpture.

►►► Santa Maria della Salute 94A3
Dorsoduro
Salute means health, and this church was built as thanks for the city's deliverance from the plague of 1630, when 45,000 Venetians died. (A similar pledge 54 years earlier had resulted in the building of Palladio's Redentore.) Built on 100,000 wooden piles, the church occupies a prime position on the Grand Canal, making it one of the city's great landmarks. The sacristy contains several paintings by Titian and Tintoretto's *Marriage at Cana*.

►► San Pantalon 94B2
Campo San Pantalon, Dorsoduro
A shortage of money left San Pantalon with an unfinished façade, a deficiency for which the interior more than compensates. Its ceiling—the city's most melodramatic—contains some 60 panels depicting a mass ascent into Heaven: *The Martyrdom and Apotheosis of San Pantalon*. It was painted by Antonio Fumiani between 1680 and 1704. The church's smaller paintings include Veronese's last work, *San Pantalon Healing a Boy*, and Antonio Vivarini's *Coronation of the Virgin*.

►► San Salvatore 95B4
Campo San Salvatore, San Marco
A noted Renaissance church, San Salvatore contains several tombs, including that of Caterina Cornaro (see Asolo, page 118), and a pair of paintings by Titian; an *Annunciation* (right-hand wall) and a *Transfiguration* over the high altar.

*Marble drapery in
Santa Maria Assunta*

Il Redentore
Leading Italian architect
Andrea Palladio designed
only two churches in
Venice. One was San
Giorgio Maggiore (see
page 101), the other Il
Redentore, commissioned
in 1576 by the Senate to
mark the end of a plague.
Its prominent position on
the Giudecca and eye-
catching façade make it
one of the city's landmarks,
best seen across the water
from Dorsoduro.

San Stae
San Stae is close to a
vaporetto stop on the
Grand Canal, and at the
heart of a neighborhood of
tiny squares and narrow
canals that sees relatively
few tourists. Its statue-
filled baroque façade is
one of the Grand Canal's
most striking sights.

Campo San Zaccaria
The square outside San
Zaccaria has a checkered
past. San Zaccaria itself
was built as a shrine for
Zaccharias, father of John
the Baptist, who is buried
under the second altar on
the right. The convent
alongside was once notorious for its licentiousness.
Most of the nuns were
reluctant internees, incar-
cerated because of
parental pressure or
because their fathers were
too poor to provide
dowries.

▶▶▶ **San Sebastiano**   94A1

Campo San Sebastiano, Dorsoduro
Newly restored (though infrequently open), San Sebastiano
belongs almost entirely to Paolo Veronese, who is buried
in the church and who left in it the greatest single collection of his paintings. The best are: three ceiling panels
depicting the *Life of St. Esther*; two paintings in the sanctuary, *San Sebastian* and *St. Mark and St. Marcellian*; the
walls of the *barco* (nuns' gallery); the painted organ doors;
and the ceiling panels of the sacristy.

▶▶ **Santo Stefano**   94B3

Campo Francesco Morosini, San Marco
As well as being a handsome, highly decorated church,
Santo Stefano is notable for its Gothic portal, its "ship's
keel roof" (like an upended wooden hull)—one of only
two in the city—and a calm, airy interior whose sacristy
contains late works by Tintoretto.

▶▶▶ **San Zaccaria**   95B4

Campo San Zaccaria, Castello
Massive San Zaccaria is chock-full of paintings, the most
celebrated being Giovanni Bellini's *Madonna and Four
Saints* (second altar on the left). It is worth paying the
small admission fee to see Tintoretto's *Birth of John the
Baptist* (in the Cappella di Sant'Atanasio). The Cappella di
San Tarasio has three composite altarpieces by Antonio
Vivarini and Giovanni d'Alemagna (1443).

Scattered across the 520 square miles of Venice's lagoon (the *Laguna Veneta*) are some 40 islands, many of them deserted, others home to sights that merit as much attention as the city itself.

Getting there
To reach the islands of the lagoon, take *vaporetti* from Piazzale Roma or the Fondamente Nuove: line 1 and line 4, a summer-only service known as the *turistico*, cross to the Lido (along with many others); line 52 goes to San Michele and Murano; line 12 from the Fondamente Nuove takes in Murano, Burano and Torcello.

Burano▶▶ While Burano's menfolk attended to the fishing, the island's women spent hours making the famous Burano and Venetian-point lace. Traditionally each woman specialized in a single stitch (there are seven in all), passing the lace between one another during its creation. Today the island's many craft shops sell local and factory-made foreign lace. Before leaving, visit the **Scuola dei Merletti**, an interesting lace museum and school, and allow time to wander the village's streets of neat and brightly painted houses.

Lido▶ Ranged over the lagoon's largest sandbank, the Lido is a fully fledged seaside resort, once Europe's most fashionable (Thomas Mann's *Death in Venice* is set there) but now a more downbeat—and in places dingy—conglomeration of big hotels, crowded beaches and murky water. It is, however, worth taking the *vaporetto* here from San Marco for the sublime spectacle of the Venetian skyline—one of the world's great views.

Murano▶▶ Murano is a workaday and slightly down-at-heel place dedicated almost entirely to glass-blowing. The glass furnaces moved here from the city in 1291 as a precaution against fire. For centuries thereafter the island's craftsmen were European leaders in their field. Nowadays the streets are crammed with shops hawking glassware—some of it exquisite, some of it hideous by turns. Be sure to visit the furnaces themselves to see glass being blown—admission to most is free (many lie along the Fondamenta dei Vetrai). To see examples of Murano glass past and present, and to learn about glass techniques, visit the glass museum, the **Museo Vetrario**. The church of **San Pietro Martire** has two good paintings: Veronese's *St. Jerome* and Giovanni Bellini's *Madonna and Child*.

Murano glass; not to everyone's taste, but certainly distinctive

Torcello▶▶▶ The best day trip from Venice, this rustic and peaceful little island is easily explored. Most people are here to see **Santa Maria Assunta**, Venice's first cathedral, home to magnificent 11th- and 12th-century mosaics, but the 11th-century church of Santa Fosca and the small Museo dell'Estuario are both also worth a visit.

Venice in peril

Venice is in more peril than most historic cities, threatened on several fronts by air and water pollution, sinking foundations, flooding and the constant assault of mass tourism.

Subsidence Only a couple of decades ago Venice was threatened with catastrophe. The main culprits were the water-hungry industries on the mainland, whose exploits lowered the water table and threatened to undermine the city's foundations. Two large aqueducts to pipe water from mainland rivers saved the day in 1973.

Local subsidence, though, continues to be a threat. Most of the city's buildings rest on pilings driven into the mudflats of the lagoon—or in the case of poorer houses, shored up on a loose cement of rubbish and rubble. With the lagoon now subject to increasingly frequent low tides, air can reach the pilings and accelerate their rate of decay.

Flooding Floods in Venice are nothing new, but severe inundations in 1966, 1979 and 1986 have made them the focus of the city's planners. Winter flooding is caused by strong southeast winds and seasonally high tides. Recently they have grown more frequent—not, research shows, because of global warming, but through human interference in the lagoon over the last century in the form of land reclamation and the deepening of channels.

Solutions The solution is to be a tidal barrier built across the lagoon's three main entrances. Opinion of the boom's likely efficacy is divided and many conservationists argue it does not address the city's basic problems: the more general but ultimately more critical ones of a declining population, slowly stagnating lagoon, and the choice between preserving Venice for the Venetians—more housing and industry—and turning the city into an historical fossil preserved for profit and posterity.

The flood of 1966
On November 4, 1966, Venice's sea walls (*murazzi*) were breached by the combined effects of gale-force winds, an earth tremor and two successive high tides, and the city found itself under 3ft. of water. There were no injuries and no paintings lost (unlike Florence, flooded on the same day).

Air pollution
Smog is another problem. Sulphur dioxide from mainland factories combined with the lagoon's humid and salty air produce an intensely corrosive combination. The conversion of domestic heating systems from oil to gas has lessened the problem, but local industry still pumps 50,000 ton of toxins into the atmosphere annually.

Water pollution
Venice's sewage is treated, but most of its sinks and baths empty straight into the lagoon. For years the cleansing effects of daily tides and the work of natural biological agents (marine life) preserved the ecological equilibrium. The increased use of phosphate-rich detergents and fertilizers, however, has upset this—over $250 million was spent on the problem in 1988, but the building of the barrier, which will further disturb tides, does not augur well for the lagoon's health.

You may need waterproof shoes on even the sunniest days in Venice

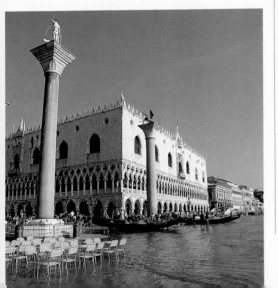

Numerous *palazzi* not mentioned in the gazetteer line the Grand Canal, several with literary connections. From San Marco west some of the more eminent include the Pisani-Gritti, home to English critic John Ruskin in 1851; Palazzo Corner, designed by Sansovino; Palazzo Barbaro, where Henry James wrote *The Aspern Papers*; the Palazzo Mocenigo, once home to Lord Byron; Corner-Spinelli and Palazzo Grimani, both stately Renaissance piles; and Vendramin-Calergi, where Wagner died in 1883 (home of the Casino).

Stroll—Dorsoduro
Walk on the waterfront along Fondamenta delle Zattare for lovely views across the lagoon to the Giudecca. Finish at Santa Maria della Salute.

Inside the Doge's Palace

Museums & Galleries

▶▶▶ Accademia   94A2
Campo della Carità, Dorsoduro
The Accademia is Venice's greatest art gallery, a superlative collection of Venetian paintings, many gathered from churches and palaces around the city. Masterpieces by all Venice's painters adorn its walls, the highlights of which include Giovanni Bellini's *Madonna Enthroned* and Carpaccio's *The Presentation* (Room II); Mantegna's *St. George*, Giorgione's *Tempest* and some of Bellini's *Madonnas* in Rooms IV–V; Titian's *St. John the Baptist* (Room VI); three Veronese masterpieces in Room XI; six 18th-century *Scenes from Venetian Life* by Longhi (Room XVII); and two narrative fresco cycles—*The Miracles of the Relics of the Cross* (Room XX) and Carpaccio's *The Legend of St. Ursula* (Room XXI). There is just one Canaletto (in Room XVII).

▶▶ Ca' d'Oro e Galleria Franchetti   94C3
Canal Grande, Cannaregio
Named after the now-vanished gilding (*oro*—gold) that covered its elaborate façade, this is Venice's most famous *palazzo*, currently home to a well-presented and varied art collection. Its showpieces are Mantegna's *St. Sebastian* and A. Vivarini's polyptych of *The Passion*. There are also lesser pieces by Titian, Giorgione and Tintoretto, and numerous rewarding works by less prominent artists and sculptors.

▶ Ca' Pesaro 94C3

Canal Grande, Santa Croce

A highpoint of Venetian baroque, this 17th-century Grand Canal palace is as worth seeing for its original interior as for the pair of modest museums under its roof—the Museo Orientale (oriental art), and the Galleria d'Arte Moderna (works from past Venice Biennales).

▶▶ Ca' Rezzonico e Museo del Settecento Veneziano 94B2

Canal Grande, Dorsoduro

This palace's "Museum of 18th-century Venice" evokes the splendor of the city's last great flowering through magnificently decorated rooms crammed with tapestries, furniture, costumes, silks, brocades, lacquerwork—even a contemporary puppet theater and chemist's shop. You may find the trappings gaudy, but the frescos of the Tiepolo family and the touching Venetian scenes by Longhi and Guardi merit the entrance price alone.

▶▶▶ Collezione Guggenheim 94A3

Calle Cristoforo, Dorsoduro

Millionairess Peggy Guggenheim's gallery—housed in an 18th-century **palazzo** on the Grand Canal—has one of the world's most important collections of modern art. Rooms are arranged by style (Dadaism, Cubism, Surrealism) and contain all 20th-century art's top names.

▶▶ Museo Correr 95B4

Piazza San Marco

This is Venice's main historical museum, a vast and occasionally dull showcase for documents, weapons, coins, ducal regalia and a wealth of miscellania relating to the city over the centuries. Some knowledge of Venetian history is needed to get the most from the exhibits. The art gallery upstairs is second only to the Accademia.

▶▶ Museo Storico Navale (Naval Museum) 95B5

Campo San Biagio, Castello

Housed near the Arsenale (the Republic's old naval base), this museum is the best collection of all things maritime in Italy. With plenty of background on gondolas, the displays range from models of galleys used against the Turks to manned torpedoes from World War II.

▶▶▶ Palazzo Ducale (The Doge's Palace) 95B4

Piazzetta San Marco

The Doge's Palace was the seat of power in Venice for almost a thousand years, but most of the present building dates from the 15th century.

You need at least a morning to do the palace justice (arriving early helps avoid the crowds). Be sure to tarry over the main entrance (Porta della Carta) and courtyard; the staircase (Scala dei Giganti): the Anticollegio, with paintings by Titian and Veronese; and the Sala del Maggior Consiglio, the council chamber, famous for Tintoretto's huge oil painting, *Paradiso*.

The Bridge of Sighs
The famous Ponte dei Sospiri links the Palazzo Ducale with its prisons (the name supposedly comes from the sighs of condemned prisoners). For the most part the prisons harbored only petty criminals (Casanova was imprisoned here in 1755 for 15 months). Hardcore convicts were kept in the less salubrious Piombi (the Leads), under the palace's roof, or in the Pozzi (Wells), 18 dark and dank cells in the palace's bowels.

Venetian landmark: the Bridge of Sighs

VENICE

Campo Santa Margherita
This square, ringed by 14th-century houses, is the social heart of the Dorsoduro district. It has an attractive food and vegetable market, and lots of relaxed bars, haunts of students from the university. Nearby is the Scuola Grande dei Carmini, rich in Tiepolo frescos.

The Scuole
The *scuole* of Venice were religious confraternities administered by wealthy Venetians as charities for the needy. The main ones took their names from their patron saints, or from the nationality of their founders. Many acquired tremendous prestige, reflected in their works of art, among the most remarkable in Venice.

San Rocco
The *scuola* of San Rocco was always chiefly concerned with the relief of the sick—as was its patron, San Rocco (or St. Roch). The saint was held especially useful in cases of bubonic plague, an illness from which he was saved by divine intervention. Paintings all over Italy (and especially in Venice) often show him pointing to a plague sore on his thigh.

The Torre dell'Orologio, Piazza San Marco

►► **Palazzo Mocenigo** 94C2
Salizzada San Stae, Santa Croce
Once owned by one of Venice's grandest families, this palace's nine rooms must still look much as they did in their 18th-century heyday. Each is richly gilded and painted, and decorated with period furniture and Murano glass chandeliers.

► **Palazzo Querini-Stampalia** 95B4
Campiello Querini, Castello
The splendor of this 16th-century **palazzo** suggests the scale of Venice's former wealth and power. Its 20 rooms contain the art collection and furnishings of one of the city's leading 18th-century families. The paintings are not the city's best, but there are one or two persuasive works, notably the chronicles of Venetian life by Pietro Longhi, Giovanni Bellini's *Presentation in the Temple* and some popularist, if inept, portrayals of *Venetian Festivals* by Gabriele Bella.

►►► **Scuola di San Giorgio degli Schiavoni** 95B5
Calle Furlani, Castello
Schiavonia (the name refers to Slavs) was what Venetians called Dalmatia, a coastal strip along the eastern Adriatic, and a dominion of the Republic for centuries. The *scuola* established by the city's resident Slavs contains Vittore Carpaccio's poetic frieze of frescos illustrating the lives of St. George, St. Tryphon and St. Jerome (the patron saints of Dalmatia).

►►► **Scuola Grande di San Rocco** 94B2
Campo San Rocco, San Polo
"One of the three most precious buildings in Italy," said John Ruskin of San Rocco, grandest of the city's *scuole*. He was referring to Tintoretto's series of over 50 visionary Biblical scenes that took 23 years to complete. The paintings were executed after the artist had won the commission in a bitterly fought competition.

Start your exploration in the Sala dell'Albergo, almost one wall of which is covered in a magnificent *Crucifixion*. Pictures on its entrance wall depict scenes from The Passion (1567). In the main upper hall, painted later (1581), the wall panels contain New Testament scenes, the ceiling inventive Old Testament episodes. There are more Tintorettos on the ground floor (1587) and in the neighboring church of San Rocco.

Landmarks

▶ **Arsenale** *95B5*

Ride *vaporetto* No. 52 and you pass through the arch and flanking towers that mark the entrance to the Arsenale. This vast naval dockyard in the east of the city was where the great ships of the Venetian empire were built and berthed. Most of the old basins and docks are now deserted, or used by the Italian navy, but glimpses from the outside still evoke their past scale and splendor.

▶▶▶ **Monumento al Colleoni
(Colleoni Statue)** *95C4*

Campo Santi Giovanni e Paolo, Castello
Bartolomeo Colleoni, a native of Bergamo, served Venice as one of its leading *condottieri*, or mercenaries, from 1448. At his death he left a portion of his wealth to the state, on condition that a statue of him be raised in front of the Basilica di San Marco. The Republic took the money, but cheated by erecting the statue in front of the Scuola di San Marco. In the statue itself, however, they did Colleoni proud, commissioning the Florentine sculptor Andrea Verrocchio to produce one of the masterpieces of Renaissance sculpture (1481–8).

The Rialto
Venice's earliest settlers were drawn to the stable land and defensive position on the Grand Canal's *rivo alto* (high bank). In time the area (and name) developed into the Rialto, the city's commercial heart. In the "Bazaar of Europe," textiles, precious stones, silks, spices and exotica from the Orient were traded. Europe's first state bank opened here in the 12th century, and finance flourished—as did prostitution. The Rialto still has a busy market, concentrated on the Ruga degli Orefici (souvenirs), Campo San Giacomo (fruit and meat) and Campo Battisti (fish).

109

▶▶▶ **Ponte di Rialto (Rialto Bridge)** *94C3*

The Rialto Bridge with its three pedestrian walkways and two rows of shops is one of the city's best-known landmarks. Built between 1588 and 1591, it replaced a wooden bridge whose central portion could be raised to allow the passage of ships (many paintings, like Carpaccio's *Miracles of the True Cross* in the Accademia, show what this and earlier bridges looked like).

▶▶ **Torre dell'Orologio (Clock Tower)** *95B4*

Piazza San Marco
Crowds invariably gather around this curio, a brightly enameled clock-face and digital clock linked to moving statues. The face indicates the hours, phases of the moon and movement of the sun through the signs of the zodiac. Two bronze figures of Moors strike the hours.

The elegant Rialto Bridge, once the only crossing of the Grand Canal

Walking in Venice

In a city as beautiful and free of cars as Venice, walking makes the perfect option for getting around. One of Venice's greatest pleasures is escaping the crowds to lose yourself in its magnificent labyrinth of alleys and canals, so treat the suggestions below as no more than starting points for your own exploration.

Venetian words

An open space (piazza) in Venice is called a *campo, campiello* or *campazzo*. Alleys are *calle, calletta* or *callesella* (occasionally *ruga*, analogous to the French *rue*). A *ramo* is the branch of a *calle*. *Salizzada* refers to the first alleys paved with stone; *fondamenta* (or *riva*) means the path alongside a canal (used as the "foundation" for the canal's buildings). A canal is a *rio*; a *rio terra* is a canal which has been filled in.

Canal Grande Venice's single best excursion is not a walk at all, but a boat trip on one of the *vaporetti* which ply up and down the Grand Canal (Nos. 1, 82, 3 or 4). Buy one of the many guides or maps devoted solely to the canal to identify its key buildings (there are 200 separate palaces alone). Boats make frequent stops if you want to see anything on the way.

Piazza San Marco In and around Piazza San Marco you can wander between some of the city's most famous sights—the Basilica di San Marco, Campanile di San Marco, Palazzo Ducale, Museo Correr, Libreria Sansoviniana and the Ponte dei Sospiri ("Bridge of Sighs").

The west Start at the Accademia and head west towards the Fondamenta Gheradini, home to a lovely fruit and vegetable market, and then make for the Scuola Grande dei Carmini, San Pantalon, the Scuola Grande di San Rocco and Campo San Polo. Then move north toward the Grand Canal (and a boat to the center) via Campo San Giacomo dell'Orio and the churches of San Giacomo and San Stae.

The east Eastern Venice is one of the city's quieter areas. Start at Campo Santa Maria Formosa and its eponymous church, just northeast of Piazza San Marco. Then take in Santi Giovanni e Paolo and its lovely square and Colleoni monument. Proceed to San Francesco della Vigna, the Arsenale, the Museo Storico Navale, and the Scuola di San Giorgio degli Schiavoni.

The Ghetto Venice's was the world's first ghetto (the word comes from the word *getar*, to found, or *geto*, foundry, after the metal-working industry that dominated the area until 1390). Jews were segregated here from 1516 on. The district's low, crowded houses are distinctly different from the rest of the city. Its heart is in Cannaregio, north of Rio Terra San Leonardo.

Taking the weight off their feet: visitors outside St. Mark's

Transportation and shopping

Getting around The *vaporetto*, or water bus, is the principal means of traveling Venice's canals (*motoscafi*, or motor launches, are similar but quicker). The system is initially confusing, but you soon get the hang of the numbered routes. The city map (pages 94–5) shows the main stops, each of which usually has a ticket office, route maps and timetable. Tickets can also be bought in shops with an ACTV sign (ACTV is the public transport company). Tickets cost a flat fare, though if you are making several journeys buy 24- or 72-hour tourist tickets or a discounted 10-ticket block (a *blochetto*). The *Biglietto Isole* allows you to visit Murano, Burano and Torcello. Remember to date stamp your ticket at each pier before boarding. Tickets must also be bought for large pieces of luggage. Services run about every 10 minutes. Seats in the prow are the most coveted spots—they offer the best views.

Walking—the city's only other means of transportation—is helped by yellow signs pointing directions to the main destinations. Given Venice's complexity, no map is totally accurate: Hallweg, Falk, FMB or Kummerly and Frey are the best.

Shopping Venice has always been a city where goods are bought and sold. These days, the vast number of visitors means prices are inflated and much of its merchandise little more than tourist junk. But shops can still be found selling the quality crafts for which the city has traditionally been renowned—fabrics, glass, leather, metalwork, paper, and woodwork. The island of Burano is especially known for its lace, Murano for its glassware—though much can be horribly kitschy. Metalwork and woodwork (furniture) shops are found around Campo San Barnaba. For the most distinctive of Venetian souvenirs—carnival masks and hats—visit **Tragicomica** (Campiello dei Meloni, San Polo) and **Mondonovo** (Rio Terra Canal, Dorsoduro 3063, just off Campo Santa Margherita).

The most fashionable shopping areas are the Mercerie—the streets between Piazza San Marco and around the Rialto bridge. The busiest area is the Strada Nova leading from the railroad station to the heart of the city.

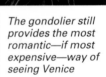

Hiring a gondola
Gondola fares are priced at a set rate—though few gondoliers adhere to this, so confirm the price *and* duration of a trip before setting off. Rates are doubled between 8:00 at night and 8:00 in the morning. Useful tips are to take rides in the late afternoon, when the Grand Canal is less crowded, and to start from a station on the Canal (rides on the lagoon are more choppy).

The gondolier still provides the most romantic—if most expensive—way of seeing Venice

Traghetti
Since the Grand Canal has only three bridges, it can often save time to use the *traghetti* (two-man gondola ferries) that cross the canal between special piers (at several points).

Carnival masks make stylish and unusual souvenirs

Accommodations

Alternatives to Venice
Price and availability of accommodations can be a problem in Venice, and though it may not be an ideal arrangement, you might consider seeing the city as one or more day trips from a base in nearby towns. Padua (see page 124) and Treviso (see page 125) are good options, both less than half an hour by train from Venice.

Many visitors willingly pay extra for a room with canal view

Reservations and high season Venice has around 200 hotels. While most are well run, a few have become slovenly, taking for granted the constant flow of visitors that fills the city virtually year round. It is almost essential to reserve a room in advance during July and August, and wise to do so for the rest of the high season—which runs from mid-March to late October. Christmas and Easter must also be considered peak periods—together with the two weeks of Carnevale in February.

Prices Hotel rates are generally higher than in Rome or Florence, which in the upper brackets puts them among the highest in western Europe. Off-season rates can be far more reasonable—but this is when many hotels close. It is now often impossible to avoid paying for a breakfast, whether you take it or not, and charges for air-conditioning—a definite plus in summer—can be hefty. Relatively few hotels have restaurants, but where they do, half-board deals often involve unappetizing dinners (and you lose the chance to eat out).

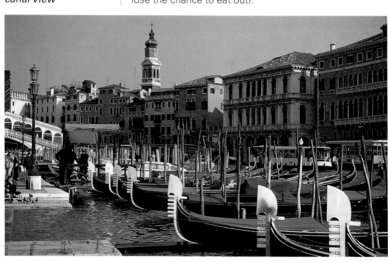

Finding a room
If you arrive without a room, head straight for one of the tourist offices run by the A.V.A. (the Venetian Hoteliers' Association). They have booths at the Santa Lucia train station, Marco Polo airport, or the Autorimessa Comunale in Piazzale Roma. The lines may be long, but each will find you a room, taking a L10,000, L20,000 or L30,000 deposit according to the category of hotel (deductible from your first night's bill).

Rooms Because of the constraints imposed by planning regulations, Venice's old hotels often have a wide variety of rooms—so ask to see several before parting with any money. Rooms with canal views often command a premium, worth paying if it avoids a dark and miserable back room. Singles are notoriously bad, so lone travelers might consider taking a double room in a cheaper hotel. Lounges are frequently minimal in all but the grandest hotels.

Noise and location The best hotels lie on the Grand Canal near San Marco; the cheapest in the streets around the railroad station off Rio Terra Lista di Spagna. Wherever your hotel, be certain when making reservations to find its exact location (and remember you may need to carry your luggage). Even without cars, Venice has its share of nocturnal traffic. Church bells and pedestrian chatter can also reverberate noisily in narrow streets. Dorsoduro is one of the quieter areas.

Food and drink VENICE

Restaurants Mass tourism has not been good for Venetian cuisine. Restaurant prices are high, cooking unimaginative and service indifferent. Good restaurants can be found—usually in the upper price bracket—and even an average meal can be made memorable by a waterfront setting. As a general rule, places away from San Marco and in the quieter eastern and northern parts of the city, are good areas to search out cheaper and more authentic *trattorie*.

If you are watching your budget, most restaurants offer a *menù turistico*, a set price menu. Quality and quantity, however, are usually inferior to eating *à la carte*. Most places, large or small, close once a week, often on Sunday or Monday.

Cafés and bars Given Venetian prices, cafés and bars are more than ever the great standby if you want cheap snacks and sandwiches. Between-meals nibbles in the city are known as *cichetti*, typically including *polpette* (meatballs), *carciofi* (artichoke hearts), eggs, anchovies, and *polipi* (baby squid). All are traditionally washed down with *un ombra*, a glass of wine—literally a "shadow," from the idea of coming out of the sun for light refreshment. For a treat, indulge yourself in one of the city's more famous and venerable bars (see panel).

Venetian cuisine Fish and seafood form the basis of Venice's cuisine, as prawns, squid and octopus in *antipasti*, in *zuppa di pesce* (fish soups), or as *granseola* (Murano crabs), *sarde in saor* (marinated sardines), *baccalà* (salt cod) and *seppioline nere* (cuttlefish cooked in its own ink). *Risotto* is the first course *par excellence*, whether with seafood, vegetables, or ingredients like snails, tripe and quails. *Bigoli* is a local pasta, often served with a tuna (*tonno*) sauce. Thick soups are also popular, especially *pasta e fagioli* (pasta and beans). Cornmeal *polenta* is another staple, often an accompaniment to the famous *fegato alla veneziana* (calves' liver and onions).

Wine
Good local wines include Friulian whites like Tocai and Pinot Bianco and reds like Merlot, Refosco and Raboso. The best drink is *prosecco*, a delicious, light sparkling wine. It is cheap and available in any bar—simply ask for *un prosecco*.

Bars—The Top Three
Venice's most famous café is *Florian* in Piazza San Marco, opened in 1720 and patronized ever since by the famous and notorious—Proust, Wagner and Casanova included. Both Florian and its competitor, the less pretty but equally notorious *Quadri* across the square, charge stratospheric prices—but they are worth it for a once-in-a-lifetime treat. Much the same goes for the legendary *Harry's Bar*, Calle Vallaresso, San Marco.

113

One of the world's great settings for an al fresco meal

A

2780m
Mte Coglians

anto Stéfano
di Cadore
Paluzza
Pontebba
Tarvisio
Ampezzo
Tolmezzo
Chiusaforte

**R I U L I -
E N É Z I A
I U L I A**

A23
Venzone
Gemona
del Friuli

Maniago
Tarcento

Spilimbergo
San Daniele
del Friuli
Tricésimo

Aviano

Cividale
del Friuli
SLO

Udine

Pordenone
Codróipo
Gorizia
San Vito
al Tagliamento
Palmanova
zzáno
écimo
A28
Castions
di Strada
Gradisca
d'Isonzo

A4
Cervignano
del Friuli
Monfalcone
Latisana
Aquiléia
Duino
A4
**Borgo
Grotta Gigante**
Portogruaro
*Laguna di
Marano*
**Castello
di Miramare**
Santo Stino
di Livenza
Lignano
Sabbiadoro
Grado
TRIESTE

an Donà
di Piave
*Golfo di
Trieste*
Múggia

Eraclea
Cáorle

lésolo
Lído di lésolo

*Golfo
di Venézia*

HR

0	10	20	30	40	50 km
0		10		20	30 miles

4   5

Essentials

Aquileia: The basilica
Cividale dei Friuli: The town, Tempietto Lombardo
Dolomites: The mountains, Grande Strada delle Dolomiti (drive)
Padova (Padua): Cappella degli Scrovegni (Giotto frescos)
Trento: Duomo, Castello del Buonconsiglio
Trieste: San Giusto
Verona: The city, Arena, Piazza dei Signori, San Zeno
Vicenza: Basilica, Santa Corona, Teatro Olimpico, Palladian palaces

Tourist information

Bolzano: Piazza Walther 8 (tel: 0471/970 660).
Cividale del Friuli: Largo Boiani 4 (tel: 0432 /731 398).
Padua: (Padova) Railway Station (tel: 049/875 2077).
Trento: Via Alfieri 4 (tel: 0461/983 880).
Trieste: Railway Station (tel: 040/420 182).
Verona: Via Dietro Anfiteatro 6 (tel: 045/ 592 828).
Vicenza: Piazza Matteotti 12/Piazza del Duomo 5 (tel: 0444/544 122).

Scenic drives

(*Veneto*) SS48/SS51 around Cortina d'Ampezzo; SS203 Belluno–Agordo–Cortina d'Ampezzo; SS141 Bassano del Grappa–Monte Grappa; (*Trentino*) SS612 Trento–Cembra–Cavalese–San Martino di Castrozza; SS421/SS237/SS239 Mezzolombardo–Andalo–Molveno–Tione di Trento–Madonna di Campiglio; (*Alto Adige*) SS241/SS48 Bolzano–Canazei–Cortina d'Ampezzo; SS508 Bolzano–Val Sarentina–Vipiteno; SS44 Vipiteno–Passo di Monte Giovo–Merano; SS621 Brunico–Valle Aurina–Canova.

The Northeast Venice exerts such a pull that few visitors escape its clutches to explore the rest of northeast Italy—the regions of the Veneto, Trentino-Alto Adige and Friuli-Venezia Giulia. Yet in many ways this is a region whose attractions are among the best of their kind. Among its landscapes are the Dolomites, the most spectacular mountains in Europe. Architecturally, the region contains the villas of Andrea Palladio, one of the most influential of all architects. Padua has one of Italy's great fresco cycles, and Verona is undoubtedly among the country's finest Roman and medieval cities. Ethnically, too, the region is fascinating, a melting pot of Italian, Slav and German-speaking peoples. Even some of Italy's most famous wines originate in the northeast—notably the ubiquitous Soave and Valpolicella.

The Veneto Modern-day Veneto is the heartland of Venetia, the mainland territories ruled by the Venetian Republic between the 14th and 18th centuries (though Venetia's domain also included much of present-day Friuli-Venezia Giulia). Like most northern regions it divides neatly into plain, low hills and mountains. The plain is prosperous and densely populated, which means sightseeing involves braving sprawls of industry and modern housing. Any unpleasantness, however, is worth enduring to see Verona, Shakespeare's setting for *Romeo and Juliet*, and as beautiful today as it must have been when the play was written. Vicenza, too, deserves a day's visit, mainly for its Palladian architecture. Padua, by contrast, is disappointing, though its modern horrors should be overlooked for as long as it takes to see Giotto's frescos and the Basilica di Sant'Antonio. Few places stand out among the lesser towns, though Asolo provides a restful retreat from the bustle of the cities.

Trentino-Alto Adige This strange, multicultured hybrid is a region where unresolved historical problems have come home to roost. Southern Trentino (capital Trento) is Italian-speaking, while Alto Adige, or Sudtirol (capital Bolzano) is mainly German-speaking. Alto Adige was ceded to Italy at the end of World War I, having previously been part of the Austro-Hungarian Empire. As a result, everything here has more than a tinge of the Teutonic. Ethnic differences have led to inevitable tensions (including acts of terrorism), though a large measure of autonomy has, for the most part, kept the lid on nationalist ambitions.

While the disputes are generally out of sight, the region's bilingualism and brisk efficiency are immediately noticeable. Most of the area's pleasures, however, are those that transcend cultural differences. Trento and Bolzano both have their charms (along with Merano), but the mountains of the Dolomites provide the region's main attraction. Their magnificent scenery can be enjoyed by car or train, but hiking (and skiing) facilities are so outstanding in this area that it would be foolish not to attempt a little walking.

Alto Adige's cuisine has a decidedly Teutonic flavor. Be prepared for *knödel* (dumplings), often in a clear broth (*suppe*); *wienerschnitzel* (breaded veal cutlets); *sauerkraut*; *blau forelle* (mountain trout); *speck* (a special ham); *gröstl* (a meat, onion and potato pie); goulash; and—

of course—the ubiquitous apple strudel. Delicatessens are full of excellent cheeses, pickles, hams, and sausages. Bakeries have many types of black and rye bread, as well as Viennese-type pastries (be sure to try *krapfen*, a cake with jam and whipped cream).

Friuli-Venezia Giulia This region is more ethnically jumbled than Trentino-Alto Adige, comprising a cocktail of Italian, Slavic, and central European cultures that fills Italy's extreme northeastern corner. A potentially fascinating area, its peripheral position puts it beyond the ambitions of most visitors. Its coastal plains are not much to look at (though the lagoons have a beauty of sorts), but two of their little towns—Aquileia and Cividale del Friuli— can hold their own with any in Italy. The old Austro-Hungarian port of Trieste has an old-world atmosphere and makes a perfect base for local excursions.

Piazza delle Erbe, the social heart of Verona

THE NORTHEAST

Grado
Isolated in the heart of the Venetian lagoons (6½ miles from Aquileia) is Grado, a wonderfully atmospheric place. The town's centerpiece is Sant'Eufemia, a church that has changed little since it was built in 579, its highlight a 6th-century mosaic floor. Grado is also a beach resort, with enormous beaches, warm water, and safe swimming (the town's name comes from its gently graded shoreline). Boats run here from Trieste (four per week), a lovely way to visit the town.

Caterina Cornaro
Caterina Cornaro was a scion of one of Venice's most powerful families. Through marriage she became queen of Cyprus, but was eventually duped by Venice into abdicating. In return she received Asolo, where she lived and held court for 30 years. In 1509 she was forced out by Emperor Maximilian, and fled to Venice, where she died a year later.

Villa Barbaro
The Villa Barbaro at Maser, northeast of Asolo, is not only one of Palladio's finest villas, but also contains a virtuoso group of frescos by Veronese, considered one of Italy's finest examples of *trompe l'oeil*.

▶▶ **Aquileia** *115C5*

Today Aquileia is a sleepy agricultural town. Little at first glance suggests it is the region's most significant archeological site. In its day, however, its trading links and defensive position made it the fourth most important Italian city in the Roman Empire (after Rome, Milan and Capua). By the 4th century, it was also a patriarchate, a region ruled by a bishop-prince, or patriarch.

The first patriarch, Teodoro, built a sumptuous **basilica**▶▶▶ in 313, remodeled in the 10th century and now—despite damage from earthquakes—the region's most impressive medieval building. Its most breathtaking feature is a vast mosaic floor, considered among the world's finest early Christian mosaics. Almost as noteworthy are the Cripta degli Scavi, a crypt containing parts of the 4th-century church; the tombs of several patriarchs; and the crypt's 12th-century frescos.

Elsewhere there are numerous **Roman remains**▶▶, together with two intriguing museums—the **Museo Paleocristiano**▶ and **Museo Archeologico**▶.

▶▶ **Asolo** *114C3*

Asolo is a romantic medieval hill town, full of churches and tiny squares, and set in the Dolomites' bucolic foothills. Of all the Veneto's small towns, it is perhaps the most beautiful, and its wooded and villa-studded countryside the most charming. Fittingly, it lends its name to an Italian verb, *asolare*, which means to pass one's time in pleasant aimlessness.

The actress Eleonora Duse was born in Asolo in 1859. Notorious as much for her tempestuous love affairs as for her performances, she frequently retreated to the town to escape gossip and scandal, and after her death in Pittsburgh during an American tour was returned to her birthplace to be buried. The **Museo Civico**▶ houses many mementoes of her, together with memorabilia connected with the English poet Robert Browning, one of the town's other notable inhabitants.

▶ **Bassano del Grappa** *114C2*

Formerly renowned for its school of painting, this town in the foothills of the Alps is now better known for its colorful pottery and—as its name suggests—a noted *grappa* (a type of *eau de vie*). Local-born painter Jacopo Bassano (1516–92) dominates the **Museo Civico**▶, which includes his famous *St. Valentine Baptizing St. Lucilla*. More famous still is the town's covered wooden bridge, the much rebuilt 13th-century **Ponte Coperto** or **Ponte degli Alpini**▶.

▶ **Belluno** *114C3*

Belluno's old town occupies a lofty position high above the confluence of the Ardo and Piave rivers. To the west it is framed by the saw-toothed mountains of the Dolomiti Bellunesi, the most southerly and least explored of the Dolomite ranges. For the rest, the town is full of old arcaded streets, ancient fountains, and Renaissance *palazzi*. **Piazza del Duomo**▶ is the most beautiful of the squares, the Venetian-style Palazzo dei Rettori the best known of the palaces. The Gothic church of **Santo Stefano**▶, the Museo Civico and the elegant Piazza delle Erbe are also worth a visit.

► **Bolzano (Bozen)** 114D2

Capital of the mostly German-speaking Alto Adige, Bolzano is a congenial base for exploring the Dolomites (see pages 120–1). Its Gothic **Duomo**► (repaired after World War II) neatly combines modern altars with fragments of medieval fresco. Its carved spire and green-tiled roof are eye-catching, but less interesting than the fine sandstone Gothic pulpit and famous *Porta del Vino* (Wine Door). This is embellished with reliefs of vines and peasants tending their vineyards, commemorating a special license granted to the church to sell wine in 1387.

Elsewhere, the **Chiesa dei Domenicani**► contains the town's best paintings, several 14th-century Giottoesque frescos. The **Museo Civico**► offers archeological fragments and an excellent folklore section, with wood carvings, costumes, old household objects and several reconstructed interiors. Take the *funivia* (cable car) to Soprabolzano (literally "over Bolzano"), from where a tiny tramway takes you 4 miles to the hamlet of Collalbo and the "Earth Pyramids," a bizarre rock "forest" of eroded spires and pinnacles.

Below: elegant traditional houses in Bolzano
Below right: market day in Bassano del Grappa

Monte Grappa
From Bassano del Grappa take the winding mountain road 19 miles north to Monte Grappa, 5,857ft. high, where you can take in some of the grandest panoramas in the area.

Castello Rancolo
You can visit one of several castles in the Val Sarentina valley north of Bolzano. Castello Rancolo (13th- to 19th-century) is the nearest and most impressive, with guided tours of its rooms, many of which are decorated with 15th-century frescos.

Drive
One of the best of the many scenic drives near Bolzano is the SS508, which follows the Val Sarentina to Vipiteno (39 miles).

What's in a name
The Dolomites are so-called because of the dolomite rock, or magnesium limestone, which is their main constituent. The rock itself was named after the 18th-century French geologist Diendonne Sylvain Guy Tancrède de Gratet de Dolomieu.

The Tre Cime di Lavaredo with the Rifugio Locatelli *(refuge) beneath*

▶▶ **Cividale del Friuli** *115C5*

Important as one of the few places in Italy where there is some tangible record of the Lombards (see panel), Cividale is a lovely place, filled with a tangle of medieval streets, ancient bridges and interesting churches.

The 15th-century **Duomo**▶▶ boasts several remarkable works, including an embossed early 13th-century *pala*, or silver altarpiece. Off the right aisle, the Museo Cristiano contains the octagonal *Baptistery of Callisto*, commissioned in the 8th century by Cividale's first bishop-patriarch and made from 5th-century Lombard fragments of marble and stonework. Alongside stands the *Altar of Ratchis*, carved in 749, and one of the few surviving masterpieces from the Lombard era.

To the Duomo's left, the **Museo Archeologico**▶▶ houses Lombard weapons, tools and jewelry, but the town's finest monument to the era is the **Tempietto Lombardo**▶▶, an old temple whose carved stucco arch is a peerless example of Lombard sculpture.

The coming of the Lombards
The Lombards swept into Italy after the fall of the Roman Empire. A Teutonic warrior race, they had descended from Scandinavia to occupy the Danube. They came south in AD 568, under their king, Alboino. The entourage included 40,000 men, women and children, supported by a huge retinue of slaves, wagons and livestock. They established three Italian dukedoms, the first of which had Cividale as its capital (the other two were Pavia, in Lombardy, and Spoleto, in Umbria).

▶▶▶ **Dolomiti (The Dolomites)** *114D2*

No other European mountains approach the scenic spectacle of the Dolomites, a group of 30 or so self-contained massifs in a wide arc from Lake Garda to the Austrian border. Set apart from the rest of the Alps by their geology, they are ancient coral reefs that have been compressed, uplifted, and weathered. This largely explains the incredible crags and rock pinnacles that are their hallmark, and the peculiar, pinkish-orange limestone that forms most of the massifs.

Many mountain roads offer views unparalleled in Italy (see page 121) but it would be a shame to come here and not attempt a little walking (see pages 122–3). On a first visit, the best way to come to grips with the area is to concentrate on one or two massifs. The most famous is the **Dolomiti di Brenta**▶▶▶ in the west, with Madonna di Campiglio as the best base. Several massifs are also easily accessible from Bolzano (Sciliar, Puez-Odle) and from Cortina d'Ampezzo (Sesto, Cristallo, Marmarole and Fanes-Sennes-Braies).

THE GREAT DOLOMITES ROAD

Drive **La Grande Strada delle Dolomiti**

La Grande Strada delle Dolomiti—the Great Dolomites road—was opened in 1909 to link Bolzano with Cortina d'Ampezzo and runs for 66 miles through some of the most spectacular mountain scenery in Europe. You can add many scenic options to this itinerary, especially if you make the return loop to Bolzano.

From Bolzano the road enters the Val d'Ega, a corridor of gorges and waterfalls that offers thrilling views of the Catinaccio and Latemar massifs. Mountain-cradled Lago di Carezza is one of the road's more famous viewing spots. The road then continues over high passes, skirting thick forests and wild countryside, and constantly unfolding breathtaking vistas as it hairpins towards Canazei. Here the SS641 offers a tortuous alternative to the Strada, breasting the Marmolada massif, glaciers and Lago di Fedaia before the last leg to Cortina d'Ampezzo.

The Passo Sella with Sassolungo in the background

Anyone who loves mountains and the activities associated with them will be entranced by the Dolomites. They offer an unbeatable combination—stupendous scenery, hikes to suit every ability and some of the best skiing in Europe.

Monte Civetta walk
Start from the village of Alleghe, 23 miles southwest of Cortina (use the SS638 and SS203 roads). Take the path from the village to the *Rif. A Tissi* via Lago Coldai and *Rif. Sonino* (tremendous views of Civetta's huge rock walls). For a longer walk continue from *Tissi* south to *Rif. Vazzoler* and thus to Listolade on the SS203 (9 miles south of Alleghe). Use Kompass map *Alpi Bellunesi* (No. 77).

122

Walking

On no account should you come here without tackling at least one walk. It need not be difficult: there is ample choice between easy low-level strolls and more demanding high-level walks. Towns and starting points are often high up, so even what look like "mountain climbs" are often easier than they first appear. Access to all the main centers is easy; maps are excellent and widely available; paths are well-marked and well-trodden; and accommodations are cheap and plentiful. Refreshment stops (*rifugi*) are rarely more than an hour apart, and there are numerous cable cars to take the sting out of the longer ascents.

The only problem is knowing where to start. Numerous guidebooks are published, and tourist offices have lists of walks. The best approach is to settle on one massif and a single base, and start with a recognized "classic."

The Passo di Giau, La Gusela

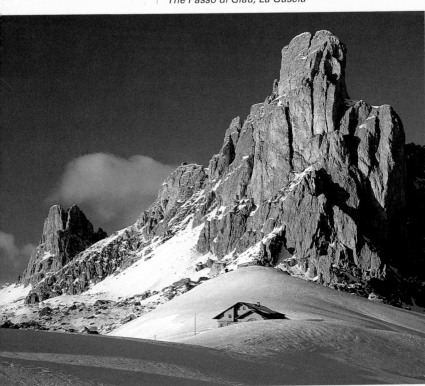

Dolomiti di Brenta Use Madonna di Campiglio (4,950 feet) as your base. It offers plenty of accommodations, and numerous circular walks you can complete in a day. The easiest is to take the Grostè ski lift to *Rif. G. Graffer* (7,748 feet) and follow trail 316 to the *Rif. Tuckett* (7,498 feet). From here you can follow paths 317 or 328/318 back to Madonna. Alternatively, walk from Madonna to *Rif. Vallesinella* (an easy hour's stroll on trail 375) then climb to the *Rif. Brentei* (317/318), one of the Dolomites' most popular refuges. For a longer walk, continue on path 318 up the spectacular Val Brenta Alta towards *Rif. Pedrotti*. Double back the same way to the *Brentei*, or drop to the Val Brenta and back to Madonna on trail 323 or 391 (all walks are marked on the Kompass map *Dolomiti di Brenta* No. 73).

Dolomiti di Sesto This is the easternmost Dolomite massif. Cortina is a good overall base, but Sesto or Dobbiaco are the closest villages to the best-known walk, which follows path 5/102 up the Val Fiscalina from San Giuseppe (south of Sesto) to the *Rif. Locatelli* with extraordinary views of the much photographed Tre Cime di Lavaredo (see illustration on page 120). Paths 101/104 give closer views of these peaks and longer walks. There is another easier approach to the Tre Cime from *Rif. Auronzo* to the south (reached by road from Cortina). The Tabacco map *Cortina-Dolomiti di Sesto* (No. 1) covers the whole area.

Skiing

In the Dolomites, the choice of both ski slopes and resorts is almost endless. Even the tiniest of villages has some slopes on offer, together with stores, hotels and outfitters.

The main centers for skiing are perhaps **Cortina d'Ampezzo**, east of Bolzano in the heart of the mountains, and **Madonna di Campiglio**, west of Trento, on the fringe of the Dolomiti di Brenta. Both towns are crowded and decidedly upscale, but for your money you get all the various trappings of top-class international resorts.

For similar facilities—but in cheaper and less chic surroundings—try the resorts in the Val Gardena (such as **Ortisei Canazei**), or in the **Val Badia** south of **Brunico** (itself one of several modest resorts in the Val Pusteria). There are also good cross-country options (*sci di fondo*), two of the best centers being Ortisei and Dobbiaco in the Val Pusteria.

Accommodations
Almost every hamlet in the Dolomites has a superb range of accommodations. Most are aimed at skiers, which means that summer rates are very competitive. Hotels are comfortable and of higher overall quality than in much of Italy. Do not be afraid to spend a night in a mountain refuge—they are not the preserve of hardened mountaineers. Accommodations are in dormitories, but they are snug and friendly places. Most open daily from June to September. Details from tourist offices.

Skiing in the Dolomites at Vigo di Fassa

123

Settimane Bianche
Ski resorts' bargain periods are known as *settimane bianche* (white weeks). They usually fall in January and February when slopes are at their emptiest and snow conditions are often unreliable. Prices on passes and accommodation are reduced.

Excursion from Merano
The tiny church of San Procolo lies in the hamlet of Naturno in the lovely Val Venosta (9 miles west of Merano). It contains exceptional wall paintings from the 8th century—the oldest in the entire German-speaking world. The trip is best combined with a drive into the Tessa mountains, an Alpine massif northwest of Merano. From Naturno, pick up the road west of the hamlet which strikes north up the Val di Senales. This provides a breathtaking 15-mile route into the mountains.

▶▶ **Merano (Meran)** 114D2

Sedate, mountain-ringed Merano is a fossil from a bygone age, full of belle epoque memories, leftovers from the turn of the century, when its mild climate, thermal springs and "grape cure" made it a favored spa with monied Europeans (the cure—reputedly used since Roman times—involves a two-week diet of fresh grapes). Among the many parks and promenades, the most famous is the **Passeggiata d'Inverno e d'Estate▶**, a path by the banks of the River Passirio. Above the town is the Passeggiata Tappeiner, a path that winds through gardens and vineyards offering views of Merano and its valley.

The town center is at its best around Via dei Portici, where rustic houses sit alongside more recent neoclassical and art-nouveau buildings. Nearby are the Gothic **Duomo▶** and ivy-clad **Castello Principesco▶**—the main things to see—together with a handful of churches and the modest Museo Civico. But Merano is mainly a place to relax in, preferably—if you can afford the cures—at the **Terme**, the largest of the town's spa facilities.

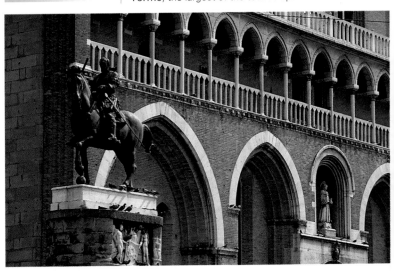

The condottiere *Gattamelata rides proudly outside St. Antony's basilica, Padua*

▶▶▶ **Padova (Padua)** 114B3

Padua is an ugly city, worth enduring for two not-to-be-missed sights. The **Cappella degli Scrovegni▶▶▶** is home to one of Italy's greatest fresco cycles: Giotto's 32-panel series of paintings on the lives of Christ and the Virgin Mary (1303–9). Like the artist's cycle in Assisi (see page 168), it marked a turning point in Western art, introducing a fluency and naturalism into painting that departed from the formality of Byzantine art.

In the **Basilica di Sant' Antonio▶▶** is buried St. Antony of Padua, one of Italy's most revered saints (patron saint of the lost and found). Outside the church stands the famous statue of Gattamelata, a noted Venetian *condottiere*. Inside, are Donatello's bronze reliefs illustrating the life of St. Antony; high altar figures of the Madonna and Saints (also by Donatello); St. Antony's votive-filled chapel; and the 14th-century frescos in the Beato Luca and San Felice chapels.

VIA ELETTRICA TRENTO-MALÈ S.p.A.	A
DA	
TRENTO	
GARDOLO	
LAVIS	
ZAMBANA	
NAVE S. ROCCO	
MASETTO	
MASO TABARELLI	●
S. MICHELE	
MEZZOCORONA	
MEZZOLOMBARDO	
SPORMAGGIORE	

▶ **Trento (Trent)** *114C2*

Italian-speaking capital of Trentino, Trento is best known for the Council of Trent, a meeting at which the Catholic hierarchy between 1545 and 1563 debated ways to turn Europe's rising tide of Lutheranism. Its opening and closing sessions took place in the **Duomo▶▶**, heart of the present town, whose austere nave contains an unusual arcaded stairway, traces of old fresco and a modest copy of Bernini's *baldacchino* in St. Peter's, Rome. Outside, on the east wall, look for the church's famous "knotted columns," a memorial to the skill of the town's medieval masons. Alongside the Duomo, the Palazzo Pretorio contains the **Museo Diocesano▶**, a small museum displaying 16th-century Flemish tapestries, carved altarpieces and painted chronicles of the Council of Trent.

Elsewhere, Trento is nicely uncommercialized, and a pleasure to wander through for an hour or so. Via Belenzani, with its rows of Renaissance *palazzi*, is the most singular street. As you explore, try to take in the church of Santa Maria Maggiore and the **Castello del Buonconsiglio▶▶**, for centuries the home of Trento's prince-bishops. Inside, it houses the Museo Provinciale d'Arte and the *Ciclo dei Mesi*, a lovely 15th-century fresco cycle depicting the months of the year.

Trento's prince-bishops
From the 13th century on, Trento's bishops enjoyed considerable power, reveling in the unique position of being able to act as the Papacy's representatives in clerical matters and as arbiters for the Holy Roman Empire in secular affairs. This evenhandedness was one reason the Council of Trent was held in the town. Their autonomous balancing act continued for 800 years, ending when the Habsburgs secularized the principality in 1802.

▶ **Treviso** *114B3*

Drawn away by Venice's siren call, few people have much time for Treviso. Yet its old center is an alluring mixture of canals, frescoed façades, shady porticoes, and medieval fragments. The Dominican church and seminary of San Nicolò▶▶ is the main monument, filled with frescos and decorated tombs. The **Duomo▶**, which has paintings by Tintoretto and others, is also diverting, while **Via Carlo Alberto▶**, heart of an appealing market district, is the best single street. Also explore the central Calmaggiore area, with many old *palazzi*, the Peschiera (Fish Market), and two excellent museums: the **Museo Civico▶**, with works by, among many others, Titian and Bassano, and the **Museo della Casa Trevigliana▶**, a gorgeous 14th-century house and museum of applied arts.

For wine lovers, the wine roads Strada del Vino Rosso and Strada del Vino Bianco start from Conegliano, just 14 miles north of Treviso, with plenty of opportunities to sample wine.

An evocative glimpse of Treviso

THE NORTHEAST

Trieste's old harbor

Miramare
The most popular excursion from Trieste is to Miramare, a beautifully situated castle built for Archduke Ferdinand Maximilian between 1856 and 1870 (located 4 miles north of the city). It is a marvelously kitschy and eclectic building (open to the public), though Triestini prefer to come here for the beaches.

Grotta Gigante
Borgo Grotta Gigante, 9½ miles from Trieste, is near the largest publicly accessible cave in the world. The Grotta Gigante can reputedly accommodate St. Peter's, Rome, with room to spare (it is 353ft. deep by 686ft. wide).

▶▶ Trieste   115B5
Trieste has little to see, if truth be told, but it rates as one of northern Italy's most atmospheric and distinctive cities (it also has lovely surroundings and a rugged coastline). At the crossroads of three cultures, it has been shaped by Italian, Slavic and middle-European influences. Once the chief port of the Austro-Hungarian Empire, its most tangible memorials relate to this golden age—notably several neoclassical districts and a handful of wonderful turn-of-the-century coffeehouses (**San Marco** in Via G Battisti and **Tommaseo** in Piazza Tommaseo are the most famous).

To glimpse the city's earlier past, visit **San Giusto▶▶**, the Romanesque-Gothic cathedral (with its origins in the 6th century), filled with frescos and some outstanding 12th-century mosaics. Close by, the Museo di Storia e d'Arte▶ chronicles the city's history from Roman times (the city was the Roman port of Tergeste). It is easily seen in conjunction with the **Museo Sartorio▶**, a series of gloomily decorated rooms redeemed by a noted ceramics collection and some 270 Tiepolo drawings. You should also climb to the Castello (1470–1630) for its views and small museum of weapons and armor.

▶ Udine   115C4
Once a bastion of the Roman Empire's northern frontier, Udine is today one of Italy's more urbane and airy little towns. At its heart lies the monumental **Piazza della Libertà▶▶**, dominated by the Palazzo del Comune, one of many buildings around the town to bear a Venetian stamp (the town was ruled by Venice from 1420 to 1797). To the south, the main attractions of the **Duomo▶** are several paintings by Giovanni Battista Tiepolo, a painter who also left frescos in the **Oratorio della Purità▶** and **Palazzo Arcivescovile▶**.

Be sure to climb to the 16th-century **Castello▶**—from the Piazza della Libertà (you pass the lovely Loggia del Lionello *en route*). Paintings in the castle's museum include works by Tiepolo, Caravaggio, Carpaccio, and Bronzino. Also leave time for San Francesco, a neat little Renaissance church, and for the collection of Friulian crafts, costumes and folk art in the **Museo Friuliano delle Arti e Tradizioni Popolari▶**.

Opera

Opera's emotional drama and sensuality are perfectly suited to the Italian temperament—"more heart than mind," said Giacomo Puccini—and there is nowhere better to enjoy a performance than in Italy itself, whether under the stars in Verona's amphitheater or in one of the country's many great opera houses.

Opera's roots lie in the traditional Italian mystery plays, the *maggi*, and the madrigal comedies of the 16th century. The composer Jacopo Peri produced the first *opera in musica*, literally a "work in music," in 1600, a performance of *Euridice* to mark the marriage of Maria de' Medici to Henry IV of France. This and other early pieces were little more than spoken recitals with a light musical backing. The first composer to use a full orchestra was Claudio Monteverdi (1567–1643), whose *La Favola d'Orfeo* (1607) is held to be the first operatic masterpiece.

The first public opera house, the Teatro di San Cassiano, opened in Venice in 1637, followed by others all over the country. By 1700 there were 17 in Venice alone. About 2,000 new operas were staged during the 18th century.

The golden age Opera's 19th-century golden age was heralded by the almost simultaneous arrival of Rossini, Donizetti and Bellini. All enjoyed success at an early age, were often in fierce competition, and burned out quickly, the first two dying relatively young (Rossini's last triumph came at the age of 40). Italian opera's greatest genius was perhaps Verdi. The son of a semiliterate peasant, Giuseppe Verdi (1813–1901) wrote such masterpieces as *Rigoletto* (1851), *La Traviata* (1853), *Aida* (1871) and *Otello* (1887).

Harsh critics
In the 18th century, Italian audiences were notorious for their rowdiness and uncompromising criticism. Charles Dickens noted their "uncommonly hard and cruel character" and thought them "always to be lying in wait for an opportunity to hiss."

127

Giacomo Puccini
The curtain fell on the golden age with the death of Verdi's successor, Giacomo Puccini, responsible for many highlights of the operatic canon, such as *La Bohème* (1896), *Tosca* (1900) and *Madame Butterfly* (1904).

The Roman Arena in Verona, scene of a summer opera season

THE NORTHEAST

The pleasing exterior of Verona's Duomo

Opera in the amphitheater
Even if you are no fan of opera, seeing a performance in Verona's Arena is an unforgettable experience. The season runs throughout July and August, when the city is crowded and accommodations difficult to find. You can get tickets from the box office (Arch 6 of the Arena); from the *Ente Lirico*, Piazza Brà 28—or from scalpers outside the Arena (who sell at little over face value). Most seats are unnumbered, so arrive early—the build-up is fun anyway—and be sure to rent a cushion and bring a sweater.

Romeo and Juliet
Shakespeare's Capulets and Montagues were based on true families (the Cappelli and Montecchi). Their feuds were also real enough, though the characters of Romeo and Juliet are fictional inventions. Nonetheless, it is hard to resist the so-called *Casa di Giulietta* (Juliet's House) on Via Cappello. The house and courtyard are pretty and there's even a balcony, though, as Arnold Bennet pointed out, it is "too high for love, unless Juliet was a trapeze artist, accustomed to hanging downwards by her toes."

"There is no world without Verona walls, /But purgatory, torture, hell itself./ Hence—banished is banish'd from the world—And world's exile is death..."

William Shakespeare (*Romeo and Juliet*).

▶▶▶ Verona *114B1*

Verona is one of northern Italy's loveliest and most artistically alluring cities. You should try to spend several days here—a couple seeing the city sights and soaking up the atmosphere, and a few exploring nearby towns like Vicenza, Padua, and Mantua. Verona's picturesque center, evocatively set on the fast-flowing Adige river, is scattered with Roman and medieval remains together with churches, monuments, and a labyrinth of old streets—every bit as romantic as when Shakespeare chose Verona as the setting for *Romeo and Juliet*.

In the center Start a tour in Piazza Brà, the city's mammoth main square. It holds the 1st-century A.D. **Arena▶▶▶**, one of the largest surviving amphitheaters of the Roman world. Built to hold 20,000 spectators, it still provides the stage for the city's famous summer opera season (see panel). You need not pay for a performance, however, to see its interior, nor to enjoy the cityscape from its upper tiers.

Via Mazzini▶, the center's elegant main street, leads to a far more intimate square: **Piazza delle Erbe▶▶**, the city's heart and social meeting place. Renaissance palaces and medieval townhouses surround it on all sides, echoing to the bustle and commotion of a colorful fruit and vegetable market.

Alongside it lies one of Italy's most magical piazzas, the **Piazza dei Signori▶▶▶**, once the city's chief public *piazza*, hence its trio of 12th-century civic buildings: the Loggia del Consiglio, a council meeting chamber; the Palazzo del Governo, seat of Verona's medieval rulers; and the

Palazzo della Ragione, a Gothic ensemble whose **Torre dei Lamberti**▶▶ offers dizzying views of the city.

In its lower corner are the **Arche Scaligere**▶▶▶, among the most accomplished Gothic funerary monuments in Italy. They are the tombs of the Scaligeri, principally Cangrande I ("The Big Dog"), a protector of Dante and patron of the arts. His grinning figure looks down from the equestrian statue atop his tomb, distinct from other clan members, whose canopied graves lie behind a wrought-iron palisade (decorated with ladders, the family's emblem and a pun on their name—*scala* means "ladder").

Going north Not far away is **Sant'Anastasia**▶, Verona's largest church, the focus of the city's most captivating medieval quarter. Here, too, is the **Duomo**▶, distinguished by its exterior carvings and Titian's *Assumption* (first altar on the left). Behind the church, cross the river for the **Teatro Romano**▶—a ruined Roman theater—and the modest Museo Archeologico. Above the museum, climb the steps to the Castel San Pietro to enjoy one of the city's best views. **San Giorgio in Braida**▶, just to the west, is worth a look for the *Martyrdom of St. George* by Veronese.

Going west More paintings await in the **Castelvecchio**▶▶▶, a fortress and former Scaligeri seat, now home to the Museo Civico d'Arte. Before you reach its paintings, the castle's maze of courtyards, chambers and passages is a fascinating diversion in its own right. Foremost among the artworks are Madonnas by Pisanello, Carlo Crivelli and Giovanni Bellini; Tiepolo's *Heliodorus*; and Tintoretto's *Nativity* and *Concert in the Open*. Behind the castle the evocatively fortified Ponte Scaligero (1355) crosses the river to Piazza Arsenale, part of a large city park where you can take a break from sightseeing. Wander north and recross the river and you come to **San Zeno Maggiore**▶▶▶, widely regarded as northern Italy's most magnificent Romanesque church. Exterior details to admire include the ivory-colored façade; the huge rose window and its *Wheel of Fortune*; the reliefs of the main portal; and the extraordinary 12th-century bronze panels of the door. Inside, frescos cover many surfaces, overshadowed by Mantegna's compelling *Madonna and Saints* above the high altar.

A glass of wine
Verona is known for its historic *osterie*, old-fashioned wine shops, popular stops for a glass of sparkling *prosecco*, Soave or one of the cheap Bardolino or Valpolicella reds. Try *Bottega dei Vini*, Vicolo Scudo di Francia (off Via Mazzini); *Cacciatore*, Piazza Isolo; and *Osteria delle Vecete*, Via Pellicciai; or *Osteria del Duomo*, Via Duomo.

Wine fair
Italy's biggest wine fair, *Vinitaly*, takes place in Verona every April, with ample opportunities for the public to sample wines from all over Italy.

129

Rulers and patrons
Though ruthless in pursuit of power, the Scaligeri were great patrons of the arts. Both Giotto and Dante were guests of the family: Dante dedicated his *Paradiso* to Cangrande I.

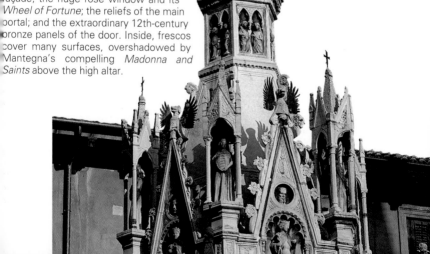

The splendid tomb of Cangrande I

Villa Valmarana ai Nani
Hundreds of villas are scattered around Vicenza's countryside. Some of the best—like the Villa Valmarana—are only a stone's throw from the city. Valmarana is known for its fresco cycles by Giambattista and Giandomenico Tiepolo, poetic and cheerful depictions of classical stories and idealized country life.

Villa Cordellina-Lombardi
This villa near Montecchio Maggiore, 8 miles south-west of Vicenza, has further notable frescos by Giambattista Tiepolo.

Basilica di Monte Berico
This gaudy 17th-century basilica commemorates two apparitions of the Virgin, held to signal Vicenza's deliverance from plague in 1426. Pilgrims throng its interior, but for lay visitors its lures are its views of the city and two exceptional paintings: Montagna's *Pietà* and Veronese's handsome *Supper of St. Gregory the Great.*

▶▶▶ **Vicenza**   *114B2*

Vicenza is a showcase for the architectural genius of Andrea Palladio (see opposite), who over many years designed or restructured most of the city's finest buildings. Otherwise, it is a wealthy city, grown fat on the back of a booming electronic sector, Italy's largest textiles industry, and the printing business.

Piazza dei Signori▶, site of the old Roman forum and still the city center, contains the **Basilica**▶▶▶, Palladio's first project and the building with which he made his reputation. Its tremendous colonnades buttress the earlier Palazzo della Ragione, a medieval law court whose crumbling exterior had defied all previous attempts at repair. The **Loggia del Capitano**▶ across the piazza is also by Palladio, though never completed. Before leaving the square, enjoy the sights and sounds of Piazza delle Erbe's fruit and flower, market, and take a drink in the Gran Caffè Garibaldi, an old-world coffeehouse overlooking the Basilica.

Corso Andrea Palladio▶▶, the center's main street, is lined with palaces, some by Palladio, some by Vincenzo Scamozzi, his chief disciple: the best are Bonin-Thiene (No. 13); Capra (No. 45); Pagello (No. 47); Thiene (No. 67); Braschi (No. 67); the **Palazzo del Comune**▶ (No. 98); and the **Palazzo da Schio**▶. To complete a Palladian tour, visit the **Teatro Olimpico**▶▶▶, Europe's oldest indoor theater and perhaps Palladio's finest work. The tourist office alongside has information on the architect's villas around Vicenza, and other city-center palaces like the Valmarana-Bragna and Porta-Festa. The most famous of Palladio's villas is on the outskirts of town. La Rotonda was a pleasure pavilion whose design was widely copied, particularly in the United States at Thomas Jefferson's home, Monticello.

No visit is complete without seeing the church of **Santa Corona**▶▶, site of two sublime paintings: Veronese's *The Adoration of the Magi* and Giovanni Bellini's *The Baptism of Christ*. The **Museo Civico**▶ houses works by Veronese, Bassano, Montagna and Tintoretto.

Setting up shop: craft fair in Vicenza's Piazza dei Signori

Andrea Palladio

Andrea Palladio was among the most important Italian architects of the 16th century. Through his reworking of classical idioms he became one of the most influential figures in the development of Western architecture.

Born in Padua in 1508, Palladio was apprenticed to a sculptor at an early age. At 16 he moved to Vicenza and enrolled in the guild of bricklayers and stonemasons. He soon found employment as a mason in a workshop specializing in monuments and decorative sculpture. He later became the protégé of Count Giangiorgio Trissano, a humanist poet and scholar, who guided his studies, directing him to the works of ancient Roman architects like Vitruvius (active 46–30 BC). During this period Palladio probably met Alvise Cornaro, the architect responsible for importing the Roman Renaissance style into northern Italy. He also came into contact with Vicenzan high society, whose leading pillars were to employ him to design their palaces and country villas. He embarked on the first of these— the Villa Godi—in 1540.

The legacy of Rome In 1541 and again in 1547 Palladio visited Rome, studying not only the works of Rome's High Renaissance masters— men like Bramante and Peruzzi—but also the city's Roman antiquities, whose classical forms were to inspire much of his work. The fruit of his studies appeared in the variety and proportional subtlety of the many

palaces he built over the next 30 years. Of the many classical ideas that informed his buildings, perhaps the most distinctive was the use of the ancient Greco-Roman temple front as a portico (as in La Rotonda).

Another visit to Rome in 1554 produced his book *L'Antichità di Roma*, which for 200 years remained the standard guidebook to Rome. Even more influential still were *I Quattro Libri dell'Architectura* (1570), four books that together form perhaps the most important architectural treatise ever published.

The last years After 1570 Palladio was preoccupied with church design in Venice, producing Il Redentore, San Giorgio Maggiore and the façade of San Francesco della Vigna. Remarkably, he never received a civic or private commission from the city. His last work was Vicenza's Teatro Olimpico in 1580, the year of his death.

Top: La Rotonda, near Vicenza
Above: Palladio's Venetian masterpiece, San Giorgio Maggiore

Above: Florentine monk, a link with the past
Below: Florence's unmistakable roofscape

132

Map labels:

Museo Stibbert
Museo di San Marco
Giardino dei Semplici
Istituto Botanico
Giardino della Gherardesca
Cenacolo di Sant' Apollonia
San Marco
PIAZZA SAN MARCO
Università
Accademia di Belle Arti
Santissima Annunziata
Galleria dell'Accademia
PIAZZA DELLA SANTISSIMA ANNUNZIATA
Museo Archeologico
Palazzo Medici-Riccardi
Spedale degli Innocenti
VIA CAVOUR
VIA DEGLI ALFANI
VIA DEI SERVI
BORGO PINTI
DELLA
oteca enziana
VIA DEI PUCCI
VIA BUFALINI
Ospedale di Santa Maria Nuova
Teatro della Pergola
Santa Maria Maddalena dei Pazzi
VIA DEI PILASTRI
PIAZZA DEL DUOMO
Duomo
Museo dell' Opera del Duomo
VIA SANT' EGIDIO
Museo Storico Topographico (Museo di Firenze Com'era)
BORGO PINTI
VIA FIESOLANA
Campanile di Giotto
VIA DELL' ORIUOLO
DEL CORSO
VIA DEL PROCONSOLO
BORGO DEGLI ALBIZI
PIAZZA G SALVEMINI
VIA PIETRAPIANA
Casa di Dante
Badia Fiorentina
nichele
VIA GHIBELLINA
Museo Nazionale del Bargello
Casa Buonarroti
VIA DELL' AGNOLO
LLA CONDOT
VIA DE' LEONI
PIAZZA SAN FIRENZE
Teatro Verdi
San Firenze
VIA GIUSEPPE VERDI
VIA GHIBELLINA
BORGO ALLEGRI
PIAZZA DELLA SIGNORIA
a della Palazzo Vecchio
ioria
Galleria gli Uffizi
VIA DEI NERI
VIA DEL BENCI
PIAZZA SANTA CROCE
VIA DI SAN GIUSEPPE
ARNO
VIA DI CASTELLANI
Museo di Storia della Scienza
PIAZZA MENTANA
CORSO DEI TINTORI
Museo Horne
Santa Croce
VIA MAGLIABECHI
LUNGARNO GEN DIAZ
LUNGARNO DELLE GRAZIE
Biblioteca Nazionale Centrale
PZA DEI CAVALLEGGERI
LUNGARNO DELLA ZECCA VECCHIA
LUNGARNO TORRIGIANI
DE' BARDI
PONTE ALLE GRAZIE
Arno
0   200 m
0   200 yards
Palazzo Torrigiani
3
LUNGARNO SERRISTORI
VIA DI SAN NICCOLO
San Miniato al Monte
4
PIAZZA GIUSEPPE POGGI

Florence (Firenze) Tuscany's main attraction is as a city-sized shrine to the Renaissance. Florence's churches, palaces and museums are crammed with enough fine art to last a lifetime. Its streets, on the other hand, are surprisingly dour, hunched up with dark *palazzi* and filled with traffic and tourists. One or two notable exceptions aside, therefore, it is a city where your time is best spent indoors, poring over paintings or sculpture. Not that the city is without its visual appeal. Few sights are as impressive as a first view of Piazza del Duomo, the Ponte Vecchio or the Piazza della Signoria. But these are aberrations—more points of departure than places to linger. Florence has cafés for relaxation, and gardens, of course, but head for Siena if you want atmospheric streets and medieval charm.

FLORENCE

Festivals
Florence's foremost event is the **Maggio Musicale Fiorentino**, one of Europe's leading festivals of opera and classical music (April–early July). The **Estate Fiesolana**, a festival of chamber and symphonic music is held at Fiesole (June–late August). *Box Office* at Via della Pergola 10r has information on all events (tel: 055/242 361).

The highlights Piazza della Signoria offers the Palazzo Vecchio and the Loggia della Signoria (or Loggia dei Lanzi), Piazza del Duomo the Duomo and Baptistery, while Piazza della Repubblica, between the two, is a 19th-century square on the site of the Roman forum. From these central piazzas it is only a matter of minutes to the city's three great galleries: the Uffizi (paintings) and the Bargello and Museo dell'Opera del Duomo (sculpture). Other buildings offer similar star attractions—Michelangelo's *David*, housed in the Accademia, for example, or the sculpture-filled façade of Orsanmichele. The city is so rich in art that its second-ranked picture gallery—the six-museum complex of the Palazzo Pitti, surrounded by the Boboli Gardens—is better than most cities' best.

The churches Where Florence's galleries chronicle the Renaissance in its entirety, its churches tend to be monuments to particular artists. Most contain individual works of genius: San Marco (Fra Angelico); San Lorenzo (Michelangelo); Santa Croce (Giotto); Santa Maria del Carmine (Masaccio and Masolino); and Santa Maria Novella (Masaccio, Ghirlandaio and Filippino Lippi).

Origins Ancient *Florentia* was reputedly founded in 59 BC by Julius Caesar (though there was an earlier Etruscan settlement in the hills at nearby Fiesole). Florence emerged from the Dark Ages as an independent city state, prospering through banking and trade in wool and textiles. Ruled first by mercantile elements (the Primo Popolo), it later passed to the guilds (the Secondo Popolo) and in 1293 to the quasi-republican Signoria (a council drawn from the major guilds).

Guelph and Ghibelline Florence's rise to power, however was blighted by the Guelph and Ghibelline conflicts that affected many Italian city states (fights between supporters of the Pope and Emperor respectively). Often these were a cover for local rivalries, the most famous being the divisions in the Guelph camp between "Black" and "White" factions (Dante belonged to the latter, and along with many others was expelled from the city in 1302).

The Medici A single family emerged triumphant from Florence's conflicts—the Medici, a banking dynasty founded by Giovanni de' Medici. Its members were to control Florence—and later Tuscany—for over three centuries. Their power reached its zenith under Giovanni's son Cosimo, and Cosimo's grandson Lorenzo il Magnifico (1449–92), under whose enlightened patronage Florence became the greatest city of the Renaissance. Influence slipped when Lorenzo's son, Piero, surrendered to the French in 1494, leaving the way open for Savonarola, a charismatic monk who held the city in thrall until executed by the Papacy in 1498.

Last of the Medici The family returned in 1512 with reduced power, only to be removed again in 1527 when Charles V overran Rome (ousting Clement VII, a Medici pope). They were back again just three years later, and under another (distantly related) Cosimo declared themselves Grand Dukes of Tuscany in 1569. The last of the Medici died in 1737, and the city passed by treaty to the future Francis I of Austria. Except for 15 years of Napoleonic rule, it remained under Austrian control (with nominal independence) until Italian Unification in 1860. The city was capital of Italy from 1865 to 1871.

The view from Florence cathedral's dome

Tourist information
The main tourist offices are to be found at Via Cavour 1r (tel: 055/290 832), north of the Duomo, and at Chiasso dei Baroncelli 17r (near Piazza della Signoria).

Italy's many ghosts include the poets, painters and men of letters lured by what Keats called a "beakerful of the warm south." The years between about 1720 and 1790 marked the halcyon days of the Grand Tour, a route through several European cities culminating in Rome and Naples. Without this journey no gentleman's (rarely lady's) education was complete.

Top: Thomas Cook's first tour poses for a group photograph in the ruins of Pompeii

Modern visitors
The Grand Tour's turning point came in 1864 when a Mr. Thomas Cook ran the first package tour from London to Naples. He provided food, travel, entertainment and accommodations for some 50 people, thus sounding the death knell of travel in the grand style, and ushering in the era of mass tourism. With at least 50 million visitors a year, tourism is now among Italy's top money-earners, a boon and a bane for residents—and, perhaps, for foreigners too, who are now left with only scraps of the old Italy captured in the poems, paintings, letters and journals of travelers past.

Early visitors After those who came for plunder and pillage, Italy's earliest visitors were pilgrims, drawn by Rome's shrines and churches. Their greatest incursion occurred during the Holy Year proclaimed by Boniface VIII in 1300. Although doubtless designed to line papal coffers rather than provide spiritual solace, Boniface's offer of plenary indulgences attracted some two million visitors.

Pilgrims continued to outnumber tourists until about the 16th century, when gentlemen of substance turned to Italy to add the final polish to their courtly and cultural education. Castiglione's famous book *Il Cortegiano* (The Courtier) was translated and became a bible of behavior for English courtiers. However, this was also the period in which Italy acquired its reputation for intrigue, corruption and diabolic debauchery.

Paradise of exiles By the 18th century, Italy had come to be seen either as a museum of the past, or a country where foreigners could cast off their inhibitions and indulge in its more sensuous diversions. Some came for art and inspiration; some sought escape, others health; and many were lured by the idea of a warm climate stimulating the passions.

However, the journey to the promised land often turned out to be fraught with incident and difficulty. Joseph Addison arrived at Calais and fell into the harbor; Casanova was apparently sexually molested by a policeman; and Tobias Smollett, perhaps the most miserable man ever to travel, found dirt and disappointment at every turn. Goethe wisely observed that "every foreigner judges by the standards he brings with him." Italy worked its spell on countless others, among them Milton, Montaigne, Rubens, Turner, Velázquez, Poussin, Liszt, Nietzsche, Browning, Tennyson, Melville, Mark Twain, Henry James...

San Giorgio from the Dogana, sunrise, *painted by J.M.W. Turner on his visit to Venice*

Churches

▶▶▶ Battistero (Baptistery)   *133C3*
Piazza San Giovanni
The 11th-century Baptistery is most famous for its bronze doors, whose creation is generally considered to have marked the start of the Florentine Renaissance. The south (entrance) doors—cast in 1326 by Andrea Pisano—were already in place when the 20-year-old Lorenzo Ghiberti won a competition to design the others in 1401. His north doors have panels illustrating the Life of Christ; the east doors show Old Testament scenes. Inside are a lovely marble floor; a 13th-century mosaic ceiling; and Donatello and Michelozzo's tomb of the anti-pope John XXIII (a landmark of early Renaissance sculpture).

▶▶ Campanile   *133C3*
Piazza San Giovanni
"The model and mirror of perfect architecture," said Ruskin of the Duomo's bell tower, begun in 1334 to a design by Giotto. It was finished by Andrea Pisano and Francesco Talenti, and decorated with reliefs by Pisano, Donatello and Luca della Robbia (most of the originals are now in the Museo dell'Opera del Duomo). Climb the 414 steps to the top for the vertiginous views—George Eliot did, and found her "muscles much astonished at the unusual exercise."

▶▶▶ Duomo (Santa Maria del Fiore)   *133C3*
Piazza San Giovanni-Piazza del Duomo
The cathedral was started in 1296 following a design by Arnolfo di Cambio, but was only consecrated in 1436, after contributions by several more architects—notably Filippo Brunelleschi, whose magnificent dome is one of the miracles of medieval engineering.

    The spartan interior is a little disappointing, its only major works of art two equestrian frescos: a portrait by Uccello of *Sir John Hawkwood*, a famous English mercenary, and a study of *Niccolò da Tolentino*, by Andrea Castagno.

The Gates of Paradise
According to legend, Michelangelo described the Baptistery's east doors as "so beautiful they are worthy to be the Gates of Paradise." Their name may actually come from the fact that the district between the Baptistery and Santa Reparata was known as *Paradiso*. Lorenzo Ghiberti included a self-portrait in the frame of the left-hand door. He is the bald, smiling man—the fourth head from the top of the right-hand band. The original doors are being replaced by copies, the restored originals going to the Museo dell'Opera del Duomo.

Baptisms
Every 25 March (New Year's Day in the old Florentine calendar), it was the tradition for all children born in the city over the last 12 months to be brought to the Baptistery for a mass baptism. This made it both the civic and religious symbol of the city.

The Duomo, Florence

The Annunciation
Until the end of the 18th century the Florentine New Year began on March 25, the festival of the Annunciation—hence the popularity of paintings of the Annunciation and of the church of Santissima Annunziata, a fashionable spot for society weddings. The festival is still marked by a large annual fair in Piazza Santissima Annunziata.

Michelangelo's Tomb
Michelangelo's body was brought back from Rome in 1574 and buried in Santa Croce following a magnificent memorial service in San Lorenzo. His tomb is immediately on the right of the church as you enter. Michelangelo is said to have chosen this spot personally. The reason?—On the Day of Judgment, when the graves of the dead fly open, the first thing he would see would be Brunelleschi's dome on the Duomo.

Mercato Centrale
Be sure to visit this market near San Lorenzo, the largest covered food hall in Europe (built in 1874). It is a fantastic medley of fruit, vegetable, meat, and fish stalls, plus all kinds of bars and specialty food shops (tripe, pasta, olive oil etc). It is open Monday–Saturday 7AM–2PM and also Saturday 4–8PM. The streets around it are crammed with stalls selling cheap bags, belts, shoes and clothes.

▶▶ **Orsanmichele** 133B3
Via dei Calzaiuoli
Built originally as a granary, Orsanmichele became a trade hall for the city's guilds and later a place of worship. Each guild commissioned a piece of sculpture for the church's exterior, eliciting works from artists such as Ghiberti, Verrocchio and Donatello. Inside is a large, highly ornate marble **tabernacle** by Andrea Orcagna (1355–9).

▶ **Santissima Annunziata** 133 D4
Piazza Santissima Annunziata
Several of this church's frescos repay a visit, chiefly Andrea del Castagno's powerful works (first chapel on the left) and the paintings of Pontormo, Rosso Fiorentino and Andrea del Sarto (in the entrance atrium).

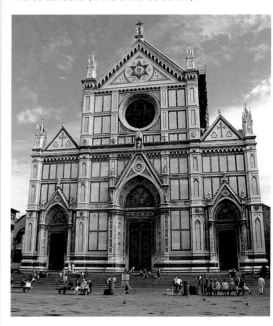
Santa Croce's 19th-century façade

▶▶▶ **Santa Croce** 133A4
Piazza Santa Croce
Florence's most famous church is renowned for its frescos and the tombs of some of the city's most illustrious personalities. The key frescos are two cycles by Giotto, painted in the Peruzzi and Bardi chapels right of the altar. One has scenes from the life of St. Francis, the other episodes from the lives of St. John and John the Baptist. The frescos nearby are by Taddeo Gaddi and his son. Among the church's 270 tombs are shrines to Machiavelli, Michelangelo, Galileo, Rossini and Dante (the last is empty, since Dante was exiled from Florence and is buried in Ravenna).

Donatello has two exceptional works in the church, a relief of the Annunciation and a wooden Crucifixion. If you revel in Renaissance architecture, Brunelleschi's Cappella dei Pazzi chapel is a masterpiece of the genre.

▶▶▶ San Lorenzo 132C2
Piazza San Lorenzo
Founded in the 4th century as the city's first cathedral, San Lorenzo later became the parish church of the Medici. Most people come here for the **Cappelle Medicée**, the family's mausoleum (entered via a separate entrance behind the church). It contains four tombs, two of them sculpted by Michelangelo: one for Lorenzo (grandson of Lorenzo the Magnificent), carved with reliefs representing *Dawn and Dusk*, the other for Lorenzo the Magnificent's youngest son Giuliano, decorated with figures representing *Night and Day*. Michelangelo also designed the Biblioteca Laurenziana, an extraordinary Medici library (located in the cloister off the main church).

▶▶▶ Santa Maria del Carmine 132A1
Piazza del Carmine
This church contains Masaccio's famous Brancacci fresco cycle, one of the great Renaissance masterpieces. Masolino da Panicale started the cycle in 1425, and was joined by Masaccio (then aged 22), first as an assistant, later—when his genius became apparent—as an equal. The paintings were a turning point in Renaissance art, demonstrating innovative use of perspective, increased drama and naturalism, and a virtuoso handling of light and space. They were completed by Filippino Lippi 60 years after Masaccio's untimely death (at the age of 25).

▶▶▶ Santa Maria Novella 132C1
Piazza Santa Maria Novella
Santa Maria Novella's gloomy interior hides several of Florence's foremost frescos, most notably Masaccio's 1428 *Trinity*, one of the first Renaissance paintings to master the principles of perspective. Crowds gathered at its inauguration, unable to believe a painting could create a "recession" in a solid wall. The Cappella Strozzi is lavishly frescoed by Filippino Lippi, and the apse contains frescos by Domenico Ghirlandaio. Be sure to see the richly decorated **cloisters▶▶**, the Chiostro Verde, with frescos by Paolo Uccello, and the Cappella degli Spagnuoli.

▶▶▶ San Miniato al Monte 133A4
Florence's finest Romanesque church perches above **Piazzale Michelangelo▶▶** —a stunning vantage point that offers some of the city's most memorable panoramas. If you do not relish the walk up the hill, take the regular No. 13 bus from the station or Piazza del Duomo. The beautiful multicolored façade dates from the 11th century, its pediment crowned by an eagle, a symbol of the guild entrusted with the church's well-being. The interior is distinguished by the unusual raised choir and large crypt, by an old pulpit and fragments of inlaid pavement (1207) and by the walls' 15th-century frescos.

> **Art lesson**
> "All the most celebrated sculptors and painters since Masaccio's day have become excellent and illustrious by studying their art in this chapel."
> Giorgio Vasari on the Brancacci Chapel.

> **San Miniato**
> San Miniato (St. Minias) belonged to a Christian community that settled in Florence in the 3rd century. After his martyrdom (he was beheaded), his corpse is said to have carried his severed head across the Arno to the site of the present church.

139

Stained glass in Santa Maria Novella

Italy's most famous gallery, the Uffizi. Most of its contents were left to the city by the Medici family

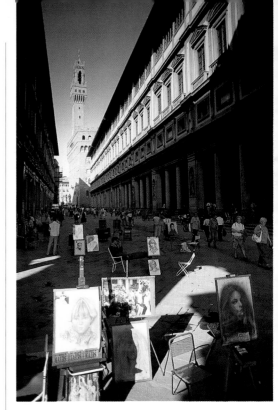

Palazzo del Bargello
The building housing the Bargello's collection was once home to the *Podestà*, the city's chief magistrate, its courtyard the site of numerous executions. It was the Florentine custom to paint the condemned prisoners—artists as eminent as Botticelli undertook the commissions—whose portraits were hung on the palace's exterior walls. The building took its present name in the 16th century, when the chief of police—the *Bargello*—took up residence.

David's deformities
Michelangelo's *David* was originally destined to reside in front of the Duomo. It was intended as a piece of public sculpture, not a gallery exhibit, which explains its deliberate deformities—the huge head, overlong arms and overlarge hands—all of which serve to increase its monumental effect. Started when the artist was 26, it took three years to complete, and when finished was the largest statue sculpted since Roman times.

Art Galleries

►►► Bargello, Museo Nazionale del   *133B3*
Via del Proconsolo 4
Italy's preeminent collection of Renaissance sculpture starts in style, opening with four Michelangelo masterpieces, including a serene *Apollo*, before moving on to the flamboyant art of Cellini and Giambologna. Second-floor highlights include famous works by Donatello, and reliefs by Ghiberti and Brunelleschi, which took first and second place in the competition to design the Baptistery doors.

►►► Galleria dell'Accademia   *133D3*
Via Ricasoli 60
Most visitors come here for one thing—Michelangelo's *David*, the most famous male nude in the history of art. The gallery contains six other figures by Michelangelo—a *Pietà*, an unfinished *St. Matthew*, and *Four Slaves*, the latter still deliberately "imprisoned" in their stone.

►►► Galleria degli Uffizi   *133A3*
Piazzale degli Uffizi
Some of the world's best-known Renaissance paintings are here. Three majestic altarpieces by Cimabue, Duccio and Giotto open proceedings, followed by six rooms of Sienese and Gothic art. Then come the familiar names: Room VII (Fra Angelico, Paolo Uccello and Piero della Francesca); VIII-IX (Pollaiuolo and Filippo Lippi); and X-XIV (Botticelli). Later rooms include canvases by Leonardo da Vinci, Michelangelo, Raphael, Caravaggio and many more.

Museums & Palaces

▶▶ **Casa Buonarroti
(Michelangelo Museum)**   *133B4*

Via Ghibellina 70

Michelangelo never lived in this house, which belonged to his nephew, and its jumble of memorabilia includes only two accredited original works: the *Madonna della Scala*, his earliest known sculpture (executed when he was just 16), and the *Battle of the Centaurs*, carved not long afterwards. He is also credited with a *Crucifix*, discovered in Santo Spirito in 1963.

▶ **Museo Archeologico**   *133C4*

Via della Colonna 36

The Archeological Museum's rambling collection embraces Greek, Roman and Egyptian objects, but is of most interest for its Etruscan exhibits. It suffered terribly in the 1966 flood, and ongoing restoration work means many of its treasures are still not on show.

▶▶ **Museo dell'Antica Casa Fiorentina**   *133B2*

Via Porta Rossa 13

The museum occupies the Palazzo Davanzati, part of which has been furnished and decorated to suggest the appearance of a 14th-century Florentine house. Its rooms range from a typical kitchen to a frescoed bedchamber, all filled with fascinating period detail, including art, furniture, fabrics, tapestries, lace, and domestic objects from the 14th to 18th centuries.

Markets

Two of Florence's markets lie close to the Casa Buonarroti: Piazza dei Ciompi's Mercato delle Pulci, the city's flea market, and the Mercato di Sant'Ambrogio, a rambunctious food market missed by most tourists.

Stroll—Giardino dei Semplici

Close to San Marco and the Archeological Museum is the Giardino dei Semplici, created by Cosimo I as a medicinal and botanical garden in 1545. A peaceful spot for a stroll, it retains its original layout, with medicinal herbs, Tuscan plants, flowers, and shady avenues. The entrance is at Via La Pira 4.

141

▶▶▶ **Museo dell'Opera del Duomo**   *133C3*

Piazza del Duomo 9

The sculpture collection is drawn from works removed from the Duomo, Campanile, and Baptistery. On the ground floor are reliefs from the cathedral's first façade (the present façade is a 19th-century addition).

Upstairs (after passing a *Pietà* by Michelangelo), you can see two masterly sculptures by Donatello—the *Prophet Habakkuk* and *Mary Magdalene*—and two contrasting *cantorie* (choir lofts), one also by Donatello and the other by Luca della Robbia. In the last room stand several of Ghiberti's original bronze panels from the Baptistery doors, together with a silver altarpiece by Pollaiuolo and Verrocchio.

Sculpture in the Museo dell'Opera del Duomo

Museo Stibbert

One of the city's more off-beat museums lies a half mile north of San Marco at Via Stibbert 26. Its 64 rambling rooms contain a 50,000-piece private collection, ranging from snuffboxes to paintings, but best known for one of the world's greatest assemblages of armor and militaria.

Henry James on Fra Angelico:

"He apparently never received an...impression of evil; and his conception of human life was a perpetual sense of sacredly loving and being loved..."

Filippo Lippi

Filippo Lippi (1406–69) was a notorious womanizer—despite being a monk. Vasari said he was "so lustful that he would give anything to enjoy a woman he wanted...and if he couldn't buy what he wanted then he would cool his passion by painting her portrait." On one occasion, Cosimo de' Medici—despairing of a commission ever being completed—locked him in the studio of the Palazzo Medici, only for Lippi to escape down a rope of knotted sheets.

Loggia della Signoria

Many of the statues outside the Palazzo Vecchio are copies—not those in the nearby Loggia della Signoria, however, an open loggia which contains two great originals: Benvenuto Cellini's bronze *Perseus* and Giambologna's *Rape of the Sabine Women*.

▶▶▶ **Museo di San Marco (Fra Angelico Museum)** *133D3*

Piazza San Marco 3

Cosimo de' Medici rebuilt the monastery of San Marco for the Dominicans in 1437. During the work, Fra Angelico—himself a Dominican monk here from 1436 to 1447—frescoed much of the building, creating the paintings as a hymn to God. The peaceful ex-monastery is now a veritable memorial to this most sublime of Renaissance painters. The Ospizio dei Pellegrini (Pilgrims' Hospice) near the entrance contains around 20 works, mostly collected from churches around Florence. The Sala Capitolare (Chapterhouse) across the cloister contains a powerful *Crucifixion*, but Fra Angelico's single greatest work, the *Annunciation*, is on the stairs leading to the monks' dormitory cells, all 44 of which contain Biblical vignettes frescoed by the artist and his assistants.

▶ **Museo di Storia della Scienza (History of Science Museum)** *133A3*

Piazza dei Giudici 1

This fascinating little museum, recently overhauled, explores the technological side of the Renaissance and the period's close links between art and science. It includes antique clocks and instruments, a reconstructed alchemical laboratory, surgical and anatomical models, and much material connected with Galileo.

▶▶ **Palazzo Medici-Riccardi (Medici Palace)** *133C3*

Via Cavour 1

This monolithic Renaissance palace was designed for Cosimo il Vecchio in 1444 and enlarged two centuries later by its new owners, the Riccardi family. Two windows in the ground floor arches are attributed to Michelangelo, and were copied in numerous *palazzi* around the city. The only part of the Medici wing to survive, is the chapel, which contains limpid frescos of *The Journey of the Magi* by Benozzo Gozzoli, a pupil of Fra Angelico (its figures are portraits of members of the Medici family). A second-floor gallery has a painting by Filippo Lippi, for whom Cosimo established a workshop in the palace.

The Pitti Palace

▶▶ **Palazzo Pitti**   *132A2*

Piazza de' Pitti

The Pitti family commissioned this colossal palace around 1460 in an attempt to outdo the Medici—only for the Medici to buy them out in 1541. It now houses six separate museums. Of these the Galleria Palatina is by far the most important, though its impact would be greater if the paintings were better hung and the rooms less labyrinthine. Nonetheless, its highlights include 11 Titians and 14 Raphaels, a good selection of works by Andrea del Sarto, and paintings by Perugino, Caravaggio, Velásquez, Rubens, and Van Dyck.

▶▶ **Palazzo Vecchio**   *133B3*

Piazza della Signoria

What this palace lacks in grace it makes up for in grandeur. Its imposing bulk and sturdy campanile loom over Florence's main piazza. Started in 1299, it was built to house the *signoria*, the city's ruling council, whose members were selected from Florence's seven major guilds. Most of its public apartments are worth a look, particularly

> **Museo di Zoologia**
> This museum (also known as *La Specola*) is a stone's throw from the Palazzo Pitti (at Via Romana 17). Most visitors come for the *Cere Anatomiche*—Anatomical Waxworks—open only Tuesday and Saturday 9–noon). It contains over 600 models made between 1775 and 1814, ranging from entire corpses to arms, legs and organs, each minutely dyed and detailed to reveal nerves, muscles, and blood vessels. The most famous room shows four wonderfully graphic tableaux of Florence during the plague.

143

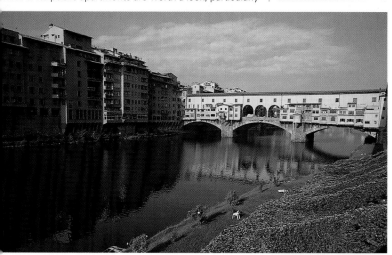

the Salone dei Cinquecento, full of statues and second-rate frescos by Vasari. Off the *Salone* lies the Studiolo, a tiny masterpiece of Mannerist decoration. The Sala dei Gigli features frescos by Ghirlandaio and a newly restored *Judith and Holofernes* by Donatello.

▶ **Ponte Vecchio**   *132A2*

This bridge and its picturesque huddle of overhanging shops is one of the city's most familiar landmarks. It was built in 1345, and its shops once included butchers, grocers and blacksmiths, all of whom were removed in 1593 on the orders of the Medici Ferdinand I. The bridge contained a private corridor between the Medici offices in the Uffizi (*ufficio*—office) and the family's palace (the Palazzo Pitti). Unfortunately for the shopkeepers Ferdinand objected to slabs of meat and other produce not fitting for the ducal passage. Since then the bridge has been the preserve of jewelers and goldsmiths.

Top: Ponte Vecchio
Above: buildings on the 14th-century bridge

Walking in Florence

Florence's occasionally gloomy streets are not as appealing to wander through as those of some other cities, but almost any itinerary takes you to churches, palaces, art galleries, and museums of immense individual interest.

Stroll—Giardino di Boboli
The Boboli gardens behind the Palazzo Pitti have innumerable peaceful corners for quiet strolls or leisurely picnics. Above the gardens looms the Forte di Belvedere, from where there are unforgettable panoramas of the city. Access to the Belvedere is possible from the Costa San Giorgio, a lane behind Santa Felicità.

A dramatic corner of Santa Maria Novella

Piazza del Duomo A wander around Piazza del Duomo and the adjacent Piazza San Giovanni introduces you to three of the city's landmarks—the Duomo, Battistero and Campanile. Stroll along the cathedral's southern exterior and you come to the Museo dell'Opera del Duomo.

Piazza della Signoria to Santa Croce From Piazza del Duomo follow Via dei Calzaiuoli, Florence's main street. Stop off at Orsanmichele, and in Piazza della Signoria, the city's main square. The piazza contains the Palazzo Vecchio and Loggia della Signoria (and the Uffizi is nearby). Heading east you can then take in the Bargello and some of the attractive streets that lead to the church of Santa Croce.

Santa Maria Novella to the Museo di San Marco Start at the church of Santa Maria Novella. Cross Piazza dell'Unità Italiana to its east and take Via del Melarancio to San Lorenzo and the Cappelle Medicée. See the Palazzo Medici-Riccardi before cutting up to look around the Mercato Centrale, Florence's busy covered market. Then head north to see Sant'Apollonia and Andrea del Castagno's important but surprisingly little known fresco of the *Last Supper*. The Galleria dell'Accademia and Museo di San Marco lie a short distance east.

If you have time this walk can also encompass a trio of more minor sights around Piazza della Santissima Annunziata: the Museo Archeologico, Santissima Annunziata and the Spedale degli Innocenti.

Oltrarno This walk takes in some of the city's quieter reaches south of the River Arno. Start either at the Museo di Storia della Scienza or the Ponte Vecchio. Pop into the church of Santa Felìcita to see one of Florence's greatest Mannerist masterpieces, Pontormo's *Deposition*, and then walk west to see Santo Spirito and Santa Maria del Carmine. Finish at the Palazzo Pitti and Giardino di Boboli (see panel).

Getting around Walking is the most practical way to see Florence—most of the city's sights are close together and traffic is restricted in the city center. Orange A.T.A.F. buses can be used to cover larger distances, or to visit outlying spots like San Miniato al Monte. Most services stop in Piazza del Duomo (see panel—Useful Bus Routes). Tickets are valid for 70 or 120 minutes (for any number of journeys). They must be bought before boarding and are available from *tabacchi* or automatic machines around the city; 24-hour passes are also available. A few buses displaying a sign of a hand holding a coin have ticket machines on board which accept change.

If you are **driving**, the *zona a traffico limitato* (Z.T.L.)—the city center traffic restrictions—will prevent you taking your car into the center between 7:30AM and 6:30PM Monday to Friday. You can usually enter to unload luggage at hotels but must then leave the restricted zone and park elsewhere.The main parking lots are Fortezza da Basso (behind the train station); Piazza Vittorio Veneto; Piazza del Carmine; Piazza Piave; Piazza Mentana; and Piazza Santa Maria Nuova. All become busy and all are pay parking lots.

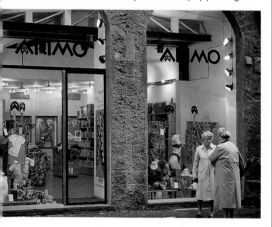

Quality does not come cheap in Florence

Shopping Florence is a good shopping center, particularly known for its **leather goods**. The most exclusive stores, including the big-name designer boutiques, are concentrated on Via dei Tornabuoni and its two smaller tributaries, Via Strozzi and Via della Vigna Nuova (**Gucci** among them, which was founded in Florence). Borgo Ognissanti is also crammed with top-quality shops. For slightly cheaper clothes and leatherware visit the market stalls around San Lorenzo, or the **Leather Guild**, Piazza Santa Croce 20r, one of several outlets in Florence where you can watch craftsmen at work.

Jewelry is also of a high standard, with many stores on and around Ponte Vecchio (though prices are high—and beware the fakes sold by some of the street traders). For **antiques** visit Via Maggio, Borgo Ognissanti or the riverside streets like Lungarno Corsini. Specialty **food** stores can be found around the Mercato Centrale. For wines and liquors try **Biagini**, Via dei Banchi 57, off Piazza Santa Maria Novella.

Useful bus routes
No. 7 Station–Duomo–Fiesole;
No. 10 Station– Duomo–Museo di San Marco;
No. 13 Station–Duomo–Piazzale Michelangelo–San Miniato;
No. 15 San Marco–Via del Proconsolo–Ponte alle Grazie–Palazzo Pitti–Piazza Santo Spirito–Piazza del Carmine–Fortezza da Basso.
Maps and timetables are available from the A.T.A.F. office at Piazza del Duomo 57r.

Bicycle rental
Bicycles (and scooters) can be rented from several points in the city. Try *Bicicittà* outlets at Piazza Pitti, Fortezza di Basso and Via Alamanni (opposite the train station).

Farmacia S M Novella
Be sure to visit this shop, an original monastic pharmacy almost unchanged since the 16th century. It is as famous for its furniture and decor as its products, which include special soaps, face creams, medieval cures and Dominican herbal remedies. *Via della Scala 16.*

Marbled paper
Florence is one of the few places where you can find marbled paper, a craft brought to Venice from the Orient in the 12th century. The oldest outlet (1856) and *the* place to buy is **Giannini**, Piazza Pitti 37r—though it is also the most expensive.

Department stores
Upscale *Coin* is at Via dei Calzaiuoli; mid-range *Standa* at Via Panzani 31; and lower-priced *Upim* at Via degli Speziali 3–23.

Accommodations

Hotel agencies
As well as the ITA agency you might try **Florence Promhotels**, Viale A Volta 72 (tel: 055/570 481) and **Toscana Hotels 80**, Viale Gramsci 9 (tel: 055/247 8543). Both take reservations by phone or mail.

A Room with a View
The *pensione* which features in E. M. Forster's well-known Florence-set novel is the **Jennings-Riccioli**, Corso Tintori 7 (tel: 055/244 751)—though restoration has removed much of the atmosphere evoked in the book. The hotel in which the film of the book was shot was the **Quisisana e Ponte Vecchio**, damaged by a terrorist bomb in 1993, and now, sadly, closed.

Picnics
Picnics cut cost and make pleasant outings in their own right. Buy food from *alimentari* or markets like the Mercato Centrale, Sant'Ambrogio (in Piazza Ghiberti near Santa Croce) or Piazza Santo Spirito. Then retire to the Semplici or Boboli gardens, or squares like Santissima Annunziata, Santa Croce, or Santa Maria Novella.

Florence is undeniably one of Europe's tourist meccas, and although it has well over 400 listed hotels, it is a city where high-season accommodations are at a premium. If you arrive late in the day during July and August, you may find it difficult to secure a room in almost any category of accommodation.

Ideally, of course, you should reserve well in advance, but all is not necessarily lost even if you turn up without a reservation. Florence has several agencies who find rooms at a set price for a small commission (which can usually be deducted from your first night's bill). Vacant rooms may only be available on the outskirts of the city, so make sure that you know where your hotel is and how to get to it.

Informazioni Turistiche Alberghiere (I.T.A.) is the best-known of these agencies (see also the panel on this page). They have two year-round offices: one is inside the train station, open daily 8:30AM–9PM (tel: 055/282 893) while the other is in the AGIP service station at Peretola on the A11 highway west of the city (tel: 055/440 790). Seasonal offices (operating between April and October) are located at the Fortezza da Basso (tel: 055/471 960) and the Chianti-Est service area on the A1 highway.

Choosing a hotel Most budget hotels are near the station (on Via della Scala, Via Nazionale and Via Faenza). Some—but not all—are fairly grim, and certain areas are best avoided at night. The district around Ognissanti has some of the more plush hotels. The quietest spots are in Oltrarno (where there is also more chance of rooms). The residential area around the Teatro Comunale is also a good base (Corso Italia).

Do not judge a hotel by its exterior, for plain façades on gloomy *palazzi* often conceal wonderful Renaissance interiors. Atmospheric and charming villa and palace hotels are widespread in the city center. Rooms can vary greatly within a building, so ask to see a variety. Noise is as much a factor as it is in any Italian city.

The terra cotta pantiles of a Florentine roofscape

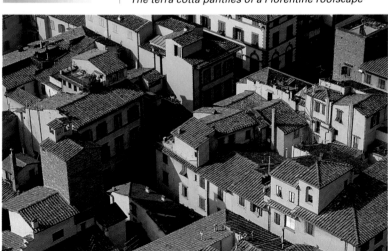

Food and drink

Florence likes to claim it introduced cooking to the French—when Catherine de' Medici took a group of Florentine chefs to Paris on her marriage to the future Henry II of France. The city's cooking is now wholesome and down-to-earth, centered around basic ingredients like olive oil, top-quality meat, and fresh vegetables. Restaurant prices are a little high, as you would expect in a tourist town, but the overall quality is usually reliable and occasionally exceptional. Florentines eat a bit earlier than some other Italians—around 12:30 for lunch, 7:30 for dinner. As a general rule, cheap places cluster around the station, the top spots on the main streets, and the quieter *trattorie* in Oltrarno.

Anyone at all interested in Tuscan food should be sure to visit the Mercato Centrale on Via dell'Ariento near San Lorenzo.

Specialties Florence's most famous dish is the ubiquitous *bistecca alla Fiorentina*, a thick, heavily seasoned Val di Chiana steak grilled over an open fire. Appetizers are likely to include *crostini* (toasts covered in truffle, olive or liver paste) or strong hams and salamis (boar sausage is common—*salsiccia di cinghiale*). First-course favorites are thick soups like *ribollita* (literally "reboiled"), *pappa al pomodoro* and *panzanella*, all variations on a theme of vegetables, beans, oil and bread. The city's most traditional dishes are today rather scarce—things like tripe, pumpkin soup, cocks' combs and kidneys—though they can still be found.

Drinking The best place to sample wine is in a traditional *vinaio*, or wine shop, which—like most bars—often also sells sandwiches and snacks (see panel). Chianti is the obvious local drink, but most big Tuscan wines are usually available—Brunello, Vino Nobile and others. Outdoor cafés are not as big a feature as in some cities, but they exist, together with several famous but rather touristy bars living on past reputations.

Taking a break in Piazza della Signoria

Bars and cafés

Piazza della Signoria's *Rivoire* is the city's classiest and most elegant café, closely followed by Piazza della Repubblica's grand but more sterile *Gilli*, *Giubbe Rosse* and *Paszkowski*. *Giacosa*, Via dei Tornabuoni 83r, is good (and claims to have invented the Negroni cocktail). *Robiglio*, Via dei Servi, and *Manaresi*, Via de' Lamberti 16r, both claim to serve Florence's best cup of coffee. *Caffè*, Piazza Pitti 11–12r is a lovely old-world spot. For a perfect *vinaio* visit *Vini e Panini*, Via Cimatori 38r.

Ice cream

Florence's—some say Italy's—best ice cream is found at *Vivoli*, Via Isola delle Stinche 7r (between the Bargello and Santa Croce). Follow the crowds.

Enoteca Pinchiorri

This is among Europe's finest restaurants. The wine list matches the quality of the cooking—over 80,000 bottles of fine Italian and French wines. Prices are stratospheric, but for a one-time treat this cannot be beaten. Via Ghibellina 87 (tel: 055/242 777).

TUSCANY

Tuscany (Toscana) In exploring Florence—with all its treasures—you barely scratch the surface of Tuscany's artistic heritage. Almost every town in Tuscany boasts attractions that could occupy a day's sightseeing. Siena deserves at least that, its calm medieval ambience the perfect foil for Florence's frenetic, tourist-filled streets. Little known Lucca is as graceful a town as any in Italy, often overlooked in favor of Pisa, curiously lackluster once you have seen the Leaning Tower and its surrounding ensemble. Lofty Volterra, too, has its medieval moments, but is better known for its fine Etruscan museum. Arezzo might be ignored altogether, except for its great frescos, while nearby Cortona seduces with its fine and atmospheric streets. Pienza and Montepulciano, too, are both as attractive for their own sakes as for any outstanding art and architecture they offer.

The villages The siren call of Tuscany's towns leaves little time for its villages. No trip to the region, though, would be complete without a visit to San Gimignano and its famous towers, still an evocative sight despite thousands of summer visitors. Fewer people find their way to Sovana, well off the beaten track, but well worth a trip for its charm, churches, and Etruscan tombs. Nearby, Sorano and Pitigliano complete a fine trio of villages. South of Siena are more villages (see Drive, page 155), most notably Montalcino—famous heart of the Brunello wine region. In this same area, lost in lovely countryside, stand three beautiful abbeys—Sant'Antimo, San Galgano, and Monte Oliveto Maggiore.

The landscapes Chianti encapsulates for many people Tuscany's archetypal landscape. There is more to the region, however, than just vineyards and soft, rolling hills. In the far north, for example, rise the mountains of the Orecchiella and Alpi Apuane, famed for their marble and their scenic splendor. Caught between them is the green valley of the Garfagnana. Along much of the coast stretches the Maremma, an often melancholy but nonetheless evocative plain edged with low hills. One corner contains the Monti dell'Uccellina, a glorious pocket of coastal landscapes protected by the Parco Naturale della Maremma. South of Siena lie the *crete*, the region's strangest landscape, bare clay hills checkered with prairies of rippling wheat. In the east are the Casentino, Mugello and Pratomagno, all Chianti's scenic equals, but all still largely unexplored by foreign visitors.

Eating Italians who should know better dismiss Tuscans as *mangiafagioli*—bean eaters. The region's cuisine may be simple, but it is hearty and varied, based on excellent olive oils and the finest ingredients. Meals often start with *crostini* (small pieces of toast with liver, olive, or tomato pastes), followed by soups like *ribollita* (a thick bread, bean, and vegetable broth). Meat dishes include *lepre* (hare); *arista* (pork loin with garlic and rosemary); *pollo alla diavola* (grilled, marinated chicken); and the famous *bistecca alla fiorentina* (a steak grilled over charcoal). Meats often appear *alla cacciatore* ("in the way of the hunter"), simple roasts in a rich sauce of tomatoes, garlic, and olives. Wild boar and game birds are also common. For dessert you might find *zuccotto* (sponge cake with cream and chocolate) or *panforte* (a spicy cake of nuts and candied fruit from Siena). Many menus also offer *cantucci*, small almond biscuits traditionally served at the end of a meal with Vin Santo (see below).

Wine Chianti needs little introduction, a wine of infinite variety and quality, sometimes sublime, often insipid. Of greater repute is Brunello di Montalcino and its younger cousin, Rosso di Montalcino. Almost as famous is Vino Nobile di Montepulciano, at its best one of Italy's more majestic reds. Less well-known are the excellent Carmignano, Pomino, Cercatoia (from Lucca) and Morellino di Scansano. Whites include the impeccable Villa Antinori Bianco, the rare Torricella, and variable Vernaccia di San Gimignano. The semi-sweet Vin Santo (Holy Wine) is a famed dessert wine, though its quality is inconsistent.

Scenic drives
SS146/SS451 Montepulciano–Pienza–San Quirico–(Montalcino)–Buonconvento–Monte Oliveto Maggiore; SS222 (*Chiantigiana*) Siena–Castellina in Chianti–Greve–Florence; SS68 Volterra–(San Gimignano)– Colle di Val d'Elsa; SS70/SS208 (Florence)–Pontassieve–Poppi–Camaldoli–Bibbiena–Chiusi della Verna; SS324 Castelnuovo di Garfagnana–San Pellegrino in Alpe–Pievepelago–San Marcello Pistoiese–Pistoia.

Scenic railroads
For a look at the Garfagnana and its mountains, ride the little branch line from Lucca to Aulla (two hours). For a plodding journey around the *crete*, some of the region's most distinctive scenery, take the trains from Siena to Grosseto.

Miniature garden in Castellina in Chianti

TUSCANY

152

Part of The Legend of the Holy Cross *by Piero della Francesca in Arezzo's San Francesco church*

▶▶ Arezzo 149C4

An otherwise unexceptional provincial town, Arezzo is distinguished by one of Tuscany's most famous fresco cycles—Piero della Francesca's *Legend of the Holy Cross* in the **church of San Francesco▶▶▶**. The frescos, created between 1452 and 1466, tell the story of the cross used to crucify Christ, and represent one of the largest collections of this enigmatic artist's work (see panel for other noted paintings by him to be seen nearby). Elsewhere, the town offers the **Pieve di Santa Maria▶▶**, an attractive Romanesque church with a striking façade and a high altar polyptych by Pietro Lorenzetti, a *Madonna and Child with Saints* (1320). Behind the church rises the **Piazza Grande▶** a dramatically sloping medieval square, and above it the **Duomo▶**, which contains another Piero della Francesca fresco, *Mary Magdalen*. Alongside stands some lovely stained glass and the tomb of Guido Tarlati, perhaps designed by Giotto. The **Fortezza Medicea▶** is a good spot for picnics, and provides a belvedere for views over the hills of the Casentino.

▶ Casentino 149D4

The Casentino is one of Tuscany's hidden corners. A large, mountain-ringed basin, it embraces the Arno's upper reaches—an undulating agricultural region—and the huge tracts of one of Italy's wildest primeval forests, the **Foresti Casentinesi▶▶** (a proposed national park). Most of the little villages have something of interest, and away from the slightly spoiled valley floor the upland roads are a scenic delight. **Poppi▶** is a picturesque village, centered on a 13th-century castle and fine 12th-century abbey, the Badia di San Fedele. Beautifully situated **La Verna▶** near Chiusi della Verna has a monastery founded by St. Francis—it was here that he received the stigmata (a breezy walk behind it leads to La Penna (4,234 feet) for some fine views). The village of Caprese Michelangelo, birthplace of the great artist whose name it bears, lies just 7 miles south.

►► Chianti
148C3

Chianti's vineyards and wooded hills form the quintessential Tuscan landscape. They also form a veritable "Paradise of Exiles" for hordes of foreign expatriates, an influx that has undoubtedly spoiled certain hilltowns (in summer at least). Other villages—Radda in Chianti and Gaiole in Chianti, for example—are tarnished by a surprising amount of light industry. The region's real pleasures, therefore, are to be found in driving the back roads, exploring the smaller villages and sampling wine at any one of several hundred vineyards open to the public. **Greve in Chianti►** lies at the heart of Gallo Nero ("Black Cockerel") country; the consortium of this name is responsible for some of the region's better wine. The village holds a large wine fair every September, and is chock-full of wine shops (the best is Piazzetta Santa Croce's Enoteca di Gallo Nero). Elsewhere, one of the most interesting *cantinas* to visit is the Castello di Brolio at **Brolio►**.

►► Cortona
149C4

Legend claims hilltop Cortona to be older than Troy, though today the town's appearance is medieval, with old churches and ancient corners dotted around its precipitous cobbled streets. The Renaissance church of **Santa Maria del Calcinaio►►**, one of the finest in this part of Italy, stands out as you approach. Piazza della Repubblica forms the town center, close to the **Museo dell'Accademia Etrusca►►**, a fine little Etruscan museum, and to the **Museo Diocesano►►►**, a small but superlative gallery that contains Fra Angelico's *Annunciation* and *Madonna and Child*.

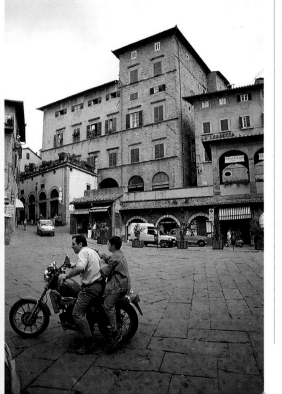

Strada Chiantigiana
For a representative slice of Chianti scenery follow the *Strada Chiantigiana*, the name given to the SS222 road from Siena to Florence. Designed as a *Strada del Vino* (Wine Road), it also cuts through some of the region's less spoiled countryside by way of Castellina and Greve in Chianti.

Wine
Chianti was the world's first officially designated wine-producing area. In 1716 Cosimo III defined the boundaries within which vineyards could claim the *Chianti* name. Now there are seven separate wine-producing zones and over 7,000 registered vineyards. As a result, Chianti is not one wine, but many, with great variety in taste, type and quality. Standards have improved recently, with the best wines most often found in the *Chianti Classico* (*Gallo Nero*) and *Chianti Rufina* zones. Better Chiantis mature at between four and seven years. Recent vintage years have been 1985 and 1986.

Piazza della Repubblica in the hilltop town of Cortona

TUSCANY

Portoferraio on Elba

►► **Elba, Isola di**   *148B2*

The island of Elba is a world unto itself within Tuscany, hardly a part of the region at all. Its excellent white-sand beaches, limpid waters, and lush interior landscapes attract a flood of visitors (over a million in August alone). **Portoferraio**►► is the capital, reached by ferry from Livorno and Piombino on the Tuscan mainland. **Marina di Campo**► on the south coast has the largest beach, but is also the island's biggest and brashest resort. The beautiful part of the island centers around its highest point, Monte Capanne (3,362 ft.), close to two lovely hilltowns—Poggio and **Marciana**►►—and on the spectacular cliff scenery of the west coast. In the southeast corner, **Capoliveri**►► provides access to a string of small popular resorts.

► **Forte dei Marmi**   *148D2*

Forte dei Marmi was once the main port for exports of marble from the Alpi Apuane. Today it is the most upscale town on the Riviera della Versilia, the string of beach resorts that lines the Tuscan coast north of Pisa. Palm-lined boulevards and a first-rate beach are hardly enough to explain why the town has such an exalted reputation (and prices). It is, however, a favored retreat for writers and artists, and a good base for excursions into the Alpi Apuane to the east.

► **Garfagnana**   *148D2*

North of Lucca, the Garfagnana embraces the Serchio valley and the staggering mountain ranges of the Alpi Apuane and the Orecchiella. Its towns are undistinguished, though **Bagni di Lucca**► preserves something of the romantic beauty that attracted Byron, Browning and Shelley in the 19th century. **Barga**►► has a Romanesque gem in its honey-stoned cathedral. The Grotta del Vento about 5.50 miles west of Barga is Tuscany's most spectacular cave. In the **Orecchiella**►► drive the magnificent mountain roads to San Pellegrino in Alpe with its **Museo della Campagna** ►►, an outstanding ethnographic museum.

SOUTH OF SIENA

Drive Through Tuscany's heart

A glorious drive which takes you through the heart of the Tuscan countryside, visiting vineyards, abbeys, Roman baths and historic hill towns.

Start in **Montepulciano** (page 158), and after a look around take SS146 west to **Pienza** (page 158), an essential stop, then drive down to **San Quirico d'Orcia**► for its Romanesque church, the Collegiata. Just south, detour to **Bagno Vignoni**►► to see the sulphurous hot springs in the village square. Continue past the hilltop village of Castiglione d'Orcia to the romantic ruined abbey of **Sant'Antimo**►►.

After **Montalcino** (page 157), wind down to Buonconvento, home to an excellent art gallery, the **Museo d'Arte Sacra**►►. Climb through beautiful countryside to the wonderfully situated and remote **Abbazia di Monte Oliveto Maggiore** (page 157). Continue to Siena (SS438) or return by country roads to Montepulciano.

Note: you can start this drive from Siena, taking the SS326 toward Sinalunga, then the SS438 to Asciano, a gorgeous road through the *crete* (bare, deeply fissured hills that characterize the landscape south of Siena).

Certosa di Pisa
You can visit this fascinating 14th-century Carthusian monastery from either Pisa or Lucca (12.50 miles). Guided tours show you the frescoed main church, eleven tiny chapels and the cloister, with its three-room suites of cells and gardens. Monks lived here in solitude and silence except on Sundays, when they were permitted to speak and eat together. Note the message above the gate as you leave: *Egredere sed non omnis:* "Leave, but not entirely," addressed to monks sent on missions into the outside world.

▶▶▶ **Lucca**   148D2

Lucca is Tuscany's most likable town after Florence and Siena. Its Roman grid of streets is enclosed by tree-lined walls▶▶—that you should walk for the views—and dotted with palaces, museums, and Romanesque churches.

San Michele in Foro▶▶▶ is the most beautiful of the churches, its muted interior overshadowed by perhaps Italy's most intricate and inspired façade. Home to more precious works of art is the **Duomo di San**

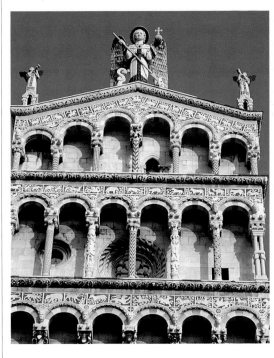

Façade of Lucca's San Michele church

Martino▶▶▶. The main portal has carvings by Nicola Pisano, while the nave is dominated by the Tempietto, a gaudy octagon built to house the *Volto Santo*. This highly venerated icon is supposed to be a true effigy of Christ carved at the Crucifixion (it is probably a 12th-century fake). Beyond it lies the 15th-century **tomb of Ilaria del Carretto** by Jacopo dell Quercia, one of Italy's most exquisite Renaissance masterpieces.

San Frediano▶▶ stands in the town's northern reaches, distinguished outside by a 13th-century mosaic, inside by a beautiful 12th-century font. Nearby is the **Piazza del Anfiteatro▶▶**, a medieval square built in and around the old Roman amphitheater.

Lucca's museums and galleries are not exceptional: the **Pinacoteca Nazionale▶** is as interesting for its extravagantly decorated rococo rooms as for its paintings, but best for art lovers is the **Museo Nazionale Guinigi▶** with good paintings, sculptures, furniture, and applied arts. The birthplace of composer Giacomo Puccini, Via di Poggio 30, houses a small museum of Puccini memorabilia.

▶▶ Maremma 148A3

The Maremma stretches from Pisa to the border with Lazio, an area of empty, often melancholy countryside that for centuries has been covered in marsh and wild tracts of *maquis*. Drainage of the region was started by the Etruscans (and finished by Mussolini). Vestiges of its ancient landscapes, however, are preserved in the sublimely beautiful **Parco Naturale della Maremma▶▶**, well worth a visit. The park headquarters are at Alberese, from where a special bus takes you into the park (private traffic is banned from the area).

Tuscany's finest beach lies north of the park, the almost completely uncommercialized **Marina di Alberese▶▶▶**. More developed resorts include **Porto Ercole▶** and **Porto Santo Stefano▶**, upscale spots on Monte Argentario, a mountainous promontory close to the Laguna di Orbetello (some of Italy's best bird-watching territory). To the north are **Punta Ala▶**, a chic, purpose-built resort, and **Castiglione della Pescaia▶**, a moderate resort and fishing village.

Inland, **Massa Marittima▶▶** offers a perfect medieval piazza, with one of Tuscany's best small cathedrals. Other more far-flung villages well worth exploring are Sovana (see page 163), clifftop Pitigliano, Roccalbegna and Castagneto Carducci.

▶▶ Montalcino 149B4

A lovely, if unassuming hilltown, Montalcino produces one of Italy's most prestigious red wines—Brunello di Montalcino. The smart *enoteca* in the Rocca (castle) is one spot to sample it (the ramparts offer the bonus of good views). No visit to the town is complete, however, without

Vineyards
Two outstanding vineyards can be visited around Montalcino: the Fattoria dei Barbi (4 miles to the southeast), which also has a renowned restaurant attached, and the Villa Banfi (11 miles southwest), the area's largest and most modern producer.

Abbey of Sant'Antimo, south of Montalcino

a drink of some sort in the **Fiaschetteria Italiana**, a wonderful 19th-century café in Piazza del Popolo. Around the town, which is well worth an hour's stroll, there are also several little churches and a pair of modest museums.

▶▶▶ Monte Oliveto Maggiore, Abbazia di 149B4

No monastery can be more beautifully situated than Monte Oliveto Maggiore, founded in the 14th century by the Olivetans, or "White Benedictines," a breakaway group who strove to return to the simple ideals of the Benedictine order. Its great treasure is a 36-panel fresco cycle on the life of St. Benedict, by Il Sodoma and Luca Signorelli. The wooden choir is also outstanding.

Sant'Antimo
The 12th-century Benedictine abbey of Sant'Antimo (6 miles south of Montalcino), ranks high in Tuscany's pantheon of Romanesque buildings. Its setting, frescos and carvings are delightful; on Sunday mornings a small group of French Cistercians often celebrate Mass with a Gregorian chant.

TUSCANY

158

The Leaning Tower of Pisa

▶▶ **Montepulciano**   149B4

Hilltop Montepulciano is a perfect blend of medieval, Renaissance and baroque ingredients. As added spice it also has the further attraction of Vino Nobile di Montepulciano—the "king of wines." An important Renaissance church, Sangallo's **San Biagio▶▶**, stands just outside the walls. Within them, Piazza Grande's ancient *palazzi* compete for attention with the **Duomo▶▶**, best known for its Michelozzo sculpture and an altarpiece by Taddeo di Bartolo. Be sure to climb the tower of the Palazzo Comunale for its views, and to explore the quiet backstreets, as delightful as any in Tuscany.

▶▶ **Pienza**   149B4

Pienza is a planned Renaissance town, created by Pope Pius II (and named after him) out of Cortigiano, the village of his birth. The transformation began under Bernardo Rossellino in 1459, the architect responsible for most of the town's buildings. It was cut short by Pius' death, but not before the consecration of the **cathedral▶▶**, a handsome pile with a redoubtable wooden choir and altarpieces executed by the leading Sienese artists of the day. More paintings (and papal vestments) are displayed in the **Museo Civico▶** to the cathedral's left. The **Palazzo Piccolomini▶▶** alongside contains richly appointed papal apartments and offers sweeping views from its courtyard. Churches worth a glance include San Francesco and the Pieve.

▶▶▶ **Pisa**   148D2

Pisa's **Leaning Tower▶▶▶** needs no introduction. A surprising number of people, however, overlook the other magnificent buildings in Piazza del Duomo—otherwise known as the *Campo dei Miracoli* (Field of Miracles). The tower was intended as a campanile for the **Duomo▶▶▶**, a stunning creation famous for its pulpit (by Giovanni Pisano) and paintings by Cimabue and Ghirlandaio. Giovanni's father, Nicola, sculpted a similarly fine pulpit in the **Baptistery▶▶▶** nearby. In the cemetery, or **Camposanto▶▶**, look for the Cappella Ammannati's frescos illustrating *The Triumph of Death* (many other paintings were lost as a result of bombing during World War II). The **Museo dell' Opera del Duomo▶▶** is something of a mixed bag of sculpture and paintings. The **Museo delle Sinopie▶** contains sketches for the Camposanto's vanished frescos. It is worth remembering that you can buy a single ticket to see all Piazza del Duomo's main sights.

▶▶ Pistoia
148D3

Pistoia's quiet provincial demeanor conceals a superb medieval interior. Its heart is the **Piazza del Duomo▶▶**, site of several stern *palazzi*, the Gothic Baptistery and the 12th-century Duomo. The cathedral boasts possibly the greatest piece of silverware in Italy, the Dossale di San Jacopo. Started in 1287 and not completed until the late 15th century, this amazing altarpiece weighs over a ton and features 628 sculpted figures. Of the town's many churches, two deserve special attention: **San Giovanni Fuorcivitas▶▶** and **Sant' Andrea▶▶**, the latter home to a pulpit by Giovanni Pisano, a masterpiece of Italian Gothic sculpture.

▶▶ San Galgano, Abbazia di
148B3

San Galgano may not be Tuscany's best preserved building—the roof has collapsed and the nave is a grassy square—but it is by far its most romantic and atmospheric. Founded in 1218 by the Cistercians, it was for a period Tuscany's leading monastic center. Be sure to walk to the nearby **Chiesetta di San Galgano▶▶**. The effort is rewarded by fine views and fragments of 14th-century fresco.

▶▶▶ San Gimignano
148C3

Few places look as thoroughly medieval as San Gimignano. Its famous crop of towers—a "Renaissance Manhattan"—together with its art-filled churches make it one of the most popular excursions from Florence or Siena. Endure the crowds to climb the Torre Grossa in Piazza del Popolo, one of the town's 14 surviving towers (out of an original 72). Also fight your way into the **Collegiata▶▶▶**, beautifully and comprehensively frescoed by three separate artists, including Taddeo di Bartolo, whose *Last Judgment* must be one of Tuscany's most wonderfully gruesome paintings. Climb to the Rocca (castle) for its views, and to the church of **Sant'Agostino▶▶** for Benozzo Gozzoli's fresco cycle on the life of St. Augustine.

Pistols
Pistoia was one of Italy's most violent medieval towns—Michelangelo called its inhabitants "enemies of heaven"—which makes it only fitting that it should be responsible for the word "pistol." A *pistole* was originally a dagger, but the name came to be used for the small firearms made in the town during the 16th century.

Vernaccia di San Gimignano
Once one of Tuscany's greatest white wines, Vernaccia vintages are these days pale imitations of their former selves. Pale and flowery wines have largely replaced the aged, golden wine of times past. Good wines are still produced, however, notably by Falchini and Teruzzi & Puthod.

159

Many-towered San Gimignano

▶▶▶ **Siena**   *148C3*

Florence's long-term historical rival is still its main rival for the attentions of visitors. Siena is the medieval city *par excellence*, more intimate and, for many who get to know it, ultimately more appealing than the Tuscan capital, notwithstanding all the latter's artistic bounty.

The Campo, Siena's magnificent heart

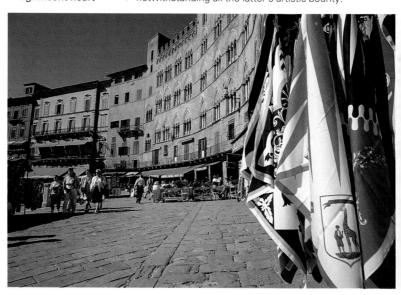

The Campo Siena's heart is the sloping semicircular Campo, Italy's greatest square and scene of the famous Palio (see page 162). At its lowest edge stands the Palazzo Pubblico►►►, long Siena's town hall, but also home to the Museo Civico. Numerous paintings line its walls, none more famous than two frescos attributed to Simone Martini in the Sala del Mappamondo: a *Maestà* (1315) and the *Portrait of Guidoriccio da Fogliano*, a lovely courtly image of a *condottiere* on horseback.

Almost equally as notable are the frescos in the next room, the Sala dei Nove: Ambrogio Lorenzetti's *Allegories of Good and Bad Government*, panels which most entertainingly illustrate the consequences of good and bad government. If you can face the 503 steps, climb the adjacent **Torre del Mangia**►► next door for all-embracing views of the town. Before leaving the square, pay through the nose at least once for a drink at one of its many cafés—worth it just to enjoy the piazza and all its myriad comings and goings.

Monteriggioni
This must-see village, 7 miles north of Siena on the SS2, rivals San Gimignano as the most evocative and complete medieval ensemble in Tuscany. Its fame rests on its perfectly preserved 13th-century walls, a formidable set of fortifications that look out from their unspoiled hilltop site over the surrounding countryside.

Siena's cathedral.
Below: dome and campanile; bottom: interior

161

The Cathedral A short walk away the decorated façade of the **Duomo**►►► makes an exuberant introduction to a still more impressive interior. Of particular note are the inlaid marble pavement, Nicola Pisano's great pulpit, Donatello's bronze pavement (north transept), and the Piccolomini altar, partly sculpted by Michelangelo. Above all, though, see the Libreria Piccolomini (off the left aisle), with Pinturicchio's recently restored frescos on the life of Pope Pius II (Aeneas Piccolomini).

The baptistery, below the east end of the cathedral, contains one of Siena's leading Renaissance treasures, a baptismal font decorated with bronze panels illustrating *Scenes from the Life of John the Baptist* by Donatello, Lorenzo Ghiberti, Jacopo della Quercia and other artists.

More paintings Behind the Duomo, the **Museo dell'Opera del Duomo (Cathedral Museum)**►► contains the greatest of all Sienese paintings, a *Maestà* by Duccio (1311). For a full résumé of the city's art, however, visit the **Pinacoteca Nazionale**►►►, crammed with room after room of gorgeous paintings by—among others—Duccio, Simone Martini, Pietro and Ambrogio Lorenzetti, Sassetta, and Bartolo di Fredi.

The Palio

Siena's Palio is no mere tourist attraction. This horse race, run twice yearly in the Campo, is not only Italy's most spectacular festival, it is also a symbol of the intense rivalries that still rage between the town's medieval *contrade*, or districts.

Origins The Palio has taken place almost every year since medieval times (though the custom may well go back further). It takes its name from the *pallium*, a banner embroidered with an image of the Virgin and presented to the race's winner. Originally run through the town's streets, the pageant moved to the Campo during the 16th century.

The *contrade* Siena has 17 *contrade* (districts), each with its own flag and heraldic motif (usually an animal), as well as its own church, museum and social center. (At one time there were reputedly 59 *contrade*.) Allegiance to the *contrada* of your birth is still absolute—after a conventional baptism, children are baptized again in their *contrada* fountain. Each *contrada* holds an annual parade, and the *alfieri*, the famous flag-throwers, can often be seen practicing in the streets.

Only ten *contrade* may take part in the race, so lots are drawn to make the selections. Horses are also drawn by lot, though *contrade* select their own jockeys, many of whom are drawn from the *butteri*, the traditional cowboys of Tuscany's Maremma region. Other representatives of the *contrade* well in evidence are the flag-bearers, drummer, captain, grooms, and pages.

The race The races are run on July 2 and August 16, but the days beforehand are filled with numerous processions and pageantry. Trial races are run, parties held, and—most importantly—the horses are blessed in church (dung produced in the church is taken as a good omen). Meanwhile, jockeys can be bribed or ambushed before the race, and alliances are forged and broken between different *contrade*. Huge bets ride on the result. In the race itself, which lasts just 90 seconds, anything goes except interfering with a rider's reins. Despite the obvious dangers, no one—supposedly—has ever been killed, thanks, say the Sienese, to the protection of the Virgin Mary (in whose honor the race is run). Even if you are not in Siena on race day—when the town is hugely crowded—national television broadcasts the race live.

Anything goes in the world's most colorful horse race

▶▶▶ Sovana   149B4

Tiny Sovana is as historically interesting a village as you will find in Italy. For centuries it was controlled by the Aldobrandeschi, a noble clan who held sway over much of the region. The election of a family member, Hildebrand, as Pope Gregory VII in 1073, brought it great wealth (reflected in buildings now out of all proportion to the village's size).

There is just one street, and one tiny square, Piazza del Popolo. On its left side stands **Santa Maria▶▶▶**, a glorious Romanesque church, remarkable for its frescos and 9th-century ciborium (altar canopy). Along a country lane lies the **Duomo▶▶▶**, whose 8th- to 12th-century interior contains fascinating early carvings and a wonderfully intimate crypt. The countryside around the village is scattered with hundreds of **Etruscan tombs▶▶**, notably the Tomba della Sileno, Tomba del Sireno and **Tomba Idebranda▶▶**, considered Tuscany's finest single tomb.

▶ Viareggio   148D2

Viareggio—Tuscany's "Biarritz"—is almost Florence-on-the-Sea, with kids and Italian families flocking here in summer from the region's landlocked capital. In the 19th and early 20th centuries it was a fashionable resort, vestiges of its heyday still visible in the town's famous Liberty and art-deco buildings. It is still a relatively sedate spot, with the Versilia coast's best facilities and beaches.

▶▶ Volterra   148C3

Dark and Etruscan Volterra broods over a strange, empty countryside from its magnificent hilltop position. **Piazza dei Priori▶▶**, its central square—of stage set medieval perfection—is dominated by the Pisan-style Duomo and baptistery, the former noted for its pulpit and Benozzo Gozzoli's fresco *The Magi*. For more paintings, visit the **Pinacoteca Comunale▶**, the star of which is Rosso Fiorentino's extraordinary *The Descent from the Cross*, a particularly good example of the Mannerist genre. Etruscan fans should also visit the **Museo Etrusco Guarnacci▶▶**, one of Italy's major archeological museums. Also wander the town's outskirts to see its many Roman remains, the *balze*—deeply eroded cliffs and gullies—and the shady gardens of the pleasant **Parco Archeologico▶**.

Some of Volterra's extensive Roman remains

UMBRIA AND LE MARCHE

Umbria Umbria has emerged from Tuscany's shadow, no longer its poorer sister, but a beautiful and varied region in its own right. Its narrow borders harbor a dozen or more hilltowns, each crammed with artistic and architectural treasures. Its pastoral countryside has earned the title *il cuore verde d'Italia* (The Green Heart of Italy). It is also Italy's mystical heart, the birthplace of St. Benedict and St. Francis.

The hilltowns Umbria's hilltowns are the highlight of any visit to central Italy. Pink-stoned Assisi, birthplace of St. Francis, contains a superlative fresco cycle by Giotto. Perugia, its more stern neighbor, has a warren of dark medieval streets and countless churches and galleries. Orvieto possesses Italy's finest Gothic cathedral. Spoleto and Gubbio (the "Umbrian Siena") are both delightful medieval towns. Lesser and less-visited places also have their charms, notably Todi, the epitome of a hilltown; Spello, steep and sleepy; and Montefalco, a lofty belvedere with a fine little art gallery.

The countryside Part of Umbria's charm is its soft, gentle countryside. Some is spotted with light industry, but off the main roads the region is a picture of pastoral perfection—all olive groves, oakwoods, vineyards and silver-hazed hills rolling into the distance. Lago Trasimeno provides a watery contrast close to Perugia, while in the east a wild counterpoint is provided by the Valnerina and Monti Sibillini. The unspoiled scenery around Norcia—the equal of any in Italy—contains the Piano Grande, one of the country's most poetic landscapes.

Le Marche (The Marches) Some people predict that the Marches will follow the tourist-filled track of Tuscany and Umbria. Virtually unknown, it has all the ingredients for a popular tourist destination—scenery, beaches, and historic towns. Its landscapes vary from the mountains of the Apennines to the jumbled hills and valleys near the coast.

Vineyards carpet the slopes up to Assisi

UMBRIA AND LE MARCHE

Violin workshop in Ascoli Piceno

Scenic drives
(*Umbria*): SS209 Terni–San Pietro in Valle–Triponzo–Visso; Visso–Castelluccio–Piano Grande–Norcia; Spello–Monte Subasio–Assisi; SS79 bis Orvieto–Todi; (*Marche*): San Leo–Carpegna–Pennabilli–SS258–Sansepolcro; SS78 Ascoli Piceno–Amandola–Sarnano.

Urbino is unmissable, thanks to its great Ducal Palace, while San Leo and Ascoli Piceno are lesser spots of which any region would be proud. On the coast there are outstanding resorts, notably around Monte Conero and Ancona.

Gastronomy Umbria's gastronomic credentials are almost unknown to foreigners. It is one of only two areas in the country where truffles are found in abundance (the other is around Alba in Piedmont). These strange delicacies have been prized since Roman times for their aromatic, not to mention aphrodisiac qualities. They grace the dishes of many restaurants, especially around Norcia and Spoleto. In Norcia, too, you can eat wild boar, together with Italy's most celebrated salamis, and the miniature lentils of Castelluccio.

The Marches' best-known specialty is Ascoli Piceno's delicious *olive all'ascolana*—hollowed-out green olives stuffed with minced meat and fried in olive oil. Its other great delicacy is *vincisgrassi*, a rich lasagne filled with *prosciutto*, cream and black truffles. Up and down the coast, there are also at least seven different versions of *brodetto* (fish stew). Each town claims the perfect recipe. Ancona's is most famous, perhaps because it contains 13 types of fish. South of Monte Conero the broth is thickened with flour, saffron is used, and slices of bread are toasted. To the north, flour is omitted, vinegar is added, and the bread is eaten untoasted and rubbed with garlic.

Wine Tuscany for a long time outranked Umbria in wine as in much else, but Umbria is now at least the equal, and often the superior of its neighbor. The wines of Torgiano's Lungarotti, the Rubesco Riserva in particular, are among the most distinguished in Italy. Other Umbrian wines are like the region itself—subtle and understated—none more so than the vintages of Montefalco. Try the rare Sagrantino, Rosso di Montefalco and Grechetto (the classic Umbrian white), preferably from producers like Adanti, Caprai, and Benincasa. Also look out for Antinori's Cervaro della Sala (which has the potential to become one of Italy's great whites). More humble but still acceptable drinks include Orvieto (white) or Colli Altotiberini (red).

►   **Ancona**   *164C3*
Ancona is a busy and unattractive port, worth a call only to see the Romanesque church of **San Ciriaco►►** and the newly-refurbished **Museo Nazionale delle Marche►►**, a wide-reaching archeological collection of paleolithic and Roman remains.

The town takes its name from the Greek *ankon* (elbow), probably after **Monte Conero►►** to the south (6½ miles). This wild promontory is the only land formation to disturb the ruler-straight coastline that runs for hundreds of miles from the Venetian lagoons to the Gargano peninsula. You can explore its rugged interior by walking from several centers, or by driving one of two scenic roads to the churches of Santa Maria di Portonovo and Badia di San Pietro. To see its spectacular cliffs and seascapes take boat trips from Portonovo, Sirolo or Numana, three popular and picturesque resorts on the so-called **Riviera del Conero►**.

► ► **Ascoli Piceno** 164B3

After Urbino, Ascoli Piceno is the Marches' most enticing historic town. Much of its center still conforms to the layout of the old Roman colony, built after the defeat of the *Picini*, an early Marchese tribe. At its heart lies **Piazza del Popolo► ►**, whose ensemble of medieval buildings creates one of Italy's loveliest squares. Admire it over coffee from the art-deco surroundings of the Bar Meletti, then take a closer look at the Palazzo del Popolo and the church of **San Francesco► ►**. To the south stands the **Duomo►** whose prize exhibit is a ten-paneled altarpiece by Carlo Crivelli, a Venetian artist who is also represented in the **Pinacoteca Civica► ►** nearby.

The most picturesque part of town (with many medieval watchtowers), lies at the top of Via del Trivio above the River Tronto (walk down Via della Luna for the best views). The area harbors the Gothic church of San Pietro Martire and the more appealing SS Vicenzo ed Anastasio, an 11th-century church built over a primitive 6th-century crypt.

Tourist information
Ascoli Piceno: Piazza del Popolo (tel: 0736/252 391).
Assisi: Piazza del Comune 12 (tel: 075/812 450).
Gubbio: Piazza Odersi 3–5 (tel: 075/922 0790).
Perugia: Palazzo dei Priori 3 (tel: 075/23 327).
Orvieto: Piazza del Duomo 24 (tel: 0763/41 772 or 0763/42 562).
Spoleto: Piazza Libertà 7 (0743/220 311).
Urbino: Piazza del Rinascimento 1 (tel: 0722/2613 or 0722 2441).

Ascoli Piceno's beautiful Piazza del Popolo

167

San Damiano
This church lies in a secluded spot amid olive groves, preserving the humility and mystical atmosphere usually associated with St. Francis but absent in much of the town. It was here that the saint received his calling from God, and where he composed his famous *Canticle to the Sun*. St. Clare also lived here and the smoke-blackened church, cloister and refectory are little changed from her day. (The church is a pleasant 15-minute walk from Assisi.)

168

St. Francis's Tomb
St. Francis was buried in great secrecy to prevent his remains being stolen or desecrated (medieval relics had enormous spiritual and financial value). His tomb was so well hidden that it was only discovered in 1818 after almost two months of excavations.

▶▶▶ **Assisi** 164B2

St. Francis's burial place, the **Basilica di San Francesco▶▶▶**, is the premier sight of this lovely medieval town. Its Lower Church is somber and atmospheric, the walls covered in frescos and decorative motifs: see Simone Martini's frescos of the life of St. Martin (first chapel on the left); the ceiling vaults above the high altar (by Giotto and assistants); and Pietro Lorenzetti's powerful *Deposition* and *Crucifixion* (in the left transept). Steps in the nave lead to Francis's tomb (see panel).

The Upper Church's soaring Gothic lines provide a startling contrast, its walls covered by one of Italy's most famous fresco cycles, Giotto's *Life of St. Francis* in 28 huge panels. Do not overlook the faded frescos above, by a trio of Roman artists, nor the delicate wooden choir. To the rear, the **Museo-Tesoro della Basilica▶▶** is rich in paintings and precious objects.

Basilica of St. Francis in Assisi

Other sights Elsewhere, see **San Pietro▶**, an expertly restored 11th-century Romanesque church; **Oratorio dei Pellegrini▶**, a lavishly frescoed 15th-century pilgrims' hospice; **Piazza del Comune▶▶**, the town's central square, on the site of an old Roman forum, with the 1st-century Tempio di Minerva; the Basilica di Santa Chiara, St. Clare's burial place; and the **Duomo▶**, dull inside, but fronted by a glorious Romanesque façade. From the Duomo walk up to the restored Rocca Maggiore (castle) for remarkable views.

Saints

Umbria is Italy's mystical heart, the *terra dei santi*—land of saints. The region was the birthplace not only of Francis and Benedict, founding fathers of Western monasticism, but also of a multitude of lesser saints including St. Clare, St. Rita and St. Valentine.

Light and landscape Few would deny the strange mystical light that illuminates Umbria's gray-hazed hills. Nor would many dispute the soft-edged beauty of the region's countryside—a landscape that epitomizes pastoralism and seems made for peaceful introspection. Could it be that these abstract qualities have helped nurture the region's wealth of saints and mystics?

History Umbria's history and position also have a bearing on its preponderance of saints. One of the Romans' most important consular roads, the *Via Flaminia*, cut through the region, not only linking Rome with the Adriatic, but also providing a conduit for eastern monks and other early Christians fleeing persecution. Umbria's green hills were the first place they came to, many settling in the region's woods and caves, perfect sanctuaries in which to pursue lives of monastic contemplation.

Montefalco
Nowhere shows Umbria's preponderance of saints better than Montefalco, a little village that produced eight saints. You can see the 3rd-century bones of San Fortunato (abbey of that name) and the mummified bodies of Illuminata and Chiarella (church of Sant'Agostino) and St. Clare (convent of Santa Chiara).

St. Benedict Tiny Romanesque churches all over Umbria mark the graves of the region's holy men and women. Each town had its bishop—who was invariably sanctified—each village its saint (or saints). The caves of three such early hermits can still be seen at Sant'Eutizio, a Benedictine abbey north of Norcia. It was through contact with these men—St. Spes, St. Fiorenzo and St. Eutizio—that Norcia's St. Benedict (480–547) found his vocation. This apparently minor event was of incalculable importance, for it led ultimately to the creation of the Benedictine Order. (Benedict, incidentally, is the patron saint of Europe.)

St. Francis More than 600 years were to elapse before the birth of Umbria's other great saint, St. Francis (1182–1226). A humble but revolutionary spirit, he took Christianity back to its basic principles—"poverty, chastity and obedience." Among his many followers was St. Clare, who formed the Poor Clares, the Franciscans' female wing. Like many orders springing from Umbria's soil, it spread throughout Europe and survives to this day. (Francis is the patron saint of Italy.)

St. Francis of Assisi with one of his animal friends

Porte della Morte
Gubbio's famous "doors of death" are narrow, bricked-up doors wedged into many of the town's medieval façades. They were supposedly used to carry a coffin out of the house. Having been tainted by death, it is said, they were then permanently sealed. In fact, their purpose was probably defensive, the narrow entrance behind the door being easier to defend than the main doors. The best examples are in Via dei Consoli.

Monte Ingino
A visit to this hill above Gubbio is a must: walk up the path behind the Duomo or take the cable car from Porta Romana. There are great views from a little bar and you can see the *ceri*, large wooden "candles" used in the Corsa dei Ceri, an exuberant 900-year-old pageant held annually on May 15.

Wine
Orvieto's fertile volcanic soils partly account for the high reputation of its wine, once so prized that architects working on the Duomo were happy to be paid in it. These days newer and drier Orvietos rank less highly, though the old-style *Orvieto abboccato* is making a comeback through such wines as Decugnano dei Barbi's Pourriture Noble and Bigi's Vigneto Orzalume. Other good producers are Antinori, Dubini and Barberani.

► **Bevagna**   *164B2*

Plain-bound Bevagna, ancient *Mevania*, was founded by the Romans as a way station on the *Via Flaminia*. These days it sits within its medieval walls, a serene backwater whose central **Piazza Silvestri►►** is one of Italy's most perfect medieval squares. On it stand two exquisite Romanesque churches, San Michele and San Silvestro. To one side a monumental staircase leads up to the 13th-century Palazzo dei Consoli, its interior a lovely galleried theater converted in 1886.

Near Bevagna are Foligno, with a tight medieval core that survived World War II bombs, and the 11th-century Abbazia di Sassovivo with Umbria's finest cloister.

Taking it easy in Gubbio

►►► **Gubbio**   *164C2*

Umbria has few sights more enchanting than Gubbio's old streets, orange-tiled houses and mountain-backed setting. Start a tour just below the old town in Piazza di Quaranta Martiri, where the church of **San Francesco►►** has an engaging fresco cycle (1510) by Ottaviano Nelli, one of Umbria's earliest important painters. Opposite stands the **Loggia dei Tiratori►**, Italy's best-surviving example of a now rare type of building: wool was stretched out under its arches to dry evenly away from the heat of the sun.

Up in town, interest centers on the vast **Palazzo dei Consoli►►►**, a looming 14th-century palace (and bell-tower) that houses a small art gallery and museum. The latter is noted for the Eugubine Tablets, seven 2nd- to 1st-century BC bronzes inscribed in Latin and Etruscan. Nearby, the **Duomo►** and **Palazzo Ducale►** are worth a glance, so too the churches of Sant'Agostino and Santa Maria Nuova, both with more paintings by Ottaviano Nelli.

►► **Montefalco**   *164B2*

Known as the *Ringhiera dell'Umbria* (Balcony of Umbria) for its expansive views, Montefalco (the Falcon's Mount) is a delightful, somnolent village with a maze of medieval streets and alleys. The new art gallery in the church of **San Francesco►►►** is exceptional, built around Benozzo Gozzoli's superlative fresco cycle, *The Life of St. Francis*. Two other churches deserve a look for their paintings—**Sant'Agostino►** and **Sant'Illuminata►**.

▶▶ Norcia 164B2

Norcia's stolid mountain- and market-town atmosphere comes as a surprise after the more bucolic charms of Umbria's western hilltowns. Although short of sights, it is an agreeable place and, for gourmets, one of the culinary capitals of Italy. Famous for its cheeses and truffles, it also has the reputation for producing the country's best sausages and salami (so widespread is its fame that a butcher's shop elsewhere in Italy is often called *Un Norcino*). Shops around the main square, Piazza San Benedetto, sell all manner of delicacies, from "mules' testicles" to the ubiquitous boars' heads.

The square also contains the town's most notable buildings, namely the Castellina , a redoubtable papal fortress (1563), and the church of **San Benedetto▶**, reputedly built over the birthplace of St. Benedict. Just off the square is a temple to Umbrian and Norcian cuisine, the wonderful old medieval hotel and restaurant, the **Grotta Azzurra**.

Words of praise
Pope Leo XIII described Orvieto's Duomo as the "Golden Lily of Italian cathedrals"; the historian Jacob Burckhardt considered it the "greatest polychrome monument in the world."

▶▶ Orvieto 164A1

Orvieto's celebrated crag, or *rupa*—the rim of an ancient volcano—attracted the Etruscans (who called it Volsinii), and later the Romans. These days it is perhaps Italy's finest Gothic **Duomo▶▶▶** that lures the invading hordes. Its awe-inspiring façade alone took over 300 years to complete, and employed 33 architects, 152 sculptors, 68 painters and 90 mosaicists. Started in the 13th century, it was built to celebrate the Miracle of Bolsena (in which the host being used in a Mass at nearby Bolsena dripped blood onto the altarcloth). Inside is Luca Signorelli's *Last Judgment* (1504), one of the great Italian fresco cycles, and a wealth of lesser paintings by local 14th-century artists.

The rest of the town is less impressive, but allow an hour or more to see the frescoed church of **San Giovenale▶▶**; the church of **San Andrea▶**; the Museo del Duomo's eclectic collection; the Museo Faina's Etruscan artifacts; the Etruscan tombs; and the **Pozzo di San Patrizio▶▶** (St. Patrick's Well) an impressively engineered 16th-century well cut into the rock on which Orvieto stands.

Orvieto's great Gothic cathedral glimpsed down a side street

Drive The heart of Umbria

A short drive which links six hilltowns and climbs over Monte Subasio—wild uplands with immense views—before dropping to Assisi.

The direct drive north from **Spoleto** (page 176) to Trevi on the SS3 is not pretty. For a better taste of Umbria's pastoral countryside follow the minor mountain roads to Montefalco via either Castel Ritaldi or Giano dell'Umbria (the more scenic route if you have time).

Otherwise, start in **Trevi**, (page 177) which with Todi is perhaps Umbria's most spectacularly sited hilltown. Then cross the plain to **Montefalco** (page 170) allowing a good hour for its churches, views, and art gallery. As a possible detour, take in **Gualdo Cattaneo▶** another perfect little hill village. Drop down to sleepy **Bevagna** (page 170) for its square and Romanesque churches, and then circumvent Foligno on your way to **Spello** (page 175). Allow an hour or

so to see Pinturicchio's frescos and the town's medieval streets, churches and Roman remains.

North of Spello follow signs to **Collepino▶**, an isolated hamlet, and take the well-made gravel road over Monte Subasio. In spring the mountain is smothered in orchids, narcissi, and other wildflowers. Views from the top—the road reaches 3,960 feet—are exceptional. As the road drops to **Assisi** (page 168), visit the Eremo delle Carceri, a beautifully situated Franciscan monastery. If you do not want to take the gravel road, use the main SS3 to Assisi, or the minor road from Collepino to Assisi via **Armenzano▶**.

Trevi, proud on its hilltop above the Vale of Spoleto

►► Perugia

164B1

Perugia's industrial outskirts are unappealing, but once you are in the old center, Umbria's capital is as attractive as any of the region's hilltowns. Much of Perugia is closed to traffic, so leave your car in one of the big peripheral parking lots and ride the escalators (*scala mobile*) to the center. Alternatively, park at the railroad station and take a bus to Piazza Italia on Corso Vannucci. Corso Vannucci contains most of the sights, a bustling street, crowned by Piazza IV Novembre, the **Duomo►** and **Fontana Maggiore►►►**. The fountain, one of Italy's loveliest, was sculpted by Nicola and Giovanni Pisano. Palazzo dei Priori, a gaunt, grandiose medieval pile, is home to the **Galleria Nazionale dell'Umbria►►►**, 33 rooms documenting the development of Umbrian art. The paintings include canvases by Perugino and Pinturicchio, as well as works by non-Umbrians like Fra Angelico and Piero della Francesca. More fine frescos by Perugino reside in the **Collegio del Cambio►►►**. Close by lies the **Sala del Collegio della Mercanzia►**, a 15th-century chamber lined with superlative wooden paneling.

Walk down **Via dei Priori►** to see the **Oratorio di San Bernardino►**, adorned with bas-reliefs by Agostino di Duccio. Then visit the Arco di Augusto, an Etrusco-Roman arch, and the outlying churches of Sant'Agostino and **Sant'Angelo►**. Across the town, **San Domenico►** boasts an exceptional Gothic tomb, while its cloisters house the **Museo Archeologico Nazionale dell'Umbria►**. Beyond it lies Perugia's grandest church, the sumptuously decorated **San Pietro►►**.

► Pesaro

164D2

Pesaro's 2½ miles of beaches make it a popular package-tour destination, but the influx of visitors does little to tarnish the town's stylish appearance. Behind the elegant white-stucco hotels of the waterfront stands a pleasant old center, its most enticing street the porticoed Corso XI Settembre. Of the sights, the **Museo Civico►►** stands out, mainly for Giovanni Bellini's glittering polyptych, *The Coronation of the Virgin*. It also has a fine ceramics section—the fame of Pesaro's majolica once rivaled that of Faenza (see page 84).

Perugia, capital of Umbria, retains its medieval heart

Pasticceria Sandri
Perugia's most atmospheric bar is at Corso Vannucci 32, a turn-of-the-century Viennese-style café with lots of brass, wood paneling and frescoed ceilings. Try some of the town's nationally renowned Perugini chocolates. The best place to sample Umbria's wines is the *Enoteca Provinciale*, Via Ulisse Rocchi 16.

Rossini
Opera composer Gioacchino Rossini was born in Pesaro in 1792. His home at Via Rossini 34 has a small museum and his works are performed during the town's summer festival.

Weight for weight, truffles are the world's most expensive foodstuff. They have been prized for their earthy and aromatic flavor since Roman times (when they were believed to have been formed by lightning striking the earth). They are subterranean fungi of the class *Ascomycetes*, part of the *Tuber* genus.

Sagre
You may come across a truffle *sagra* in an Umbrian town or village. This is a festival held to celebrate the truffle harvest (similar festivals take place in honor of many products of the Italian countryside, such as wine, fruit, vegetables—even sausages).

174

What, where and why Truffles are unable to carry out photosynthesis, and therefore live symbiotically with certain forest plants (using their chlorophyll). Anything from the size of peas to footballs, they thrive best in calcareous soils, and amid oak and hazel woods. Numerous other factors influence distribution, however, notably climate and drainage—one of the reasons why commercial production has proved elusively difficult.

Finding truffles Dogs, rather than sows, are now used to hunt truffles (sows are attracted by the truffles' perfume, which closely resembles the musky pheromones of the male pig—unfortunately the sows often become uncontrollably excited when close to the truffle). In order to keep the valuable find secret, a truffle hunter will generally dig only at night. Equipped with torch and trowel, he searches in the spot where his dog sniffed out the truffles earlier in the day.

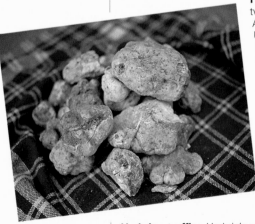

Types and uses Italy has two key truffle areas—near Alba, in Piedmont, and in Umbria around Norcia and Spoleto. Each has its distinct specialties, for there are at least nine types of edible truffle—though only six are well known. Restaurants usually serve them grated over pasta or omelettes (*frittate*). Shops sell truffle paste, or truffles preserved under oil (at a price). The real thing is rare, so beware of substitutes.

Umbrian truffles Umbria's most common truffle is the black winter truffle (*tartufo nero*), gathered from a few inches underground between mid-November and mid-March. The white truffle (the Alba, or Acqualagna truffle), is found as much as 20 inches underground (from October 1 to December 31). The rarer *scorzone*, or summer truffle, occurs near the surface (May 1 to November 30), rather like the prized *bianchetto* or *marzulo* truffle (November 15 to March 15). Musk and *uncinato* are the other two varieties.

▶▶ Piano Grande   164B2

In the Monti Sibillini east of Norcia lies one of the strangest and most magical landscapes in Europe. The Piano Grande is a vast upland plain, 3,960 feet high and covering 16 square miles, surrounded by barren whale-backed mountains. In spring the plain is smothered in poppies, buttercups and narcissi, as well as rarities like tulips, orchids and fritillaries. Walking opportunities are excellent, and the surrounding slopes form an ideal playground for hang gliders.

Hang gliders line up for takeoff on the Piano Grande

▶▶ San Leo   164D1

Although less famous than nearby San Marino, San Leo is by far the more attractive destination. Machiavelli thought its castle▶▶—hung on a vast cliff—Italy's greatest military fortress, and Dante used it as a model for the landscapes of *Purgatorio*. The little village below has a lovely cobbled square, on which lies a rude 9th-century Pieve▶▶, or parish church, and a Romanesque Duomo▶.

▶ San Marino   164D1

The little independent republic of San Marino trades ruthlessly on its rather bogus autonomy. According to tradition it was created around AD 300 by a stonemason fleeing religious persecution (with him was Leo, founder of nearby San Leo). This makes it the longest surviving republic in Europe—its status was acknowledged even by Napoleon. It still has its own mint, postage stamps and international football team. From afar, its tremendous hilltop setting is inviting; close to, the streets are crammed with tourists and souvenir shops. Only the views merit the trip up here.

▶▶ Spello   164B2

Spilling down the lower slopes of Monte Subasio, Spello's pink-stoned medieval houses present an alluring picture from the Vale of Spoleto. Built as a colony on the *Via Flaminia*, the old Roman road between Rome and the Adriatic, it still preserves a modest crop of Roman monuments. The best are two gateways, the Porta Venere and the Porta Consolare, the town's old entrance (across from the Porta Consolare be sure to try the award-winning ice cream of the **Bar Ennio**). Midway up the street the church of **Santa Maria Maggiore**▶▶ harbors a fresco cycle by Pinturicchio that ranks with his masterpieces in Rome and Siena's Libreria Piccolomini. Higher still, two little churches are worth a peek—Gothic **San Andrea**▶, dark and atmospheric, and baroque San Lorenzo.

Excursion from Spello
Follow signs from Spello's northern gateway to La Baita or Collepino for access to Monte Subasio. The views are magnificent, and there is plenty of opportunity for walking over the mountain's open grassy ridges.

Enchanting Spello

Festival dei Due Mondi
Spoleto's "Festival óf the Two Worlds" is Italy's most prestigious international arts festival. It came to the town in 1958 as an Italo-American co-venture, a sister festival being held in Charleston, West Virginia. Tickets and information for its wide-ranging performances are available from the tourist office and the festival box office, Piazza del Duomo 9. Be warned, though, that the town is crowded during the festival (late June–July): hotel rooms are at a premium.

Below: frescos in Todi's cathedral
Bottom: Todi has a dramatic situation

▶▶▶ Spoleto 164B2

Spoleto becomes many visitor's favorite Umbrian town. During the 7th century it was the capital of the Duchy of Spoleto, one of the Lombards' three Italian dukedoms. Before that it was a preeminent Roman colony and one of the ancient Umbrians' main citadels (traces of their 6th-century BC walls are still visible).

The largely modern lower town contains a trio of worthwhile churches: **San Gregorio▶**; San Ponziano (notable for its crypt and Romanesque façade); and 4th-century **San Salvatore▶▶▶**, one of Italy's oldest churches. In the upper town, picturesque **Piazza del Mercato▶** is the spot for a *cappuccino* before taking in its nearby sights—the crypt of **San Ansano▶** with 6th-century frescos; the Arco di Druso, a Roman triumphal arch; and **Sant'Eufemia▶▶**, the town's most celebrated Romanesque church. These only whet the appetite, however, for the **Duomo▶▶▶**, central Italy's loveliest, and the **Ponte delle Torri▶▶▶**, a monumental 14th-century bridge and aqueduct. The Duomo's highlight is Filippo Lippi's apse frescos. If you cross the *Ponte,* you can walk above Spoleto's breathtaking wooded gorge, or stroll to **San Pietro▶▶**, whose façade's Lombard-Romanesque sculptures are considered some of Italy's finest.

▶▶ Todi 164B1

Todi is the rising star of Umbrian hilltowns, a small market center at heart, but increasingly well known to Italians and foreigners alike. Its position is phenomenal, perched proudly above the Tiber on a great pyramid of a hill. Three sets of concentric walls—Etruscan, Roman and medieval—center on **Piazza del Popolo▶▶**, a matchless ensemble of medieval palaces crowned by the plain-faced elegance of the Romanesque **Duomo▶▶**. **San Fortunato▶▶** is the town's premier church, its airy interior hidden behind an unprepossessing façade. A stroll through the tranquil public gardens takes you alongside **Santa Maria della Consolazione▶▶▶**, considered by many to be Italy's most perfect Renaissance church.

▶ **Trasimeno, Lago (Lake Trasimeno)**   *164B1*

Trasimeno, the largest lake on the Italian peninsula, is only moderately pretty, but is nonetheless popular with campers, beach addicts and watersports lovers Passignano▶ is the busiest resort. The nicest all-round spot, however, is Castiglione del Lago▶▶. Here you can swim off sandy beaches, or take boat trips to Isola Maggiore▶, the prettiest of the lake's three islands. North of the lake, roads around the mountains offer quiet drives and marvelous views: Castel Rigone▶ is the best little village to make for.

▶ **Trevi**   *164B2*

Trevi's glory is its position, perhaps the most impressive of any Umbrian hilltown. The tidy medieval center is a delightful area to wander through, its little alleys known for their intricately patterned cobblestones. The Duomo▶ retains a Romanesque shell (the interior is baroque). The small Pinacoteca▶ has good Umbrian paintings, but the town's best art is Perugino's pictures in San Martino▶ and Madonna delle Lacrime▶.

▶▶▶ **Urbino**   *164C2*

Urbane and majestic, Urbino is one of the least known of Italy's great Renaissance cities. Raphael and Bramante were both born here, and in the 15th century the court of Duke Federico da Montefeltro became one of the most civilized and sophisticated in Europe. Federico's extensive and elegant Palazzo Ducale▶▶▶ is home to the Galleria Nazionale delle Marche▶▶▶ with two mysterious masterpieces of Piero della Francesca: *The Flagellation* and the *Madonna di Senigallia*. Almost as alluring are Raphael's *La Muta*, Uccello's *Miracle of the Host*, and Titian's *Resurrection* and *Last Supper*. Among the rooms, Federico's personal study stands out—the tiny Studiolo, renowned for its *intarsia* (inlaid wood).

Lake Trasimeno

Olive oil
Although less well known than the oils of Tuscany, Umbria's olive oil is prized by Italians, particularly that of Trevi and the Vale of Spoleto. You need not buy fancy bottles: the widely available *Monini* oils are some of the best.

VALNERINA AND MONTI SIBILLINI

Drive **From Spoleto**

Historic Spoleto

A scenic drive through one of central Italy's most enchanting valleys, followed by mountain roads through the Monti Sibillini and across the wild Piano Grande.

Start in Spoleto and negotiate the twisting SS395 to Piedipaterno (fine views). Follow the Nera river on

SS209 toward its source at the quiet market town of Visso, sometimes through gorges and mountains, elsewhere through farmland and water meadows. You then climb to the village of **Castelluccio**, one of Italy's highest settlements (4,917 feet), and cross the eerie desolation of the Piano Grande before dropping along a snaking road to **Norcia** (page 171). The gentler terrain from here takes in Cascia, birthplace of St. Rita. More mountains, pastoral countryside and half-forgotten hill villages follow— Monteleone di Spoleto, Caso and Gavelli. Few tourists ever see this exceptional countryside, and the roads are likely to be deserted.

At **Sant' Anatolia di Narco**, if you have time, detour south before returning to Spoleto. Just after the hamlet of **Sambucheto** watch for the sign to San Pietro in Valle. The 8th-century monastery church is important as one of the few surviving memorials to the Lombards.

178

Walking in Umbria

Umbria is unusual for central Italy in having several marked trails and sufficiently detailed maps to make hiking a possibility. There are three main areas: the Monte Cucco park; Gualdo Tadino; and the Monti Sibillini National Park.

Parco Naturale del Monte Cucco This park protects a lovely tract of limestone mountains east of Gubbio. For information visit the Centro Nazionale di Speleologia, Corso Mazzini 9, Costacciaro (on the SS3, 30 miles north of Foligno). They issue a 1:16,000 map of the 30 marked trails in the area (Kompass sheet No. 664 is also useful). The most popular routes begin in the Val di Ranco: trail 1 climbs to the 5,168-foot summit of Monte Cucca via Pian delle Macinarie: trail 2 is the descent (round trip four hours). Another favorite is the walk along the Valle delle Prigioni from Pascelupo to Pian di Rolla (four-hour round trip).

Gualdo Tadino Gualdo Tadino is on the SS3, 20 miles north of Foligno. Several marked paths push into the hills east of the town, all marked on the Kompass 1:50,000 map *Assisi-Camerino* (No. 665). The most dramatic climbs the Valle del Fonno gorge, returning via the Passo della Sportella (16 miles: four hours). Another popular route follows the pilgrim trail up Monte Serra Santa (4,696 feet), reached on the extremely well-worn trail No. 122. From the summit you can drop into the Valle del Fonno or follow a path south along the ridges of Monte Nero and Monte Penna. A track drops to Gaifana (16 miles south of Gualdo), or you can continue on the main ridge to Nocera Umbra (via Monte Alago).

Parco Nazionale dei Monti Sibillini This national park offers some of the best walking in central Italy. You can choose between high mountain routes or easy strolls around the Piano Grande. Numerous trails are marked on the Kompass 1:50,000 map *Monti Sibillini* (No. 666). The most ambitious of these climbs Monte Vettore (8,171 feet) from the road at Forca di Presta. Several paths radiate from Castelluccio: try the pastoral stroll up the Valle di Canatra, or the exhilarating ridge walk along the western rim of the Piano Grande (via Poggio di Croce and Monte Vetica).

The Vale of Spoleto: there are several marked paths (red-and-white waymarks) around Spoleto

From Umbria into the Marches
On the eastern flanks of the Parco Nazionale dei Monti Sibillini (the Marches side) the classic walks are from the village of Foce to Lago di Pilato, a spectacular hike up a steep-sided valley, and the climb to Monte Sibilla from Montemonaco.

Assisi
A few paths have been marked from Assisi. The best day's walk follows trail No. 50 from the Porta Cappuccini and Rocca Minore, climbing over Monte Subasio via the Eremo delle Carceri, and dropping down to Spello.

LAZIO AND ABRUZZO

Lazio and Abruzzo Rome cannot help but overshadow Lazio and Abruzzo. There is so much to see in the city you might easily overlook its neighboring regions altogether. But after a few days seeing the capital's sights, it makes sense (if only for a change) to use Rome as a base for day-trips into Lazio. Further afield, greater relief from Rome's maelstrom awaits in the mountains of the Abruzzo, the unexplored haunt of wolves and Italy's last brown bears.

Lacklustre Lazio After the grandeur of Rome, Lazio can seem anticlimactic. In the north, its melancholy hills are redeemed only by Bolsena and its lake and the nature reserve around Lago di Vico, its featureless coastal plains by the Etruscan sites at Cerveteri and Tarquinia. Other historic centers are few and far between, some of the best attractions being provided instead by the villas and gardens at Caprarola and Viterbo.

To the south the countryside is more inspiring, from the tiny Circeo national park with lovely coastal landscapes to

Lake Bolsena, with its islands and Etruscan sites, is one of Lazio's most attractive areas

182

Above: take a trip to the Villa d'Este to see its dazzling water gardens

the limestone heights of the Ernici and Simbruini mountains (see Subiaco, page 193). Parts of the coast have decent resorts, principally Sperlonga, and if you are feeling more adventurous, the island of Ponza has yet to be discovered by most foreign visitors. Few of the region's towns merit a special journey—with the notable exception of those you can see from Rome.

Excursions from Rome Most of the excursions you want to make into Lazio are best made as day-trips from Rome. Of these the most enticing is Tivoli. Here you can see the Villa d'Este, with some of Italy's loveliest gardens, and the ruins of the Villa Adriana (Hadrian's Villa), the largest villa ever built in the Roman Empire. More imperial echoes await in Ostia Antica, Rome's old seaport, a collection of ruins as impressive as any in Rome itself. Palestrina, too, has fine old remains, together with a good museum and tremendous views. Panoramas are also part of Frascati's appeal, the most famous and easily accessible of the Castelli Romani, a coronet of towns in the volcanic hills south of Rome.

All these trips can be made by public transportation, not to be scorned given Rome's appalling traffic problems.

The most distant attractions you can see in a day are probably Cerveteri and Tarquinia's Etruscan tombs (not to mention their museums, and the smaller Etruscan sites at Sutri, Blera, and Norchia). The best of the more remote prospects are the mountains as well as the Benedictine monasteries of Subiaco.

St. Benedict's monastery in the mountains around Subiaco

Scenic drives
(*Lazio*): Viterbo–Lago di Vico–Caprarola–Ronciglione; SS411 Arsoli–Subiaco–(Filettino)–Campocatino–Fiuggi.
(*Abruzzo*): Abruzzo National Park SS83 Alfedena–Opi–Pescasseroli–Gioia dei Marsi & SS479 Sulmona–Scanno–Villetta Barrea; SS5/5bis Sulmona–(Secinaro)–Celano–Rocca di Mezzo–L'Aquila; SS80/A 24 L'Aquila–Montorio al Vomano–L'Aquila; SS17bis L'Aquila–Campo Imperatore.

Scenic railroads
The main Rome–Pescara line has a picturesque section between Avezzano and Sulmona. The Abruzzo's small branch lines are tempting to ride for their own sake. The short line from Sulmona to L'Aquila, for example, (and its continuation to Rieti) runs through good countryside. The best trip of all is from Sulmona to Castel di Sangro, which climbs high into the mountains on the eastern flank of the national park.

Seaside Lazio Southern Lazio's best beaches are at Sperlonga, Gaeta, Sabaudia and San Felice Circeo. Rome's seaside resorts—Lido di Ostia, Fregene and Ladispoli—are not recommended, being largely crowded and polluted. To the north, Santa Severa and Santa Marinella have reasonable beaches and pretty pinewood surroundings. Huge, undeveloped beaches stretch out from the hamlet of Chiarone, where Lazio meets Tuscany. Abruzzo's pleasantest seaside towns are Pineto (13 miles north of Pescara) and Vasto (41 miles south of Pescara).

Sun umbrellas line up on Santa Marinella's popular beach

Abruzzo Few people venture into the Abruzzo's desolate interior, despite road and rail links that put it within easy reach of Rome. Yet its rewards are immense, particularly if you are in search of wild mountains and villages where life is still harsh and strangers a novelty. Roads lead to the heart of the Abruzzo National Park, which has plenty of well-organized trails and interesting villages, and to the Gran Sasso d'Italia, the highest point on the Italian peninsula. Good paths in both areas allow endless hiking opportunities (see page 194), but there are also plenty of routes into the mountains for drivers. If you are driving, it is rewarding to explore the roads around the Abruzzo's three other great massifs—the Maiella, Monte Velino, and the Monti della Laga (see Scenic Drives panel).

The region is not solely about mountains, however, for as well as any number of remote hill villages, the Abruzzo has a couple of bracing towns that are interesting spots in their own right. Sulmona was the birthplace of Ovid (and where confetti was invented), while L'Aquila contains a neat little museum and several captivating churches.

Molise Molise is a tiny region lodged south of the Abruzzo (until 1963 it was part of the old Abruzzi region). Gentler than the Abruzzo, the Matese mountains are still wild and impressive. Towns and villages are less interesting, though Termoli on the coast is a reasonable beach resort, and Isernia has a good archeological museum. Around Isernia there is lovely rolling hill country.

Essentials
Cerveteri: Banditaccia tombs
Gran Sasso: Campo Imperatore
Ostia Antica: The ruins
Parco Nazionale d'Abruzzo: Walks, drives
Tarquinia: Museo Nazionale, Monterozzi tombs
Tivoli: Villa d'Este, Villa Adriano, Villa Gregoriana
Viterbo: Villa Lante, Bomarzo

Tourist information
L'Aquila: Via XX Settembre 8 (tel: 0862/22 306).
Subiaco: Via Cadorna 59 (tel: 0774/85 397).
Sulmona: Via Roma 21 (tel: 0864/53 276).
Tarquinia: Piazza Cavour 1 (tel: 0766/856 384).
Tivoli: Largo Garibaldi (0774/21 249).
Viterbo: Piazza del Sacrario 1 (tel: 0761/304 795).

LAZIO AND ABRUZZO

Market in L'Aquila

▶ **Alatri** *180B3*

Alatri's medieval appearance belies its antiquity, for its gateways, Cyclopean walls and mighty fortified **acropolis**▶▶ date back to the 6th century BC. The ramparts offer impressive views and the streets are filled with medieval monuments, the most noteworthy being Santa Maria Maggiore, famous for its 14th-century wooden sculpture of the Madonna of Constantinople. While in the area, visit nearby **Anagni**▶ another medieval town, renowned for its magnificent Cattedrale.

▶ **L'Aquila** *180C3*

The Abruzzo's capital was for centuries the second most important town in southern Italy after Naples. Today on first acquaintance it appears dour and depressing. Further exploration reveals a lively mountain town that combines medieval and modern in equal measure. Your first stop should be the castle's **Museo Nazionale d'Abruzzo**▶▶, the Abruzzo's foremost museum, a fascinating potpourri of exhibits ranging from a stuffed mammoth to displays of sacred art, local pottery, and the cream of the region's paintings. Close by stands **Santa Maria di Collemaggio**▶▶, the Abruzzo's premier piece of church architecture, known for its arched portal and intricate pink-and-white marble façade. The church of **San Bernardino**▶▶ contains the tomb of San Bernardino of Siena, who died in the town (the Sienese visit L'Aquila on his feast day, bearing gifts of Tuscan oil).

▶▶ **Bolsena, Lago di** *180C1*

Lake Bolsena is the largest volcanic lake in Italy. One of the best trips locally is the boat ride out to **Bisentina**▶▶, one of the lake's two islands (the other is Martana—both are probably remnants of the old volcanic crater). Bisentina offers not only views and scenery, but also Etruscan tombs, a Farnese family villa and five quaint little chapels. Boats run from **Capodimonte**▶, an attractive resort that extends into the lake on a castle-tipped promontory. Other towns in the fertile hills around the lake include **Gradoli**▶, at the heart of a large wine region, Etruscan **Montefiascone**▶ and medieval **Bolsena**▶, a relaxed and likable place that makes the best overall base for excursions around the lake. Civita, 9 miles east of Bolsena, is an eerie and half-deserted ghost town in a lunar landscape.

▶ **Caprarola** *180C2*

Easily seen in conjunction with Viterbo and Lago di Vico (see page 193), Caprarola is a little village almost entirely given over to the **Palazzo Farnese**▶▶. One of the high points of 16th-century mannerism, it is a building, said Stendhal, "where architecture married nature." Created as a castle in 1520, it was completed as a Farnese palace in 1559 by Vignola, one of the leading architects of his day. Many rooms are closed to the public and others are missing their period furniture. Several features, however, still

Ninety-nine
Emperor Frederick II reputedly created L'Aquila in 1242 by amalgamating 99 local castles and villages. The town has had a fondness for the number ever since. The town hall bell chimes 99 times at 9:09PM, and near the station stands the Fontana delle 99 Cannelle, a 99-spouted fountain.

Est! Est!! Est!!!
Est! Est!! Est!!! is a wine from the Bolsena region. A bishop is said to have instructed his retainer to search out taverns with the best wine and indicate his choice by chalking "Est" ("It is here") on the relevant hostelry. When he reached Montefiascone, the wine was so good he excitedly scrawled Est! Est!! Est!!!. The satisfied bishop is buried in Montefiascone, reputedly having died from overdrinking.

stand out, notably Vignola's famous monumental staircase (the Scala Regia) and the beautifully frescoed Sala del Mappamondo. Outside there is a large park and two gardens—a south-facing summer garden and an east-facing winter terrace.

▶ **Castelli Romani** *180B2*

The 13 villages of the Castelli Romani are descendants of the medieval castles built by the popes and Rome's leading patrician families. They nestle in the Albani hills south of Rome. Although they provide welcome relief from Rome's heat and hassle, many have been spoiled by wanton modern building, but much of the wooded surroundings, and lakes like Albano and Nemi, remain worth seeing; they serve as favorite destinations for Sunday-lunch excursions from Rome. **Frascati▶** is the most famous of the villages, thanks to its wine and villas. Castel Gandolfo is well known, mainly as the pope's summer residence. **Rocca di Papa▶**, **Grottaferata▶** and **Albano Laziale▶**, however, are the most picturesque *Castelli*.

▶▶ **Circeo, Parco Nazionale del** *180A3*

The smallest of Italy's national parks, Circeo was created to preserve a portion of the Pontine marshes following Mussolini's 1930s reclamation projects. It is a wonderfully diverse patchwork of lakes, coastal dunes, and forests. Wild boar and fallow deer roam the woods, and the wetland areas are renowned for their resident and migrating species of birds. Walking opportunities are myriad, and you can take boat trips around the lakes and lagoons.

Frascati
Frascati's famous and unassuming white wine is the mainstay of simple Italian restaurants the world over. In the Middle Ages, the Albani's foresters built huts of *frascata*, the brushwood that gave Frascati its name and the wine its symbol: the *frasca*, or branch, hung over the doors of taverns when the new vintage was ready.

Information
Parco Nazionale di Circeo's information center is at Via Carlo Alberto 107, Sabaudia (tel: 0773/511 386). It provides a detailed and useful map. Many of the park's gentle marked trails fan out from the center itself. For a more challenging morning's hike climb Circeo's one high spot, Monte Circeo (1,478ft.), a wooded and rocky promontory whose summit affords magnificent views over the park.

185

Capodimonte on Lake Bolsena. Boat trips on the lake start from here

The Etruscans are one of the most enigmatic and mysterious of ancient civilizations. At their height between 800 and 400 BC they controlled much of central Italy (*Etruria*) through a twelve-strong confederation of cities.

Death and life
"Death...to the Etruscans was a pleasant continuance of life, with jewels and wine, and flutes playing for the dance. It was neither an ecstasy of bliss, a heaven, nor a purgatory of torment. It was just a natural continuance of the fullness of life. Everything was in terms of life...the things they did, in their early centuries, are as natural and easy as breathing." D. H. Lawrence, *Etruscan Places*.

Norchia
The ruins of Etruscan *Orcia* lie west of Vetralla, 18 miles east of Tarquinia off the SS1bis. As well as several monumental tombs, some with great sculpted façades, the village has a medieval castle and 12th-century parish church, San Pietro.

History Where the Etruscans came from is one of history's great conundrums. Most evidence points to a mixture of seafarers and indigenous tribes whose ethnic links were with Asia Minor, and whose trading ties were with Greece. One reason for their shadowy past is depressingly banal—their cities were made almost entirely of wood, so that almost nothing of them remains. The culture's finest memorials are what has been found in their tombs, and this has given the Etruscans a reputation as a gloomy and introspective race. In truth, they seem to have been a lively and imaginative people, with highly developed social, cultural, and political systems.

The Etruscan legacy Another reason we know relatively little of the Etruscans is that the Romans deliberately set out to absorb—and then obscure—the culture of their predecessors. Etruscans were probably Rome's earliest settlers (and even provided its earliest kings). Much of their alphabet and language passed into Latin (and thus into other European tongues). The Romans also inherited many of their gods and divinities, their rituals and divinations, even their circuses and gladiatorial games. Much of this assimilation had taken place by the 3rd century BC, by which time Rome had defeated most of the Etruscan cities.

Museums and monuments Grandiose monuments to the Etruscans lie scattered all over ancient *Etruria*, from the stone-cut amphitheater at Sutri to the vivid wallpaintings of Tarquinia. Most of the smaller artifacts have been removed from tombs (or *necropoli*), for the Etruscans (like the Egyptians) left the dead with all they would need in the afterlife. Almost every Etruscan site, large or small, has a museum to display them, but their prize exhibits have gone to the Vatican museums and Rome's Villa Giulia (see page 47). These are the world's finest Etruscan museums, so if possible visit them before exploring the Etruscan sites.

Cerveteri Cerveteri, ancient *Kysry* (Roman *Caere*), was one of the leading Etruscan cities, its preeminence based on mineral riches and long-established trading prowess. Over 5,000 tombs lie in the **Necropoli della Banditaccia**, laid out as streets and houses to create a literal "city of the dead." Only 50 or so have been excavated (though many have been ransacked over the centuries).

No clue to its occupant remains in this empty Etruscan tomb

Some are curious pillboxes carved from the living rock, others earth-covered tumuli that ripple over the surrounding countryside. Of the 12 show tombs—all near the site's entrance—try to see the *Tomba dei Capitelli* and the *Tomba dei Letti Funebri*. Round off a visit with a trip to the Museo Nazionale Cerite, a modest collection of Etruscan artifacts housed in Cerveteri's 16th-century Castello Orsini.

Tarquinia In its day Tarquinia boasted a population of 100,000 and was probably the Etruscans' cultural and political capital. Now it is a strangely drab and half-derelict town, only redeemed by its museum and tombs, the most famous of any in Italy. The **Museo Nazionale** offers a small but excellent collection, its centerpiece, a pair of winged terracotta horses, perhaps the most beautiful Etruscan sculpture in existence. Its other exhibits include the inevitable funerary urns, some scintillating jewelry, and several tombs reconstructed to house their wallpaintings under controlled conditions.

The 6,000 original tombs honeycomb the Monterozzi plateau east of the town. To protect their delicate frescos, however, only a handful are open to the public at any one time (to guided tours). Their Hellenistic-style paintings span around 500 years, the earliest concentrating on mythical and ritualistic scenes, the later on the social (and sexual) context of Etruscan daily life.

Sutri About 11 miles southeast of Vetralla (on the SS1bis), Sutri is one of the more rewarding of the lesser Etruscan sites. A picturesque medieval town, it occupies a narrow rocky ridge—the type of site favored by the Etruscans for their cities. Its overgrown amphitheater was carved from the living rock (and seated 6,000 people).

Boxers on an Etruscan vase

In the city of the dead, Cerveteri

LAZIO AND ABRUZZO

Olive terraces backed by the snow-covered Gran Sasso ridge

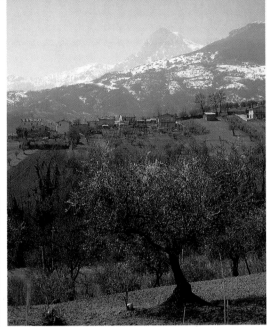

Albergo Campo Imperatore
This hotel is famous as the place where Mussolini was imprisoned after the Italian surrender in 1943. He was sprung from the remote eyrie in a daring aerial raid, and taken north by the Germans to establish the puppet Salò Republic.

Walking
Although it is easy to tour the environs of the Gran Sasso by car, there are numerous straightforward walking opportunities. For maps and information visit L'Aquila's tourist office in Via XX Settembre 8 (or the regional office in Piazza Santa Maria Paganica 5— tel: 0862/410 808). Also helpful is the Italian Alpine Club (C.A.I.) office at Via XX Settembre 15 (open weekdays 6–7PM).

Abbazia di Casamari
Take in the Abbey of Casamari as part of a car tour of southern Lazio (it lies just west of Isola del Liri, 25 miles west of Montecassino). Founded by the Benedictines in 1035, rebuilt in 1140 and now fully restored, it is a fine example of French-inspired Cistercian-Gothic architecture. The church (1217) is the three-star highlight, though all the abbey's old components are of interest (these include the cloister, pharmacy, refectory and chapterhouse).

▶▶ **Gran Sasso d'Italia** *180C3*

At 9,610 feet, the Gran Sasso d'Italia (Big Rock of Italy) is the highest point on the Italian peninsula (Etna in Sicily and many Alpine peaks are higher). Thousands of walkers and climbers are attracted to its slopes, drawn by its magnificent snow-capped ridges and the famous **Campo Imperatore▶▶**, a vast mountain-ringed upland plain.

Access is easiest from L'Aquila. It is only 66 miles on the A24 highway to the turn-off at Assergi and the hamlet of Fonte Cerreto (3,696 feet). Here there are a couple of hotels, a restaurant and a cable car (*funivia*) which takes you to the **Albergo-Rifugio Campo Imperatore** (7,025 feet), the starting point for most walks. It can also be reached by driving across the Campo Imperatore on the SS17bis (16 miles from Fonte Cerreto). The easiest of the hikes—no more than a two-hour round trip—is trail No. 10 to Monte della Scindarella (7,336 feet). The classic walk is trail No. 3, which goes close to the summit (Corno Grande).

▶ **Montecassino** *181A4*

The huge bulwarks of the abbey of Montecassino can be seen from miles around. Its superlative position was perhaps the reason St. Benedict chose it as the headquarters for the Benedictine movement in 529 (though legend said he was guided here by three ravens). For centuries it was one of the most important monasteries in the Christian world, disseminating the Benedictine ideal. It has been rebuilt many times, most notoriously after the entire building—except the crypt—was destroyed by Allied bombing on February 15, 1944. As the Nazis' regional headquarters it was an essential target, yet the abbey's destruction has been a cause for controversy ever since. The old buildings have been faithfully rebuilt, though almost inevitably the reconstruction is a sterile and soulless affair. The war cemeteries are much visited, and the views—from the middle cloister in particular—are exceptional.

Tivoli

Many visitors to Rome take time out from the sights of the capital to visit Tivoli. The crowds and endless cavalcade of tour buses are a small price to pay for the Villa d'Este, Italy's most famous gardens, and the Villa Adriana, the ruins of the Roman Empire's greatest imperial palace.

Villa Adriana (Hadrian's Villa) Tivoli, ancient *Tiber*, was known for its travertine marble—from which much of imperial Rome was built—and as a retirement home for Rome's most prosperous citizens. It had so many villas, wrote Horace, that "the Tibertine soil no longer has ploughland." The greatest, the Villa Adriana, is about 3 miles from the present town. Started in AD 125, it was built to Hadrian's own design, his intention being to recreate some of the outstanding buildings he had seen during his travels. Work eventually took 10 years, the villa and its gardens extending over a site larger than Imperial Rome itself—making it the Empire's largest and costliest palace.

To make sense of the ruins, study the model near the entrance, an attempt to reproduce the villa's original appearance. Simply wandering the lovely site, full of trees and secluded corners, is a pleasure in itself, but make a special point of seeing the Teatro Marittimo, a colonnaded palace built in the middle of an artificial lagoon.

The Villa d'Este The Villa d'Este started life as a convent, but in 1550 was converted into a country retreat for Cardinal Ippolito d'Este, the son of Lucrezia Borgia and the Duke of Ferrara. The villa now is slightly dilapidated, overshadowed by its gardens, and its fountains and formal terraces rank as some of the most beautiful in the world.

Their main attractions are the *Viale delle Cento Fontane* (Avenue of a Hundred Fountains), and two outstanding individual fountains: Bernini's elegant *Fontana di Biccierone* and the *Fontana dei Draghi* (Fountain of the Dragons), built for Pope Gregory XIII, whose symbol was a short-tailed dragon. All the gardens' byways repay exploration, but be sure to find the little path leading to the *Rometta*, a model of Rome. Also leave time to see Tivoli's third—and often overlooked—villa, the **Villa Gregoriana** (and its famous Aniene waterfalls).

189

Water is the dominant feature in the gardens of the Villa d'Este

Highlights of ancient Ostia
Ostia Antica's site is large, so allow plenty of time for exploration—you could take a picnic and make it a day-trip from Rome. Don't miss the Terme di Nettuno, noted for their mosaics; the amphitheater; and the Piazzale delle Corporazioni with the offices of the port's 61 main shipping agents. Many are still fronted by mosaics denoting the trade carried out. Also hunt for the *thermopolium*, a Roman-era bar, complete with marble counter and wall paintings illustrating the menu.

▶▶ **Ostia Antica** *180B2*

Once ancient Rome's port, Ostia Antica is now Italy's best-preserved Roman town after Pompeii (its ruins are as good as any in Rome itself). The setting is lovely, with the ruins scattered among vines and wildflowers, the paths shaded by elegant stands of parasol pines.

The colony started life as a fishing village at the mouth (*ostium*) of the Tiber, but grew as the Empire expanded trading a host of commodities with the furthest-flung imperial outposts. In the end the weight of trade exceeded the port's capacity. Coupled with the constant accumulation of silt, this led to Ostia's decline and the building of a new port, *Portus Romae* (near present-day Fiumicino).

The sprawling site centers around the Decumanus Maximus, the old main thoroughfare, from which innumerable streets branch off. Each is filled with theaters, temples, workshops, houses and the famous *horreae*, old warehouses used principally to store grain. Equally interesting are the many *insulae*, old Roman four- and five-story apartment buildings.

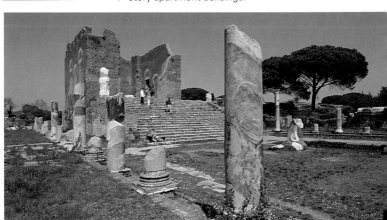

The impressive ruins of Ostia Antica

Modern Ostia
Ostia Antica is not to be confused with the modern town of Ostia nearby. This is Rome's closest seaside resort, but it is immensely crowded and commercialized, and the water and sand are often dangerously filthy.

▶ **Palestrina** *180B2*

Present-day Palestrina is largely medieval in flavor, but it rests over the ruins of *Praeneste*, an important Etruscan site founded in the 7th century BC. The city was famous for the Tempio di Fortuna Primogenia, which was the seat of an ancient cult and important oracle. The temple was enlarged under the Romans in the 4th century BC, the exact scope of the complex only coming to light after bombing during World War II.

The current town is still built on a series of vast terraces which correspond to the levels of the original temple, fragments of which lie dotted around the streets. Most of the temple treasures have been removed to Rome's Villa Giulia or to Palestrina's own Museo Nazionale Archeologico Prenestino. Among the latter's many busts, reliefs and funerary headstones, the star attraction is the outstanding 1st-century BC *Mosaic of the River Nile*, a detailed narrative describing the story of the river from its source to its delta.

SOUTHERN LAZIO

Drive The Roman countryside

A tour which encompasses pretty pockets of countryside and the most interesting towns within striking distance of Rome.

Make your way from Rome on the Via Tiburtina, not an attractive road—but few in the city's environs are—and see the Villa Adriana and Villa d'Este at **Tivoli** (page 189). Press north and make the short detour to **Anticoli Corrado▶** an unspoiled hill-town, and then follow country roads through the prettiest portion of the journey to **Subiaco** (page 193). Spend time seeing the Benedictine monuments and, if time allows, explore the wild mountains of the Monti Simbruini to the east.

Monti Simbruini For centuries the Simbruini mountains have supplied Rome with drinking water (their name means "heavy rain"). They are now part of the Apennines Natural Park. By car you can explore the park's Zompo waterfalls; the Piano di Campoli (one of the region's many impressive karstic plains); and the

scenic road from Subiaco to Jenne and Vallepietra, which has fine views over the Aniene gorge, one of the park's several deep ravines. Wind through the hill country to the south to **Palestrina** (page 190), birthplace of the great 16th-century composer who took his name from the town, then return to Rome by way of **Frascati▶** and the Colli Albani.

Medieval Anticoli Corrado, with its wonderful hilltop setting

191

Ferries to Ponza
Daily ferries run year-round from Formia and Terracina on the Lazio coast (more frequently in summer). Journey time is 2 hours 30 minutes. Faster hydrofoils run from the same ports in high season, and from Anzio, with connections from Ponza to Ischia and Naples. Connections to Ventotene, the archipelago's other main island—flatter, smaller and less verdant—run daily from Formia and Ponza (except Sunday).

San Benedetto monastery, on a rocky ridge above Subiaco

▶▶ **Ponza, Isola di** *180A1*

Romans—but not foreigners—have discovered Ponza, the largest island of the Pontine archipelago off the coast of southern Lazio. Ferries sail to Ponza Town, a beautiful fishing village of pastel-colored houses curved around a small harbor. Most people wanting to swim, however, pass over its small beach in favor of Chiaia di Luna, a slender crescent of sand about ten minutes' walk away. To escape the summer crowds, you could take small boats from the port to more secluded coves like Spiaggia Santa Lucia. You can also rent bikes and motor scooters, and a regular bus connects with La Forna, the island's other sizeable village.

▶▶ **San Clemente a Casauria** *181B4*

Among the Abruzzo's finest medieval buildings, this Cistercian abbey was founded in the 9th century and restored in the 12th century, creating a beautiful example of transitional Romanesque-Gothic architecture. The splendid portico ushers you into an interior whose simplicity is disturbed only by an elaborate pulpit. Other treasures include a 13th-century Paschal candelabrum and a ciborium taken from an early Christian sarcophagus. The crypt is the most striking feature to survive from the earliest church.

San Clemente is situated just off the A25 highway near the Torre de' Passeri exit (18 miles north of Sulmona). If it is locked ask the warden in the house nearby to let you in.

▶ **Sperlonga** *180A3*

Southern Lazio's most beautiful tract of coastline stretches between Gaeta and Sperlonga. The latter is the area's nicest and most fashionable resort, its whitewashed houses perched high on a rocky promontory. Although it fills up in summer, there is plenty of room on the beach, and if the hotels are full you should find beds at nearby Terracina ▶, another likable little resort.

▶▶ **Subiaco** *180B3*

St. Benedict retreated to caves around Subiaco in the 5th century, where he composed his famous *Rule*, one of the cornerstones of Western monasticism. Of 12 monasteries founded in his wake, only two survive. The **Convento di Santa Scholastica**, 25 minutes' walk from the town, has been largely restored, though the beauty of its three cloisters remains unsurpassed; fifteen minutes further, the **Convento di San Benedetto** contains the saint's original cave, the *Sacro Speco*, which is adorned with numerous 14th-century Sienese frescos. Subiaco itself is a winning little hilltown.

Vaulted cloister of Santa Scholastica monastery, near Subiaco

▶ **Sulmona** *181B4*

Sulmona is a bracing mountain-ringed town, ideal as a base for exploring the country around L'Aquila and for excursions into the Abruzzo national park (see pages 94–5). It was the birthplace of both Ovid, the great Roman poet (43 BC–AD 17), and confetti (see panel). Its particular sights are few, but the streets are appealing in themselves. Before you start exploring, take time out in Piazza XX Settembre's **Gran Caffè**, a lovely turn-of-the-century bar. Then see the **Annunziata**▶▶, a mixture of church, palace and poorhouse; the Gothic Fontana del Vecchio; the Duomo's 12th-century Byzantine relief; and the portal of **San Francesco delle Scarpe**▶.

▶ **Vico, Lago di** *180C2*

Lago di Vico is a secret little lake in the crater of an old volcano, surrounded by the forest-covered slopes of the Monte Cimini. The area is a nature reserve, with lots of lovely short walks, and a scenic drive, the **Via Ciminia**▶▶, which traverses the old crater's summit ridges.

▶ **Viterbo** *180C2*

Historic towns in northern Lazio are few and far between, which is perhaps why Viterbo has a reputation out of all proportion to its appeal. A favored retreat for numerous medieval popes, today it is a gloomy town, best seen quickly before moving to some of the sights nearby (the Villa Lante, Bomarzo, and Lago di Vico). Most of its old buildings lie on **Piazza del Plebiscito**▶ and **Piazza San Lorenzo**▶▶, both fine medieval squares, and in the picturesque quarter around Via San Pellegrino.

Confetti
Real *confetti* are sugared almond confections bound with wire and ribbons into elaborate flowers. They have been made in Sulmona since the 15th century. Since then they have played a part in weddings the world over. These days, of course, colored paper is thrown, though traditional white *confetti* are still used at Abruzzese nuptials.

193

Beauty...
Sacheverell Sitwell called the Villa Lante, in Bagnaia, 3 miles east of Viterbo, "the most lovely place of the physical beauty of nature in Italy or in all the world." Its grounds contain some of Europe's most beautiful Renaissance gardens. The formal gardens are seen by guided tour, but you are free to wander in the adjoining parkland.

...and the beasts
In Bomarzo, 7 miles northeast of Bagnaia, are Lazio's most extraordinary gardens, the Parco dei Mostri (Monster Park), designed in 1552 by the Duke of Orsini. Grotesques, moss-covered sculptures and huge, fantastical stone creatures give the effect of a surreal 16th-century theme park of fantasy and horror. Though commercialized, the garden is worth the high admission.

Parco Nazionale d'Abruzzo

The Abruzzo national park is central Italy's natural jewel, a superbly administered wilderness area that provides wonderful hiking country and a refuge for wolves and brown bears as well as a host of other flora and fauna.

Information
For information on the park, visit Pescasseroli's central information office (Via Piave, tel: 0863/91 461) and the large park center/museum close by. Opi, Barrea, Villetta Barrea and Civitella Alfedena also have smaller, summer-only information centers.

Abruzzo national park, one of Europe's last great wildernesses

The lie of the land Most of the park's 98,800 acres comprise a jumbled collection of Apennine mountain massifs. Most reach about 5,940 feet, though the highest point is Monti della Meta (7,415 feet). The Sangro valley cuts through their heart, scattered about with the area's only villages—Barrea, Villetta Barrea, Civitella Alfedena, Opi and Pescasseroli. All of these have a handful of hotels and campsites. The most developed spot is Pescasseroli, home to the park's main museum and information center. Old ways still predominate hereabout: national costume is sometimes seen, sheep farming flourishes, and you are as likely to encounter old men bringing firewood from the forests on donkeys as you are to meet tractors.

History Italy's environmental protection record is generally poor, but in the Abruzzo national park it can claim one of the best-administered parks in Europe. It started life—like many Italian parks—as a royal hunting reserve. This was dismantled in 1877 and an embryonic park created in its place in 1917. Most of the real work, however, has been done in the last 20 years. Early opposition has largely been overcome through initiatives to promote the local economy. A fine balance has been struck between the range of facilities—such as excellent marked paths—and the need to protect the wilderness in its natural state.

Walking The park has over 150 numbered and well-marked trails of all standards, most of them marked on the park's own 1:50,000 map, available from park centers. Perhaps the most popular is the five-hour round trip from Civitella Alfedena to the Valle delle Rose (trail I1). Sightings of the park's 500-plus chamois are almost guaranteed. There are easy strolls in

194

the Canala valley immediately north of Pescasseroli, and in the Val di Fondillo east of Opi (one of the park's loveliest and most popular areas). Near Pescasseroli try trail B2 (to Monte di Valle Carrara, 2½ hours), or C3 to the Valico di Monte Tranquillo (2½ hours). Another favorite is the two-hour hike from Barrea to Lago Vivo, or the walk in the Camosciara—another pretty area—to the Belvedere della Liscia (two hours).

Flora The park claims over 1,200 species of plants and trees (and 267 types of fungi). Around two-thirds of its area is covered in ancient forests of beech and maple (beautifully colored in autumn), interspersed with ash, hawthorn and hornbeam, and blossom-bearing trees like wild apple, pear, cherry, and blackthorn. Spring ushers in swaths of asphodels, crocuses, gentians and snowdrops, easily seen on even the shortest walks, followed by wild orchids and rarities like endemic irises and Apennine edelweiss.

Wolves Italy has an estimated 150–200 wolves. Their numbers are increasing all the time, despite constant human harassment and the ever-increasing threat from feral dogs (the country has 800,000 wild dogs, which interbreed with wolves and challenge them for their food sources). The park has perhaps 15–20 individual wolves in the wild, plus several that are kept in special reserves near Civitella Alfedena and Pescasseroli. These are used for study and to preserve the thoroughbred characteristics of the Apennine wolf.

Bears The park's most jealously protected fauna are Italy's last Apennine brown bears (*Ursus arctos marsicanus*). Although descended from Alpine forebears, the Abruzzo's bears have developed enough indigenous features to be classified as a subspecies (named after the *Marsicano*, the generic name for much of the park, deriving from the Marsi, one of the area's earliest tribes). Bears were common until the 16th century, and bounties were still paid on every bear killed until as recently as 1915. About 80–100 are thought to survive, and numbers are gradually increasing. Sadly, the possibility of a sighting is minimal.

Chamois
The beautiful and graceful chamois are some of the most easily seen of the park's 40 species of mammal. Like the park's bears they are descended from Alpine ancestors, but have developed individual characteristics that allow them to be considered a subspecies (*Rupicapra rupicapra ornata*). The Valle delle Rose above Civitella Alfedena is one of their favored haunts. Many of the park's 500-strong herd are being introduced into other parts of the Abruzzo.

195

Birds
Over 300 species of birds have been spotted within the national park. The park centers (and park map) identify areas where you are likely to see particular birds—notably the ten or so pairs of golden eagles that nest in the region.

The Apennine brown bear clings precariously to existence in the national park, while numbers of wolves are steadily increasing

CAMPANIA

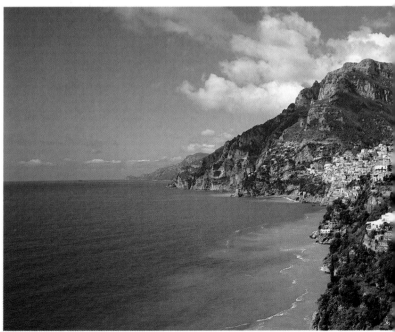

Campania To the Romans Campania was *campania felix* (the happy land), a sort of dream vacation destination—all views, fine wines, sunny skies, and bountiful countryside. It is hardly surprising, therefore, that some of the country's greatest ancient sites are here. The Greek temples at Paestum look much as they must have done 2,000 years ago; so too, the remarkable Roman cities of Pompeii and Herculaneum, buried and preserved for posterity by the ash and mud of erupting Vesuvius—Goethe's "peak of hell rising out of paradise." Visitors still come to Campania in droves, to see the ancient sites certainly, but also to enjoy the unrivaled coastal scenery of the Sorrentino peninsula and the islands of Capri and Ischia.

Naples Nowhere is quite like Naples. On first acquaintance it appears a sprawling, teeming city, the epitome of the urban nightmare. Many people leave at the earliest opportunity. Many more, intimidated by its reputation, avoid it altogether. The Neapolitans, however—some of the wiliest and liveliest Italians going—like to say that you hate the city after a day, love it after a week, and never want to leave after a year. It is well worth testing the theory, perhaps not over a year, but certainly over several days. With your valuables safely hidden, and your courage in both hands, wander the streets, visit one of Europe's finest museums, and—perhaps most importantly—sample pizza in the city where it was born.

Island idylls History's hedonists have long luxuriated on Campania's famous islands. Tiberius, for one, built a dozen villas on Capri to indulge his sexual whims. Later

Positano, a jewel of the Amalfi coast

CAMPANIA

residents have included dancer Rudolph Nureyev and droves of artists and writers. These days day-trippers make up the bulk of the visitors, diminishing the island's social cachet but unable to tarnish its incomparable beauty. Brave the crowds to share in the escapism, and leave time, perhaps, to visit the region's other islands—Ischia and tiny Procida—less beautiful, just as crowded, but equally alluring.

Campanian coasts Where Grand Tourists once visited the Bay of Naples, package tourists now settle for the Sorrento peninsula—Italy's most renowned stretch of coastline. Whitewashed towns like Amalfi, Positano and Ravello rear up high above a turquoise sea, fringed by plunging cliffs and a stunning mountainous backdrop. Crowds flock to the region as they do to the islands—but its beauty is one that commercialism cannot taint. The area's main town, Sorrento, is less striking and often busy with package tours, but nonetheless makes an appealing and convenient base. You might also want to explore the Cilento, Campania's less sybaritic coastline, a long arc of cliffs, beaches, and small resorts that skirts the mountains near the Calabrian border. See it after Paestum, and use Santa Maria di Castellabate as a base.

Pasta and pizza Two culinary staples originated in Campania—the pizza, and that most archetypal of pastas, spaghetti. Naples *is* the pizza's homeland (so ignore the killjoys who claim it was created earlier elsewhere). The classic Neapolitan versions are *napoletana* (tomatoes, anchovies and mozzarella) and *Margherita* (created for Italy's first queen, using basil, tomato and mozzarella to suggest the colors of the Italian flag). Be sure to try a pizza in one of the city's old *pizzerie* such as Da Michele or Trianon da Ciro. Alternatively, buy it by the slice (*pizza taglia*). Other local specialties are: the famous *insalata caprese* (Capri salad)—slices of tomato and mozzarella; fish and seafood, mussels (*cozze*) and clams (*vongole*) in particular (though watch your wallet, for seafood can be expensive).

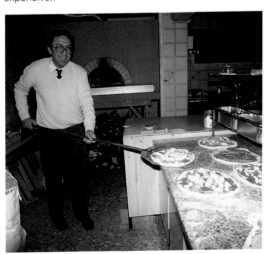

Pizza made in the traditional wood-fired oven

▶▶▶ **Amalfi** *196B2*

Formerly one of the Mediterranean's leading sea-powers, Amalfi is the largest town on Italy's most breath-taking coastline. Although it can often be dreadfully congested, its hotels and restaurants are generally more affordable than many in the area.

Poised romantically between the mountains and the sea, the town's narrow streets and dark passage-ways weave among monuments which testify to its former grandeur. The Romanesque **Duomo▶▶**, dominating the central square from the top of a large flight of steps, shows more than a hint of Saracen influence, even stronger in the adjoining **Chiostro del Paradiso▶▶** (Cloister of Paradise), full of palms and voluptuously intertwined twin columns.

Amalfi is known for its high-quality paper, and you can visit Europe's oldest working paper mill, as well as a small paper museum, the Museo della Carta. The **Museo Civico▶** houses the *Tavole Amalfitane*, a codex of maritime law which held sway over the entire Mediterranean until 1570.

199

▶ **Benevento** *196C2*

Benevento was bombed heavily in World War II, and its center—despite a certain atmospheric appeal—still has a battered and half-built feel. Nonetheless it remains one of the more interesting towns of the Campanian interior. The best sights are Roman, notably the 2nd-century AD. **Arco di Traiano▶▶** (also known as Porta Aurea) and the ruins of the 20,000-seat **theater▶**. Also worth at least a glance is the church of Santa Sofia, part of a Benedictine abbey founded by the Lombards in 760. Its cloisters hold the **Museo Sannio▶**.

▶ **Campi Flegrei** *196B1*

The "fiery fields," west of Naples, are the Phlegrean Fields of classical myth, Homer's and Virgil's entrance to Hades. They are also the Elysian Fields, long eulogized for their transcendental beauty. Nearby Naples has largely destroyed the beauty, though one or two spots deserve a visit, and there are still signs of the volcanic activity that gave the region its name.

Amalfi's highly decorated Duomo

Tourist information
Amalfi: Corso Roma 19 (tel: 089/871 107).
Benevento: Via N. Sala 31 (tel: 0824/21 947).
Capri: Piazzale Cerio II (tel: 081/837 5308).
Naples: Piazza del Gesù (tel: 081/552 3328).
Pompeii: Via Sacra 1 (tel: 081/861 0913).
Ravello: Piazza Vescovado 13 (tel: 089/857 096).
Sorrento: Via L de Maio 35 (tel: 081/878 2104).

Vesuvius (Vesuvio) is neither the world's highest nor most dangerous volcano, but the catastrophic eruption that buried Pompeii and Herculaneum has made it one of the most famous. "Many a calamity has happened in the world," wrote Goethe, "but never one that has caused so much entertainment to posterity as this one."

The big bang On August 24, AD 79 Vesuvius had been belching smoke and debris for several days. Early that morning, however, its basalt plug collapsed, unleashing the full force of the volcano. A huge cloud blotted out the sun, raining dust, stone, and lava on to the surrounding countryside. Pompeii was buried within hours, some 2,000 of its inhabitants killed by falling rocks and asphyxiating gases (many of its 20,000 population had already left). That evening, the volcano's internal walls disintegrated, sending further torrents of ash over the town (Herculaneum was engulfed at this point by a flood of superheated mud). Only late on August 26 did a feeble light return to the region.

Statistically, Vesuvius' next eruption is overdue, but if you are still interested in peering down into the crater of the famous volcano, it is easily reached

Vesuvius today What you see today when you look up at the volcano from Naples is actually the truncated cone of Monte Somma (3,736 feet). Vesuvius proper (4,214 feet) rises from its floor, a cone created by the eruption of AD 79. Vesuvius has erupted around a hundred times since that fateful morning, the last in 1944. This works out at a strike rate of around once every 20 years, so the next cataclysm is long overdue. When it arrives Naples will be in the firing line—which makes it odd that there are no contingency plans to deal with an eruption.

Reaching the crater There are several ways to get a closer look at Vesuvius. The easiest is to take the Circumvesuviana, a local railroad that runs in a broad circle around the volcano (2 hours). Alternatively, you can take the railroad as far as Ercolano, where six SITA buses daily leave the station for the cafés and souvenir shops at Vesuvius' former chairlift station (*seggovia*). You can also drive to this point (or take a taxi from Ercolano—but fix a price first). From here it is a 30-minute climb to the summit (wear stout shoes). Views into the crater and over Naples are breathtaking. You can walk around the crater (2 hours), but watch out for the crumbling paths and rickety fences.

Pompeii

Pompeii's fate was the archeologists' fortune, for the volcanic eruption of AD 79 that buried it left posterity not only the world's finest surviving Roman town, but also an unparalleled insight into the minutiae of 1st-century life. An instant in the city's existence was captured by the disaster that overwhelmed its people.

History Pompeii (Pompei in Italian) was never as famous in its own time as it is today. It started life in the 6th century BC as a Greek trading post. After falling to the Samnites, it became a thriving Roman colony. Much was damaged by an earthquake in AD 63, the remainder obliterated by Vesuvius 16 years later. The city remained forgotten until around 1600, when the study of ancient texts suggested its existence. Excavations began in 1748 and have since revealed most of the site.

Sightseeing The site is huge, and even spending a day here still leaves many stones unturned. Some houses are little more than foundations, and after a time one ruin looks much like another, so be selective. Also be sure to see Naples' Museo Archeologico, which contains most of the site's movable treasures.

The civic buildings Almost the first area you encounter (at the site's western entrance) is the **Forum**, the center of Roman civic life. Its surviving buildings include the **Basilica** (a business center and law courts), market place, and temples to Apollo, Venus, Jupiter and Vespasian. In the **Antiquarium** close by are body casts taken from the volcanic ash, figures whose contorted shapes graphically illustrate the horror of that fateful morning. Beyond the forum lie the **Terme Stabiane**, the town's earliest bathhouses. Still preserved are swimming pools, men's and women's sections, even small niches in the changing room for clothes. Alongside runs **Vico del Lupinare**, one of the main red-light districts. A small brothel at one end has several bed stalls and frescos describing the services on offer.

More salutary performances took place in the 5,000-seat **Teatro Grande** and the smaller indoor **Teatro Piccolo** (or *Odeon*). The 20,000-seat **Anfiteatro**, built in 80 BC, is Italy's oldest surviving amphitheater, and one of the most complete in the Roman world.

Casa dei Vetii This is Pompeii's best-preserved and most artistically rewarding house. Once the home of two wealthy merchants, it possesses the

Waiting for the visiting hordes at Pompeii

Pompeii

Pompeii possesses one of the most complete of all Roman amphitheaters

Pompeii

POMPEI

PORTA DI CÁPUA

Staz Scavi

Entrata
PORTA DI NOLA

PORTA DI SARNO

Casa d Gladiatori

Casa di M L Frontone

sa degli norini orati

Casa d Nozze d'Argento

Casa di Obellio Firmo

Casa di Pinario Ceriale

Villa di Giulia Felice

Casa di Cecilio Giocondo

VIA DI NOLA

Casa del Centenario

VIA DELL' ABBONDANZA

Casa di Venere

Casa di Loreius Tiburtinus

Anfiteatro

Casa di Trebio Valente

Terme Centrali

AUGUSTALI

FORTUNA

Augusta AUGUSTALI

Casa di G Rufo

VIA DEI AUGUSTALI

Casa di Rufo

Casa d Larario

Casa d Sacerdote Amandus

Grande Palestra

Macellum

Terme Stabiane

Fullónica di Stefano

Casa dell'Efebo

VIA NOCERINA

Tempio di espasiano

VIA STABIANA

Casa d Criptopórtico

Entrata

VIA DELL' ABBONDANZA

Casa d Citarista

Casa del Menandro

PORTA DI NOCERA

Edificio di Eumachia

Tempio di Iside

Casa d Amanti

Necropoli

Comizio

Teatro Grande

Teatro Piccolo

Casa di Giuseppe II

Caserma d Gladiatori

PORTA DI STABIA

Tempio Dorico

VIALE AI TEATRI

VIA PLINIO

SS 18

0 100 200 m
0 100 200 yards

203

site's finest wall paintings. The frieze of the cupids is of special note. The vestibule contains the famously well-endowed Priapus, not to mention a roomful of explicit erotica (usually closed). Phallic symbols appear all over Pompeii, probably attempts to ward off the evil eye.

Three houses The largest of the town's houses is the Casa del Menandro, a patrician villa with a lovely peristyle and many appealing frescos. Other noteworthy homes include the Casa del Fauno, source of many of the finest paintings in Naples' museum; and the **Casa di Loreio Tiburtino**, an elegant mansion whose structure is typical of many of the town's grander homes. In its courtyard, or atrium, stands the *impluvium*, a basin for collecting rainwater. To the rear spreads the peristyle, an open area of columns and fountains. Around it extend the house's private apartments.

Dogs and Dionysus Other well-kept houses include the Casa degli Amorini Dorati, Casa di M L Frontone, Villa di Giulia Felice and Casa del Centenario. You might hunt out the **Casa del Poeta Tragico**, a middle-class home built in Pompeii's final days. It is known for the sign above its door—*Cave canem*—"Beware of the Dog." Some 15,000 graffiti have been found around Pompeii, many salacious, others political or cultural. Finally, be certain to visit the **Villa dei Misteri**, for beautiful frescos describing the initiation of women into the Dionysiac mysteries.

Vesuvius, now quiet, broods over the ruins of Pompeii

Capri practicalities
Boats and hydrofoils run year round to Capri from Sorrento and Naples (Molo Beverello). During the summer there are also connections from Ischia and towns along the Amalfi coast. Buses link the island's main centers (including the Blue Grotto). Accommodation is limited in July and August (reservations essential). Capri's reputation for high prices is deserved. To save money, use Sorrento as a base: a couple of day-trips at most are enough to see the island.

The Blue Grotto
Capri's most famous sight—La Grotta Azzurra—is an overrated, frustrating and over-priced experience. First you have to pay for a boat to take you from Marina Grande; then you cough up an entrance fee; then you pay for a small boat to whisk you in and out of the turquoise-hued grotto. You are better off taking the more rewarding two-hour boat trips around the whole island.

▶▶▶ Capri 196B1

Capri's legendary beauty attracts day-trippers by the thousand. Most people come for sybaritic pursuits—Augustus called the island *Capri Apragopolis* (City of Sweet Idleness)—which means lazy walks, lovely views, and sipping drinks from flower-decked terraces.

Boats dock at Marina Grande, from where you can take a funicular to the village of **Capri▶▶▶**, whose central *piazzetta* is the place to see and be seen. Nearby, visit the Certosa San Giacomo, a crumbling monastery, and the Giardini di Augusto, gardens with tremendous views of the coast's cliffs. Below, the steep Via Krupp leads to Marina Piccola, the best place to swim (though it becomes uncomfortably crowded in summer). **Anacapri▶▶** is the island's other main village, linked by chairlift to Monte Solaro (1,967 feet), a good spot for views over the island.

▶ Caserta 196C1

Caserta's Palazzo Reale is Italy's largest royal palace (1,200 rooms, 1,790 windows and 94 staircases). The so-called "Versailles of Naples" was begun in 1752 for the Bourbon King Charles III and finished 20 years later. Size for its own sake, however, is the palace's most impressive feature. Its apartments—though suitably painted, stuccoed and decorated—are insipid and uninspiring places. The gardens, by contrast, are enchanting. Caserta Vecchia (Old Caserta), a medieval village, is 6 miles to the north.

▶▶ Ischia 196B1

Although this island is less pretty and less chic than Capri, Ischia's spas, beaches and hot springs still make it popular. The southern shores are nicest, around the villages of Fontana and **Sant'Angelo▶▶**, and the old volcanic peak, **Monte Epomeo▶▶**, is well worth climbing for the views. The town of **Ischia▶** divides into Ischia Porto, the tourist center, and Ischia Ponte, the less-commercialized fishing village. Its only real sight is the Castello, an old Aragonese fortress.

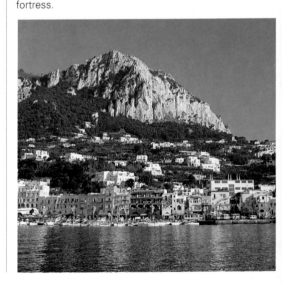

The lovely island of Capri has attracted pleasure-seekers since Roman times

Herculaneum

When Vesuvius erupted in AD 79 it destroyed at least two towns. Although Pompeii is the better known, nearby Herculaneum (Ercolano) is almost equally as interesting—and its size makes it an easier place to visit.

Origins Whereas Pompeii was a thriving commercial town, Herculaneum was a chic residential suburb, built to take advantage of the area's sea breezes and magnificent views. Houses here belonged to wealthy patrician families, and were built as sophisticated villas a cut above the town houses of Pompeii's business class. The wave of superheated mud that swept over the town in AD 79, however, was no respecter of class or property, and it entombed the town until its rediscovery in 1709. Excavations began in earnest in 1927, but since then less than half the site has been revealed.

The site Herculaneum lies at the seaward end of modern Ercolano's main street. Allow about two hours to see its highlights. On the whole it is better preserved than Pompeii, though there are fewer communal spaces or impressive civic buildings. Instead it preserves its Roman grid plan, based on two main streets—the *Cardine IV* and *Decumano Inferiore*. Only about 15 of the houses are open at any one time. Among the public buildings, note the **Terme**, a bathhouse with its benches and basins intact (plus separate warm, hot and cold rooms); the *palaestra* (gymnasium), dominated by a lovely fountain; and the remnants of the 2,500-seat theater.

The Casa dei Cervi
The house which best evokes Herculaneum's luxurious past is the Casa dei Cervi (House of the Deer), by virtue of its elegant gardens and its statues: one of a drunken Hercules (Ercolo), the town's legendary founder, the other of two groups of deer being hunted by dogs.

205

Herculaneum, risen from the mud of Vesuvius

CAMPANIA

▶▶ **Napoli (Naples)** 196B1

Naples is a place that arouses fierce passions. On the one hand it is chaotic and crime infested (guard your valuables), racked by pollution, poverty and grinding inefficiency. On the other it is the most Italian of cities (and yet unlike anywhere in Italy)—the place where family, food, and religion reign as strongly as ever; the place that gave birth to the pizza, Sophia Loren, and *O Sole Mio*; a city that was once so beautiful it formed the culmination of the Grand Tour.

To enjoy it you need to keep an open mind, but even if you take one look and want to leave, you should brave the city streets to see the **Museo Archeologico Nazionale**▶▶▶, one of Europe's greatest museums (see opposite page). Otherwise, sights are few. However, eating and soaking up atmosphere are as much a part of the Naples experience as sightseeing.

What to see Start a tour near the waterfront with the Castel Nuovo, (or Masdio Angioino) built in 1279 by Charles of Anjou (related to the French monarchy) and refurbished by Alfonso I of Aragon as a royal palace two centuries later (the Aragonese were an illegitimate branch of the Spanish monarchy, rulers of Naples until succeeded in 1734 by the Bourbons). Behind it lies the **Teatro San Carlo**▶▶, one of Europe's grandest opera houses (open to guided tours).

Among the churches, the **Duomo**▶ is less than arresting, notable only for the phials of San Gennaro's blood and fragments of a basilica founded by Constantine in AD 324 (Santa Restituta). Nearby **San Lorenzo Maggiore**▶ is a fine Gothic church, and **Santa Anna dei Lombardi**▶ offers excellent pieces of Renaissance sculpture.

The city's most worthwhile sight (after the museum) is the picture gallery of the **Palazzo Reale di Capodimonte**▶▶ to the north of the city. Most Italian masters are represented, including Raphael, Michelangelo, Botticelli, Giovanni Bellini, Filippino Lippi, Simone Martini and many more.

Staying It's best to avoid the mainly grim hotels near the station (around Piazza Garibaldi). Better budget options cluster between Piazza Dante and the Duomo. Further out, the upscale hotels congregate in the Mergellina district on the western side of the Bay of Naples.

Naples' grand arcade, the glass-domed Galleria Umberto I

Naples' Museo Nazionale Archeologico is among the best archeological museums in Europe. Its collection covers classical sculpture, finds from Campania's ancient sites, as well as the finest artifacts and wall paintings taken from Pompeii and Herculaneum.

The museum's exhibits are poorly labeled and whole sections are often closed—though even if you see only a fraction of what it has to offer you should come away satisfied. Invest in an English-language guide if you want to be thorough—they are on sale at the ticket office.

The ground floor The ground floor is devoted mainly to sculpture, the bulk of it from the Farnese collection, established in the 17th century by one of Rome's leading patrician families (mostly from sites in Lazio and Campania). Its most astounding pieces are the *Farnese Hercules*, a triumphant muscular figure, and the *Farnese Bull*, the largest sculptural group to have survived from antiquity (restored after its discovery by Michelangelo). Both came from the Terme di Caracalla in Rome.

Other outstanding works include the famous *Javelin-thrower*; the Augustan-era *Eurydice and Hermes*; the *Venus Callipyge* (literally "Venus of the Beautiful Bottom"); and a figure of *Doyphorous* from Pompeii, one of the most accomplished Roman copies of a Greek original.

The upper floors Many upper floor rooms are devoted to mosaics and wall paintings, the majority removed from either Pompeii or Herculaneum. Among the mosaics look in particular for the *Battle of Issus*, a wonderfully realistic tableau showing Alexander the Great in battle with the Persians. Also hunt out the *Seascape* (a squid attacking a lobster), the *Street Musicians*, *Sorcerers* and *The Meeting of the Platonic Academy*.

Smaller exhibits
Leave plenty of time to study some of the smaller exhibits, too. Other rooms contain a wealth of artistic objects and household items from Pompeii. Two famous examples are the Tazza Farnese, a cup of veined sardonyx, and a 115-piece table service from the Casa del Menandro. Elsewhere, pieces of gladiatorial equipment—helmets, swords and trumpets—compete for attention with everyday items like shoes, pans, even dates, olives, onions, and cakes.

207

Maiden gathering flowers, *wallpainting from Stabiae*

CAMPANIA

▶▶▶ **Paestum**   *196A2*

Poseidonia was founded by the Greeks in the 6th century BC and renamed *Paestum* when it became a Roman colony in 273 BC After falling into virtual abandonment in the 9th century, the site was rediscovered in the 18th century. Today it is dominated by three honey-colored temples, among the greatest surviving Greek temples of antiquity.

The best-preserved is the **Tempio di Nettuno▶▶▶**, (actually dedicated to Hera) built in the 5th century BC Despite its age only the roof and a few interior walls are missing. Alongside it stands the so-called **Basilica di Hera▶▶**, larger but more ruined than its neighbor (its nine-column width makes it broader by three columns than the Parthenon). Somewhat apart rests the **Tempio di Cerere**, built around 500 BC. The colony's Roman monuments are less impressive—piles of rubble in most cases—though the excellent on-site museum fills in many of the gaps. Its most celebrated exhibits are a statue of Zeus; many 6th-century BC metopes (friezes); eight bronze hydrias (water vessels); and several rare painted Greek panels.

The superb Temple of Neptune at Paestum

▶▶ **Positano**   *196B2*

Few places are as picturesque as Positano, a pyramid of whitewashed houses spilling down from the mountains to the sea. Despite its small size it is one of the most monied and exclusive resorts on the Amalfi coast. This generally makes hotels an expensive proposition, but there are plenty of cafés and restaurants in which to while away an idle afternoon (as well as a couple of popular little beaches). Nearby **Praiano▶▶** is even smaller than Positano, but rapidly beginning to match it for prices and popularity.

► **Procida, Isola di**   *196B1*

Tiny Procida is less varied and spectacular than Capri or Ischia. It is, therefore, less popular, which means the possibility of swimming and eating in relative peace and quiet. Ferries and hydrofoils run here from Ischia, Pozzuoli, and Naples (Mergellina). Chiaiolella has the most attractive of the beaches, while the islet of Vivara's peaceful olive groves are the nicest places to walk.

►►► **Ravello**   *196B2*

"Closer to the sky than the seashore," wrote André Gide of Ravello, an enchantingly beautiful small town whose lofty setting (1,155 feet) offers stupendous views of the Amalfi coast. Panoramas aside, Ravello's main attractions are quiet lanes and two magical, romantic villas. The **Villa Cimbrone**►► is known for its wild gardens, lush and full of overgrown arbors and lichen-covered terraces. They shelter Ravello's loveliest spot—a belvedere providing unrivaled views of the coast. The **Villa Rufolo**►►is slightly less spectacular, a Saracen-Romanesque building begun in the 11th century. Home over the centuries to several popes, its most famous guest was Richard Wagner, who used its gardens as the inspiration for his opera *Parsifal*.

Ravello's Duomo, a handsome 11th-century church renovated in 1786, has fine bronze doors (1179)—modeled on those of Amalfi's cathedral—cast with 54 scenes from the Passion. Inside are two pulpits from the 12th and 13th centuries, decorated with mosaics and reliefs. There is also a small museum of antiquities.

Otherwise in Ravello there is little to do—one of its charms. It is also relatively quiet: being away from the coast, it has fewer visitors than Amalfi and Positano, and most of the tourists have left by mid-afternoon, making Ravello a tempting place to stay.

209

Top: Ravello
Above: pulpit, Ravello cathedral

► **Salerno**   *196B2*

Salerno is a dusty, modern ramshackle city, most famous as the site of the Allied landings of September 9, 1943. Its workaday atmosphere and scant sights do little to entice visitors, though its position makes it a convenient base for exploring Amalfi, Positano, and Ravello. The small medieval quarter is worth a few minutes for the **Duomo**►, whose bronze doors and inlaid pulpits (1173) resemble those of Amalfi and Ravello. The adjacent Museo del Duomo contains an early medieval altar-front, embellished with 54 ivory panels, the largest work of its kind.

Grotta di Smeraldo
About 8 miles along the coast road from Positano to Amalfi is the Grotta di Smeraldo, named after the eerie emerald glow that bathes its stalagmites and stalactites. An escalator takes you to the grotto from the road, or drive to Amalfi and take a boat (trips every two hours).

Terra di Lavoro
Northwest of Capua stretches the *Terra di Lavoro*, literally the "Land of Work," long one of Campania's prime agricultural regions. It is perhaps best known for its herds of water buffalo, which yield the milk that makes Italy's finest mozzarella cheese.

Excursions in the Cilento
The Cilento's rugged interior is scarcely explored, but almost any drive along its remote roads offers numerous scenic rewards. Try in particular the mountain roads in the north around the Monti Alburni; the desolate road from Laurito to Padula (on the A3 highway); the SS18 from Vallo di Lucania to Scario; and the short SS447 loop from Palinuro to Centola and Camerota.

► **Santa Maria Capua Vetere** 196C1

The approaches to Capua are unprepossessing—endless impoverished and semi-derelict suburbs—making it hard to believe that during Roman times this was the second most important city in Italy after Rome. Invading Arabs destroyed the old city around AD 830. Its **amphitheater►►**, once second only in size to the Colosseum, is these days in a fairly poor state of preservation: most of the seats and arches have collapsed—only the network of tunnels around the arena remains largely intact. Close by lies Italy's finest surviving **Mithraeum►►**, a temple to the Persian god Mithras. Its underground chamber has a vaulted ceiling painted with stars. Modern Capua, about 13 miles away, offers the **Museo Campano►**, which houses archeological finds from the ancient city. The **Duomo**, destroyed in 1942, has been rebuilt, but a 9th-century campanile survives.

► **Santa Maria di Castellabate** 196A2

Santa Maria is one of several small resorts clinging to the coast of the **Cilento►►**, a wild mountainous region recently added to the list of Italy's proposed national parks. A low-key place, the village gathers around a small harbor, a clean, golden beach stretching away to the north. **San Marco►**, 13 miles south, is another picturesque fishing village, dead in winter, but buzzing with life in summer. The region's spectacular coast road (the SS267-447) links with other resorts, most notably Acciaroli and cosmopolitan **Palinuro►**. You might also take a look at the rather patchy Roman ruins at *Velia*, close to the village of Marina di Velia.

►► **Sorrento** 196B1

Sorrento is popular with package tourists (80 percent of whom are British). It is easy to see why, for the town is an attractive and unpretentious place, perfectly placed for excursions to Pompeii and Herculaneum (via the Circumvesuviana railway), and for trips to Amalfi, Positano and Ravello—there is a local bus service. Boats run around the Sorrento peninsula to these towns, and in summer ply regularly to the islands of Capri and Ischia.

The great pleasures of Sorrento itself are its lush, shady gardens and its views. The belvedere behind the Museo Coreale is a favorite viewing point, and there are few sights to equal a dramatic Sorrento sunset. You can swim locally at nearby Marina Grande, at Regina Giovanna (on Punta del Capo), or the Villa di Pollio, a small park with old Roman ruins. Otherwise there is little to do but relax—something for which the town is tailor-made.

Sorrento, boats at rest

THE SORRENTO PENINSULA

Drive The Amalfi Coast

This drive takes in the Amalfi Coast, Italy's most spectacular stretch of coastline, and its dramatically situated towns and villages.

Start from the end of the A3 highway spur at Castellammare di Stabia, just a few miles east of Naples and Pompeii, and then follow the coastal road (the SS145) to **Sorrento** (page 210). Notice the tangle of roads beyond Massa Lubrense leading to the tip of the peninsula. Beyond Sorrento continue on the SS145, climbing to the ridges of the craggy mountains (the Monti Lattari) that form the peninsula's rocky backbone. The next 24 miles past **Positano** (page 208), **Praiano** and **Amalfi** (page 199) are some of the most breathtaking of any road in Europe. Just past Amalfi head inland to **Ravello** (page 209), and then either loop further inland to climb the slopes of Monte Cerreto, or return to Amalfi to pick up the the SS163 coast road to Vietri sul Mare and **Salerno** (page 209).

The popular resort of Sorrento, on the dramatic Amalfi Coast

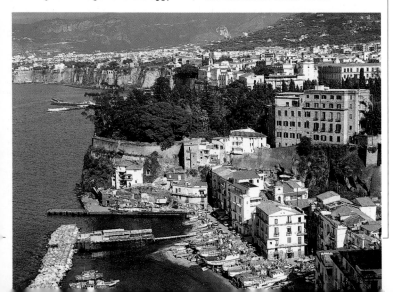

THE DEEP SOUTH

Essentials
Alberobello: The *trulli*
Bari: Basilica di San
Nicola, San Sabino
Castel del Monte: The
castle
Gargano: Beaches, Monte
Sant'Angelo
Lecce: Basilica di Santa
Croce, the town
Matera: The *sassi*
Martina Franca: Grotte di
Castellana
Taranto: Museo Nazionale
Trani: The Duomo
Troia: The Duomo

Tourist information
Bari: Corso Vittorio
Emanuele 68 (tel: 080/523
5186).
Lecce: Via Monte San
Michele 20 (tel: 0832/54
117) and Via Zanardelli 66
(tel: 0832/56 461).
Matera: Via di Viti de
Marco 9 (tel: 0835/331 983).
Taranto: Corso Umberto
121 (tel: 099/432 383).
Trani: Via Cavour 140 (tel:
0883/588 825).
Tropea: Viale Stazione 10
(tel: 0963/61 475).
Gargano: (Vieste) Corso
Lorenzo Fuzzini 8 (tel:
0884/707 495).

RI
Mola di
Bari
ugno
lássima   Grotte di
Castellana
Turi   Monópoli
aviva   Castellana Grotte
conti   Pútignano   Fasano
del   Noci   Alberobello   **Ostuni**
le   Martina   **Brindisi**
              Franca
Massafra   Mesagne
Grottáglie   San Pietro Vernotico
za   Francavilla   Squinzano
          Fontana   San Cataldo
TARANTO   Campi   **Lecce**
     San Giorgio   Salentina
Mataponto   Iónico   Mandúria
                    Copertino

olfo   di   Táranto   Nardò   Galatina   Otranto
              Galátone   Máglie   Capo d'Otranto
púlico   Gallípoli   Santa Cesárea

                    Ugento
lfo di   Gagliano del
gliano   Capo
                    Capo Santa Maria
no   di Léuca

A   Punta Alice
ale   Cirò Marina
ria

jovanni   *Neto*
òre
5m   *Gariglione*
Gariglione   **Crotone**
a
          Isola di
          Capo Rizzuto
anzaro   Capo Rizzuto

Golfo di
Squillace

0   10   20   30   40   50 km
0   10   20   30 miles

3   4

THE DEEP SOUTH

The Deep South Calabria, Basilicata and Apulia are the heart of the south—an area cut off for centuries by history and geography from the rest of Italy. Despite considerable efforts, it is still poorer and more backward than northern Italy, an imbalance worsening with the north's apparently increasing antagonism.

The south, with relatively little in the way of art or monuments, still evokes in atmosphere the Mediterranean Italy of old. Its landscapes are unspoiled, its villages ancient and many places never see a tourist. Its downside lies in a Byzantine bureaucracy, a decaying infrastructure, and a shortage of tourist facilities. But approach the south in the right spirit and it has much to recommend it, not least the fact that it costs less for eating and sleeping.

History The Greeks colonized all three regions, establishing cities in what become known as Magna Graecia (Greater Greece). The Romans were less influential, though Brindisi—connected to Rome by the Via Appia—became one of their most important links with the East. The Arabs and Byzantines held sway in the Dark Ages and influenced the region's architecture (Basilicata takes its name from *basilikos*, the name of the Byzantine administration). They were succeeded in the 11th century by the Normans, and later by the Swabians, most notably Frederick II (see panel) and the Angevins (French). For centuries after the south stagnated under the Spanish.

Calabria The "toe" of the Italian boot, though bereft of any special artistic treasures, has an unspoiled coastline and grand, wild interior. The eastern (Ionian) coast is largely monotonous; except for a few towns such as Stilo and Rossano, the resort-dotted western (Tyrrhenian) littoral is more spectacular. The Calabrian interior comprises sun-baked plains and the rounded, wooded slopes of the Sila mountains, a large, sometimes rather laborious area to explore, but brimming with natural beauty and half-forgotten villages.

Basilicata Basilicata is Italy's poorest region. Its towns and villages are the country's least discovered, its intractable landscapes some of Europe's least developed. The Pollino mountains and hills of the Sauro valley offer magnificent drives, while Matera has the unforgettable *sassi*, ancient cave dwellings that riddle the ravines around the town. Melfi, the Normans' first southern power base, is an attractive town and makes a good center for exploring some of the region's more appealing abbeys and castles.

Apulia (Puglia) Apulia is by far the most rewarding part of the south. Rocky and sun-bleached, or smothered in vineyards and olive groves, it offers little fine scenery, except in the Gargano, a promontory of beaches, cliffs and forest that forms the spur of the Italian boot. But whitewashed, Greek-looking villages dot the coast, and the famous *trulli* (curious, beehive-like buildings of unknown antiquity, some still in use), punctuate the countryside around Alberobello. Many towns are showcases for Apulian-Romanesque architecture, and in Lecce the Italian baroque finds its greatest expression.

►► **Alberobello** (see page 223)   *213D3*

►► **Bari**   *213D3*

Bari's almost Arabic warren of medieval streets is in marked contrast to the mundane promenades of the modern city. At its heart lies the **Basilica di San Nicola**►►►, a prototype for many of the region's great Apulian-Romanesque churches. Started in the 11th century, it was built to house the body of St. Nicholas, the patron saint of Holy Russia, pawnbrokers, sailors, and children (he is the St. Nicholas of Santa Claus fame). Inside, the ciborium (altar canopy) and episcopal throne are two of the finest such works in Italy. Note also the silver altarpiece (1684) and the precious exhibits of the church Treasury.

The **Cattedrale di San Sabino**►►► close by is another exceptional if more austere Romanesque church. Also worth seeing are the **Castello**►, rebuilt by Frederick II around 1240, and the **Museo Archeologico**►► housing Apulia's most complete collection of antiquities.

Drive 10 miles west and Bitonto's quiet maze of medieval streets makes a welcome getaway. Its fine 13th-century Apulian-Romanesque cathedral has an unusual *matroneum*, or women's gallery.

Decorated doorway of San Nicola, Bari

►►► **Castel del Monte**   *212D2*

This mighty fortress built around 1240 by Frederick II is one of the great medieval buildings of Europe. It is also one of the most mysterious, scholars having puzzled for centuries over its purpose and peculiar mathematical obsession. It is an octagonal building, built around an octagonal courtyard, flanked by eight towers which themselves are octagonal. Each of its floors contains eight rooms.

It may be that eight was a symbol of the crown, or that Frederick was imitating Jerusalem's octagonal Omar mosque. Another theory is that the castle's mathematical precision was astrological, for its proportions are supposed to relate to the movements of the planets. Others claim that it was a hunting lodge, or a refuge for pilgrims in search of the Holy Grail. In any event, it has few of the defensive features normally associated with medieval castles—only a magnificent position, its gloriously isolated bastions visible for miles around.

215

Frederick II's enigmatic fortress, Castel del Monte

Part of the rocky coastline of the Gargano peninsula

►►► (II) Gargano
212E2

The "spur" of the Italian boot is a hilly and largely wooded limestone peninsula edged with rocky cliffs, whitewashed villages, and broad sandy beaches. While the interior remains unvisited, the coast—in summer at least—is crowded and commercialized. Visit out of season, however, and the resorts are delightfully quiet.

Siponto► (Roman **Sipontum**) boasts a fine museum and the lovely 11th-century Romanesque church of **Santa Maria di Siponto**, but the Gargano starts in earnest at **Monte Sant'Angelo►►**. This windblown mountaintop eyrie was for almost 1,500 years one of Italy's most revered Christian shrines following several apparitions of the Archangel Michael in the 5th century. The most famous took place in a cave now contained in the **Santuario di San Michele►►** (note the beautiful bronze doors).

Moving around the coast, **Mattinata►** is a small resort with a magnificent beach, linked by a scenic road to **Pugnochiuso►**, set in a panoramic bay, and **Vieste►►**, the Gargano's busiest town. Nearby **Peschici►►**, however, makes a more attractive base, being quieter, prettier, and well placed for access to beaches (and numerous small grottoes).

Stonework on the Santuario di San Michele, Monte Sant'Angelo

►   Gerace
212A2

Rugged Gerace, perched on an impregnable crag, boasts Calabria's largest church, a Norman cathedral built in 1045 and enlarged by Frederick II in 1222. Its unadorned interior is supported by 20 ancient columns, many taken from the ruins of old Greek temples at nearby Locri. Be sure to see the Treasury with its exquisite Renaissance ivory crucifix. When you tire of exploring this unspoiled town, you might shop around for Gerace's distinctive local pottery.

▶▶▶ Lecce 213D4

Lecce is to the baroque what Florence is to the Renaissance. Counter-Reformationary zeal and mercantile money transformed much of the city in the 17th century. Churches, palaces—even houses and simple courtyards— were given a glorious baroque veneer of *putti*, gargoyles, garlands, stone curlicues, and wreaths of exuberant decoration. There is so much to see, it is best to wander at random, but start with the **Basilica di Santa Croce▶▶▶**, the apotheosis of Lecce's airy baroque style. Next door stands the **Palazzo del Governo▶**, designed by Zimbalo and Giuseppe Cino, architects responsible for many of the city's buildings. They also worked on **Piazza del Duomo's▶▶** cathedral and Palazzo del Seminario, as well as the Carmine, Gesù, Rosario, and Santa Chiara churches. Non-baroque sights include the ruins of the **Roman amphitheater▶**, Romanesque **SS Nicola e Cataldo▶** and the art and antiquities of the **Museo Provinciale▶▶**.

▶ Lucera 212E1

Lucera's windy hilltop site and tangle of inviting streets make it a wonderful place to explore. The **Duomo▶▶** is one of the region's more alluring medieval buildings, though the tremendous Frederick II **fortress▶▶** is more likely to command your attention. The second largest in southern Italy, it has walls that stretch over a mile.

Basilica di Santa Croce, Lecce

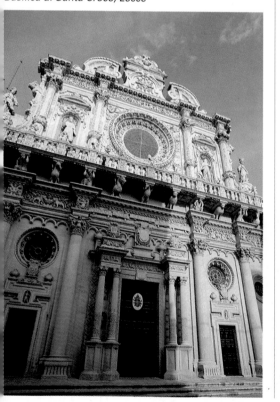

Wine tasting
Lecce's *Enoteca Internazionale* has an extensive range of Apulian, Italian and international wines served by the glass or bottle with light meals (Via Cesare Battisti 23).

The Tavoliere
Lucera's lofty position and its immense fortress look down over the plains of the *Tavoliere*, or "chess-board," named after the checkered pattern created by the region's wheatfields. The land has looked like this since Roman times, when it was parceled up into squares for distribution to retired army officers.

Romanesque Apulia

Apulia is perhaps best known for its remarkably vast number of Romanesque churches and cathedrals. Each in its way is a monument to the architectural styles bequeathed over the centuries by the region's many invaders. The influences of the Normans, Arabs, Lombards, and Byzantines all coalesce to produce the magnificent hybrid known as Apulian-Romanesque.

Why Apulia? Building a church was no easy matter. Political stability was needed for a start. Long-term projects required sustained peace and finance if they were to be completed. In Apulia, the strong government of Norman, Swabian, and Angevin rulers allowed craftsmen long periods of creative endeavor. It also meant they could travel unmolested, absorbing new trends, and moving their workshops to where demand was highest. Apulia in this respect was a religious crucible, for it lay on several vital pilgrimage routes. Its ports were also points of embarkation for pilgrims bound for the Holy Land.

Lions and griffins guard the entrance to Ruvo di Puglia's fine Apulian-Romanesque cathedral

Rome and Byzantium No two Apulian churches are alike, and no set rules govern their architectural styles, but the variety, richness of decoration, and sculptural skill that make them one of the glories of Italian medieval art are bound by a few unifying strands. The earliest classical models reached Apulian church builders via Byzantium. They contributed decorative motifs—crisp-cut and stylized—such as acanthus leaves, vine tendrils, animals and birds. Later, Roman portraiture and sarcophagi also played their part.

The Lombards Lombard sculpture also had a great influence on Apulian churches: lions, snakes, centaurs, hunters, fishes, and bizarre menageries frequently feature on church portals. Architecturally the Lombards contributed high central naves (with lower aisles), triform apsidal ends, and the arched corbel table below the roof. They also provided the beautiful lateral galleries formed of open arcades.

Arabs and Normans Norman supremacy in the 11th century brought influences from France and Normandy, notably a grandeur of design and execution. Tuscan craftsmen were employed in northern Apulia, taking the "striped" Pisan churches as their model. Oriental features filtered through from Arab Sicily, notably interlaced arches and pointed Saracenic arches. Finally, Frederick II reintroduced further classical Roman refinements.

▶▶ **Maratea** *212C2*

Pretty Maratea, on the Basilicata coast, is as pleasant as any of the resorts on the Calabrian seaboard to the south. It divides into several districts: Maratea Porto, with fishermen's cottages, bars and restaurants; hilltown Maratea Inferiore, home to most of the hotels and fun to explore; and Maratea Superiore, the upper town, from which you can climb to the evocative ruins of Maratea Vecchia (walk a little farther and you come to the top of Monte San Biagio, with magnificent views over the Gulf of Policastro and Maratea's 72-foot statue of the Redeemer). The best beaches are 3 miles away at Maratea Marina, but the coast is studded with bays where you are able to swim in complete privacy.

▶ **Martina Franca** *213D3*

Martina Franca's high-rise outskirts do not look promising, but the town center is a marvelous showcase of baroque and rococo architecture. Its centerpiece is the church of **San Martino▶▶**, fronted by a soaring baroque façade. Walk down Via Cavour and you are also treated to numerous exuberantly decorated houses and *palazzi*. The 300-roomed **Palazzo Ducale▶** should not be missed, nor the churches of the Carmine and San Domenico. Find time to wander the old **walls▶** for a lovely panorama over the *trulli*-dotted patchwork of fields and vineyards of the Itria valley. The area's prime tourist attraction lies 17 miles north of the town, the **Grotte di Castellana**, a great cave system ending in the impressive Caverna Bianca.

Scenic drives
Calabria: the SS105 Belvedere Marittimo–Castrovillari; SS177 Rossano–Cosenza; SS179/SS109 San Giovanni in Fiore–Catanzaro; SS179 Stilo–Serra San Bruno; (*Aspromonte*) SS183/184 Reggio di Calabria–Gambarie–Melito. (*Basilicata*): SS7 Potenza–Matera; SS19 Lagonegro–Rivello–Mormanno–(Rotonda)–Castrovillari. (*Apulia*): SS89 Manfredonia–Monte Sant'Angelo–Vieste–Peschici–Rodi–Garganico; SS528 Monte Sant'Angelo–Vico del Gargano; SS172 Putignano–Alberobello–Martina Franca.

219

Martina Franca: the restrained elegance of the fountain (left) contrasts with the baroque flamboyance of the architectural detail (above)

▶ **Massafra** *213D3*

Massafra bears striking similarities to Matera (see page 221). Divided in two by a deep ravine, the Gravina di San Marco, it is riddled with grottoes, troglodyte dwellings, and early Greek Christian cave churches (which date from the 9th to 14th centuries). The best churches are San Marco, La Candelora and San Leonardo. Some of the town's buildings are not well marked by signs and difficult to reach, but a dramatic baroque staircase leads clearly to **Madonna della Scala▶▶**, built around an early cave church—with delicate 12th-century frescos—and a primitive 8th-century crypt.

The Tavole Paladine at Metaponto, a temple dedicated to the goddess Hera

▶▶ **Matera** (see opposite page)   *212D2*

▶▶ **Melfi**   *212D2*

The Normans' occupation of Apulia began when 11 brothers came from Normandy offering their mercenary army in the service of local barons. In 1041 they captured Melfi and two years later elected William de Hauteville their leader. William's sons, Drogo and Humphrey, were succeeded by Robert Guiscard, recognized as "Duke of Apulia and Calabria" by Pope Nicholas II after campaigns against the Saracens (in 1059).

Dark and medieval Melfi still lies in the shadow of its Norman castle (1155), standing proud despite the earthquakes that have laid the town low over the centuries. Inside is a small museum with Greek, Roman and Byzantine finds, its prize exhibit a 1st-century Roman sarcophagus, the *Sarcofago di Rapolla*.

▶ **Metaponto**   *213C3*

Once home to Pythagoras, *Metapontion* in the 7th century BC was among the most flourishing colonies of Magna Graecia. Although its ruins today are the region's most extensive, they are spread over a large area and their effect is patchy—nor is modern Metaponto, despite its beaches, anything to write home about. The **Antiquarium**▶▶, however, is highly worthwhile, a well-presented museum of finds from the site. In its grounds is the **Tavole Paladine**▶▶, the 15-columned ruins of a 6th-century BC Doric temple. Most of the other remains lie scattered across the **Parco Archeologico**▶.

▶▶ **Otranto**   *213C4*

Greek in origin, Italy's easternmost town nestles around a small harbor. It is an attractive fishing village, becoming increasingly popular despite its mediocre beach. Its cathedral, **Santa Maria Annunziata**▶▶, is remarkable for the fresco-covered crypt (1088)—supported by 42 tiny columns—and a beautiful mosaic (1165) that runs the length of the nave. In a mixture of themes, it portrays Biblical stories, illustrates the *Months of the Year* and *The Tree of Life*, and includes characters as diverse as King Arthur, Alexander the Great, and the Queen of Sheba. Also see the town's mighty **Castello**▶ (an Aragonese fortress), and the 10th-century church of **San Pietro**▶.

Bizarrely picturesque Matera is unique for its *sassi*, cave dwellings dug from the living rock in the ravines around the town. Many have been inhabited since prehistoric times. A few have been turned into cave churches; others form an elaborate honeycomb of streets and alleys.

Disease and designer dwellings Although Matera's *sassi* appear romantic today, earlier this century they represented the ugly face of Italy, racked by unimaginable poverty and riddled with diseases like malaria, dysentery, and trachoma. Over the years their inhabitants have been rehoused in the modern apartments of the new town, only for the old caves to become the latest in designer homes for more affluent town residents. About 700 people now live in the *sassi*.

The best way to get an overall picture of the labyrinth is on the Strada Panoramica, a scenic road specially built for sightseers. To see some of the nooks and crannies, and the rock churches, slip into the smaller backstreets or employ one of the children who for a tip will take you to places you might not otherwise find.

Seeing the *sassi* The *sassi* divide into two main districts, the Sasso Caveoso (nearest the eastern end of the Strada Panoramica) and Sasso Barisano. Broadly speaking there are four types of cave: the oldest are the niches cut into the sides of the ravine, inhabited up to 7,000 years ago; the second type date from 2000 BC (and form the heart of the Sasso Caveoso); the third are 1,000 years old and lie along Via B Buozzi; the fourth are the dwellings around Via Fiorentini, most of which were excavated during the 17th century.

Rock churches Of special interest are the *chiese rupestri*, or cave churches, of which there are about 120 around the town. Most were carved by monks between the 8th and 13th centuries. Two of the best, San Pietro Caveoso and Santa Maria de Idris, lie close to one another. Both boast 14th-century Byzantine rock paintings. Santa Lucia alle Malve, a 10th-century church, is also worth a visit.

The gray labyrinth of sassi, extraordinary cave houses of Matera

One of the Greek Bronzi di Riace in Reggio di Calabria's Museo Nazionale

▶ **Reggio di Calabria** 212A2

Calabria's grim capital is worth braving only for the **Museo Nazionale▶▶**, a splendid collection of material from archeological sites all over Calabria and Basilicata. Its pride and joy, the *Bronzi di Riace*, were retrieved from the sea in a chance discovery in 1972. The two 5th-century BC sculptures depict a pair of Greek warriors, one at least believed to be the work of Phidias, regarded as the greatest sculptor of antiquity. Other prominent works include votive tablets from the Temple of Persephone at *Locri* and two paintings by Antonello da Messina, *Saint Jerome* and *Abraham and the Angels*.

▶ **Riviera Calabrese (Calabrian Riviera)** 212B2

The Calabrian Riviera is a term of convenience for a fairly uniform succession of resorts, beaches and gently unassuming countryside on the region's Tyrrhenian coast. Development is often less marked than in Italy's northern resorts, but towns still have a wide choice of hotels, restaurants, and nightlife. Most spots are crowded with Italians on vacation in summer, but sleepy and undisturbed out of season. Tropea (see page 225) is far and away the best destination, but other nice places include San Nicola Arcella; Diamante (an unusually chic resort); Amantea; and Pizzo (a reasonable alternative to Tropea).

222

Aspromonte

The "Bitter Mountain" is an incredibly wild region east of Reggio di Calabria. It is one of Italy's most isolated areas, and ways of life here have changed little in centuries. Aspromonte's mountain fastness is a traditional haunt of Calabria's kidnappers (though the area is perfectly safe). Excursions on its high roads offer astounding landscapes and ancient villages where Greek dialects are still spoken.

▶▶ **Rossano** 213C3

This picturesque little hilltown was the most important Byzantine center in the south during the 9th century. The greatest monument to its illustrious past is the *Codex Purpureus*, a beautifully illuminated 6th-century manuscript kept in the **Museo Diocesano▶▶▶**. The 188-page volume contains the Gospels of St. Matthew and St. Mark, and was probably brought to Italy by monks fleeing Muslim persecution. While you are in Rossano, do not miss 10th-century **San Marco▶▶**, Calabria's finest Byzantine church, lent a strongly Middle Eastern flavor by its palm trees and tiny cupolas. Its terrace offers a fine view over Rossano's cave-riddled gorge. The town has several other frescoed Byzantine churches, most notably La Panaghia and Santa Maria del Pilerio.

▶▶ **Ruvo di Puglia** 212D2

Ruvo's **Museo Jatta▶▶** offers a collection of the 5th- to 3rd-century BC ceramics for which the town was famous. Among its 1,700-plus terracottas is the famous red-figured Greek vase known as the *Krater of Talos*. The **Duomo▶▶** is one of the region's more important pieces of Apulian-Romanesque architecture, its rather severe façade relieved by a richly decorated portal and exquisite rose window. (Notice the griffins flanking the main doorway and the little pagan figures around the sides of the building. It is thought they may have been copied from pieces of classical pottery.)

Nobody knows the real age or origins of Apulia's *trulli*, the strange and conical dwellings that are found solely in a small region around Alberobello and nowhere else in Europe.

Practical but puzzling *Trulli* are round, single-story buildings made with uncemented stones. They are invariably whitewashed, and their tapered roofs are usually crowned with hieroglyphics—often a cross or some more arcane symbol (possibly of unknown magical significance). The oldest surviving example dates back to the 13th century, though most are no more than 300 years old. Their origins, however, are certainly more ancient.

At their most basic, the houses are practical—there is plenty of local limestone and they are simple to build; they remain cool in summer and are easily heated in winter. By these criteria, they should be found all over the Mediterranean. Why they occur only in Apulia is not known—though there is no shortage of theories.

Tax evasion? For a time it was thought they were built to outwit Ferdinand I of Aragon who, during his reign, forbade the Apulians to build permanent houses (in this way he could move laborers around as they were needed). The peasants responded by constructing houses that could be dismantled when the king's inspectors were spotted. This theory is now discredited, along with the notion that the houses were designed as a wily form of tax evasion. During Spanish rule a tax was levied on individual houses, only unfinished buildings being exempt, a clause, it is claimed, the *trulli*-owners exploited with their loose-stoned and easily removed roofs.

Greece or the Middle East A more persuasive idea links them with similar buildings at Mycenae, an idea which would connect the *trulli* with the Greek civilization of 3000 BC Apulian ports are the closest to Greece, and for centuries the region was part of Magna Graecia. On the same lines, and perhaps closer to the truth, is the theory that they were imported from the Middle East—a conjecture based on their similarity to the "sugar loaf" houses of Syria and elsewhere. They were possibly introduced by Eastern monks—and used initially as tombs—or copied by soldiers returning from the Crusades.

One of Apulia's mysterious trulli

Excursion from the Sila
The scenic SS110 meanders lazily to Serra San Bruno (22 miles), with its Certosa di Santo Stefano, founded in 1090 by St. Bruno, originator of the strict Carthusian order (the abbey is closed to women). A couple of miles away is the church of Santa Maria del Bosco, a church where you can see a cave where the saint is said to have prayed. The waters of the spring here are reputed to be effective for exorcisms.

►   **Sila**   *212B2*

Calabria's mountainous interior divides into three jumbled massifs—the Sila Grande, Sila Piccola and Sila Greca—large areas of which are protected by the Parco Nazionale della Calabria. Almost the Apennines' last gasp, they have long been famous for their forests (from about the 6th century onward, timber from the Sila provided the wooden roofs for many of Rome's churches). Today the scenery is wild and unspoiled, though the long rolling ridges and endless woods can become monotonous. Camigliatello and San Giovanni in Fiore (a less attractive town) are the main bases, Lakes Arvo, Cecita and Ampollino the most picturesque areas. Roads off the SS107 (SS177, SS179 and SS108bis) offer the best drives, and there is a superbly scenic little railway from Cosenza to San Giovanni in Fiore.

►   **Stilo**   *212A2*

Any fan of early church architecture should make a beeline for Stilo, home to **La Cattolica►►** an important if rather ramshackle Byzantine church of indeterminate age (estimates range from 10th-century to 12th-century). Its brick and stone weathered to a lovely red-brown hue, the church looks out over a rocky valley, a major retreat for Basilian monks in southern Calabria (as Rossano was for their counterparts in the north of the region). Note the upturned ancient column in the nave, reputedly a symbol of Christianity's triumph over paganism. The town has several other churches of lesser antiquity.

The rolling forested landscape of the Sila

►   **Taranto**   *213D3*

A large port and naval base, Taranto has one important tourist attraction, the **Museo Nazionale►►►**. The museum's emphasis is on Magna Graecia, embracing a wide range of Greek statues, ceramics and the world's largest collection of Greek terracottas (50,000 pieces). Its centerpiece is the *Sala degli Ori*, a room devoted to goldware. Other highlights include a pair of *korai* (figurines of young girls); a series of Roman portraits; several actors' masks; busts of Apollo and Aphrodite; and a variety of bas-reliefs and mosaics from the town's tombs.

▶▶ **Trani** *212D2*

Trani is an elegant and picturesque Apulian port, once a rival to Bari as the region's most important maritime power and still a cosmopolitan town. Today its fame rests on the **Duomo▶▶▶**, one of the area's finest examples of Apulian-Romanesque architecture. The cathedral's beauty is given added impact by the fact that it sits virtually on the sea's edge. Tremendous bronze doors, cast in 1180, usher you into a three-tiered church. Most of the interior is Norman, though part rests on the Ipogea di San Leucio, a 6th-century paleo-Christian tomb. In the rest of town, try not to miss the church of Ognissanti, built as a hospice by the Knights Templar; the Palazzo Caccetta, a 15th-century Gothic palace (Gothic buildings are rare in Apulia); and the Castello, built for Frederick II in 1233 (but since rebuilt). Also walk around the medieval quarter, centered around Via Mario Pagano, and take time out in the Villa Comunale (Public Gardens) near the seafront.

▶▶ **Troia** *212E1*

Quiet and windblown, Troia is a pretty village, distinguished by its splendid **cathedral▶▶▶**. Built in 1093, it has a sumptuous rose window, as well as a pair of 12th-century bronze doors, all tinged with the classical, Saracen, and Byzantine motifs that characterize Apulian-Romanesque architecture. Inside do take a look at the curious carved 12th-century pulpit, the capitals and the paintings, manuscripts and furnishings of the **Museo Diocesano▶**.

▶▶ **Tropea** *212B2*

A huddle of pastel-colored houses perched above the sea, and surrounded by golden beaches, Tropea is by far the nicest resort on the Calabrian coast (the Riviera Calabrese). Although fashionable and popular, the town manages to retain its charm, and has hotels and *trattorie* in most price ranges. When not enjoying Tropea's beaches, seafood or picturesque streets, visit the church of Santa Maria dell'Isola, dramatically situated on a limestone crag near the sea. Also look into the Duomo, known for two strange works of art: an inlaid 16th-century Black Crucifix, and the Madonna of Rumania, which was reputedly painted by St. Luke.

Trani's cathedral, a jewel of the Apulian-Romanesque style

225

Scylla and Charybdis
The legendary sea monsters of Homer's *Odyssey* were probably whirlpools created in the Straits of Messina by the meeting of the Ionian and Tyrrhenian seas. Ships to this day must navigate with care in these waters. *Scylla* corresponds to Calabria's modern-day village of Scilla: *Charybdis* is Cariddi on the Sicilian mainland.

The church of Santa Maria dell'Isola, Tropea

SICILY

The island of Sicily

Colorful Sicilian ceramics for the tourist market

I Strómboli

I Basiluzzo
I Panarea

Isole Eólie o Lipari

I Filicudi
I Salina
cudi

I Lípari • Lípari
I Vulcano

Torre
Faro
C di Milazzo Villafranca
Tirrena
Milazzo MESSINA Villa San
Giovanni
Gioiosa A20
Marea C Calava
Brolo
Capo d'Orlando Barcellona Pozzo
Sant'Ágata A20 di Gotto RÉGGIO DI
di Militello Patti Furnari CALÁBRIA
Caronia Naso 1287m
San Pza di Verna A18
Fratello Tortorici Novara
o Stéfano Monti 1847m di Sicilia Roccalumera
amastra Nébrodi Santa Teresa di Riva
Mistretta Mte Soro Taormina Sant'Alessio Siculo
Cerami Cesarò Randazzo Letojanni
gi Mazzaró
A Nicosia Troina Linguaglossa Giardini-Náxos
L di Bronte 3323m Fiumefreddo di Sicilia
Pozzillo Etna Riposto
onforte Agira Adrano Giarre 227
Catenanuova Regalbuto Milo A18
nna Paternò Nicolosi Trecastagni
Valguarnera Misterbianco Acireale
Caropepe A19 Aci Castello
iazza Aidone CATÁNIA
merina Ramacca Piana di
Villa Casale Catánia Golfo di Catánia
franca Palagonia
zzarino Caltagirone Francofonte Lentini C Santa Croce
Grammichele Augusta
Niscemi Melilli Golfo di
Vizzini Sortino Augusta
a 986m Palazzolo
d'Acate Giarratana Acréide Floridia Siracusa
Acate Akrai Canicattini A18
Cómiso Noto Bagni Capo Murro
Vittória Ragusa di Porco
Gela Módica Noto Ávola
Rosolini Golfo di Noto
Marina di Ragusa Scicli Íspica
Pozzallo Pachino

Capo Pássero
Capo Isola
delle Correnti

4   5

Sicily Cross the sea to Sicily and you do more than leave the Italian mainland. You cross to an island that stands on the edge of Europe, a place whose history and culture conspire to make it a world apart. Almost every Mediterranean power over the last 2,000 years has ruled its shores, not only leaving a mark on its art and architecture, but also molding its cuisine and shaping its attitude to foreigners (a breed that for some Sicilians also includes other Italians). Although subjugation—together with poverty and the Mafia—have often crippled the island, they have rarely cowed its population. As a result you will find Sicilians some of the most singular and most hospitable of Italians.

SICILY

Goethe's judgment
"To have seen Italy without seeing Sicily is not to have seen Italy at all, for Sicily is the clue to everything."
Goethe (*Italian Journey*).

History Sicily is named after its early Siculo and Sicano tribes (1250 BC). Given the 500 years of Greek domination (from 800–300 BC), it could as easily have kept its Greek name, *Trinacria* (after the island's triangular shape: Greek *treis*—three—and *akra*—point). During this period cities like Syracuse and Agrigento were among the most powerful in Europe. Roman rule followed, superseded by the Vandals and then by the Byzantines. Two centuries of Arab rule from 827 produced another golden age, followed by a further upbeat period under the Normans (1061–1194). Henry IV, son of Frederick Barbarossa, imposed a period of imperial Swabian rule, soon followed by Angevin domination under Charles of Anjou (brother of the French king). The famous Sicilian Vespers (1282), after a brief period of independence, brought in the Spanish, who ruled Sicily in one guise or another until the 19th century.

The Greek temple of Segesta in its magnificent flower-strewn setting

Art and architecture Sicily is laden with monuments from each of its historical epochs. The Greeks bequeathed the theaters of Syracuse and Taormina, and the temples of Agrigento, Selinunte and Segesta. The Romans created the mosaics of Piazza Armerina; Arabs, Byzantines and Normans left numerous fine buildings, and influenced the architecture of countless others. Swabians and Angevins built palaces and churches, many overlaid with the baroque stamp of the Spanish (most notably those in Noto and Ragusa). All the strands come together in Palermo, one of Italy's great artistic capitals, but few towns are without treasures from one or more periods.

Essentials
Agrigento: Valley of the Temples
Cefalù: The Duomo
Monreale: The Duomo, cloisters
Mount Etna: Excursions
Palermo: Palazzo dei Normanni, Cappella Palatina
Piazza Armerina: Roman mosaics at Villa Casale
Segesta: The temple, views
Siracusa: Duomo, Parco Archeologico, Museo Nazionale
Taormina: Teatro Greco, views

Landscapes The last 30 years have not been kind to the Sicilian coast. Time and again you come across ranks of derelict factories or half-built houses destroying what must once have been an idyllic coast. Cefalù and lovely Taormina are notable exceptions, and things are better on the islands—the unspoiled Egadi, for example, or the volcanic Lipari. In the interior they are better still, with landscapes as strange and spectacular as any in Italy. Modern housing has left its mark, but few could fail to be moved by Mount Etna, Europe's greatest volcano, or by the stark grandeur and lunar emptiness of the rolling interior plateaus. The mountains, too, are a revelation, especially the Madonie and Nebrodi, whose high, wooded ridges run along much of the northern coast.

Food Eating is one of Sicily's great pleasures, Greek, Arab, Norman, and Spanish influences combining to form a unique cuisine. The quality and variety of fruit and vegetables in the markets is superb, and in restaurants the array of specialties is overwhelming. Seafood figures heavily, notably mussels (*cozze*), tuna (*tonno*), sardines (*sardi*) and swordfish (*pesce spada*). Fish sauces for pasta are good, especially *pasta con le sarde*. Chillis, capers, olives, peppers and eggplant are widely used (notably in *caponata*, a local "sweet-and-sour" specialty). Sicilian desserts are legendary. Ice cream was reputedly first made by the Arabs using snow from Etna. *Cassata* is an ice cream cake, *granita* crushed ice flavored with coffee or lemon. *Zabaglione*, a frothy whip of eggs and Marsala wine, and *cannoli*, a cream-filled pastry, must both be sampled at least once.

When and how to go Spring is the best time to visit Sicily, when the weather is warm and the hills covered in wildflowers. July and August are uncomfortably hot and crowded, while September and October are pleasanter (and you can often swim as late as November).

There are several ways of reaching Sicily from the mainland, including regular car ferries to Messina from Villa San Giovanni and Reggio di Calabria. Overnight car ferries operate daily from Naples to Palermo, and once a week to Catania and Syracuse.

Mount Etna seen from Taormina

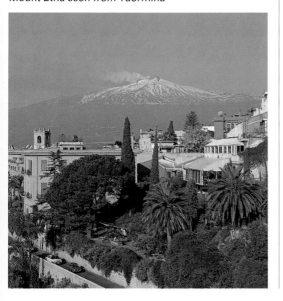

Tourist information
Agrigento: Viale della Vittoria 255 (tel: 0922/401 352).
Cefalù: Via Amendola 2 (tel: 0921/21 050).
Enna: Piazza Garibaldi 1 (tel: 0935/500 901).
Lipari: Corso Vittorio Emanuele 239 (tel: 090/981 1190).
Monreale: Piazza Duomo (tel: 091/640 2448).
Palermo: Piazza Castelnuovo 35 (tel: 091/331 861).
Piazza Armerina: Via Cavour 15 (tel: 0935/680 201).
Siracusa: Via San Sebastiano 43 (tel: 0931/677 607).
Taormina: Piazza Santa Catarina (tel: 0942/23 243).

229

Scenic drives
(*Mount Etna*): Catania–Nicolosi–Rifugio Sapienza; Linguaglossa–Rifugio Citelli–Milo; SS120 Adrano–Bronte–Randazzo.
(*Madonie mountains*): Cefalù–Collesano–Piano Battaglia–Petralia Soprana; SS286/SS120 Cefalù–Gibilmanna–Castelbuono–Gangi–Nicosia; SS117 Mistretta–Nicosia–Enna.

SICILY

The Temple of Concord at Agrigento (ancient Acragas), one of the most complete Greek temples remaining

Operatic taste
There is a famous pasta specialty named after one of the operas of Catania-born composer Vincenzo Bellini. You should be able to sample *pasta alla Norma* (a tomato and egg-plant sauce garnished with basil and cheese) in any of the trattorias on Via Etnea.

▶▶▶   **Agrigento**   226B3

Although modern Agrigento detracts from the setting, the **Valle dei Templi**▶▶▶ (Valley of the Temples) is one of Europe's greatest archeological sites. Only ruins now remain of perhaps Magna Graecia's foremost city.

The eastern zone of the site contains the **Tempio di Ercole (Hercules)**▶▶, a temple built around the time of the colony's foundation in 582 BC Nearby are the ruins of a paleo-Christian necropolis, and the tawny-stoned **Tempio della Concordia (Concord)**▶▶▶, the best-preserved Greek temple in the world after the Theseion in Athens. From here a path follows the old walls to the **Tempio di Giunone (Juno)**▶▶, a lonely and majestic ruin at the edge of the site.

In the western zone stands the **Tempio di Giove (Jupiter)**▶, planned as the Greek world's largest temple, but left unfinished after an attack by the Carthaginians in 405·BC Here, too, is a *telamone*, a monumental column carved as a human figure, and the Tempio dei Dioscuri, a fake temple built in 1832 from miscellaneous fragments.

The **Museo Nazionale Archeologico**▶▶▶, a mile from the site, houses an overwhelming collection of artifacts removed from Agrigento and its environs. Outstanding are its *telamone*; a *krater*, or vase, depicting the *Battle of the Amazons*; the *Efebo*, a statue of a young man; a statuette known as the *Sitting Venus*; and several lion's head carvings removed from the temples.

Also pop into the adjacent church of **San Nicola**▶, both for its views of the temples, and for the Greek and Roman fragments incorporated in its walls.

▶   **Catania**   227B5

Sicily's second city is a modern and industrial place, whose chaotic and unpleasant streets may deter you from exploring its handful of ancient and medieval monuments (most of which have suffered over the years from earth-quakes). The **Duomo**▶ and Sicily's largest church, San Nicolò, are worth a glance; so too the artistic and archeo-logical displays of the (often closed) **Museo Civico**▶.

Magna Graecia

Magna Graecia (Greater Greece) was the network of scattered Greek colonies that sprang up over much of Sicily and southern Italy from about the 8th century BC. Greece had an established trade with parts of Italy, most notably with the Etruscan cities of Tuscany, and it was inevitable that in time settlers should start to colonize areas near the Greek mainland. Over the centuries, the splendor of their cities came to rival and sometimes exceed those of Greece itself.

The colonies According to the historian Thucydides, the first settlers in Sicily established a foothold at Naxos (now Giardini-Naxos near Taormina) in 735 BC. They then quickly founded other colonies on Sicily's eastern coast at *Catana* (Catania), *Leontinoi* (Lentini) and *Zancle* (Messina). Within a year Greeks from Corinth had raised *Ortigia* (Syracuse), Magna Graecia's most powerful city, and five years later Megaran colonists, neighbors of the Corinthians in Greece, founded Megara Hyblaea, 15 miles to the north. Settlers from Crete and Rhodes created Gela in 689 BC, expanding westward a century later to settle *Acragas* (Agrigento). Pioneers from Rhodes founded Lipari, Sicily's last Greek colony, in 580 BC.

Sicilian riches Although the colonies retained links with Greece, they quickly became independent cities. Sicily's immense resources—especially its wheat-growing potential—brought them considerable wealth, a prosperity which can still be gauged from the splendor of the ruins in Syracuse and Agrigento. At the same time, however, the colonies were torn by internal jealousies and internecine warfare.

Greek jealousy As well as suffering civil war, the cities remained prey to two external adversaries. The first threat came from the mainland Greek states, who became jealous of Magna Graecia's increasing power. In 415 BC Athens sent an armada to attack Syracuse, suffering a defeat—after one of the greatest sea battles in ancient history—that left Syracuse and Magna Graecia at the peak of their powers.

Carthage The second threat came from Carthage, a North African power founded by the Phoenicians, who had cities of their own in western Sicily (Marsala and Palermo in particular). Battles raged between the two powers for centuries (and Carthage often sided with cities against their neighbors). In the 3rd century BC the two sides laid aside their differences and united to confront the growing power of Rome. The alliance was to no avail. The sack of Syracuse by Rome in 211 BC marked Magna Graecia's effective demise. For 700 years thereafter Sicily remained under Roman rule.

La Mattanza
Tuna are caught all over Sicily, but the most famous catch is Favignana's ritualized slaughter, *La Mattanza*. The age-old rite takes place around three times weekly in May and June. Under the head fisherman, or *rais* (an Arabic title), the fish are surrounded, netted, and then impaled and beaten to death. To many, in these days of ecological awareness, the ritual seems to be a bloodthirsty tourist attraction.

Charming Cefalù is dominated by its superb Norman-Romanesque cathedral

►► **Cefalù** 226C3

Of all Sicily's coastal towns, except for Taormina, Cefalù is perhaps the most attractive. Nestled under a huge crag, it boasts good beaches and a tangle of tempting medieval streets. Its prime attraction is the beautiful **Duomo►►►**, whose glorious mosaics (1148) are the earliest of any church in Sicily. Equally captivating is its balanced Norman-Romanesque façade, best seen from one of the outdoor cafés in the palm-fringed **Piazza del Duomo►►**. Close by lies the **Museo Mandralisca►►**, with a collection of Greek and Arab artifacts, and a famous painting by Sicily's most famous artist, Antonello da Messina, the *Portrait of an Unknown Man* (1472).

► **Egadi, Isole** 226C1

Ferries and hydrofoils run from Trapani to this archipelago just off Sicily's western coast. Favignana is the largest and most popular island, with many rocky coves but just one sandy beach, Cala Burrone. **Marettimo►►** is wilder and grander, an important sanctuary for wildlife, with gentle walks and hidden beaches. **Levanzo►** is more primitive, rocky and sunbleached, and known for the neolithic cave paintings of the Grotta del Genovese.

► **Enna** 227B4

If you explore Sicily's remote and beautiful interior, then consider making your base in Enna (the so-called "navel of Sicily"). There is little to see, but the town has a welcoming provincial air and—from its incredible crag-top position—some of the finest views on the island. Two small museums, the Museo Alessi and Museo Varisano, have displays of Greco-Roman finds and medieval church art. The **Castello►** was built by Frederick II, on a site probably used as a defensive citadel for over 5,000 years.

►► **Erice** 226C1

Erice is a tremendous mountain town, a sacred place and mighty fortress (*Eryx*) since time immemorial. Tour buses crowd in during the summer, drawn by the views from its limestone ramparts and the delightful medley of its tiny piazzas and cobbled streets, but the town has plenty of quiet corners in which to escape the throng.

►► **Etna** *227B5*

Etna (10,965 feet) is one of the world's largest and most active volcanoes. Its smoking summit is a landmark over much of Sicily. The Arabs called it *Jebel*, the Mountain of Mountains. Ancient navigators thought it the highest point on earth. Pindar described it as the "column which supports the sky." The Greeks called it *aipho* (I burn), from which the present name derives.

Etna smolders under its blanket of snow

Eruptions For all its majesty, Etna is little more than 60,000 years old—a mere stripling in geological terms. There have been about 90 major eruptions since 475 BC (when the first was recorded)—the last was in 1991. The most catastrophic came in 1669, when a 15 mile fissure opened up in the mountain (Etna has a tendency to split at the seams, unlike most volcanoes, which erupt through the central cone. Around 350 minor craters have been created by these lateral eruptions). The rent unleashed a 1¼ mile-wide tongue of magma, engulfing Catania (24 miles away) and surrounding its castle with molten lava. The eruption continued for 122 days, throwing out ash that carried over 60 miles. In places the lava took eight years to cool. Chronicles describe peasants boiling water on the rocks long after the eruption.

Around the volcano Etna is an awe-inspiring sight, and a quarter of a million people a year now visit the crater (see panel). Its environs, however, offer as much to see as the melancholy desolation of its highest slopes. For a good view of these varied surroundings you can either drive one of several scenic roads or take the Circumetnea railway that circles Etna's base, starting at Catania's Circumetnea station and finishing at Giarre-Riposto. Five trains daily ply the route. Most drivers approach from Catania, but roads from **Linguaglossa**►► and Adrano are equally spectacular—and less busy. All routes offer beautiful countryside, ranging from thick forests of oak and chestnut to the groves of orange, lemon, figs and olives that blanket Etna's fertile lower slopes.

Reaching the summit
All-included tours to Etna's summit run from Catania or Taormina. It is as easy (and cheaper), however, to make the trip by car or take the daily bus (8AM) from Catania's F.S. railroad station to the *Rifugio Sapienza* (6,207ft). From here you can walk to the summit on a rough road provided for tourist minibuses. Allow 3 to 4 hours for the walk, wear boots or stout shoes, and take plenty of warm and waterproof clothing.

SICILY

Stromboli
Stromboli is packed in summer with visitors drawn to its still-active volcano (which performs around four times hourly). Hotels are busy, so make the island a day-trip from Salina or Lipari. A path leads to the cone (3,059 ft.) from Piscita, a hamlet close to the harbor at San Vicenzo (a five-hour round walk). Many people camp near the summit to enjoy the volcano at night.

Aeolus
The Aeolian Islands were named after Aeolus, the Greek god of the winds and navigation, who kept all the world's winds in one of the islands' many caves. Ulysses was given a sack of them, and they blew his boat back to port when his curious crew opened the bag.

Antonello da Messina (1414–79)
This great Sicilian painter was one of the few southern artists to leave a mark on the Italian Renaissance. He was one of the first painters to experiment with oils, his virtuoso technique—particularly in portraiture—greatly influencing the Venetian artists of his day (Antonello himself was much influenced by Flemish art). Only a handful of his works survive in Sicily, notably in Messina, Cefalù, Syracuse, and Palermo.

▶ **Gela** 227A4

Gela is a town ravaged by textile factories and petrochemical plants. It is redeemed only by its **Museo Archeologico▶**, known mainly for the collection of 5th-century BC pottery for which Greek Gela was famous. Two and a half miles out of town is the more attractive area of **Capo Soprano▶▶**, where part of the fortifications that once surrounded the Greek city have been excavated.

▶▶ **Lipari, Isola di** 227D4

Lipari is the main island of the Isole Eolie (Aeolian Islands), a seven-island volcanic archipelago off Sicily's northern coast. The group has become popular over the last few years, visited mainly for its beaches and Stromboli's regular volcanic eruptions (see panel).

Lipari is the busiest of the islands, easily reached by regular ferries from Milazzo, Messina, Naples, and Reggio di Calabria. From its capital, Lipari, a picturesque port (with a good little museum), you can take boat trips around the coast or pick up bus connections to the rest of the island. You can also rent bikes and motor scooters (many roads offer lovely panoramas of Sicily and the archipelago). Good targets include Aquacalda, interesting for its pumice and obsidian quarries; San Calogero, which has mud baths and hot springs; and Canneto, one mile from Lipari's best beach, the Spiaggia Bianca. Much of the rugged interior also offers excellent walking.

To escape the crowds, visit outlying Panarea, tiniest and perhaps most dazzling of the islands, or the still unspoiled islets of Filicudi and Alicudi (each has a hotel and a few private rooms).

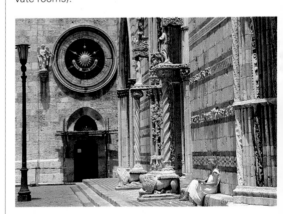

The Duomo at Messina: what is claimed as the world's largest astronomical clock is housed in the campanile

▶ **Messina** 227C5

Most people see no more of the gateway to Sicily than is absolutely necessary. Despite an enchanting view from the ferry, Messina close up is a battered and modern city (the result of earthquakes and 1943 bombing raids). If you have to linger there, try to be in Piazza del Duomo at noon for the performance of one of the world's largest astronomical clocks, or visit the **Museo Regionale▶**, graced with paintings by Caravaggio and Antonello da Messina.

▶▶▶ Monreale 226C2

Little outside the famous Norman cathedral of Monreale, 5 miles east of Palermo, suggests the splendor of what is within—the most extensive and accomplished Christian mosaics in the world. Probably the work of Greek and Byzantine craftsmen, they were started around 1174 and completed in only 10 years. The apse portrays Christ, arms outstretched, flanked by St. Peter and St. Paul (the panels show the saints' martyrdoms—crucifixion and beheading respectively). The nave's gold-backed mosaics illustrate episodes from the Old and New Testaments.

Climb the tower for its views, then visit the cloister, an elegant arcade supported by 216 twin columns (no two of which are the same). To the cathedral's rear lies a garden, filled with banyan trees and other exotic vegetation. Little else in the town is worth exploring, though the views over Palermo and the Conca d'Oro, or "Golden Shell" (the coastal area) are magnificent.

▶▶ Noto 227A5

The earthquake that devasted much of eastern Sicily in 1693 had at least one silver lining—many of the cities it razed were beautifully rebuilt in the baroque style of the day. Noto's tawny-stoned churches and palaces are the most complete expression of this transformation. It is also one of the more heavily promoted of the region's tourist attractions, so if you wish to stay—and the town makes a nice stopover—then be prepared for high-season crowds.

During rebuilding, the town's residential and religio-political districts were deliberately separated. Most of the latter's buildings lie along Corso Vittorio Emanuele, the best on **Piazza del Municipio**▶▶, one of the most harmonious little squares in Sicily. Most of the *palazzi* have beautifully decorated façades, but perhaps the most famous is the **Palazzo Villadorata**▶▶, known for its billowing balconies (situated in Via Corrado Nicolaci, first right west of Piazza del Municipio).

Thomas à Becket
Among the ranks of saints below the mosaics of Christ and the Virgin, you should be able to pick out the figure of martyred archbishop of Canterbury, Thomas à Becket, canonized in 1173 shortly before Monreale cathedral's mosaics were started (he is marked *SCS Thomas Cantb*).

Baroque splendor in Noto, one of the gems of Sicily

RAPPORTI MAFIA - POLITICA:
INFLUENZA NELLE AMMINISTRAZIONI LOCALI
VENERDÌ 7 MAGGIO 1993 · Ore 18,30
CARMINE MANCUSO
A

Many ambiguities surround the origins and identity of the Mafia. These days the old image of a criminal fraternity bound by family ties and codes of honor is a thing of the past. Mafia bosses are now slick-suited supremos (with politicians in their pockets), involved in every dubious trade from arms to heroin.

Plus ça change…
One of the earliest allusions to the Mafia came in a report from the the British consul in 1866, who wrote: "*Maffie*-elected *juntas* share the earnings of the workmen, keep up intercourse with outcasts, and take malefactors under their wing and protection."

The Mafia family
Mafia "families" are groups united in crime—which do not always include blood relations. Each takes its name from its village of origin (Corleone, for example), or the city quarter it controls (in Palermo, the *Ciaculli, Porta Nova*, etc). Each has foot soldiers, lieutenants and a *capo*, or *padrino* (godfather). Families ally themselves in *cosche*, named after artichoke crowns (to symbolize the unity of many), but the network is often fractured by disputes within and between families.

The American Mafia
The hundreds of thousands of Sicilians who emigrated to the United States at the beginning of the century were a breeding ground for Mafia-style organizations (the so-called "Black Hand"). During the period of Fascist rule many Italian *mafiosi* also fled to the U.S. Today, few doubt that there are links between Italian and American organized crime.

Mafia and mafia Everything about the Mafia is mysterious—even where its name comes from. The word may derive from the Arabic *mu'afàh* meaning "protection" (though it also means "skill," "ability," "beauty" and "safety"). It appeared in Italian for the first time around 1860. Many commentators underline the idea of mafia as a mentality, "a state of mind, a philosophy of life, a moral code, prevailing among all Sicilians" (Luigi Barzini, *The Italians*). This small "m" mafia does not mean all Sicilians are criminals (nor that they condone criminality). It does, however, have a bearing on its upper case cousin—the criminal underworld known as the Mafia.

Origins How and why the Mafia (and mafia) developed are vexed questions. The answers lie in the gap that has always existed between southerners and authority—a breach historically filled by the Mafia. Two cultural phenomena go some way to explaining it: first, the value Sicilians attach to the ability to impose one's will on others; second, the historic distrust felt by southerners for the state. This feeling stems from Sicily's catalogue of foreign rulers, as well as from the island's isolation—its rugged interior has always proved a barrier to the imposition of authority—and from the alienation of peasants from their feudal overlords, forced to work on Sicily's estates (*latifondi*) as serfs for absentee landlords in Naples or Palermo.

History Mafia activities go back hundreds of years, some say to the 12th century, when a secret sect was formed to oppose imperial rule. Under the Bourbons, ex-brigands were used to "police" the interior, often taking kickbacks instead of arresting their erstwhile colleagues. Elsewhere, middlemen known as *gabellotti* acted as mediators between peasants and landowners. By intimidating one group and becoming agents for the other they quickly grew rich, becoming a distinct class, bound by mutual self-interest, established codes of honor and a semi-formal organization.

Mussolini and the Mafia Little is known of the Mafia before World War II. It was under Fascism that Mussolini became the only political figure in Italy's history to damage the organization. Through his legendary prefect, Cesare Mori, he set about the Mafia with a lethal—and illegal—efficiency. The Mafia was dealt a dose of its own medicine. It might well have proved fatal—but for the intervention of the Americans.

The Mafia

Allied deliverance When the Allies prepared to land in Sicily in 1943 they had only one organized source of intelligence and logistical support—the Mafia. In New York they talked to men like Lucky Luciano, who provide "introductions" to the island's Mafia bosses (Luciano's 50-year prison sentence was repealed as a reward). This cleared the way for the Allies, and, in the aftermath of the invasion, also helped create the Allied Military Government. In organizing political and military control of the island, the Allies entrusted responsibility for 62 of Sicily's 66 towns and cities to men with Mafia connections. Don Vito Genovese, on whom Mario Puzio based *The Godfather*, was one of these men.

The new Mafia Allied intervention left the Mafia well placed to exploit Italy's postwar economic boom. With its criminal muscle and political connections it amassed huge fortunes (mainly from the construction business). Much of the money was "laundered" through "respectable" businesses, or used to finance the Mafia's expansion into arms and drug dealing (trades that brought immeasurable riches and changed the Mafia's character forever). Mafia tactics became increasingly ruthless as the stakes grew higher. Threats to its power were met by violent clan battles and the assassination of all who stood in its way. Despite recent "maxi-trials" of hundreds of *mafiosi*, and the "supergrass confessions" of men like Tommaso Buscetta, the Mafia's inextricable links with most aspects of Sicilian life make it highly unlikely that it will ever be eradicated.

Words
Italians call the Mafia *la piovra*, or the "octopus," because its tentacles infiltrate so many aspects of national life. The *mafiosi* themselves, however, are more circumspect. They would never address each other as such: Mafia men are *amici* (friends) or *uomini d'onore* (men of honor). They are members of *Cosa Nostra* (Our Thing) and protected by a code of silence—*omertà*.

Illustrious corpses
Since the 1970s the Mafia has murdered politicians, journalists, and anyone else who threatened its position. These *cadaveri eccellenti* (illustrious corpses) reached a peak in 1982 with the assassination of General dalla Chiesa, gunned down as he prepared to investigate links between politicians and organized crime. In 1992 Italy was shocked by the killings of Giovane Falcone, one of the most effective and highly respected of Sicily's investigating magistrates, and of Judge Paolo Borsellino.

Sicily, 1950s: The coffin of another police officer killed in the daily fight against the Mafia

Glowing mosaics decorate the arches in Palermo's 12th-century Palatine Chapel

►► Palermo 226C2

Past meets present head-on in Palermo, Sicily's capital. Norman, Arab, and baroque monuments rise amid slums and backstreets riddled with poverty and petty crime. Traffic and squalor assault the senses at every turn, ingredients in the city's strange mixture of criminal threat and decaying grandeur. Like Naples, this is not a place to suit all tastes, but in its grungy streets, its vibrant markets and magnificent art, it captures all the color and contradictions that are so peculiarly Sicilian.

History Palermo started life as an 8th-century BC Phoenician trading post (though it takes its name from the Greek *Panormus*—"all port"). Later it became a Carthaginian and then Roman stronghold. Its golden age came under the Arabs, when for 240 years (from 831) it became Europe's second most important city after Constantinople. It remained preeminent under the Normans (1072) and the Swabians (1194). Decline set in with the Angevins (1266) and—most markedly—with the Spaniards (who ruled for almost 600 years from 1282 on).

Cathedral and palace The Norman stamp is evident in the **Cattedrale►►**, at least in the exterior (1185), for the old interior was ruined by alterations in the 18th century. Its most interesting features are the royal tombs of Henry VI, Roger II and Frederick II (contained in two chapels of the south aisle). A reliquary (1631) close by contains the remains of St. Rosalia, Palermo's patron saint. The treasury is crammed with precious objects, most notably a jewel-encrusted crown removed from the tomb of Constance of Aragon, wife of Frederick II.

Close to the cathedral stands the **Palazzo dei Normanni►►►**, a monumental complex started by the Arabs and enlarged by the Normans (under whom it became one of Europe's leading courts). At its heart are the Sala di Re Ruggero (Hall of Roger II), decorated with mosaics of hunting scenes, and Palermo's undoubted artistic highlight, the **Cappella Palatina►►►**. The latter,

The Sicilian Vespers
An island-wide uprising against Sicily's Angevin rulers was sparked in 1282 by a French insult to a woman in Palermo, traditionally said to have occurred after the bell for vespers (evening service) was rung in Palermo's church of Santo Spirito.

built by Roger II in 1132, is a largely Romanesque creation, though the interior rests on Roman columns and glitters with Byzantine-influenced mosaics. The wooden ceiling is Moorish, an intricate honeycomb of exquisite carving.

Churches Nearby **San Giovanni degli Eremiti▶▶** stands on the edge of the *Albergheria* district, a fascinating quarter teeming with baroque churches, busy markets and run-down backstreets. The church (1132) retains its original Arabic-influenced domes, as well as a picturesque double cloister, filled with a wild profusion of palms, shrubs and lemon trees. It stands on the site of an old mosque (Palermo once had 200 mosques).

Three other important churches lie conveniently grouped around **Piazza Pretoria▶▶** The finest, **La Martorana▶▶**, contains good 12th-century mosaics, while both **San Giuseppe▶** and **Santa Caterina▶** have wonderfully extravagant baroque interiors.

Museum and gallery The **Museo Archeologico▶▶** is a small but excellent collection, prized for the carved friezes (or metopes) taken from the temples at Selinunte (see page 240). Other highlights include prehistoric cave paintings; lion's head fountains from temples at Himera; the *Ram of Syracuse*, a 3rd-century BC Greek bronze; and two Roman sculptures—*Hercules and the Stag* and *The Satyr Preparing to Drink*. The cream of Sicily's medieval treasures are contained in Palazzo Abatellis's **Galleria Nazionale Siciliana▶▶▶**. Paintings are downstairs, sculptures upstairs, the masterpieces including Antonello da Messina's *Three Saints* and *Annunciation*, the Arab-styled *Malaga Vase*, and a delicate 15th-century *Bust of Eleanor of Aragon*.

Convento dei Cappuccini Italy has no stranger or more eerie sight than the thousands of mummies lining the catacombs of Palermo's Capuchin convent (in the west of the city at the corner of Via G. Mosca and Via Pindemonte). The figures have parchment-yellow skin stretched across bones. All are still wearing clothes—crumbling silks and dusty top hats; each is bizarre, comical or macabre by turns.

Monte Pellegrino
Monte Pellegrino overlooks Palermo, splitting off the city from the bay at Mondello. The scenic trip to the mountain is a popular Sunday excursion (bus No. 12 runs here from the Teatro Politeama). Near the top is the Santuario di Santa Rosalia, a pilgrim church marking the spot where the bones of Palermo's patron saint were found in 1624. Paths and roads offering fine views lead towards the summit.

Fishy decisions in Palermo's market

Markets
Palermo's Vucciria market sprawls over several streets south of Piazza San Domenico. Stalls sell everything from swordfish to coffee percolators. The local delicacy, sold from stalls, is *guasteddi* (rolls filled with strips of calf's spleen, ricotta cheese, and a hot sauce). The flea market is near the cathedral on Via Papireto (the antiques neighborhood is in the same area).

Residents of the Catacombs

► Ragusa
227A4

Ragusa suffered in the same earthquake as Noto (see page 235) and was rebuilt along similar baroque lines. It is less visited than its neighbor, however, and you can wander around the atmospheric old town (*Ragusa Ibla*) in virtual solitude. The streets here are decrepit without being depressing, the locked doors and shuttered windows creating the impression of an abandoned ghost town. While exploring, be sure to visit **San Giorgio►►**, among the more stately of Sicily's baroque churches.

The unfinished Greek temple of Segesta

►►► Segesta
226C2

Segesta's windswept **Greek temple►►►** rises in glorious isolation amid beautiful countryside, perhaps the grandest and most inspiring of all Sicily's great Hellenistic monuments. Started around 425 BC, it is all that remains of ancient *Segesta*, a colony with pre-Greek roots in the 12th century BC. The temple was never finished, though from its 36 columns and well-rounded appearance you would never know. Closer up, you see that the columns remain unfluted and parts of the walls are missing, but this doesn't detract from the temple's harmonious proportions or the splendor of its natural setting.

Be sure to take the short road (1 mile) that wends through flower-strewn slopes to a small Greek theater on a barren hilltop nearby. The views are remarkable, especially at sunset, stretching to the sea across Monte Erice and the pastoral plains below.

►►► Selinunte
226B2

Founded in 628 BC and probably named after a wild parsley (*selinon* in Greek), Selinunte quickly became one of Magna Graecia's most prosperous colonies. It attracted many bitter rivals, notably Segesta, and suffered devastating attacks from the Carthaginians in 409 BC and 250 BC (blows from which it never fully recovered). The site today is among Sicily's finest, two of its original seven **temples►►►** as impressive as any on the island. Nobody knows to which gods Selinunte's temples were dedicated, so each is indicated only by a letter. They divide into two groups: the nearest to the entrance stand in a group (E, F, G)—Temple E was re-erected in the 1950s; the others lie together on the old acropolis to the west. Many of the site's treasures have been taken to Palermo's Museo Archeologico, but the ruins are still a lovely place to explore. The small fishing village and resort of Marinella just below the site makes a good base for the ruins.

Piazza Armerina mosaics

A steep, cobbled lane leads from Piazza Armerina in central Sicily towards the Villa Casale, wending through open countryside before arriving at the little forested valley that shelters the ruins (3 miles). The villa probably served as a retreat and occasional hunting lodge, possibly for Emperor Maximianus Herculius, co-emperor with Diocletian between AD 286 and 305. It was used until as late as the 12th century, when a landslip covered it, preserving the mosaics until full-scale excavations began in the 1950s. The site has been skillfully laid out, new roofs serving to protect the mosaics and to suggest how the villa might have looked in its heyday.

The mosaics All the components of a great Roman house are here, from the atrium, peristyle and baths to vast public halls and private apartments. Everything pales alongside the mosaics, however, 4,200 square yards of exquisite works that unfold dramatically from room to room. Their style is reminiscent of Roman villas in North Africa, suggesting they are the work of Carthaginian craftsmen, a notion which helps to explain some of the more exotic scenes and animals they portray. Certainly the villa's centerpiece seems set in Africa, the great *Hunting Scene* that stretches for over 198 feet along the edge of the courtyard's covered corridor. Its detailed and intertwined narrative depicts tigers, ostriches, elephants—even rhinos— being captured and caged for return to Rome's circuses and gladiatorial games.

Detail from a hunting scene: one of the extraordinary mosaics in the Villa Casale

Equally as captivating are a circus scene and chariot race, or an enchanting children's hunt, where youngsters are chased by the hares and peacocks they are supposed to be catching. Another fine room vividly (and bloodily) depicts the labors of Hercules. Most people's favorite room, however, is the one that proves there is nothing new under the sun—with a mosaic showing 10 women athletes in Roman "bikinis."

SICLIY

The baroque façade of Syracuse's cathedral

Fontana Aretusa
The Delphic oracles that first guided settlers to Syracuse spoke of the spring feeding Ortigia's Arethusa fountain. In Greek myth the nymph Arethusa rose here after swimming from Greece, transformed into a spring by Artemis to escape the clutches of the river god Alpheus. Admiral Nelson took on water from the spring *en route* for the Battle of the Nile. Today the spot is planted with papyrus and surrounded by pleasant cafés.

▶▶▶ **Siracusa (Syracuse)**   227A5

Syracuse was founded by Greeks from Corinth in 733 BC Within a hundred years it had become one of Europe's greatest cities. Today it divides into three areas: a dull modern town; Ortigia, the city's heart for 2,700 years; and the Parco Archeologico, a large area of Greek, Roman, and early Christian remains.

The old town Ortigia▶▶, part medieval and part baroque, is an island, linked to the rest of the town by a bridge. It is graced with two pretty squares—**Piazza Duomo**▶▶ and Piazza Archimede (both popular meeting places with plenty of nice cafés). See the **Tempio di Apollo**▶ Sicily's oldest Doric temple (565 BC), and spend plenty of time wandering around the port area and its old streets. Pay special attention to the **Duomo**▶▶, a fascinating patchwork of styles, its Norman walls embedded with columns from a 5th-century BC temple (much of the interior was also hacked from the temple). Further fragments hail from the 7th century, the date of the site's consecration as a Christian cathedral. The façade is 17th century.

The **Museo Nazionale**▶▶, part of the lovely Palazzo Bellomo, offers mainly medieval treasures, its highlights a ravishing *Annunciation* by Antonello da Messina and Caravaggio's *Burial of St. Lucia*. There is also much sculpture, silverware, fabrics, furniture, and religious vestments.

Syracuse: a fishing port for thousands of years

From the ancient world At the **Parco Archeologico**▶▶▶ the first thing you see after the souvenir stalls is the Ara di Ierone, the base of a colossal 3rd-century BC altar. Close by is the 15,000-seat **Teatro Greco**▶▶, the most complete theater in the Greek world (5th-century BC). Near it extends the Latomia del Paradiso, a lovely green area famous for the cave known as the Orecchio di Dionisio (Ear of Dionysius).

Half a mile from the park lies the **Museo Archeologico Nazionale**▶▶▶, a purpose-built museum whose wide-ranging collection covers finds from Syracuse, Agrigento and beyond. Its star attraction is the *Venus Anadiomene* (Venus Rising from the Sea). Also outstanding are the *kouroi* (Greek statuettes) and a *Winged Victory*.

►► Taormina 227C5

Taormina is Sicily's most beautiful town, ringed around by mountains and perched above a turquoise sea. Etna rises majestically in the background. The climate is mild, the views matchless, and its vegetation a semitropical garden of palms, bougainvillea, and orange trees.

What to see The town center forms an intimate collection of tiny streets and flower-filled balconies. Wandering its twisting alleys or exploring its dark staircases is pleasure enough, with the chance of stumbling on quiet piazzas or of catching sudden views of the sea below.

Beyond the town's backstreet charm, there is really only one sight, the magnificently sited **Teatro Greco►►►**. Built by the Greeks in the 3rd century BC, it was almost completely remodeled by the Romans. A small museum holds various archeological fragments from the site.

What to do After seeing the theater, many people confine themselves to a drink in one of the expensive but irresistible cafés on Piazza IX Aprile, Taormina's main square (or those on Corso Umberto I, its main street). You should also take time to stroll in the public gardens (on Via Croce) and to climb to the **Castello►►** for more all-embracing views. Paths and roads (and buses) beyond the castle lead to Castelmola (3 miles), a tiny crag-top village with more nice bars and fine views.

Sadly, Taormina is too enticing to have to yourself. In high season—which runs from April to September—it becomes crowded and almost a caricature of itself. The streets are thronged, their attractive shops outnumbered by souvenir stalls. Glitzy pizzerias compete at night with pounding discos. Ranks of glitterati attending film and theater festivals preen and parade. Don't necessarily be deterred, but try to come off season if possible.

Taormina alternatives
If hotel prices and high-season crowds prevent you staying in Taormina, consider putting up in Spisone and Letojanni, less elegant but more affordable resorts nearby. Better still, try Giardini-Naxos, the best place to stay near Taormina. It is a modern town, with a broad sandy beach and plenty of hotels at all prices. Regular buses run up to Taormina.

243

The Greek theater above Taormina, with Etna beyond

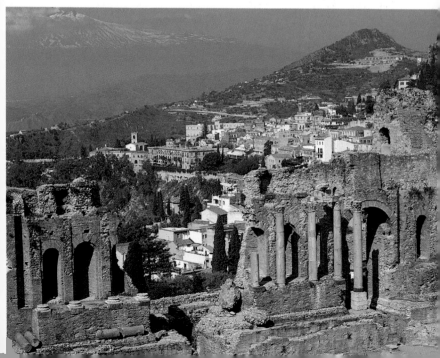

SARDINIA

Scale: 0 10 20 30 40 km / 0 10 20 miles

F Corse

Bocche di Bonifacio
Capo Testa
Santa Teresa Gallura
I Maddalena
I Caprera
Palau
Bajà Sardinia
Porto Cervo
Porto Rotondo
Golfo Aranci
Cannigione
Arzachena

E Punta Caprara dello Scorno
I Asinara
C del Falcone
Stintino
Golfo dell'Asinara
Costa Paradiso
Costa Smeralda
Luogosanto
Trinità d'Agultu
Gallura
Calangiánus
Olbia
I Tavolara
I Molara
San Teodoro

Porto Tórres
Castelsardo
I'Elefante
Tempio
Pausánia 1362m
Telti
Monti
971m
Mte Nieddu
Budoni
Sorso
Sédini
Perfugas
Mte Limbara
la Caletta
Nulvi
I. del Coghínas
Oschiri
Alà dei Sardi
Lodè
Siniscòla
Santa Lucia

D Tramaríglio
Anghelu Ruju
Olmedo
Usini
Ploaghe
Ózieri
Pattada
Buddúso
Bitti
1127m
Mte Albo
C Comino
Grotta di Nettuno
Pórto Conte
Alghero
Uri
Ittiri
Móres
Thiesi
Bultei
Bono
Orune
Cedrino
Grotta di Ispinígoli
Orosei
Villanova
Monteleone
Pozzomaggiore
Bonorva
Bolótana
Nuoro
Serra Orlos
Cala Gonone
Golfo di Orosei

C C Marárgiu
Bosa
Macomèr
Ottana
Orani
Oliena
Dorgali
Grotta del Bue Marino
Suni
Sédilo
Sopramonte
Mte Alto
Cúglieri
Abbasanta
1050m
Mte Ferru
L. Omodeo
Orgósolo
Gavoi
Fonni
Gola su Gorruppu
C Mannu
Nartolia
Losa
Ghilarza
Ovodda
Monti del Gennargentu
C di M Santu
Sínis
Cábras
Ortueri
Sórgono
1834m
Pta la Mármora
Baunei
San Giovanni di Sínis
Fordongiánus
Désulo
Aritzo
Arzana
Lotzorai
Thárros
Oristano
Samugheo
Láconi
Seúlo
Lanusei
Arbatax
Tórtoli
Golfo di Oristano
Ábbanta
Gennargentu
Barbágia
Seui
Seúlo
Barì Sardo

B Capo d'Frasca
Arboréa
Áles
Giara di Gesturi
Nurallao
Isili
Jerzu
Terralba
Gésturi
Nurri
Tertenía
Úras
Su Nuraxi
Barúmini
Marina di Árbus
Sárdara
Villamar
Las Plássas
Mándas
Escalaplano
Costa Verde
Árbus
Pabillónis
Gúspini
Sanluri
Guásila
Ballao
Gonnosfanádiga
San Gavino Monreale
Senorbi
Flúminimaggiore
Villacidro
Serrenti
Sant'Andrea Frius
San Vito
Villaputzu
1236m
Mte Linas
Buggerrú
Tempio di Antas
Monastir
1067m
Pta Serpeddi
Muravera
Nébidà
Domusnovas
Villasor
Dolianova
Iglésias
Siliqua
Assémini
Sestu
Sínnai
C Ferrato

A Portoscuso
Villamassargia
Narcao
CÁGLIARI
Quartu
Sant'Elena
Costa Rei
C Sandalo
Carloforte
Carbonia
San Giovanni Suérgiu
1116m
Capoterra
Villasímius
Calasetta
Giba
Sarroch
Capo Carbonara
Sant'Antioco
Golfo di Cágliari
I di S Pietro
Sant'Anna Arresi
Pula
Nora
I di S Antioco
Dónus de Mana
Santa Margherita
Bithia
Capo Spartivento
Costa del Sud

244

Sardinia (Sardegna) Italy's second-largest island differs from the Italian mainland in almost every respect, but for visitors its most vital difference is the lack of conventional sightseeing. You come here not for museums and monuments, but for some of Europe's finest beaches, or for the spectacle of the island's mountainous interior. The main cities, Cagliari and Sassari, are provincial spots, and—like most of the smaller towns—amount to little more than bases from which to venture further afield. If you do want to sightsee, you could happily potter around one of the island's classical or prehistoric sites (see page 249), or make a beeline for the coronet of Pisan-Romanesque churches near Sassari (see page 251).

Sea and sand Beaches are what bring most people to Sardinia. The most famous cluster around exclusive resorts on the Costa Smeralda, but there are plenty of smaller resorts, and a plethora of sandy coves and rocky inlets await those who make the effort to get off the beaten track. For the most part the sea is clean and beautifully clear, safe for swimming and ideal for any number of activities from sailing to snorkeling. Facilities at larger resorts allow you to indulge most seaside whims, though there are still plenty of unspoiled and scarcely developed spots.

The interior Sardinia's interior is varied and in many parts strikingly beautiful, ranging from gently rolling plains and endless scrub-covered hills to the upland hamlets and desolation of the Barbagia and Gennargentu mountains. Here, sheep and shepherds are often the only living creatures you encounter as you drive the lonely roads. Villages often preserve ancient customs and ceremonies, and you may still come across people in traditional costume.

Traditional lifestyle in Sardinia's interior

245

SARDINIA

Essentials
Cagliari: Museo
Archeologico, Duomo
Cala Gonone: Coastline,
Grotta del Bue Marino,
Gennargentu: Gola su
Gorruppu
Giara di Gesturi: Su Nuraxi,
Las Plassas
Oristano: Sinis peninsula
Porto Conte: Grotta di
Nettuno
Sassari: Pisan churches
(page 251)

Tourist information
Alghero: Piazza Porta Terra
9 (tel: 079/979 054).
Cagliari: Piazza Deffenci 9
(tel: 070/651 698).
Nuoro: Piazza Italia 19 (tel:
0784/32 307).
Oristano: Via Cagliari 278
(tel. 0783/74 191).
Sassari: Viale Caprera 36
(tel: 079/299 544) and Viale
Umberto 72 (tel: 079/233
534).

Mosaic in Cagliari's cathedral

History Although prehistory bequeathed Sardinia's finest monuments—its great stone *nuraghi*—the Phoenicians are the first culture of which much is known. They arrived in the 8th century BC, followed by the Carthaginians and the Romans (238 BC). During the Middle Ages, Vandals, Byzantines, and Arabs all left their mark. For a brief period, however, the island was ruled by the Giudicati, four independent duchies with close ties to Pisa and Genoa (hence the island's many Pisan-Romanesque churches). The Spanish gained control in 1479, remaining in charge until 1720, when the island passed by treaty to Piedmont's dukes of Savoy. The island joined a united Italy in 1861.

Food Sardinian cuisine is the simple food of peasant and fisherman. On the coast you can sample just about every type of Mediterranean seafood, and in the interior cheeses such as *pecorini*, *casu marzu* and the yogurt-like *gioddu* are common. First-course specialties include *malloreddus* (small dumplings); *culingiones* (ravioli); *favata* (pork and bean stew); *leppudrida* (meat and vegetable soup); and *sa fregula* (Sardinian couscous). For main courses you might be offered *aragosta* (crayfish); *burrida* (marinated fish), *porceddu* (suckling pig), or *buttarga* (tuna or mullet roe). *Sebadas* are cheese and honey pastries fried in oil; *suspirus* and *gueffus* are desserts bursting with almonds.

Facts and figures
Sardinia lies 108 miles from mainland Italy, and is 162 miles long by about 72 miles wide. It is Italy's third largest region, but has the country's lowest population density (the population is 1.6 million, a third that of Sicily). The capital is Cagliari, and there are three provincial capitals—Nuoro, Oristano and Sassari.

Wine Several of Sardinia's unique grape varieties were introduced by the Phoenicians and Carthaginians. Despite their venerable provenance, they have not always been used to best effect, and the island's wines can be idiosyncratic—to say the least. The most famous vintage is the dry, sherry-like Vernaccia di Oristano (Contini is a good producer). The basic reds are Cannonau and Monica di Sardegna, slightly overshadowed by whites like Vermentino and Torbato di Alghero (the latter is produced by Sella & Mosca, one of Europe's largest estates). Malvasia di Bosa is a prized dessert wine. *Filu ferru* (steel thread) is the local grappa, named because shepherds distilled it illegally and hid bottles underground—with a protruding piece of wire to locate them later. Almost every cork in a bottle of Italian wine, incidentally, comes from the cork oak forests of northern Sardinia.

► **Alghero** *244D1*

Alghero is one of Sardinia's busiest resorts, saved by its proud Catalan roots and down-to-earth fishing harbor from the tackiness that often blights tourist towns. There were so many Catalans here in the 14th century that the region became known as *Barcelonetta* (Little Barcelona). Many streets and monuments take Catalan names—*carrer* not *via*, for example; *plaça* not *piazza*; and *iglesia* for church, not *chiesa*).

Among the cobbled streets within the medieval walls, look for the town's seven large 15th-century towers, particularly the **Porta Torre►** and **Torre Sulis►**, and fine Aragonese-Gothic buildings like the **Casa Doria►**, **Palau Reial►** and **Palazzo d'Albis►**. The octagonal *campanile* is all that survives from the original 16th-century **Duomo►**. San Francesco is the most interesting church.

►► **Cagliari** *244A2*

A large port, lots of industry and around 250,000 people should make Cagliari an unappetizing prospect. In fact it is a pleasant place, blessed with a neat medieval center, several modest monuments, and a hinterland of exquisite beaches and flamingo-filled lagoons. The old citadel above the harbor was founded by the Phoenicians, the forerunner of a port that over the centuries has remained one of the most important in the Mediterranean.

The **Citadella dei Musei-Museo Archeologico►►** is the island's premier museum, home to the cream of its prehistoric, pre-Roman and medieval treasures. Of these, the most important are the bronze figurines and other displays devoted to Sardinia's ancient Nuraghic culture (see page 249). The **Duomo►** nearby is known for its crypt and two Pisan pulpits (1165). Elsewhere, see the **Torre San Pancrazio►**, which with the Torre dell'Elefante formed the cornerstone of the city's medieval defences, and **San Saturnino►►**, Sardinia's oldest church (5th-century).

Sunday market in Cagliari

Marshland wildlife near Alghero

247

Boat trips
Two of the best coves south of Cala Gonone are Cala di Luna and Cala Sisine. Boats run to both, offering views of the deep gorges that cut through the coast's 2,970 ft.-high mountains. Boats also visit the *Grotta del Bue Marino*, reputedly one of the last refuges of the Mediterranean monk seal (*bue marino*), and a magical spot filled with stalactites and stalagmites.

L'Elefante
This little curiosity stands 2½ miles out of Castelsardo on the SS134. It is an odd elephant-shaped rock that hangs over the road. Inside are several *domus de janas* tombs (see page 249), many etched with mysterious symbols and bull's head motifs. At Sedini (9 miles) another five-chambered *domus* has been turned into the Gothic church of San Andrea (1517).

The lovely bay at Cala Gonone

▶▶   **Cala Gonone**   244C3

Sardinia is so well known for its beaches that it is easy to forget the tremendous variety of its other coastal scenery. None is more spectacular than the east-coast mountainous cliffs surrounding the bay at Cala Gonone. Approach the area on the SS125 if possible (from Arbatax), a majestic road that climbs to over 3,300 feet as it wends through some of the island's wildest scenery. Its most breathtaking stretch offers views over the gorge of the Gola su Gorruppu▶▶▶.

Cala Gonone itself is approached from Dorgali, a town growing increasingly busy as more people discover the beauty of the coastline. Until a few years ago the bay and its tiny hamlet were accessible only from the sea. New hotels and villas that have sprouted since the building of a road have not yet spoiled the area's incomparable scenery. The best way to the area is to take a boat trip, either to marvel at the views, or to be dropped at one of the secluded coves up and down the coast (see panel).

▶▶   **Castelsardo**   244D2

Castelsardo, on the north coast, is a citadel town, founded in 1102 by the Genovese, whose formidable castle offers sweeping views over the sea and the town's maze of medieval streets. Similar views are to be had from the cliff-edge Duomo, worth popping into for its 15th-century icon, the *Madonna degli Angeli* by an unknown local painter. For beaches follow the scenic road to Porto Torres, fringed by a broad crescent of sand and turquoise seas.

Castelsardo is also known for its handicrafts, many of which are of dubious quality and authenticity. Bargains are to be had, though, if you rummage through the junk and stick to the weaving and palm-leaf baskets for which the town is most famous. Cork and coral goods, rugs, wrought iron and Sardinian masks (*mamathones*) are also available.

Prehistory

Sardinia's prehistoric monuments provide some of the island's most memorable sights, from the great stone nuraghi that dot the countryside to the delicate bronze figurines of Cagliari's archeological museum. That almost nothing is known of the culture which produced them only adds to the appeal of ancient remains as mysterious and intriguing as any in Europe.

The earliest ruins The Sardinians could have come from almost anywhere: were they descended from Sardus, legendary son of Hercules, or from the Shardana tribes of ancient Libya? Or did they come from one of the countries around the Mediterranean? Nobody knows. Their earliest memorials are the *domus de janas* (elves' dwellings), tiny tombs cut into the rock which date from 2000–1800 BC. According to popular tradition they were the homes of elves, witches, and fairies. Their other major monuments were the *tombe dei giganti* (giants' tombs), believed by locals to be the graves of their gigantic ancestors—in fact they were the temples and mausoleums of the nuraghic tribes that dominated prehistoric Sardinia from 1500–500 BC.

Tombe dei Giganti
Sardinia's most significant concentration of *tombe* are at Anghelu Ruiu (6 miles north of Alghero on the road to Porto Torres). About 35 tombs riddle the hillside, eerie chambers connected by corridors and sloping passages. Some have lintels carved with symbolic shapes. Others are protected by a large standing stone.

Nuraghi These same tribes also left the 7,000 or more nuraghi that scatter the island. These enigmatic structures are visible everywhere—on hills, at roadsides, or half-buried in scrub—either singly or in clusters. Most are conical in shape, with a round vaulted interior, linked by corridors and stairways to an upper terrace. Many are more than two or three stories high. No two are the same. Some may have been dwellings, others fortified citadels.

The Sant'Antine nuraghe

Statuettes Sardinia has yielded around 500 nuraghic statuettes, quirky bronze figurines between 6 inches and 18 inches tall, probably made around the 8th century BC from copper and tin ore imported from as far afield as Etruria and Cornwall. Many were votive offerings, made to decorate nuraghic temples. They show immense vigor and invention, depicting not only people—anything from warriors to nursing mothers—but also objects such as houses, boats, gods, nuraghi, and domestic animals.

These figures marked the apogee of nuraghic culture. Around 1000 BC Sardinia began to fall prey to invading Phoenicians and Etruscans, far more skilled than the local tribes in the art of warfare (whose only weapons, according to the chroniclers, were stones and boulders rolled from hilltops).

Finding nuraghi
Sardinia's best nuraghi are Su Nuraxi, outside Barumini; Losa, near Abbasanta; and Sant' Antine, between Macomer and Sassari. The most interesting of the smaller sites are Palmavera, west of Fertilia; Serra Orrios, near Dorgali; Bruncu de Madili, near Gesturi. You should have no trouble in discovering many more for yourself.

SARDINIA

Sardinian bread
Sardinia has over 300 types of bread. Be sure to try the best known, the old-fashioned *pane carasau*. Round, dry and wafer thin, it was originally made by shepherds because it would keep for long periods. It is eaten crisp or softened by adding a few drops of water. Bread is shaped into flowers, animals—even lace— for weddings and christenings.

A quiet stretch of the Costa Smeralda

▶▶ **(La) Costa Smeralda**   *244E3*

The Emerald Coast started life as one resort—**Porto Cervo**▶▶—an upscale resort village built by the Aga Khan in the 1960s. Since then it has come to describe the string of chic resorts that have sprung up along Sardinia's northeastern coast. Many of its villages are in the Porto Cervo mold—undeniably chic and tasteful, but also rather soulless and lacking in local color. As oases of hedonistic retreat, however, they can hardly be bettered.

Other spots are still quite undeveloped, giving you Porto Cervo's beaches and facilities at a fraction of the cost. Close to **Santa Teresa Gallura**▶, for example, a relaxed and carefree resort on Sardinia's northern tip, lie three of the island's best beaches—Punta Falcone, La Marmorata and **Capo Testa**▶▶. Beyond them, more beach-fringed bays stretch as far as **Palau**▶, main port for the Maddalena archipelago (see page 252). Farther east, villages like **Cannigione**▶ on the Golfo di Arzachena are also still relatively quiet. Nearby Baia Sardinia, Portisco and Porto Rotondo, however, are similar in style to Porto Cervo.

▶▶ **Gennargentu, Monti del**   *244C2*

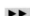

The Gennargentu is Sardinia's mountainous heart, a region of ancient landscapes and ways of life that have scarcely changed in centuries. Its isolated and self-contained farming villages offer your best hope of seeing local costumes or stumbling on age-old festivals. It is also among Europe's last wilderness areas, recently having been designated a national park. Driving is the only practical way to explore, using either Mandas or Nuoro as your base (though infrequent trains from Cagliari run through the region to Sorgono and Arbatax). Most roads here offer lonely excursions, but try the Arbatax–Dorgali (SS125) ride in particular for its exhilarating views of the **Gola su Gorruppu**▶▶▶. To reach other breezy vantage points for views follow the Fonni to Aritzo road (and the spur to Bruncu Spina at 5,181 feet), or the scenic drives from Aritzo to Arcu Guddetorgiu (6 miles northeast of Aritzo) and Seui (27 miles southeast).

THE LOGUDORO

Drive The Logudoro

This route explores Sardinia's north-west corner—the Logudoro (Land of Gold)—famous for its remote 12th-century Pisan-Romanesque churches and several of the island's grandest prehistoric nuraghi.

You could start the tour in Sassari, but by starting at **Castelsardo** (page 248), a magnificently sited old town, you have the chance of seeing not only San Pietro di Simbranos, one of the remotest of the Pisan churches, but also the famous Elefante rock and its prehistoric tombs. Tumbledown **San Antioco di Bisarcio** is the next church, followed by **Santa Maria del Regno**, a large, granite-fronted affair near Ardara (this now nondescript village was once capital of the Logudoro).

Moving southwest, you reach **San Antonio**, Pisan in style, but—as the red-and-white façade suggests—renovated by the Aragonese. Next comes **San Michele di Salvenero**, then **Santissima Trinità di Saccargia▶▶**, part of a once-famous abbey (1116), now perhaps Sardinia's most notable church.

Pick up the main road (SS131) and turn off to Borutta, beyond which stands the beautifully situated church of **San Pietro di Sorres▶**. Returning to the SS131 you come to the **Valle dei Nuraghi▶▶**, peppered with dozens of these enigmatic buildings, including the outstanding **Nuraghe Sant'Antine▶▶▶**. It dates from the 14th century BC, and centers on an impressive 53 feet bastion. Be sure to visit the **Museo di Torralba**, the best of several nuraghi museums in the vicinity (1 mile north in Torralba).

The eye-catching church of Trinità di Saccargia

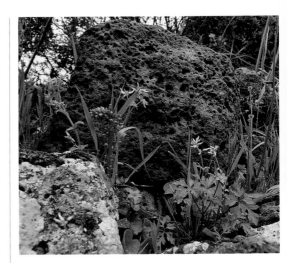

Giara di Gesturi: basalt and wildflowers

▶▶ Giara di Gesturi *244B2*

Giare are strange basalt plateaux found all over Sardinia. None are odder or more alluring than the Giara di Gesturi. About 1,980 feet high and 7 miles across, its herb- and *maquis*-covered plains stretch to the horizon, broken by outcrops of pinkish-black basalt and vast woods of cork oak (the forests contain an estimated 250,000 trees). After rain, trickling streams appear and areas of marsh form on the plateau rich in spring flowers and host to many migrating birds (the biggest such areas are Pauli Maiori and Pauli Minori). Roaming the heathland you may spot one of the plateau's famous wild horses—shy, tiny creatures similar to Shetland ponies and once common all over Sardinia. The area makes excellent walking country (for strolls long and short), and is easily accessed from surrounding villages. To get there, take the SS131 from Cagliari and after 24 miles branch east on the SS197 for Barumini: Gesturi village is 3 miles beyond. You can combine a visit to the Giara di Gesturi with a trip to **Las Plassas▶▶** a remarkable conical hill whose dramatic silhouette and ruined 12th-century castle are a landmark all around, and to **Su Nuraxi▶▶▶**, one of the island's finest nuraghi. *Su Nuraxi* means simply "the nuraghe," a blunt title for the oldest, most splendid and most extensive nuraghe in Sardinia. If you see no other nuraghi, be sure to see this one, half a mile west of Barumini.

▶ Iglesias *244B1*

Gold, silver, iron, lead and zinc have been mined from the countryside around Iglesias for centuries. The town itself bears remarkably few signs of its industrial past. On the contrary, it is a pleasant and elegant spot, whose name derives from its numerous churches (Spanish *iglesia*—church). Its hub is Piazza Sella, a lively little square, backed by an old quarter of balconied houses and quiet cobbled streets. The secluded **Duomo▶** is worth a quick glance, and there is also a museum devoted to the town's extensive mining heritage.

Buggerru
This seaside resort lies 24 miles north of Iglesias, surrounded by impressive beaches and dramatic countryside. To stay ahead of the crowd, explore the beautifully unspoiled Costa Verde north of Buggerru, reached on wild and picturesque roads from Guspini. Marina di Arbus is developed, but the cliffs and mountains to the south are still pristine.

Garibaldi and Caprera
Garibaldi first came to Caprera in 1855, seven years after his abortive attempt to form a Roman republic. In 1860 he set off from Maddalena with the thousand redshirts (the famous *Mille*), his spectacular conquest of Sicily and Naples a prelude to the creation of a united Italy a year later. He then retired to lead the life of a simple farmer on Caprera. His house, garden, and tomb are kept as a museum.

▶▶   La Maddalena   *244E3*

This seven-isled archipelago has always had a naval presence. Nelson spent 15 months in its waters pursuing the French prior to the Battle of Trafalgar. Today, the island of Maddalena still has a huge NATO base, though assaults on the islands now come only from visitors flooding in from the Costa Smeralda. Most are here for the beaches, though the islands also have their scenic side—worn granite rocks, sparse *maquis*, and wind-bent pines. Many people also come to pay homage to Garibaldi, Italy's nationalist hero, who lived for many years on the island of Caprera (see panel on page 252).

▶▶   Nora   *244A2*

Sardinia's most compelling archeological site occupies a narrow neck of land at Capo di Pula (19 miles west of Cagliari). Founded by the Phoenicians, the colony was later settled by the Carthaginians and then by the Romans. It was abandoned in the 3rd century AD, possibly in the wake of some natural disaster. Among the ruins you can see part of a burial ground, a Carthaginian temple to their chief goddess Astarte, a fine Roman theater, fragments of four Roman baths, and a miscellany of houses, streets, and well-preserved mosaic pavements. Part of the city is submerged, but still remains visible under the water close to the shoreline. Alongside the site stand the ruins of the 11th-century church of Sant' Efisio. Immediately below is a tempting sandy bay.

▶   Nuoro   *244C2*

Nuoro has a grand mountain setting but as D. H. Lawrence observed when he visited the town earlier this century: "There is nothing to see... which to tell the truth is always a relief. Sights are an irritating bore." Little has changed, though these days the town boasts a folk museum, the **Museo della Vita e Tradizioni Popolari▶▶**, Sardinia's most complete collection of costumes, handicrafts and other mementoes of its rural past. Otherwise it is a rather shabby place, useful mainly as a springboard for excursions into the former bandit country to the south.

Olbia   *244D3*

Mainland ferries dock at Olbia, a modern but not unduly industrialized port. This makes it a lively but not particularly prepossessing place, and after seeing the 12th-century church of **San Simplicio▶▶** it probably makes sense to head for the string of resorts and beaches strung along the SS125. Lanes off the main road lead to small bays and sandy beaches. More developed facilities cluster around San Teodoro (15 miles) and Siniscola (33 miles), and around the coast's most picturesque little resorts, La Caletta and Santa Lucia (both about 4 miles east of Siniscola).

Costumes
Elderly people still wear traditional dress in Sardinia's interior villages. Styles vary from village to village, but colors are usually black and white for men, scarlet and green for women. Many garments are richly embroidered, or embellished with jewelry handed down over generations. Many are extremely valuable. The *Museo della Vita* in Nuoro has an excellent display of such costumes.

Costume display in Nuoro's Museo della Vita

SARDINIA

Tharros
Little remains of *Tharros*, founded by the Phoenicians in 800 BC and later occupied by the Romans and Carthaginians. One of the most important classical sites in Sardinia nonetheless, it has the added attraction of a wild and beautiful setting, edged by clear seas and alluring beaches.

▶ **Oristano** *244C1*

You often come to Sardinian towns only to leave them again for more interesting sights in the surrounding countryside. Oristano is no exception: it serves as a base for the **Sinis peninsula**▶▶, a patchwork of lagoons and desert-like dunes east of the town. As well as providing the background to ancient **Tharros**▶▶ (see panel), this is an area of solitary churches, ghost towns, and virtually deserted white-sand beaches. As a sanctuary for flora and birds, notably flamingos, it is also a haven for botanists and naturalists. In Oristano itself, the bustling Piazza Roma and the tight historic core detain you only briefly. South of the town, however, leave time for the majestic 12th-century church of **Santa Giusta**▶▶.

Above: the marshland blooms near Oristano
Left: painting in the church of Santa Giusta, Oristano

▶▶ **Porto Conte** *244D1*

Porto Conte is the main destination for many of Alghero's visitors, a sweeping bay of fine beaches that forms part of the *Riviera del Corallo* (after the coral collected off the coast, much of which is made into jewelry sold in Alghero's shops). Two rocky promontories hold the bay in a protective embrace. The crook of the southern arm contains the **Nuraghi di Palmavera**▶▶ some 50 or so nuraghi gathered around a central domed "palace." Two good beaches occupy the promontory's southern shore, Lazzaretto and Le Bombarde.

The northern arm, Capo Caccia, rears up from the sea in a series of spectacular cliffs, easily seen by boat (from Alghero) or from the promontory's fine coastal road. It also harbors the **Grotta di Nettuno**▶▶▶, one of the Mediterranean's most fabulous sea caves. Single-file tours (on the hour) are conducted along a natural corridor past incredible displays of stalagmites and stalactites. The whole cavern is beautifully and dramatically lit. You can approach by boat from Alghero (15 minutes) or from Capo Caccia, where 600 dizzying steps—the *escala del cabriol* (goat's stairway)—drop to the cave's entrance at the foot of the cliffs.

▶ **Sant'Antioco, Isola di** *244A1*

Access to Sant'Antioco, off southwest Sardinia, is via a causeway built by the Carthaginians. Halfway across look for the two rocks known as *Su Pàra* and *Sa Mongia* (the monk and the nun), two illicit lovers turned to stone by God as they fled the island. The town of Sant'Antioco on the other side has been inhabited since Phoenician times. Its main attractions date from later, principally the early Christian catacombs under the Romanesque church of Sant'Antioco. Dark, dank and chilling, these tombs still contain skeletons, some perhaps from an earlier Carthaginian tomb on the site. A more extensive Carthaginian burial site, or *tophet*, covers a hillside nearby (follow signs from the village). The site has a small museum, numerous funerary urns and the remains of several ancient temples.

Many popular beaches dot the island, notably on the western coast, all linked by road to Calasetta and Sant'Antioco. Most are still pleasantly undeveloped.

▶ **San Pietro, Isola di** *244A1*

Carloforte▶ on San Pietro can be reached by ferry from Portoscuro (13 miles southwest of Iglesias, page 252), or from Calasetta on its near neighbor, Sant'Antioco. Although partly spoiled by a large power station, individual parts of the island are attractive, notably **Capo Sandalo▶▶** and **La Caletta▶▶**, both accessible by road from Carloforte (8 miles). The island has endless stretches of rocky shoreline, perfect for swimming and snorkeling.

Sassari *244D1*

Sardinia's second city has little to recommend it other than as a supplies stop to be visited from more agreeable spots on the coast. If you happen to pass through, spend a little time in the old quarter, whose claustrophobic maze of streets contrasts strikingly with the bland modern boulevards on the town's outskirts. See the **Duomo▶** with its intricate baroque façade, and the **Museo Sanna▶**, almost a carbon copy of Cagliari's archeological museum. It offers similar displays of nuraghic, Roman and Carthaginian artifacts, and examples of local costumes and handicrafts.

Beaches
A fine succession of beaches curves in a wide arc along the coast north of Sassari from Porto Torres to Castelsardo. All are linked by the SS200, a scenic seafront road.

Scenic drives
SS125 Arbatax–Dorgali–Nuoro; SS128/197 Nuoro–Fonni–Sorgono–Barumini; SS292 Oristano–Cuglieri–Bosa–Alghero; SS200/SS127 Sassari–Castelsardo–Costa Smeralda

255

Traces of former elegance in Sassari

Much as Sardinia's coastline is nowadays synonymous with beaches and the pleasures of sand and sea, so the interior's vast tracts of lonely, sun-baked mountains have been associated since time immemorial with banditry, kidnapping and lethal, blood-soaked vendettas.

Blood on the walls
Visitors to Orgosolo now search in vain for traces of its violent past, though locals have painted many houses with murals depicting some of the village's more blood-curdling historical episodes.

Sardinian banditry has flourished for centuries

The beginnings Banditry (the word comes from the Catalan *bandejat*, or *bandeado* in Spanish) has plagued Sardinia from Roman times. It has its roots in the traditional animosity and conflict of interests between the shepherds of the mountains—who required land for grazing—and the more peaceable peasants of the lowlands who sought to tame the land for cultivation. At its simplest, lawlessness probably started with the looting of a few sheep, or the rustling of a few cattle, even today not seen as terribly heinous crimes among shepherds, who are more likely to be outraged at the theft of money, or the more practical items needed for everyday existence.

The blood feud If banditry's simple give and take were breached, or its basic rules broken—notably when blood was spilled—then blood feuds and vendettas (*bardana*) could develop that might escalate over decades to embrace not simply individuals but entire villages and districts. One notable *disamistade*, or enmity, for example, festered for years in Orgosolo, deep in the Barbagia mountains, banditry's traditional fortress, prompted by the disputed inheritance of the village's chief clansman. From 1903 over the course of 14 years virtually every member of the two families involved was wiped out. Between then and 1954 the village (population 4,000) had on average a killing every two months.

Capture de deux voyageurs français par des brigands en Sardaigne

Robbery and kidnapping Simple highway robbery also became endemic, particularly after the war. One of the more infamous heists was the holdup of 250 people in broad daylight in 1952 while the local police force celebrated its annual *festa*. Another came in 1973 when thieves made off with 230 sheep from the state agricultural penal colony. More recently, and more alarmingly, kidnapping has become the crime of choice, Sardinia's harsh interior providing the perfect cover for captors who know the terrain better than their pursuers. The numbers have soared. Between 1945 and 1965 there were 58 reported kidnappings on the island (and none on the Italian mainland); in just three years from 1979 to 1982 there were 22 abductions.

Arriving
Passports only (no visas) are required for visitors from the U.K. and other E.U. (European Union) countries, the U.S., Canada, the Republic of Ireland, Australia, and New Zealand.

Air Direct scheduled flights from the U.S. fly to Rome and Milan. From the U.K. and Europe, you can fly into Rome, Venice, Milan (Verona), Turin, Bologna, Genoa, Florence, Pisa and Naples. Most long-haul flights fly to either Milan (Malpensa) or Rome (Leonardo da Vinci). Charter flights operate to the main cities plus Ancona, Alghero, Brindisi, Cagliari, Catania, Lamezia (Calabria), Olbia, Palermo, Pescara, Rimini, and Verona.

Rail Trains run directly to Rome, Milan, Venice and Naples via Calais and Paris from London (Victoria) and other major European cities. Motorail services are available on some routes.

Road Entry to Italy by road is best made via the Mont Blanc tunnel (France); the Brenner Pass (Austria); and the St. Bernard tunnel, Chiasso, or Simplon Pass (from Switzerland).

Camping
Most Italian campgrounds are on the coast or around lakes. Many Italian campgrounds open seasonally (typically June–September) and are extremely busy during July and August (so reserve ahead or arrive by 10AM). Tourist offices have full details of current prices for grounds, but if you are camping extensively invest in the widely available *Campeggi e Villaggi Turistici,* published by the Touring Club of Italy (T.C.I.).

Car breakdowns see page 261.

Car rentals see page 262.

Children
All but budget hotels accept children and it is normal to take young children to restaurants in the evening. Diapers, accessories and baby foods are widely available. Children under four ride free on buses, trams and trains, and enjoy free admittance to museums and galleries. Children

between four and 12 qualify for half-price reductions.

Climate
Despite its basically mild winters and warm summers, Italy has a surprisingly varied and extreme climate. In winter Venice and Milan are nearly as cold as New York City and you can ski in several parts of the country during September. The best months for sightseeing are April, May, June, September and October, though rain and cold linger in northern and mountain areas throughout spring and fall. July and August are the hottest months everywhere. Winters can be severe, particularly in the Alps and fog-bound plains of Lombardy and Emilia-Romagna.

Crime
The sheer number of visitors to Italy makes them an obvious target for the unscrupulous, especially in the larger cities and more depressed areas of the south. Of the horror stories told of unwitting tourists fleeced by Italy's criminal elite, however, few have much basis in fact. Common sense and a few precautions should keep you safe.

● Always carry cash in a belt or pouch—never in a pocket.

● Do not carry large amounts of cash: use credit cards or travelers' checks.

● Wear your camera and never put it

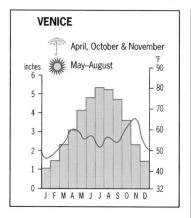

VENICE

April, October & November

May–August

CATÁNIA

March, October & November

May–September

down on café tables—and beware of strap-cutting thieves.

● Do not flaunt valuables—better still, leave them at home.

● Leave all jewelry in the hotel safe (not rooms). Chains and earrings worn in the street are easily snatched by bold thieves.

● Women should hold bags across their front, never hung over one shoulder, where they can be easily rifled or grabbed.

● Be careful of pickpockets on crowded buses or where large groups of tourists congregate (particularly if you are confronted by gangs of determined-looking gypsy kids, who will jostle you and rifle through your pockets).

● After dark, women especially should not linger in noncommercial parts of town, in parks, or around railroad stations.

● When driving always lock your car and never leave luggage, cameras or valuables inside.

Report any theft to your hotel and then to the police at the local *questura* (police station), many of which have a special department to deal with tourists' problems. They will issue documents (*denuncia*) to forward with any insurance claims. If you lose a passport report the loss to the police and then contact your consulate or embassy. To contact the police in an emergency, call 113.

Customs regulations
You may bring home up to $400 of foreign goods duty-free, provided you've been out of the country for at least 48 hours and haven't made an international trip in the past 30 days. Each member of the family is entitled to the same exemption; exemptions may be pooled.

For the next $1,000 of goods, a flat 10% rate is assessed; above $1,400 duties vary with merchandise. Travelers 21 or older are allowed one liter of alcohol, 100 cigars, and 200 cigarettes, and one bottle of perfume trademarked in the United States. Antiques and works of art over 100 years old are duty-free. Exceed these limits, and you'll be taxed at the port of entry and additionally in your home state.

Gifts under $50 may be mailed duty-free to stateside friends or relatives, with a limit of one package per day per addressee. Perfumes over $5, tobacco, and liquor are banned.

For *Know Before You Go*, a free brochure detailing customs regulations, contact the U.S. Customs Service (1301 Constitution Ave., Washington, D.C. 20029, tel: 202/927 6724.

Travelers with disabilities

Italy is not an easy country for people with physical disabilities, though facilities are slowly improving and staff at airports, stations, and museums are helpful (St. Peter's and the Vatican museums are wheelchair accessible). Italian State Tourist Offices in foreign countries (see page 270) provide a list of hotels equipped for people with disabilities, and addresses of helpful Italian associations in main cities. Some high-speed trains have wheelchair lifts (wheelchairs must be carried free by law): buses do not, though seats are reserved for passengers with disabilities.

Useful addresses

● **Australia:** Barrier-Free Travel, 57 Albyn Road, Strathfield NSW 2135 (tel: 02/742 5918).

● **Canada:** Canadian Rehabilitation Council for the Disabled, 45 Sheppard Avenue E, Suite 801, Toronto, Ontario M2N 5W9 (tel: 416/250 7490)

● **Republic of Ireland:** National Rehabilitation Board, 24–5 Clyde Road, Ballsbridge, Dublin 4 (tel: 01/684181).

● **New Zealand:** Disabled Persons Assembly, P.O. Box 27–186, 63 Hinkey Street, Wellington (tel: 04/857828).

An alternative form of travel in Rome

● **U.K.:** RADAR, 25 Mortimer Street, London W1 8AB (tel: 0171-637 5400); Holiday Care Service, 2 Old Bank Chambers, Station Road, Horley, Surrey RH6 9HW (tel: 01293 774535).

● **U.S.:** S.A.T.H. (Society for the Advancement of Travel for the Handicapped), 347 Fifth Avenue, Suite 610, New York NY 10016 (tel: 212/447 7284).

Domestic travel

Air Alitalia, its domestic affiliate A.T.I. and several smaller national carriers offer frequent services between cities and islands. Prices are high and it is often cheaper and more convenient to travel by train. Students and passengers between 12 and 25 qualify for 25 percent discounts on certain Alitalia flights, and there are 30 percent reductions on some night flights, plus 50 percent savings for family groups.

Boat The F.S. (see under **Rail**) and numerous private companies provide car ferries and hydrofoils to Sicily, Sardinia, Elba and the Tuscan archipelago, the Tremiti islands (Apulia), the Sicilian islands and the Bay of Naples islands. There are connections to Corsica, Malta, Tunisia, Egypt, and Israel. Car ferry reservations for summer travel to Sardinia and Elba should be made several months in advance.

Bus Long-haul buses (*pullman*) operate between most Italian cities, but timetables, departure points and frequency can be hard to pin down. It's best to ask about services at tourist offices or to visit the local bus terminal (*autostazione*), often situated outside the town's railroad station. Tickets must usually be bought before you travel from *tabacchi* (tobacconists) or the bus terminal. For city buses see page 268.

Rail Train is the best way of traveling around Italy without a car. The system is cheap and efficient. Except for a few private lines, the network is run by the Ferrovie dello Stato (F.S.). There are six basic train categories: *Super Rapido*, *Rapido* and *Inter City*, which stop only at major stations and charge a 30 percent supplement (*un supplemento*) that must be bought in addition to the normal ticket. *Espressi* and *diretti* stop at more stations, while *locali* stop at every station along the line.

● **Tickets** (*biglietti*) are available as a one-way (*andata*) or round-trip (*andata e ritorno*) in first (*prima*) or second class (*seconda classe*). Be sure to validate return tickets in yellow platform machines before traveling.

● **Fares** are calculated on a kilometric basis and are some of the cheapest in Europe. Round-trip (3-day) tickets are discounted 15 percent on distances up to 150 miles, and 30 miles on a day-round-trip.

● **Validity** Tickets are valid for one day from the day of issue up to 150 miles, plus an extra day of validity for each additional 120 miles up to a maximum of 6 days. If you are buying your ticket in advance—advisable at busy stations— be certain to specify your day of travel.

● **Reservations** Stations usually have separate ticket windows for reservations and sleepers (*cucetta*), the former worth considering for long journeys in summer when trains can be crowded.

● **Reductions** of 30 percent are available for families with a *Carta Famiglia* (Family Card); for travelers between 12 and 26 with a *Carta Verde* (reductions are 20 percent June 26–August 14): and for men over 65, women over 60 (with a *Carta d'Argento*). Cards are available from main stations and are valid for a year (except June 26–August 14 and December 18–28 for *Carta d'Argento*). Children between four and 12 travel half fare.

● **Passes** The F.S. issue three main passes: the *Chilometrico*, valid for 1,800 miles of travel over a maximum of 20 journeys; the

Biglietto Turistico Libera Circolazione, a travel-as-you-please card available for 8, 15, 21 and 30 day periods (1st and 2nd class); and a *Flexi Card* allowing 4 days' unlimited travel within a 9-day period (or 8 days within 21, or 12 within a month).

● **Timetables** If you use trains regularly be sure to buy the *Pozzorario*, a cheap biannual timetable widely available in bookstores and station kiosks.

Driving

While many city centers are congested, the rest of Italy has a superb network of *autostrade* (limited access highways), *superstrade* (main roads) and *strade statali* (minor roads). Tolls are charged on the *autostrade*.

Accidents If you have an accident, place a warning triangle 165 feet behind the car and call the police (tel: 112 or 113). Do not admit liability or make statements that might later incriminate you. Ask any witness(es) to remain, make a statement to the police and exchange names, addresses, car details and insurance companies' names and addresses with other driver(s) involved.

Breakdowns Put on your blinkers and place a warning triangle behind the car. Call the Automobile Club d'Italia (A.C.I.) 24-hour emergency number (tel: 116) and give the operator your location, car registration and make. Roadside assistance will be given, or the car will be towed to the nearest A.C.I. affiliated garage. The service is free to any visiting motorist driving a foreign registered vehicle.

For information on routes, road conditions, gas stations and garages that repair foreign makes of cars, contact the Automobile Club d'Italia (A.C.I.), Via Marsala 8, Rome (tel: 06/49 981). For road conditions call 1941/1942.

CONVERSION CHARTS

FROM	TO	MULTIPLY BY
Inches	Centimeters	2.54
Centimeters	Inches	0.3937
Feet	Meters	0.3048
Meters	Feet	3.2810
Yards	Meters	0.9144
Meters	Yards	1.0940
Miles	Kilometers	1.6090
Kilometers	Miles	0.6214
Acres	Hectares	0.4047
Hectares	Acres	2.4710
U.S. Gallons	Liters	3.7854
Liters	U.S. Gallons	0.2642
Ounces	Grams	28.35
Grams	Ounces	0.0353
Pounds	Grams	453.6
Grams	Pounds	0.0022
Pounds	Kilograms	0.4536
Kilograms	Pounds	2.205
U.S. Tons	Tonnes	0.9072
Tonnes	U.S. Tons	1.1023

MEN'S SUITS

U.K.	36	38	40	42	44	46	48
Rest of Europe	46	48	50	52	54	56	58
U.S.	36	38	40	42	44	46	48

DRESS SIZES

U.K.	8	10	12	14	16	18
France	36	38	40	42	44	46
Italy	38	40	42	44	46	48
Rest of Europe	34	36	38	40	42	44
U.S.	6	8	10	12	14	16

MEN'S SHIRTS

U.K.	14	14.5	15	15.5	16	16.5	17
Rest of Europe	36	37	38	39/40	41	42	43
U.S.	14	14.5	15	15.5	16	16.5	17

MEN'S SHOES

U.K.	7	7.5	8.5	9.5	10.5	11
Rest of Europe	41	42	43	44	45	46
U.S.	8	8.5	9.5	10.5	11.5	12

WOMEN'S SHOES

U.K.	4.5	5	5.5	6	6.5	7
Rest of Europe	38	38	39	39	40	41
U.S.	6	6.5	7	7.5	8	8.5

Documents Visitors bringing their own (foreign registered) car to Italy must be at least 18 years of age and carry the vehicle's registration documents (logbook) and a full, valid driver's license (*patente* in Italian). Third-party insurance is compulsory; an international green card, though not compulsory, is recommended. A foreign driver's license is acceptable if accompanied by a translation, available free from the ACI or the Italian State Tourist Office in the country of origin. The translation is not required for the new, pink E.U., U.K. or Republic of Ireland license.

Gas Gasoline (*benzina*) in Italy is among the most expensive in Europe. Diesel (*gasolio*) is cheaper.

Gas stations follow normal store hours (closed 1 to 4PM) and most close all day on Sunday (except on the *autostrade*). Self-service and 24-hour pumps which take L10,000 and L50,000 notes are increasingly common.

Parking Parking is often a nightmare in towns: parking spots (*parcheggi*) are invariably full and most historic centers are partially or fully closed to traffic. Try to leave your car in guarded parking areas, and never leave valuables or luggage in parked vehicles. Cars may be towed away if illegally parked: contact the local offices of the *Vigili Urbani* to effect recovery.

Renting a car Leading rental firms have offices in most cities and airports and, with local agencies, are listed in *Yellow Pages* under "Autonoleggio." Fly-drive deals can be organized through travel agents. Drivers must be over 21 and hold a valid license (an international driver's license is sometimes required).

Rules of the road Italian traffic rules follow the Geneva Convention and Italy uses international road signs. Driving is on the right and you should yield at intersections to vehicles coming from your right. The speed limit in built-up areas is 50 k.p.h.: outside urban areas it is 110 k.p.h., unless otherwise marked (when it is usually 90 k.p.h.). The limit on motorways is 130 k.p.h. for vehicles over 1,100cc. Carrying warning triangles and wearing front seat belts are compulsory.

Electricity
The current is 220 volts A.C., 50 cycles, with plugs of the two "round" pin type: a travel plug is useful. In older hotels and houses you will find two-pin plugs of different specifications, but adapters are widely available.

Embassies and consulates
All major countries are represented by an embassy in Rome. They include:
Australia: Via Alessandri 215 (tel: 06/854 271)
Canada: Via G. Bastia de Rossi 27 (tel: 06/841 5341)
Republic of Ireland: Largo Nazareno 3 (tel: 06/678 2541)
New Zealand: Via Zara 28 (tel: 06/440 2928)
U.K.: Via XX Settembre 80a (tel: 06/482 5441)
U.S.: Via Vittorio Veneto 119a (tel: 06/46 741)

Emergency telephone numbers

Police (*Carabinieri*) **112**
Emergency services (police, fire, ambulance) **113**
Fire (*Vigili di Fuoco*) **115**
Car breakdown **116**

Etiquette
● Do not wear shorts, short skirts or skimpy tops in churches.

● Do not intrude (or cause any sort of disturbance) while church services are in progress.

● Many churches forbid the use of flash with cameras, or ban photography altogether.

● There are still few nonsmoking areas in restaurants and public places. Smoking is banned on buses and subways.

● Topless sunbathing is tolerated on out-of-the-way beaches.

● Bargaining is no longer appropriate in shops, though in markets (except food markets) and budget hotels you may be able to negotiate lower rates.

Health
Visitors from E.U. countries can claim treatment free from the Italian Health Service. Get Form E111 from any main post office before traveling. If you need treatment, exchange the form at a *Unita Sanitaria Locale* (U.S.L.) office in Italy—see *Yellow Pages* for locations. The Local Health Unit will provide you with a Certificate of Entitlement and a list of doctors and dentists who provide treatment free of charge. If a doctor refers you to a hospital, you will be given a further certificate for free treatment in certain hospitals. If you go directly to a hospital, give your E111 to the authorities there (if you have proof of E.U. citizenship, you will be treated even if you have no E111). Keep all paperwork for any retrospective claim for costs. Though Italian hospitals may be a little disorganized, and the lines long, the standards of care and treatment are very high.

Key health points to remember are:

● Vaccinations are unnecessary for entry into Italy unless you are traveling from a known infected area.

● Take out health insurance; keep all receipts for medicines and treatment from doctors, dentists and hospitals.

● For minor ailments visit a pharmacist (see **Pharmacies**, page 266).

● If you need a doctor (*un medico*), ask at your hotel or drugstore, or consult the *Yellow Pages* under "Unita Sanitaria Locale" (U.S.L.).

● If you need first aid, visit the emergency department (*pronto soccorso*) of the nearest hospital (*ospedale*).

● If you need an ambulance (*ambulanza*) call the emergency services (tel: 113) or the Red Cross.

263

TRAVEL FACTS

● Water is safe to drink unless marked *acqua non potabile*.

● To avoid heat exhaustion and sunstroke drink plenty of water, wear a hat and do not spend long in the sun.

● Levels of air pollution are high in most Italian cities.

● Snakebites are rarely fatal. If bitten, try to note the snake's appearance, and visit a doctor or pharmacy for the appropriate serum.

● Condoms (*profilatici*) are available over the counter at drugstores and some supermarkets.

Language
Italians respond well to foreigners who make an effort to speak their language. In the more high-class hotels and restaurants, or in tourist cities, you should have few problems.

Courtesies:

Good morning: buon giorno

Good afternoon/good evening: buona sera

Good night: buona notte

Hello/goodbye (informal): ciao

Goodbye: arrivederci

Please: per favore

Thank you (very much): grazie (mille)

You're welcome: prego

How are you? (polite/informal): come sta/stai?

I'm fine: bene

I'm sorry: mi dispiace

Excuse me: mi scusi

Excuse me (in a crowd): permesso

All Italian words are pronounced as written, with each vowel and consonant sounded. Major points to remember include:

● Use the polite, third person (*Lei*) to speak to strangers: use the second person (*tu*) to friends or children.

● The letter **c** is hard, as in the English "cat" except when followed by **i** or **e**, when it becomes the soft *ch* of "children."

● The same applies to **g** when followed by **i** or **e**—soft in *giardino*, as in the English "giant"; hard in *gatto*, as in "gate."

● Words ending in **o** are almost always masculine gender (plural: **i**); those ending in **a** are feminine (plural: **e**).

Lost property
● Report losses to your hotel, then to the local police station (*questura*). Most larger bus terminals and railroad stations have lost property offices.

● Report loss or theft of passports to the police and then contact your embassy or nearest consulate.

● If you lose your travelers' checks or credit cards, notify the police, then follow the instructions given with the cards and checks and inform the issuing company's nearest office.

Maps
Excellent 1:200 000 Touring Club Italiano (TCI) maps, ideal for driving and route planning, are widely available in Italy. For walking maps, the main publishers are **Kompass, Tabacco, Multigraphic** and **Istituto Geografico Centrale** (IGC).

Newsstands and bookstores sell maps, but adequate street maps of towns and cities are usually available from local tourist offices.

Media
Italy's main national newspapers (*giornali*) include the authoritative Milan-based *Corriere della Sera* (center-right); the Turin-based *La Stampa*; and the Rome-based *La Repubblica* (center-left). The biggest-selling papers are sports papers like the pink *Gazzetta dello Sport* and *Corriere dello Sport*. The leading news magazines (*riviste*) are *L'Espresso*, *Panorama*, *Europeo* and *Epoca*.

Foreign-language newspapers and magazines are available in major tourist areas at 2PM on the day of issue. The European editions of the *Financial Times*, *Guardian* and *International Herald Tribune* are widely available at newsstands (*edicole*).

Italian radio and television offer a vast range of national and local stations. Standards are low, with local networks geared mainly to advertising, pop music and old films. National stations are better, dividing equally between the three channels of the state RAI network and the stable of channels owned by Silvio Berlusconi (*Canale 5, Rete 4* and *Italia Uno*).

Money matters

The unit of currency is the *lira* (plural *lire*), abbreviated to L, and is issued in denominations of: (notes) L1,000, L2,000, L5,000, L10,000, L50,000, L100,000; and (coins) L5, L10 (both rare), L50, L100, L200, L500. A L200 telephone token (*gettone*) can be used as a coin.

Italy is no longer plagued by a change shortage, but L50,000 and L100,000 notes can still cause problems. All the zeros can be confusing, so check change and all monetary transactions carefully.

Import and export

Visitors are advised to contact their banks for current information, but at present there are no restrictions on foreign currency brought into Italy. Up to L400,000 may be imported. To export more than L1,000,000 or the equivalent of more than L5,000,000 in foreign currency, you must sign form V2 at Customs on entry, and show it to Customs on leaving. Keep all your receipts and the stubs of your transactions.

Travelers' checks are free of upper limit restrictions, and all major checks as well as Eurocheques are widely recognized. L300,000 may be charged to each Eurocheque, and most banks and exchange outlets allow you to cash up to three checks daily.

Credit cards (*carta di credito*) are slowly gaining acceptance in larger hotels, shops and restaurants, but an establishment may refuse a card, even though it displays a sticker for one of the principal cards. It is worth checking well before you have to pay the bill. Also be sure it is impossible for stubs to be tampered with once you have signed. Some cards (Visa, Amex) can be used for cash at certain banks and from automatic machines. Many gas stations still will not accept cards.

Exchange Most banks will change foreign currency and travelers' checks—look for the sign *cambio*—but lines are often long and the service slow.

Special exchange outlets may offer marginally worse exchange rates, but they avoid frustration. Along with bureaux at airports and main railroad stations they are also open beyond normal banking hours. In the last resort big hotels will change money, but at poor rates.

265

National holidays

Stores, banks, offices and schools are closed on the following days:

January 1 (New Year's Day)
January 6 (Epiphany)
Easter Monday
Easter Sunday
April 25 (Liberation Day)
May 1 (Labor Day)
August 15 (Assumption)
November 1 (All Saints' Day)
December 8 (Immaculate Conception)
Christmas Day
December 26 (Santo Stefano)

Street café in Verona

When a public holiday falls on a Tuesday or Thursday it is customary to make a *ponte* (bridge) to the weekend and take the Monday or Friday off as well.

Opening times

Archeological sites Many sites are open all day from 9AM to one hour before dusk, but it is always wise to check times with local tourist offices.

Banks are open weekdays 8:30AM to 1:20PM, and some larger banks may open from 3 to 4PM.

Churches generally open around 7AM and close towards noon, opening again between 4 and 7PM Many churches remain closed except on Sundays and religious holidays: major cathedrals and basilicas like St. Peter's often remain open all day.

Museums and galleries run by the state usually open

No 129838

F. SARANDREA DIS.

REPUBBLICA ITALIANA
MINISTERO PER I BENI CULTURALI E AMBIENTALI
UFFICIO CENTRALE PER I BENI AMBIENTALI,
ARCHITETTONICI, ARCHEOLOGICI, ARTISTICI E STORICI

B

BIGLIETTO D'INGRESSO

LIRE 6000

I.P.Z.S. - OFF. C.V. - ROMA

TTO FINO ALL'USCITA.

Tuesday to Sunday from 9AM to 1 or 2PM; almost all shut on Mondays. A few also open from 4 to 7PM, on selected days. Afternoon hours during winter are more restricted, especially in smaller galleries.

Parks and public gardens usually open from 9AM to an hour before dusk.

Post offices usually open Monday to Friday 8 or 8:30AM to 2PM (to 12:30PM on Saturday). Main offices often stay open for some services until 8PM Offices everywhere close at noon on the last working day of the month.

Restaurants and bars close once a week for a *riposo settimanale.*

Stores and offices are normally open from 8:30 or 9AM until 1PM, reopening at 3:30 or 4 to 7:30 or 8PM. Most close on Sundays and on Monday mornings, and food stores may also close on Thursday afternoons. Garages are shut on Sundays; barbers and hairdressers on Sundays and Mondays. Supermarkets and department stores usually open 9:30AM to 8PM.

Pharmacies

A drugstore (*farmacia*) is identified by a green cross. Pharmacies keep the same hours as shops, but also open late on a rotation basis. When closed (during lunch, holidays or at night), they display a list of pharmacists open nearby.

Staff are well qualified to give advice on minor ailments, and can dispense medicines over the counter, including some only available by prescription in other countries. Brand names differ from country to country, so take your used-up medication to a pharmacist to help with identification. Remember to bring any prescription or doctor's notes that might be required to obtain medicine.

Police

Dial 113 in an emergency; in other situations go to the local police station (see **Crime** on pages 258–9).

Police on the street divide into:

● The semi-military *carabinieri*, with sharp-looking black uniforms.

● The *polizia statale,* in blue uniforms, who perform most day-to-day policing.

● The *polizia urbana* and *vigili urbani*, who deal mainly with traffic control and parking offenses.

Police registration In theory, you should register at a *questura* within three days of entering Italy. In practice no one does (hotels pass on their register instead).

Post Offices
See **Opening Times** on page 266.

Stamps (*francobolli*) can be bought from tobacconists (*tabacchi*) showing a blue "T" sign, the post office (*posta* or *ufficio postale*).

Mail to and from Italy can take three weeks. *Raccomandata* (registered) or *espresso* (express) are quicker. Letters can be sent *poste restante* to a town's main post office by addressing them *Fermo Posta*, followed by the name of the town. Take a passport when collecting mail: there is a small fee to pay. Filing can be haphazard, so check under your first and last names.

Telex, fax and telegrams can be sent from larger post offices.

The Vatican runs its own postal service, known for its efficiency. There are post offices in the square in front of St. Peter's in Rome.

Public transportation

Buses The urban bus (*autobus*) services of most towns and cities run along similar lines. Usually you must buy a ticket in advance from a machine, a newsstand, a *tabacchi*—or even from station bars—then validate it in a machine on the bus (roving inspectors and spot fines await anyone without a ticket). Tickets in some cities are valid for one journey, others for any number of journeys within a given time limit. Usually you enter a bus by its rear doors (marked *salita*) and leave by the center doors (*uscita*). A bus stop is known as *una fermata.*

Subway Several cities have an underground system (*la metropolitana*), which provides the quickest way across the city. Tickets must be bought beforehand from stores, kiosks or subway stations.

Taxis Always check that your taxi is a registered cab and that the meter is running. Supplements to the meter fare are levied for additional passengers, for luggage, journeys after 8PM and on Sundays and public holidays. Many cities have set rates from the airport to the city center. It can be difficult to hail taxis on the street, and most congregate at taxi stands. You can phone for cabs either through your hotel or by consulting *Yellow Pages.*

Senior citizens

Many discounts are available when visiting Europe, but some may require membership in a specific club. A 30 percent discount on rail fares is offered to senior citizens with a *Carta d'Argento* (Silver Card), available from mainline stations—see **Reductions** on page 261 for details.

Student and youth travel

Students and young travelers can enjoy reductions for train and some air travel (see pages 260 and 261) as well as discounts to museums, galleries and archeological sites by showing an I.S.I.C. card. There is free entrance to state museums for under-18s. Specialist youth travel agents Centro Turistico Studentesco e Giovanile (C.T.S.) have over 90 offices throughout Italy.

Bicycles and scooters

Bicycle and scooter rental outlets are increasingly springing up in popular tourist areas. Most rent by the hour or day and require a credit card or passport as deposit.

Telephones

● Italy's main telephone company (S.I.P.) provides public telephones in many bars, on the street and in special S.I.P. offices, all of which are marked by a red or yellow sign showing a telephone dial and receiver.

● Most Italian phones accept L100, L200, and L500 coins as well as a L200 token, or *gettone*, which can be bought from most bars and *tabacchi*; the oldest phones, usually found in bars, may well only accept these tokens.

● Public phones are increasingly being modified to accept phone cards (*schede telefoniche*), on sale in L5,000, L10,000 and L15,000 denominations from *tabacchi*, or stores with a SIP sticker (remember to tear the corner off the card before using).

Telephone services
Operator 15
International operator
(Europe) 15
International operator
(Intercontinental) 170
International Directory
Enquiries 176
Police 112/113
Emergency services 113
ACI car breakdowns 116
Post office enquiries 160
Time 161
Road reports 1941/1942
Snow reports 162
Alarm call service 114

International calls
To call abroad from Italy dial 00, then the country code, followed by the town or city code, then the number (omitting the first zero in any town or city code). To call Italy from the U.S. dial 011 39 plus the town code (minus any zero) and number. Country prefixes from Italy include:
Australia 00 61
Canada 001
Republic of Ireland 00 353
New Zealand 00 64
U.K. 00 44
U.S. 001

● Peak period during weekdays is from 8AM to 1PM, off-peak from 1PM to 8PM, and the cheapest rates are at all other times. The cheap international rate is at weekends and 8PM to 8AM during the week.

● Note that the Italian telephone system is currently undergoing another of its major overhauls and many numbers in this book will change as a result: free S.I.P. announcements give new numbers.

● For international calls use phone cards or a *telefono a scatti*, where you speak first and pay later: these special cabins are found in some bars and hotels, post offices, some tourist offices and in most S.I.P. offices.

● To make a collect or reverse charge call dial 15 (Europe) or 170 (Intercontinental) and ask to make *una chaimata con pagamento a destinazione*.

Time
Italy is 6 hours ahead of Eastern Standard Time, 7 hours ahead of Central Standard Time, 8 hours ahead of Mountain Standard Time and 9 hours ahead of Pacific Standard Time. Montréal is 6 hours behind Italy, London is 1 hour behind, and Sydney is 8 hours ahead during the summer.

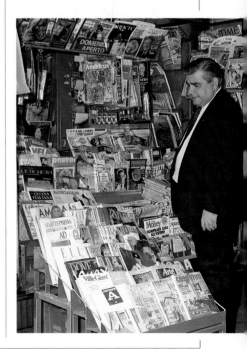

Tipping

● A 10 to 15 percent service charge (*servizio*) is usually added to restaurant bills, but waiters expect a small tip in addition.

● Taxi drivers should be tipped 10 percent.

● For quick service in bars you might wish to do as the locals do and slap down a L100 or L200 coin with your receipt when ordering.

● Tip hotel staff (porters, doormen, room service) around L1,000–L2,000 depending on the standard of hotel.

● Movie and theater ushers expect a small tip for showing you to your seats.

● Give something to custodians or sacristans if they have opened up churches or museums especially for your benefit, or outside normal opening hours.

tourist office known as an *Azienda Autonoma di Soggiorno e Turismo* (A.A.S.T.). Most follow normal store hours and offer maps, information and help with finding accommodations. (The *Ente Provinciale per il Turismo* (E.P.T.) is a complex bureaucracy that doesn't do much to dispense information.) Villages may only have a small office known as a *Pro Loco*, with limited opening hours.

Toilets

Public rest rooms are rare in Italy, found mainly in railroad stations and larger museums, and most of the time you have to use the grim facilities in bars and cafés. Ask for *il gabinetto* or *bagno* and do not confuse *signori* (men) with *signore* (women). Some larger places may have an attendant and small dish for tips—leave around L200.

Tourist offices

The tourist system is currently being reorganized, but most towns, main railroad stations and airports have a

Valeting and laundry

While Italy boasts very few coin-operated laundromats, virtually every town and village has an old-style cleaners (*una tintoria*). Service is friendly and efficient, and clothes come back pressed, packaged, and looking as good as new. Most places also offer dry-cleaning (*lava a secco*).

Youth hostels

Italy has about 50 youth hostels (*Alberghi per la Gioventù*) affiliated to Hostelling International (H.I.). Dormitory beds can be hard to come by without reservations in summer (many hostels close off season). In theory you should be a member of your national youth hostel association, but in practice many hostels allow you to join on the spot, or they simply charge a higher fee to nonmembers.

HOTELS AND RESTAURANTS

HOTELS AND RESTAURANTS

$$$ = expensive
$$ = moderate
$ = budget

ACCOMMODATIONS

ROME

The telephone code for Rome is 06.

Ambasciatori ($$$) Via V Veneto 70 (tel: 47 493). Long-established and recently refurbished luxury hotel; impeccable service and facilities.

Carriage ($$) Via delle Carrozze 36 (tel: 679 3312 or 699 0124). Renovated old world elegance near the Spanish Steps.

Columbus ($$) Via della Conciliazione 33 (tel: 686 5435). Renaissance *palazzo* and gracious atmosphere; near St. Peter's and a favorite of visiting cardinals.

Della Lunetta ($) Piazza del Paradiso 68 (tel: 686 1080). Cheap, large but dowdy rooms; busy location near Campo dei Fiori.

Excelsior ($$$) Via V Veneto 125 (tel: 4708). One of Rome's top hotels; polished and prestigious, but relaxed and appealing atmosphere.

Fiorella ($) Via del Babuino 196 (tel: 361 0597). Friendly, popular place whose eight rooms near Piazza di Spagna must be reserved in advance.

Grand ($$$) Via Vittorio Emanuele Orlando 3 (tel: 4709). No longer a fine location, but still the haunt of V.I.P.s and visiting royalty.

Hassler ($$$) Piazza Trinità dei Monti 6 (tel: 678 2651). Grand position above Spanish Steps and one of Rome's top hotels.

Hotel d'Inghilterra ($$$) Via Bocca di Leone 14 (tel: 672 161). Favorite of 19th-century writers and artists; at the heart of Rome's shopping district.

La Residenza ($$) Via Emilia 22 (tel: 488 0789). Good value rooms in converted town house off Via V Veneto.

Locarno ($$) Via della Penna 22 (tel: 361 0841). Atmospheric old favorite in side street near Piazza del Popolo.

Lord Byron ($$$) Via G de Notaris 5 (tel: 361 3041). Parkland setting away from center in leafy Parioli; exclusive and perhaps most splendidly decorated of Rome's luxury hotels; noted restaurant.

Margutta ($$) Via Laurina 34 (tel: 322 3674). Pretty, with average rooms in quiet loc tion near Piazza del Popolo.

Perugia ($) Via del Colosseo 7 (tel: 679 7200). On quiet side street near Colosseum.

Pomezia ($) Via dei Chiavari 12 (tel: 686 1371). Bargain rooms near Piazza Navona.

Portoghesi ($$) Via dei Portoghesi 1 (tel: 686 4231). Once a bargain, now no longer cheap, but still popular; near Piazza Navona; fine roof terrace and views.

Raphael ($$$) Largo di Febo 2 (tel: 682 831). Beautiful, stylish and favored by politicians (it stands opposite the parliament).

Sistina ($$) Via Sistina 136 (tel: 4890 0316). Quiet and reliable hotel near Piazza di Spagna; lovely terrace.

Smeraldo ($) Via dei Chiodaroli 11 (tel: 687 5929). Refitted, comfortable and popular hotel 2 minutes from Campo dei Fiori.

Sole ($) Via del Biscione 76 (tel: 6880 6873). Well-known backpackers' favorite; busy rooms off Campo dei Fiori.

THE NORTHWEST

Aosta

Europe ($$$) Piazza Narbonne 8 (tel: 0165/236 363). Central 5-story hotel renovated in 1991.

Rayon du Soleil ($$) Saraillon 16 (tel: 0165/262 247). Traditional hotel in the hills above Aosta; quiet with views.

Asti

Alermo ($$$) Via E Filiberto 13 (tel: 0141/595 661). Best hotel in town.

Cavour ($) Piazza Marconi 18 (tel: 0141/530 222). A good, modern and cheap hotel in the town center.

Rainero ($$) Via Cavour 85 (tel: 0141/353 866). Oldish family-run hotel near station.

Cinqueterre

Porto Roca ($$$) Monterosso (tel: 0187/817 502). Quietly situated on a hill near the town. Sea views.

Genova (Genoa)

Agnello d'Oro ($) Vico delle Monachette 6 (tel: 010/262 084). Centrally placed near the station; simple but air-conditioned.

Bristol Palace ($$$) Via XX Settembre 35 (tel: 010/592 541). Top-class hotel in the fashionable part of the city.

Major ($) Vico Spada 4 (tel: 010/293 449). A bargain; central, modern and clean.

Pagoda Residence ($$$) Via Capolungo 15, Nervi (tel: 010/326 161). Idiosyncratic small hotel 6 miles out.

Riviera di Levante

Cenobio dei Dogi ($$$) Via Cuneo 34, Camogli (tel: 0185/770 041). Modernized former summer villa of Genoa's doges, high above the town.

Piccolo Hotel ($$) Portofino (tel: 0185/69 015). Small and modern, overlooking the harbor; attracts younger set.

Royal Sporting ($$) Via dell' Olivo 345, Portovenere (tel: 0187/900 326). Modern beach hotel near village; excellent sports facilities.

San Pietro ($$) Portovenere (tel: 0187/900 616). Quietly located in a castle near beach. Restaurant serves local seafood.

Splendido ($$$) Portofino (tel:0185/269 551). About as luxurious and expensive as an Italian hotel gets.

Riviera di Ponente

Eden ($) Passeggiata Cadorna 20, Alassio tel: 0182/640 281). Small friendly hotel by the beach, 10 minutes from town center.

Grand Hotel Capo Ampelio ($$$) Via Virgilio 5, Bordighera (tel: 0184/264 333). Quietly located, this hilltop villa has been sympathetically converted.

Grand Hotel del Mare (($$$) Via Portico della Punta 34, Bordighera (tel: 0184/262 201). Top-quality hotel on a hill above the beach; great views and good facilities.

Paradiso ($$) Via Roccastorone 12, San Remo (tel: 0184/571 211). Quiet modern hotel set in its own garden.

Royal ($$$) Corso Imperatrice 80, San Remo (tel: 0184/53 91). Luxury hotel near the casino where the top people stay.

Torino (Turin)
Alfieri ($) Via G Pomba 7 (tel: 011/839 5911). Best of Turin's many cheap hotels.

Jolly Ligure ($$) Piazza Carlo Felice 85 (tel: 011/55 641). Large, centrally situated hotel in a restored and modernized old building.

Principi di Piemonte ($$$) Via Gobetti 15 (tel: 011/562 9693). Elegant hotel patronized by the rich and famous.

Victoria ($$) Via Nino Costa 4 (tel: 011/561 1909). Central, pleasant and modern, decorated in idiosyncratic style.

LOMBARDY AND EMILIA-ROMAGNA
Bergamo
Agnello d'Oro ($) Via Gombito 22 (tel: 035/249 883). One of the few cheap places in the old town.

Excelsior San Marco ($$$) Piazza della Repubblica 6 (tel: 035/366 111). Top hotel with renowned restaurant, the *Tino Fontana*.

Bologna
Apollo ($) Via Drapperie 5 (tel: 051/223 955). Clean, spacious and central.

Corona d'Oro ($$$) Via Oberdan 12 (tel: 051/236 456). Old hotel, once a printing house.

Orologio ($$) Via IV Novembre 10 (tel: 051/231 253). Reserve well in advance for this quiet, central and popular hotel.

Roma ($$) Via Massimo d'Azeglio 9 (tel: 051/226 322). Traditional hotel:

Como, Lago di
Barchetta Excelsior ($$$) Piazza Cavour 1, Como (tel: 031/3221). Refurbished hotel with lakefront setting (not all rooms have a view of the lake).

Du Lac ($$) Piazza Mazzini 32, Bellagio (tel: 031/950 320).

Lakeside hotel in village center; great views from roof terrace.

Tre Re ($$) Via Boldoni 20, Como (tel: 031/265 374). Modernized 16th-century palace by the cathedral with popular and delightful terrace restaurant.

Villa d'Este ($$$) Via Regina 40, Cernobbio (tel: 031/511 471). The most famous and expensive hotel in the Lakes region: marble staircases, chandeliers, etc, plus every facility you could possibly wish for.

Ferrara
Duchessa Isabella ($$$) Via Palestro 70 (tel: 0532/202 121). You will think you are in the 16th century—the staff even wear period dress.

Ripagrande ($$$) Via Ripagrande 21 (tel: 0532/765 250). Try for rooms on the top floor of this restored medieval *palazzo* in the center of the old town.

Garda, Lago di
Catullo ($$) Piazza Flaminia (tel: 030/916 181). Recently refurbished hotel with fine views in the center of the old town.

Sirmione ($$) Piazza Castello 19, Sirmione (tel: 030/916 331). Lakeside hotel in a charming garden setting. Guests tend to return year after year.

Villa del Sogno ($$$) Corso Zanardelli 107, Gardone Riviera (tel: 0365/290 181). Beautifully situated above the lake: very relaxing.

Lago Maggiore
Des Iles Borromes ($$$) Lungolago Umberto I 167, Stresa (tel: 0323/30 431). Famous, palatial and highly expensive hotel, in business since 1863.

La Fontana ($) On the Sempione road (SS33), Stresa (tel: 0323/32 707). This small friendly place is on a busy road but does have a garden.

Milan au Lac ($$) Piazza Marconi, Stresa (tel: 0323/31 190). This is a large and traditional hotel. Watch the boats arrive and depart at the nearby dock.

Mantova (Mantua)
Bianchi Stazione ($) Piazza Don E Leoni 24 (tel: 0376/321 504). Good budget spot near the station.

San Lorenzo ($$$) Piazza Concordia 14 (tel: 0376/220 500). Modernized hotel in old *palazzo* in the historic center. Pleasantly characterful.

Milano (Milan)
Antica Locanda Solferino ($$) Via Castelfidardo 2 (tel: 02/657 0129). Advance reservations are essential for this popular little inn in the Brera district.

Diana Majestic ($$$) Viale Piave 42 (tel: 021/2951 3404). Lovely, smart art-deco hotel run by Cigna group.

Manzoni ($$) Via Santo Spirito 20 (tel: 02/7600 5700). Excellent central location, and popular—reserve ahead.

Rovello ($) Via Rovello 18a (tel: 02/8646 4654). Basic décor in this small budget *pensione*, a favorite with the young.

Parma
Croce di Malta ($) Borgo Palmia 8 (tel: 0521/235 643). Really a restaurant but with a few cheap rooms; situated in the center.

Park Hotel Stendhal ($$$) Via Bodoni 3 (tel: 0521/208 057). One of Parma's top hotels; well placed for sightseeing.

Torino ($$) Via Mazza 7 (tel: 0521/281 046). An agreeable and friendly place, central yet quiet.

Ravenna
Bisanzio ($$$) Via Salara 30 (tel: 0544/217 111). Smooth, comfortable central hotel:

Ravenna ($) Via Maroncelli 12 (tel: 0544/212 204). Modern hotel, handy for the station. Gets full in season.

VENICE
The telephone code for Venice is 041.

Accademia ($$) Fondamenta Bollani, Dorsoduro 1058 (tel: 521 0188). One of the city's most popular and charming hotels (reserve up to a year ahead). Ample rooms, but not always quiet or spacious; homey atmosphere, reasonable rates.

HOTELS AND RESTAURANTS

Agli Alboretti ($$) Rio Terra Sant'Agnese, Dorsoduro 882/4 (tel: 523 0058). Simple, attractive family-run hotel; modern rooms but cozy atmosphere; central location.

Ca' Foscari ($) Calle della Frescada, Dorsoduro 3888 (tel: 522 5817). Quiet, attractive and easygoing.

Caneva ($) Ramo della Fava, Castello 5515 (tel: 522 8118). Close to the Rialto but still quiet; most rooms overlook a canal.

Casa Petrarca ($) Calle delle Colonne, San Marco 4386 (tel: 520 0430). Friendly, only six rooms.

Casa Verardo ($) Ruga Giuffa, Castello 4765 (tel: 528 6127). Probably the best choice in this part of the city.

Cipriani ($$$) Giudecca 10 (tel: 520 7744). Famous and luxurious, but away from the heart of the city.

Danieli ($$$) Riva degli Schiavoni, Castello 4196 (tel: 522 6480). Famous since 1822; still celebrity-packed despite a fading reputation; rooms and suites vary; avoid the annexe.

Flora ($$) Calle Bergamaschi, off Calle Larga XXII Marzo, San Marco 2283a (tel: 520 5844). Haunt of U.K. and U.S. visitors; delightful and relaxing hotel (though some rooms are dark or very cramped); pretty garden.

Gritti Palace ($$$) Campo Santa Maria del Giglio, San Marco 2467 (tel: 794 611). Superb location and setting; elegant service and supreme old-world luxury.

La Fenice et des Artistes ($$) Campiello della Fenice 1936, San Marco (tel: 523 2333). Slightly arty hotel (thanks to clients from the nearby opera house); rooms vary in size and décor—those in the old wing are more appealing.

La Residenza ($) Campo Bandiera e Moro 3608 (tel: 528 5315). There is a feeling of genuine old Venice in this small, low-key hotel.

Londra Palace ($$$) Riva degli Schiavoni 4171 (tel: 520 0533). Distinguished atmosphere; watery views.

Metropole ($$$) Riva degli Schiavoni 4149 (tel: 520 5044). Small, subtle and exclusive hotel with canal and garden rooms.

Monaco and Grand Canal ($$$) Calle Vallaresso, San Marco 1325 (tel: 520 0211). Intimate luxury hotel on the Grand Canal; some rooms rather small; excellent service.

Pausania ($$) Fondamenta Gherardini, Dorsoduro 2824 (tel: 522 2083). Quiet, stylish 3-star hotel close to Campo Santa Margherita.

Sant'Anna ($) Corte del Bianco, Castello 269 (tel: 528 6466). Away from the center and crowds; good for families.

Santo Stefano ($$) Campo Santo Stefano, San Marco 2957 (tel: 520 0166). Tiny, immaculate 11-roomed hotel near the Accademia; modest sized rooms with nice décor.

Stefania ($) Fondamenta Tolentini, Santa Croce 181 (tel: 520 3757). Close to the station.

THE NORTHEAST
Asolo
Villa Cipriani ($$$) Via Canova 298 (tel: 0423/952 166). One of the most beautiful and alluring of all the CIGA chain's hotels.

Bolzano-Bozen
Croce Bianca-Weisses Kreuz ($) Piazza del Grano/ Kornplatz 3 (tel: 047/977 553). Pleasant and cheap hotel-café.

Grifone-Greif ($$$) Piazza Walther (tel: 0471/977 056). Venerable hotel perfectly located on the town's central square; noted restaurant.

Luna-Mondschein ($$) Via Piave 15 (tel: 0471/975 642). Established and run by the same family for two centuries, this hotel is central, tranquil and friendly.

Padova (Padua)
Bellevue ($) Via L Belludi 11 (tel: 049/862 493). Nice rooms around an ivy-covered courtyard.

Europa ($$) Largo Europa 9 (tel: 049/661 200). Well-placed but unexciting central hotel:

Trento
Accademia ($$$) Vicolo Collico 4/6 (tel: 0461/233 600). Central and amiable hotel in medieval building with modern fittings. Noted restaurant with *nouvelle cuisine* edge.

Treviso
Campeol ($) Piazza Ancillotto 8 (tel: 0422/56 601). A reliable mid-range hotel in the town center.

Continental ($$$) Via Roma 16 (tel: 0422/411 216). Conveniently situated for exploring the old town; comfortable rooms with all modern conveniences.

Le Beccherie ($) Piazza Ancillotto 11 (tel: 0422/540 871). Budget first choice.

Trieste
Duchi d'Aosta ($$$) Piazza dell'Unità d'Italia 2 (tel: 040/7351). Central and beautifully appointed hotel with elegant restaurant (*Harry's Grill*).

Hotel al Teatro ($$) Via Capo di Piazza G. Bartoli 1 (tel: 040/ 366 220). Old-style neoclassical hotel near the opera.

Verona
Colomba d'Oro ($$$) Via Cattaneo 10 (tel: 045/595 300). Quiet and comfortable hotel close to the Arena.

Giulietta e Romeo ($$) Vicolo Tre Marchetti 3 (tel: 045/800 3554). Unpretentious smallish hotel; good value and well placed for sightseeing.

Il Torcolo ($$) Vicolo Listone 3 (tel: 045/800 7512). Close to the Arena and like all Verona's hotels must be reserved in advance during the opera season.

Victoria ($$$) Via Adua 8 (tel: 045/590 566). Small, plush and quiet.

Vicenza
Campo Marzio ($$) Viale Roma 21 (tel: 0444/545 700). This modern hotel has well-equipped rooms a short walk from the city center.

FLORENCE

The telephone code for Florence is 055.

Annalena ($$) Via Romana 34 (tel: 222 402). Famous 14th-century hotel near Pitti and Boboli gardens; favorite with writers and artists over the years.
Ariston ($) Via Fiesolana 42 (tel: 247 6980). Cheap hotel east of Piazza 55. Annunziata.
Ausinia e Rimini ($) (tel: 262 203) & **Kursal** (tel: 496 547) Via Nazionale 22. Refitted hotels under the same management near the station.
Beacci Tornabuoni ($$$) Via dei Tornabuoni 3 (tel: 268 377). Famously quaint and archetypal old-world *pensione* (half board required).
Excelsior ($$$) Piazza Ognissanti 3 (tel: 264 201). Top rate luxury class hotel; part of the CIGA chain. Its renowned *Il Cestello* restaurant has magnificent views of the city from its summer roof terrace.
Grand Hotel Villa Cora ($$$) Viale Machiavelli 18 (tel: 229 8451). Venerable and opulent rooms, pool, large garden.
Hermitage ($$) Vicolo Marzio 1 (tel: 287 216). Popular with U.K. and U.S. visitors. Good 3-star overlooking the Arno.
Kraft ($$) Via Solferino 2 (tel: 284 273). Quiet, comfortable and spacious; small pool and panoramic roof terrace.
La Mia Casa ($) Piazza Santa Maria Novella 23 (tel: 213 061). Best of several hotels on this square.
Loggiato dei Serviti ($$) Piazza della Santissima Annunziata 3 (tel: 289 592). 19th-century elegance and 20th-century comfort in a quiet pleasant square.
Monna Lisa ($$$) Borgo Pinti 27 (tel: 247 9751). Cozy, rather small and much sought-after rooms, but aristocratic fittings and communal spaces; located in a Renaissance *palazzo* close to the Duomo.
Regency Umbria ($$$) Piazza d'Azeglio 3 (tel: 245 247). Quiet and charm at top prices. Noted restaurant.
Rigatti ($$) Lungarno Diaz 2 (tel: 213 022). Top two floors of 19th-century *palazzo*; airy rooms with plush antique fittings; advance reservations essential.
Sorelle Bandini ($) Piazza Santo Spirito 9 (tel: 215 308). Fine choice in Oltrarno; views, lofty rooms and lovely fittings.
Splendor ($) Via S Gallo 30 (tel: 483 427). Quiet and congenial hotel near San Marco.
Villa San Michele ($$$) Via Doccia 4, Fiesole (tel: 59 451). Small, romantic and exclusive hotel in hills outside the city.

TUSCANY

Arezzo

Continentale ($$) Piazza Guido Monaco 7 (tel: 0575/320 251). Well equipped and cheerfully furnished; near station and sights.

Lucca

Ilaria ($) Via del Fosso 18 (tel: 0583/47 558). Family-owned budget choice within easy walking distance of the main sights.
Universo ($$) Piazza del Giglio, off Piazza Napoleone (tel: 0583/493 678). Traditional; highest ranking spot in the town center.
Villa La Principessa ($$$) Massa Pisana, 2 miles from Lucca on Via Nuova (tel: 0583/379 737). Lots of old-world charm in this lovely country house set in its own park.

Pisa

Cavalieri ($$$) Piazza della Stazione 2 (tel: 050/43 290). Modern and handy for the station and airport.
Royal Victoria ($$) Lungarno Pacinotti 12 (tel: 050/940 111). River views from this *palazzo* 10 minutes from the cathedral square; comfortable with varied decor.

San Gimignano

La Cisterna ($$) Piazza della Cisterna (tel: 0577/940 328). Venerable old inn in the center of town, with highly respected restaurant.
Pescille ($$) (tel: 0577/940 186). Tasteful hotel 2 miles from San Gimignano; pool, garden and views of village.

Siena

Certosa di Maggiano ($$$) Via Certosa 82 (tel: 0577/288 180). Small and highly exclusive hotel in former monastery 1 mile outside town.
Hotel Duomo ($$) Via Stalloreggi 38 (tel: 0577/289 088). Solid central choice.
Palazzo Ravizza ($$) Via Pian dei Mantellini 34 (tel: 0577/280 462). Traditional hotel in 17th-century *palazzo*; snug and faded grandeur.
Santa Caterina ($) Via Piccolomini 7 (tel: 0577/221 105). Town house converted into a small modern hotel in the mid-1980s; garden.

Volterra

San Lino ($$) Via San Lino 26, near Porta San Francesco (tel: 0588/85 250). Central choice with pool; formerly a convent.
Villa Nencini ($$) Borgo Santo Stefano 55 (tel: 0588/86 386). Just out of town center; pool and garden.

275

UMBRIA & THE MARCHES

Assisi

Hotel Umbra ($$) Via degli Archi 6 (tel: 075/812 240). The guest rooms have terraces in this 400-year-old building in a traffic-free location.
Italia ($) Vicolo della Fortezza 2 (tel: 075/812 625). Tiny hotel just off main square.
La Rocca ($) Via di Porta Perlici 27 (tel: 075/816 467). In a quiet part of town.
Subasio ($$$) Via Frate Elia 2 (tel: 075/812 206). Lots of old world elegance close to the Basilica; rooms with views.

Gubbio

Ai Cappuccini ($$$) Via Tifernate (tel: 075/922 9234). Modern luxury in converted 14th-century monastery.
Bosone ($$) Via XX Settembre 22 (tel: 075/922 0688). In a frescoed palace in the heart of Gubbio.
Dei Consoli ($$) Via dei Consoli 59 (tel: 075/927 3335). Excellent location in central medieval street.
Hotel Gattapone ($) Via Ansidei 6 (tel: 075/927 2489). Small family-run hotel in the town center; comfortable and informal.

HOTELS AND RESTAURANTS

Norcia

Grotta Azzurra ($$) Via Alfieri 12 (tel: 0743/816 513). Perfect, amiable central hotel with a great restaurant.

Orvieto

La Badia ($$$) La Badia, 3 miles south of Orvieto (tel: 0763/90 359). Monastery converted into famous country hotel; pool andtennis courts.

Maitani ($$) Via Maitani 5 (tel: 0763/42 011). This baroque palace in the center of town offers comfortable, if not over-modern, accommodation.

Virgilio ($$) Piazza del Duomo 5 (tel: 0763/41 882). Small unassuming hotel by the cathedral; nice rooms.

Perugia

La Rosetta ($$$) Piazza d'Italia 19 (tel: 075/572 0841). You can stay in the old building or in a new wing; the restaurant is well regarded.

Locanda della Posta ($$$) Corso Vannucci 97 (tel: 075/572 8925). Lovely small hotel in the old quarter with views over the town.

Palace Hotel Bellavista ($$) Piazza d'Italia 12 (tel: 075/572 0741). Grand hotel in a 19th-century *palazzo*.

Spoleto

Aurora ($) Via dell'Apollinare 4 (tel: 0743/220 315). Small, central and quiet place in the upper town.

Dei Duchi ($$$) Viale Matteotti 2 (tel: 0743/44 541). Fine town-center hotel with garden, close to Roman amphitheater.

Gattapone ($$$) Via del Ponte 6 (tel: 0743/223 447). Tiny hotel with tempting views and lovely rooms.

Todi

Bramante ($$$) Via Orvietana 48 (tel: 075/894 8381). Converted medieval convent near S M della Consolazione.

Urbino

Bonconte ($$$) Via delle Mura 28 (tel: 0722 2463). Avoid the small top-floor rooms.

Hotel San Giovanni ($$) Via Barocci 13 (tel: 0722/28 27). Unpretentious but comfortable hotel in a converted medieval building in old Urbino.

LAZIO & ABRUZZO
L'Aquila

Grand e del Parco ($$) Corso Federico II 74 (tel: 0862/413 248). Best of the upscale hotels.

Sole ($) Largo Silvestre dell'Aquila 4 (tel: 0862/24 041). Airy, sunny rooms in a quiet street off Corso V Emanuele near Piazza del Duomo.

Parco Nazionale d'Abruzzo

Cristiana ($$) Pescasseroli (tel: 0863/910 795). Popular and welcoming wooden chalet-type mountain hotel:

Subiaco

Belvedere ($$) Via dei Monasteri 33 (tel: 0774/85 531). On the road between the town and the monasteries; has a welcoming restaurant.

Sulmona

Europa Park ($$) (tel: 0864/251 260). Large 105-room hotel in rural setting out of town on the SS17 road.

Italia ($) Piazza Tommaso 3, off Plazza XX Settembre (tel: 0864/52 308). Popular, central and cheap; Puccini was one of the first guests.

Tarquinia

Tarconte ($$) Via Tuscia 23 (tel: 0766/856 585). Modern and perfunctory, but outstanding views from some rooms and panoramic summer dining.

CAMPANIA
Amalfi

Amalfi ($$) Via dei Pastai 3 (tel: 089/872 440). Spotless rooms and terraces and citrus garden make this a good mid-range choice; reservations essential.

Hotel Luna Convento ($$$) Via P. Comite 19 (tel: 089/871

002). A lovely, converted 13th-century abbey; avoid street-side rooms.

Lidomare ($$) Via Piccolomini 9 (tel: 089/871 332). Smart, small and clean.

Miramalfi ($$) Via Quasimodo 3 (tel: 089/871 588). Quietly located modern hotel one half mile out of town, overlooking the sea.

Santa Caterina ($$$) Strada Amalfitana 9 (tel: 089/871 012). One of the area's best hotels; swimming pool and lovely grounds.

Sole ($) Largo della Zecca (tel: 089/871 147). One of several cheap places near the cathedral.

Capri

Quattro Stagioni ($) Via Marina Piccola 1, Capri Town (tel: 081/837 0041). Cozy rooms with views.

Quisisana ($$$) Via Camerelle 2, Capri Town (tel: 081/837 0788). Island's top hotel and a favorite of visiting Americans; very expensive.

Scalinatella ($$$) Via Tragara 8, Capri Town (tel: 081/837 0633). Intimate modern hotel with views, pool and luxury features.

Villa Brunella ($$) Via Tragara 24, Capri Town (tel: 081/837 0122). Tasteful hotel with terraces, views, pool and noted restaurant.

Villa Eva ($) Via La Fabbrica 8, Anacapri (tel: 081/837 2040). Secluded bliss.

Villa Krupp ($$) Via Matteotti 12, near Giardini di Augusto (tel: 081/837 0362). Quiet and small; Lenin and Gorky stayed here.

Ischia

Delle Rose ($) Via Casa Mennella 9 (tel: 081/994 682). In cheaper village of Casamicciola.

La Villarosa ($$) Via Giacinto Gigante 5 (tel: 081/991 316). Tasteful hotel in lovely garden setting. Private pool.

Regina Isabella ($$$) Piazza Restituita, Lacco Ameno (tel: 081/994 322). The island's top luxury hotel.

Napoli (Naples)

Ausonia ($) Via Caracciolo 11 (tel: 081/682 278). One of Naples' better budget hotels: seafront position in Mergellina.

Cavour ($$) Piazza Garibaldi 32 (tel: 081/283 122). One of the better hotels in this otherwise dingy and depressing area near the station.

Excelsior ($$$) Via Partenope 48 (tel: 081/764 0111). The city's top hotel.

Rex ($$) Via Palepoli 12 (tel: 081/764 9227). More bland alternative to the Excelsior in a convenient and relatively quiet location near the Santa Lucia waterfront.

Positano

California ($) Via Colombo 141 (tel: 089/875 382). Good budget choice.

Casa Albertina ($$$) Via Tavolozza 3 (tel: 089/875 143). Friendly, cheerful small hotel, run by the owner; good view from terrace and roof garden.

Palazzo Murat ($$) Via dei Mulini 23 (tel: 089/875 177). Town center location with garden setting and elegant old-world charm.

San Pietro ($$$) Amalfi Coast Road (tel: 089/875 455). The best in the area; extravagant luxury and exclusivity; very expensive.

Sirenuse ($$$) Via Cristoforo Colombo 30 (tel: 089/875 066). The town center's luxury choice; views, pool and large, tasteful rooms.

Ravello

Belvedere Caruso ($$) Via San Giovanni del Toro 52 (tel: 089/857 111). Charming old-fashioned villa hotel; lovely garden and restaurant; first choice in the range.

Palumbo ($$$) Palazzo Gonfalone (tel: 089/857 244). There are just eight attractive rooms here; stunning views; very elegant and very expensive.

Villa Amore ($) Via Santa Chiara 5 (tel: 089/857 135). Garden looking over cliffs and sea.

Villa Maria ($) Via Santa Chiara 2 (tel: 089/857 255). Small and quiet *pensione* with pretty garden and friendly ambience.

Sorrento

Bellevue Syrene ($$) Piazza della Vittoria 5 (tel: 081/878 1024). Old-style comfort in this villa hotel above the sea; garden.

Cocumella ($$$) Via Cocumella 7 (tel: 081/878 2933). Amid the orange groves of Sant' Agnello suburb, this ex-monastery is now a fine welcoming hotel

Eden ($$) Via Correale 25 (tel: 081/878 1909). Central but reasonably quiet; pleasant rooms (some at budget price).

Excelsior Vittoria ($$$) Piazza Tasso 34 (tel: 081/807 1044). Sorrento's best-known hotel, a cliff-top landmark; faded grandeur but comfortable.

THE DEEP SOUTH
Alberobello

Astoria ($) Viale Bari 11 (tel: 080/721 190). Functional hotel near the station; restaurant serves local dishes.

Dei Trulli ($$$) Via Cadore 28 (tel: 080/932 3555). Trulli-style rooms in a wooded setting.

Bari

Boston ($$) Via Piccinni 155 (tel: 080/521 6633). Medium-sized modern hotel on the edge of the Old Town; a few rooms have balconies.

Sheraton Nicolaus ($$$) Via Rosalba 27 (tel: 080/504 2626). Large chain hotel with the usual Sheraton facilities for business clientele.

Castel del Monte

Federico ($) Castel del Monte (tel: 0883/83 043). Six passable rooms and busy restaurant-pizzeria with panoramic terrace.

Gargano

Al Castello ($) Via Castello 29, Peschici (tel: 0884/964 038). Hotel with noted restaurant.

Pizzomunno ($$$) Lungomare Enrico Mattei, Vieste (tel: 0884/708 741). Most upscale beach and park resort complex on the Gargano; numerous facilities.

Rotary ($) Via per Pulsano, Monte Sant'Angelo (tel: 0884/62 146). Simple and modern hotel with views; just out of town.

Valle Clavia ($$) Valle Clavia, Peschici (tel: 0884/964 012). Stolid modern hotel near beach in pinewoods.

Lecce

Cappello ($) Via Montenegrappa 4 (tel: 0832/28 881). Near the station.

President ($$$) Via Salandra 6 (tel: 0832/311 881). Sleek, modern spot in the new business part of town.

Risorgimento ($$) Via Augusto Imperatore 19 (tel: 0832/42 125). Large *palazzo* in the baroque old town; old-fashioned charm.

Matera

Roma ($) Via Roma 62 (tel: 0835/333 912). Clean and central—but like all Matera's hotels it fills up quickly.

Trani

Lucy ($$) Piazza Plebiscito 11 (tel: 0883/41 022). Small and friendly place; airy rooms with balconies; near the seafront and public gardens.

Trani ($) Corso Imbriani 137 (tel: 0883/588 010). Reliable, modern hotel near the station.

SICILY
Agrigento

Bella Napoli ($) Piazza Lana 6, off Via Bac Bac (tel: 0922/20 435). Roof terrace overlooking the valley.

Jolly dei Templi ($$) Parco Angeli, Villagio Mose (tel: 0922/606 144). Reliable hotel in the *Jolly* chain, 5 miles southeast of the town.

Villa Athena ($$$) Via dei Templi 33 (tel: 0922/596 288). Only hotel near the temples, so busy as a result; reserve ahead.

Cefalù

Cangelosi ($) Via Umberto I 28 (tel: 0921/21 591). Cheap, central choice.

Kalura ($$$) Contrada Caldura (tel: 0921/21 354). Beautifully set hotel with private beach and panoramic terraces.

Villa Belvedere ($$) Via Mulini (tel: 0921/21 593).

HOTELS AND RESTAURANTS

Hotel with antique appeal and quiet palm-tree garden.

Enna
Grande Albergo Sicilia ($) Piazza N Colajanni 5, off via Roma (tel: 0935/500 850). Friendly, reliable and central.

Erice
Elimo ($$) Via V. Emanuele 75 (tel: 0923/869 377). Comfortable hotel in medieval town house.

Noto
Stella ($) Via F Maiore 44, corner of Via Napoli (tel: 0931/835 695). Noto's only hotel.

Palermo
Grande Albergo e delle Palme ($$$) Via Roma 396 (tel: 091/583 933). Famous and faded, but still the best hotel in central Palermo; rooms vary greatly in quality.
Orientale ($) Via Maqueda 26 (tel: 091/616 5727). Located in atmospheric 17th-century *palazzo*.
Pensione Sud ($) Via Maqueda 8 (tel: 091/617 5700). Handy for the station.
Sole ($$) Corso Vittorio Emanuele 291 (tel: 091/581 811). Best of the mid-range central hotels, though some rooms potentially noisy.
Villa Igiea ($$$) Via Belmonte 43 (tel: 091/543 744). At Acquasanta 2 miles from the center; lovely art-nouveau building and grounds; the city's most luxurious and comfortable hotel:

Piazza Armerina
Hotel Park Paradiso ($$) (tel: 0935/680 841). Located ½ mile north of the church of Sant'Andrea.

Siracusa (Syracuse)
Gran Bretagna ($) Via Savoia 21 (tel: 0931/68 765). Easily the best Ortigia choice and often full as a result. A cheap and reliable restaurant lurks downstairs.
Jolly Hotel ($$$) Corso Gelone 45 (tel: 0931/461 111). Reliable big-chain hotel close to the station and archeological zone.
Motel Agip ($$$) Viale Teracati 30 (tel: 0931/463

232). Usual motel facilities and decent restaurant. Convenient for the archeological zone.

Taormina
Jolly Diodoro ($$$) Via Bagnoli Croce 75 (tel: 0942/23 312). Chain hotel with a fine situation close to the Greek amphitheater above the town. Pleasant garden and great views.
Palazzo Vecchio ($$) Salita Ciampoli 9 (tel: 0942/23 033). Elegant and central.
San Domenico Palace ($$$) Piazza San Domenico 5 (tel: 0942/23 701). First choice for views, atmosphere and luxury; very expensive.
Svizzera ($) Via Pirandello 26 (tel: 0942/23 790). Excellent and popular choice; lovely building; clean rooms and sea views.
Villa Fiorita ($$) Via Pirandello 39 (tel: 0942/24 122). Swimming pool and small garden; rooms with fine views of the coast.

SARDINIA
Alghero
San Francesco ($) Via Machin 2 (tel: 079/979 258). At the center of the old town; quiet and clean rooms; reserve ahead.
Tarragona ($$) Via Gallura (tel: 079/952 270). Near the port.
Villa Las Tronas ($$$) Lungomare Valencia (tel: 079/981 818). Top hotel; characterful villa above the sea (with beaches) just east of the town center.

Cagliari
Firenze ($) Corso Vittorio Emanuele 50 (tel: 070/653 678). Five popular rooms, so reserve well in advance.
La Perla ($) Via Sardegna 18 (tel: 070/669 446). One of many budget options on this street.
Regina Margherita ($$$) Viale Regina Margherita 44 (tel: 070/670 342). The city's top hotel:

Costa Smeralda
Balocco ($$$) Liscia di Vacca, Porto Cervo (tel: 0789/91 555). A touch cheaper than

most hotels in Porto Cervo.
Pitrizza ($$$) Porto Cervo (tel: 0789/91 500; closed October–May). An extremely exclusive hotel:

Nuoro
Su Gologone ($$) Su Gologone, Oliena (tel: 0784/287 512). About 5 miles from Oliena village; handsome hotel, well-known and widely advertised restaurant.

Oristano
Cama ($) Via V Veneto 119 (tel: 0783/74 374). Convenient for the station and the old town; parking and air-conditioning.
Mistral ($$) Via Martiri di Belfiore (tel: 0783/212 505). Edge of town hotel with new annex in the town center.

RESTAURANTS

Note Always try to book a table at expensive ($$$) restaurants (and preferably in moderate ($$) ones as well). Few restaurants have a dress code, but a jacket (and sometimes a tie) is in order at most expensive places.

ROME
The telephone code for Rome is 06.

Al Leoncino ($) Via del Leoncino 28. Superb pizzeria one block off Via del Corso; wood oven and interior unchanged for 30 years.
Al Moro ($$$) Vicolo delle Bollette 13 (tel: 678 3495). Brusque and crowded, but some of the city's best food.
Al Piccolo Arancio ($$) Via Scanderburg 112 (tel: 678 6139). One of three fine and innovative restaurants under same management.
Baffetto ($) Via Governo Vecchio 114. Legendary pizzeria near Piazza Navona; lines common; amiable atmosphere.
Birreria Tempera ($) Via San Marcello 19. Great old beer hall behind Piazza Venezia; perfect for lunch and light snacks.

Checchino dal 1887 ($$$) Via di Monte Testaccio 30 (tel: 574 6318). Long renowned as the place to sample classic Roman dishes—tripe, brains and other rarely eaten parts; among Rome's best wine lists.

Da Giggetto ($$) Via Portico d'Ottavia 21. Famous Jewish-Roman cuisine in old-fashioned setting.

Da Nerone ($$) Via delle Terme di Tito 96 (tel: 474 5207). Best eating near the Colosseum; excellent buffet *antipasti* and homemade Tuscan wine.

El Toulà ($$$) Via della Lupa 29b (tel: 687 3498). High prices, swanky, and often rated Rome's best; plenty of famous faces.

Grappola d'Oro ($$) Piazza della Cancelleria 80. Little-known place near Campo dei Fiori; perhaps the archetypal old Roman *trattoria*.

Ivo's ($) Via di San Francesco a Ripa 157. Quintessential Roman pizzeria; fast turnover; arrive early to avoid the lines.

La Fraschetta ($) Via di San Francesco a Ripa 134. A few doors from Ivo's and quieter but almost as good; excellent desserts.

L'Eau Vive ($$$) Via Monterone 85 (tel: 654 1095 or 6880 1095). An institution, mainly because food is served by nuns; good place to go cardinal spotting; cheaper lunch menu.

Mario ($$) Via della Vite 55 (tel: 678 3818). Good value Tuscan food; 30-year old institution; invariably busy, so make a reservation.

Pierluigi ($$) Piazza de' Ricci/Via Monserrato (tel: 686 8717). Old Roman favorite; popular with locals, tourists, film stars, and expatriates alike; loud and busy, especially Sunday lunch.

THE NORTHWEST
Aosta
Cavallo Bianco ($$$) Via Aubert 15 (tel: 0165/362 214). Widely considered the best restaurant in the region; old 16th-century post house setting; elegant and extremely expensive.

La Brasserie du Commerce ($) Via de Tillier 10 (tel: 0165/ 35 613). Centrally located, small and friendly. The vegetables are especially good.

Vecchia Aosta ($$) Via Porta Pretoriane 4 (tel: 0165/361 186). Elegant and atmospheric place with local cuisine and good wines.

Asti
Falcone Vecchio ($$) Vicolo San Secondo 8 (tel: 0141/53 106). Old, intimate surroundings; large menu of local dishes.

Gener Neuv ($$$) Lungo Tanaro 4 (tel: 0141/57 270). Among Italy's top restaurants; very good but very expensive.

Genova (Genoa)
Enoteca Sola ($$) Corso Barabino 120r (tel: 010/594 513). A small, old-fashioned restaurant with light, Ligurian cooking.

Gran Gotto ($$$) Via Fiume 11r, near Piazza della Vittoria (tel: 010/564 344). Small and smart and with good food, this is one of the city's classic spots.

Sa Pesta ($) Via Giustiniani 16r, near Piazza Matteotti. For lunch only.

Riviera di Levante
Manuelina ($$) Via Roma 300, Recco (tel: 0185/74 128). One of the Riviera's more celebrated spots.

Savoia ($) Piazza IV Novembre 3, Rapallo (tel: 0185/247 021). Handy pizza place.

Terrazza Bellini ($$) Via XX Settembre 62 (tel: 0185/770 737). Not scenic, but good food.

Riviera di Ponente
Bagatto ($$) Via Matteotti 145, San Remo (tel: 0184/531 925). In the town center; serves national and regional dishes. Good local wines.

Degli Amici ($$) Via Lunga 2, Bordighera. Reasonably-priced seafood in the old town.

La Reserve Tastevin ($$$) Via Arziglia 20, Capo Sant'Ampelio, Bordighera (tel: 0184/261 322). Excellent views and seafood.

Torino (Turin)
Brek ($) Piazza Carlo Felice 18. Sleek self-service.

Da Giuseppe ($$) Via San Massimo 34 (tel: 011/812 2090). Piedmontese specialties served; popular with locals.

Vecchia Lanterna ($$$) Corso Re Umberto 21 (tel: 011/537 047). One of Italy's top five restaurants; very expensive.

LOMBARDY AND EMILIA-ROMAGNA

Bergamo
Da Vittorio ($$$) Via Giovanni XXIII 21 (tel: 035/ 218 060). One of Italy's top restaurants. Reasonably priced lunch menu. Excellent pastries.

Taverna del Colleoni ($$$) Piazza Vecchia (tel: 035/ 232 596). Handsome place in the heart of the old town.

279

Bologna
Antica Brunetti ($$) Via Caduti di Cefalonia 5 (tel: 051/234 441). Busy restaurant-pizzeria near Piazza Maggiore.

Bertino ($) Via delle Lame 55 (tel: 051/522 230). Cheap, popular neighborhood *trattoria*.

Da Cesari ($$) Via de Carbonesi 8 (tel: 051/237 710). Interesting dishes at a reasonable price.

Tre Frecce ($$$) Strada Maggiore 19 (tel: 051/231 200). Mouthwatering cooking served in a medieval *palazzo* setting.

Como, Lago di
La Pergola ($$) Pescallo (tel: 031/950 263). Enjoy freshly caught fish beside the lake, near Bellagio.

La Scuderia ($) Piazza Matteotti 4, Como. Lively pizzeria.

Sant'Anna ($$$) Via F Turati 3, Como (tel: 031/505 266). Family-run, rather sleek, business-oriented spot.

Ferrara
Da Noemi ($) Via Ragno 31a, off Corso Porta Reno. Simple, family-run place in business over 30 years.

HOTELS AND RESTAURANTS

La Provvidenza ($$$) Corso Ercole d'Este 92 (tel: 0532/21 937). Worthy and well known, so reservations advisable.

Garda, Lago di
Del Pescatore ($$) Via Piana 20, Sirmione (tel: 030/916 216). Reservations necessary for this noted fish restaurant.

Lago Maggiore
Del Pappagallo ($) Via Principessa Margherita 40, Stresa. Pasta and pizzas from wood-burning ovens.
L'Emiliano ($$$) Corso Italia 50 (tel: 0323/31 396). A discreet, elegant and high-quality restaurant.

Mantova (Mantua)
Dei Martini ($$) Piazza dell' Arco 1 (tel: 0376/372 101). A lovely restaurant with many local specialties.
L'Aquila Nigra ($$) Vicolo Bonacolsi 4, near Palazzo Ducale (tel: 0376/350 651). Lovely frescoed dining room; Mantuan specialties; reservations required.

Milano (Milan)
Boeucc ($$$) Piazza Belgioioso 2 (tel: 02/7602 0224). Venerable Milanese dining spot near La Scala, with luxurious decor and varied menu.
Grande Italia ($) Via Palermo 5. Lively central spot for pasta and pizzas.
La Giara ($) Viale Monza 10. Pugliese cooking at rustic wooden benches.
La Libera ($$) Via Palermo 21 (tel: 02/805 3603). Trendy spot in Brera district; draught beer, jazz, and delicious food.

Parma
Corrieri ($) Via Conservatorio 1. Popular with locals.
Enoteca Fontana di Parma ($) Via Farini 22a. Excellent selection of wines and light meals.
La Greppia ($$$) Via Garibaldi 39a (tel: 0521/233 686). Parma's best and smartest restaurant.

Ravenna
La Gardela ($) Via Ponte Marino 3. Fine, homely *trattoria* two minutes from Piazza del Popolo.

Tre Spade ($$$) Via Faentinci 136 (tel: 0544/500 522). Converted mill near the Duomo serving immaculate and inventive food.

VENICE
The telephone code for Venice is 041.

Agli Alboretti ($$) Rio Terrà Sant' Agnese, Dorsoduro 882 (tel: 523 0058). Pleasant, slightly upmarket place near the Accademia.
Ai Cugnai ($) Calle Nuova Sant'Agnese 857 (tel: 528 9238). A tavern, handy for the Accademia. A group of local women serve Venetian specialties.
Ai Promessi Sposi ($) Calle dell'Oca, Castello 4367. Sea-food dishes and lively bar.
Al Mascaron ($) Calle Lunga S M Formosa. Informal and often busy with Venetians.
Antico Martini ($$$) Campo San Fantin 1983 (tel: 522 4121). A Venetian institution; prices far from old-fashioned.
Da Fiore ($$) Calle dello Scaleter, San Polo 2202 (tel: 721 308). Local favorite now discovered by tourists, so book ahead.
Da Silvio ($) Calle San Pantalon, San Polo 429. Best of the options locally; garden dining in summer.
Fiaschetteria Toscana ($$$) Campo San Giovanni Crisostomo, Cannaregio 5719 (tel: 528 5281). Friendly atmosphere, setting and food make this a popular choice with locals.
Gazebo ($$) Rio Terra San Leonardo 1333a-Strada Nuova (tel: 716 380). Above average place near station; *al fresco* eating possibilities.
Madonna ($$) Calle della Madonna, San Polo 594. Large and busy fish restaurant.
Montin ($$) Fondamenta di Borgo, Dorsoduro 1147 (tel: 522 7151). Favored haunt of Pound, Hemingway, Visconti *et al*; erratic cooking, slightly overpriced, but still popular with locals and visitors alike.
San Bartolomeo ($) Calle della Bissa, San Marco 5424a. Good selection of self-service snacks.

THE NORTHEAST
Bolzano-Bozen
Cavallino Bianco-Weisses Rössel ($) Via dei Bottai 6. Popular, central and authentic *bierkeller* with up to 100 Italian and Tyrolean dishes daily.
Kaiserkron ($$) Piazza della Mostra 1 (tel: 0471/970 770). Reliable choice in the town center.

Padova (Padua)
Dotto Via Soncin 9. Reliable old-world place in the city center.
El Toulà ($$$) Via Belle Parti 11 (tel: 049/875 1822). Part of a top-ranking chain; suave and sophisticated.

Trento
Alla Mora ($$) Via Roggia Grande 8 (tel: 0461/984 675). Dine *al fresco* in the court-yard of this delightful restaurant; good, varied menu.
Chiesa ($$) Via San Marco 64 (tel: 0461/238 766). Medieval setting and dishes from medieval recipes.

Treviso
Beccherie ($$) Piazza Ancillotto 10 (tel: 0422/540 871). Lovely rustic inn in the old town.

Trieste
Antica Suban ($$) Via Emilio Comici 2 (tel: 040/54 368). On the edge of town; many good local dishes.

Verona
Dodici Apostoli ($$$) Corticella San Marco 3 (tel: 045/596 999). One of Verona's top restaurants; medieval setting.
Il Desco ($$$) Via dietro San Sebastiano 7 (tel: 045/593 358). Vies with Dodici Apostoli for the role of the city's best restaurant.
La Greppia ($$) Vicolo Samaritana 3 (tel: 045/800 4577). Good local dishes are offered here, in old-fashioned surroundings.

Vicenza
Da Remo ($$) Via Ca'Impenta 14 (tel: 0444/911 007). One of the best places to eat around here. Venetian dishes are served in a charming villa 1 mile from Vicenza.

Scudo di Francia ($$) Contrà Piancoli 4 (tel: 0444/323 322). Simply decorated central place with local specialties.

FLORENCE
The telephone code for Florence is 055.

Alle Murate ($) Via Ghibellina 52r (tel: 240 618). Increasingly popular, but still reasonably priced. Light, innovative cuisine.

Al Lume di Candela ($$$) Via delle Terme 23r (tel: 294 566). *The* place for a romantic meal (the name means "by candlelight"); small and elegant and housed in a medieval tower.

Angiolino ($$) Via Santo Spirito 36r (tel: 239 8976). Busy with locals and tourists, with wood-burning stove and charcoal grill, but cooking occasionally erratic.

Da Mario ($) Via Rosina 2r, Piazza del Mercato. Low prices, friendly atmosphere, shared tables with students and market traders; family run and traditional no-frills food.

Enoteca Pinchiorri ($$$) Via Ghibellina 87 (tel: 242 777). Often called Italy's best restaurant, though perhaps over-formal; 80,000 bottles of best French and Italian wine. Reservations required.

Il Cibrèo ($$) Via de' Macci 118r (tel: 234 1100). Sometimes over-adventurous Tuscan specialties and Italian standards with a hint of *nouvelle cuisine*; great desserts and good wine list.

Il Contadino ($) Via Palazzuolo 69r. Basic meals and backpackers' favorite.

La Capannina di Sante ($$$) Piazza Ravenna (tel: 688 345). Casual and simple place; city's best fish restaurant.

Latini ($) Via Palchetti 6r (tel: 210 916). Bustling and always busy (lines likely after 8p.m.); shared tables and deliberate quasi-rustic atmosphere.

Le Fonticine ($$) Via Nazionale 79r (tel: 282 106). Highly-rated restaurant combining Tuscan and Emilia-Romagnan dishes.

Zà-Zà ($) Piazza del Mercato 26r (tel: 215 411). Communal tables, poster-hung wood-paneled walls (canteen below) and robust no-nonsense cooking.

TUSCANY
Arezzo
Buca di San Francesco ($$) Piazza San Francesco I. Tourist filled, but offers reliable food.

Spiedo d'Oro ($) Via Crispi 12 (tel: 0575/22 873). Hearty Tuscan home cooking in this cheerful *trattoria* close to the Archeological Museum.

Cortona
La Loggetta ($$) Piazza Peschiera 3. Lovely medieval dining room, fine food and well-chosen wines.

Lucca
Buca di Sant'Antonio ($$) Via della Cervia 3 (tel: 0583/55 881). This former inn is now considered Lucca's finest restaurant. Some unusual dishes are on offer.

Da Giulio ($) Via del Tommaso 29, near Palazzo Mansi (tel: 0583/55 948). Packed and popular so reserve or arrive early.

Solferino ($$$) San Macario in Piano, 3½ miles from Lucca on Viareggio road (tel: 0583/ 59 118). Place of Tuscan-wide renown run by same family for four generations.

Montalcino
Taverna dei Barbi ($$) Fattoria dei Barbi, 4 miles southeast of Montalcino near La Croce (tel: 0577/848 277/849 357). Wonderful restaurant and vineyard.

Pisa
Da Bruno ($$) Via Luigi Bianchi 12 (tel: 050/560 818). Traditional Tuscan cooking, near the old town.

Sergio ($$$) Lungarno Pacinotti 1 (tel: 050/48 245). Smart riverside restaurant in an ancient palace. The owner cooks both well and imaginatively.

Stelio ($) Piazza Dante 11. Popular studenty pizza and pasta joint.

San Gimignano
Bel Soggiorno ($$) Via San Giovanni 91 (0577/940 375). You can enjoy local dishes and splendid views here on the top floor of a 19th-century inn.

Le Terrazze ($$) Hotel La Cisterna, Piazza della Cisterna 23 (0577/940 328). You dine overlooking the town and surrounding country in this well-known restaurant. Tuscan dishes dominate the menu.

Siena
Al Marsili ($$) Via del Castoro 3 (tel: 0577/47 154). Siena's best, so reservations are essential.

La Torre ($) Via Salicotto 7. Friendly, tiny *trattoria* just off the Campo, so arrive early to be sure of a table.

Le Logge ($$) Via del Porrione 33 (tel: 0577/48 013). Pretty and popular spot offering Tuscan specialties; reserve a table.

Volterra
Etruria ($$) Piazza dei Priori 6 (tel: 0588/86 064). No need to book at this place in the heart of town, but the local dishes are good.

UMBRIA AND THE MARCHES
Assisi
Fortezza ($$) Vicolo della Fortezza (tel: 075/812 418). Good, unpretentious food and setting.

Il Medio Evo ($$$) Via dell'Arco dei Priori (tel: 075/813 068). Beautiful medieval dining rooms and some of Umbria's best food.

Palotta ($) Via San Rufino 4. Arrive early to be sure of a table (12:30 for lunch) in this popular restaurant.

Gubbio
Fornace di Maestro Giorgio ($$) Via Maestro Giorgio 2. Located in workshop of a medieval master potter; table d'hôte menus and Umbrian dishes.

Taverna del Lupo ($$) Via Ansidei 21a. Large, busy medieval dining hall.

Montefalco
Il Coccorone ($) Via Fabbri-

Largo Tempestivi. One of Umbria's finest restaurants.

Norcia
Grotta Azzurra ($$) Via Alfieri 12. A temple to Umbrian cuisine, with noted truffle dishes and medieval dining rooms.

Orvieto
Grotta ($) Via Signorelli 15. Friendly, simple and good value *trattoria*.
Maurizio ($$) Via del Duomo 78 (tel: 0763/41 114). Self-consciously modern decor, and often touristy, but good food in central location.

Perugia
Café del Cambio ($) Corso Vannucci 29. Good for quick, cheap lunches.
Falchetto ($$) Via Bartolo 20. Sound choice just behind the Duomo; two small dining rooms and good food.
Osteria del Bartolo ($$$) Via Bartolo 30 (tel: 075/61 461). Elegant setting and occasionally exotic food.

Spello
La Cantina ($) Via Cavour 2. Excellent local specialties in pleasant medieval setting.

Spoleto
Pentagramma ($$) Via Tommaso Martini 4, off Piazza Libertà (tel: 0743/37 233). Specializes in rustic Umbrian dishes.
Sabatini ($$) Corso Mazzini 54. Clever interior and fine, innovative cooking.

Todi
Umbria ($$) Via S Bonaventura 13, off Piazza del Popolo (tel: 075/894 737). Superb outside terrace.

Urbino
Vecchia Urbino ($$) Via dei Vasari 3 (tel: 0722/4447). The best place for a treat in Urbino.

LAZIO & ABRUZZO
L'Aquila
San Biagio ($) Piazza San Biagio 1 (tel: 0862/22 139). Perhaps the most popular bet with the locals for a night out.

Tre Marie ($$) Via Tre Marie 3 (tel: 0862/410 109). The spot to come to sample classic Abruzzese food and wines; 17th-century setting and cozy atmosphere. Reserve.

Bolsena
Da Picchietto ($$) Via Porta Fiorentina 15, Bolsena (tel: 0761/799 158). Homemade pasta and lake specialties like grilled eels.

Palestrina
Coccia ($$) Albergo Coccia, Piazzale Liberazione (tel: 06/953 8172). Central, busy hotel dining room with views over town gardens.

Sulmona
Cesedio ($) Piazza Solimo 25. Family-run place near Corso Ovidio and local favorite.
Italia ($) Piazza XX Settembre. Inventive additions to traditional Abruzzese fare.

Tarquinia
Corneto ($) Via Garibaldi 12-Via Cavallotti. Not much to look at, but generous portions of pizza and pasta.

Tivoli
Cinque Statue ($$) Via Quintilio Varo 1-Largo S Angelo (tel: 0774/20 366). At the entrance to the Villa Gregoriana; veranda for *al fresco* eating.
Del Falcone ($) Via Trevio 34 (tel: 0774/22 358). Central and well-patronized rustic-look restaurant; try to reserve ahead.

Viterbo
Porta Romana ($) Via della Bontà. Local favorite.
Richiastro ($) Via della Marrocca 16. Pretty garden restaurant on cobbled street.

CAMPANIA
Amalfi
Da Bararacca ($$) Piazza Ferrari. The town's oldest restaurant; fish specialties.
Il Tari ($) Via P Capuano 9. Small and modest; good for snacks and sandwiches.
La Caravella ($$) Via M Camera 12 (tel: 089/871 029). Unpromising entrance hides

intimate interior; choice of mainly fish dishes.

Capri
Da Gemma ($$) Via Madre Serafina (tel: 081/837 0461). One of Capri's longest-established restaurants.
Il Solitario ($$) Via G. Orlandi 54, Anacapri (tel: 081/837 1382). Intimate spot with garden. Booking essential.
La Capannina ($$$) Via delle Botteghe 14, Capri Town (tel: 081/837 0732). Widely considered the island's top restaurant.
La Pigna ($$$) Via Roma 30, Capri Town (tel: 081/837 0280). Veranda and *al fresco* dining in one of Capri's favorite restaurants.

Ischia
Giardini Eden ($$) Ischia Ponte, Via Nuova Cartaromana (tel: 081/993 909). The island's top restaurant.

Napoli (Naples)
Avellinese da Peppino ($) Via Silvio Spaventa 31–5. Great favorite with tourists and locals near Piazza Garibaldi; welcoming and excellent food.
Bellini ($) Via Santa Maria di Constantinopli 80, corner of Via San Pietro (tel: 081/459 774). One of the most famous and popular restaurants with Neapolitans; somewhat slow service but great pizzas and other dishes.
Bersagliera ($$) Borgo Marinaro 10 (tel: 081/415 692). On the waterfront and touristy as a result, but still fun for a first night—and the food is good.
Ciro a Santa Brigada ($$) Via Santa Brigada 71, off Via Toledo (tel: 081/324 072). Pizza and fish specialties; favored by artists, journalists and the like.

Positano
Buca di Bacco ($$) Via Rampa Teglia 8 (tel: 089/875 699). Above the town's most fashionable café; terrace dining overlooking the beach. Reservations required in the evening.
O'Capurale ($$) Via Marina (tel: 089/875 374). Reserve

ahead for outdoor tables in the cheapest and best of the many restaurants on and near Positano's waterfront.

Ravello
Cumpa Cosimo ($) Via Roma 44 (tel: 089/857 156). Friendly and pleasant good-sized restaurant, popular with tourists. The food is good.
Villa Maria ($) Via di Santa Chiara. Romantic place with garden overlooking the sea.

Sorrento
Parrucchiano ($$) Corso Italia 71 (tel: 081/878 1321). One of the town's oldest, best and most popular restaurants; beautiful setting and tempting local dishes; reservations advised.
Sant'Antonino ($) Via Santa Maria delle Grazie 6. Popular with locals and visitors; low prices and flower-filled patio.

THE DEEP SOUTH
Alberobello
Pugliese ($) Via Gigante 4 (tel: 080/721 437). Simple, cozy restaurant where you can eat interesting local dishes *al fresco*.
Trullo d'Oro ($$) Via F. Cavallotti 29 (tel: 080/771 820). Rustic and atmospheric restaurant arranged in five *trulli*.

Bari
La Pignata ($$) Corso Vittorio Emanuele 173 (tel: 080/523 2481). The best of Bari's many fine restaurants.
Taverna Verde ($) Largo Adua 18/19, end of Corso Cavour (tel: 080/540 309). On the waterfront; extremely popular with locals; reserve in advance.

Lecce
Barbablu' ($) Via Umberto I 7. Local favorite.

Matera
Il Terrazzino ($) Bocconcino Due-Vico S Giuseppe 7. In an old *sasso* dug into the rock; outdoor terrace looks over other *sassi*; excellent pizzas and local dishes.
Lucana ($) Via Lucana 48, off Via Roma (tel: 0835/216 779). Best restaurant in town.

Trani
La Antica Cattedrale ($$) Piazza Archivio 2 (tel: 0883/586 568). Lovely old dining room; also tables outside; reserve on summer weekends.

SICILY
Agrigento
Black Horse ($) Via Celauro 8. Oddly decorated family-run *trattoria*.
Caprice ($$) Via Panoramica dei Templi 51 (tel: 0922/26 469). Popular place near the temples.
Vigneto ($$) Via Cavaleri Magazzeni 11 (tel: 0922/414 319). Reserve or arrive early to get a table on the terrace with views of the temples.

Cefalù
Al Bastione ($) Cortele Pepe, off Corso Umberto I. Fine seafood with indoor or *al fresco* eating.
Arkade Grill ($) Via Vanni 9. Excellent Tunisian cooking plus a few Italian dishes.

Erice
Monte San Giuliano ($) Via San Rocco 7 (tel: 0923/869 595). Arab cuisine influences some of the dishes served in this popular friendly place. Reserve a table.

Noto
Trieste ($) Via Napoli 17. Busy and excellent-value restaurant on the edge of the Giardino Pubblico.

Palermo
Antica Focacceria San Francesco ($) Via Paternostro 58. Marvelous turn-of-the-century institution with authentic Sicilian specialties.
Charleston ($$$) Piazza Ungheria 30 (tel; 091/321 366) or, 16 June to 25 September, Viale Regina Elena, Mondello (tel: 091/450 171). The best in the city. Moves 5 miles out of town during high season.
Lo Scudiero ($$) Via del Fante 9 (tel: 091/501 485). Relaxed atmosphere and Palermitan specialties.
Shanghai ($) Vicolo de Mezzani 34, overlooking Piazza Caracciolo. Not Chinese, despite the name, but wonderfully atmospheric place in the midst of the Vucciria market.

Siracusa (Syracuse)
Archimede ($$) Via Gemmellaro 8 (tel: 0931/69 701). Small, tasteful and popular Ortigia spot with good game and seafood.
Do Scugghiu ($) Via Scina 11, off Piazza Archimede. Local institution with huge choice of pasta dishes.
La Foglia ($$) Via Capodieci 39-41 (tel: 0931/461 569). Trendy vegetarian restaurant.

Taormina
La Griglia ($$) Corso Umberto 54 (tel: 0942/23 980). Probably the best of the many restaurants on Corso Umberto.
Pace ($) Piazza San Pancrazio 3. Bustling pizza and pasta place with outdoor tables.

SARDINIA
Alghero
Da Pietro ($) Via A Machin 20 (tel: 079/979 645). Busy vaulted restaurant in the old town; excellent seafood.
La Lepanto ($$) Via Carlo Alberto 135 (tel: 079/979 116). One of the island's leading seafood spots.

Cagliari
Antica Osteria ($$) Via Cavour 60 (tel: 070/665 870). Rivals Dal Corsaro as the city's best restaurant, but prices here are a little lower.
Da Serafino ($) Via Sardegna 109. Good value and popular with locals.
Dal Corsaro ($$$) Viale Regina Margherita 28 (tel: 070/664 318). One of Sardinia's best-known restaurants—so reservations are essential.

Oristano
Il Faro ($$$) Via Bellini 25 (tel: 0783/70 002). Recognized as one of the area's top seafood restaurants.
Tirso ($–$$) Via Tirso 6 (tel: 0783/72 506). Old restaurant in the historic center.

Index

a

Abruzzo *see* Lazio and Abruzzo
Abruzzo, Parco Nazionale d' 183, 194–5, 276
  accommodation 272–8
Agrigento 230
  accommodation 277
  eating out 283
  Museo Nazionale Archeologico 230
  Valle dei Templi 230
air travel 258, 260
Alassio 64, 72
Alatri 184
Alba 65
Albano Laziale 185
Albenga 72
Albergo-Rifugio Campo Imperatore 188
Alberobello 223, 277, 283
Alghero 247, 278, 283
Amalfi 199, 276
Amantea 222
Anagni 184
Ancona 166–7
Angelico, Fra 142
Angera 87
Anghelu Ruiu 249
Anticoli Corrado 191
Aeolian Islands 234
Aosta 64, 65, 76, 272, 279
Aosta, Valle d' 64, 76
Apulia 214, 218
Aquileia 118
Arezzo 150, 152, 275, 281
Argentera, Parco Naturale dell' 70
Armenzano 172
art and architecture
  baroque 36–7
  Byzantine 31
  classical 30
  18th, 19th and 20th centuries 38
  Gothic 32
  pre-Renaissance 33
  Renaissance 34–5
  Romanesque 32, 218
Ascoli Piceno 167
Asolo 116, 118, 274
Aspromonte 222
Assisi 165, 168, 179
  accommodation 275
  Basilica di San Francesco 168
  Duomo 168
  eating out 281
  Museo-Tesoro della Basilica 168
  Oratorio dei Pellegrini 168
  Piazza del Comune 168
  San Damiano 168
  San Pietro 168
Asti 65, 272, 279
Avigliana 77
Avise 76
Ayas, Val d' 64, 77

b

Badia, Val 123
Bagnaia 193
Bagni di Lucca 154
Bagno Vignoni 155

Baldo, Monte 85, 86
bandits 256
Bard 76
Barga 154
Bari 215, 277, 283
Barletta 215
Barrea 194
Basilicata 214
Bassano del Grappa 118
Baveno 87
Bella, Isola 87
Bellagio 83
Bellini family 98–9
Belluno 118
Benevento 199
Bergamo 82, 279
Bevagna 170, 172
bicycle and scooter rental 268
Bisentina 184
Bitonto 215
Blanc, Mont 76
Bologna 81, 82
  accommodation 273
  Archiginnasio 82
  eating out 279
  Pinacoteca Nazionale 82
  San Domenico 82
  San Giacomo Maggiore 82
  San Petronio 82
Bolsena 184, 282
Bolsena, Lago di 184
Bolzano (Bozen) 119, 274, 280
Bomarzo 193
Bordighera 72
Borromee, Isole 87
Bregagno, Monte 86
Brescia 82
Brolio 153
Brusson 77
Buggerru 252
Buonconvento 155
bus and coach services 260, 268
Byron, Lord 69, 106

c

Cagliari 247, 278
Cala Gonone 248
Calabria 214
Camigliatello 224
Camogli 69
Campania 196–211
  accommodation 276–7
  cuisine 198
  eating out 282–3
  essential sights 198
  tourist information 199
Campi Flegrei 199
camping 258
Campo Imperatore 188
Canaletto 99
Cannero Riviera 87
Cannigione 250
Capo Testa 250
Capodimonte 184
Capraia 154
Caprarola 184–5
  Palazzo Farnese 184–5
Caprese Michelangelo 152
Capri 197–8, 204
  accommodation 276
  Anacapri 204
  eating out 282
  La Grotta Azzurra 204

Carezza, Lago di 121
Cariddi 225
Casamari, Abbazia di 188
Cascata del Varone 85
Cascia 178
Casentino 152
Caserta 204
Caserta Vecchia 204
Caso 178
Castagneto Carducci 157
Castel Gandolfo 185
Castel del Monte 215, 277
Castel Rigone 177
Castelli Romani 182, 185
Castello Rancolo 119
Castelluccio 178
Castelsardo 248, 251
Castiglione del Lago 177
Castiglione Olana 83
Castiglione della Pescaia 157
Catania 230
Catholic Church 12
Cefalù 232, 277–8, 283
Cernobbio 83
Certosa di Pavia 91
Certosa di Pisa 156
Certosa di Santo Stefano 224
Cerveteri 182, 186–7
Cervo 87
Champoluc 77
Chianti 153
Chiarone 183
chiese rupestri (cave churches) 221
children 258
Cilento 198, 210
cinema 18
Cinqueterre 64, 66, 71, 272
Circeo, Parco Nazionale del 185
Civetta, Monte 122
Cividale del Friuli 120
Civita 184
Civitella Alfedena 194
climate 258
Cogne 68
Cogne, Val di 64, 68
Collalbo 119
Collepino 172
Columbus, Christopher 67
Como 81, 83
Como, Lago di (Lake Como) 80, 83, 86, 273, 279
Conero, Monte 166–7
confetti 193
conversion chart 262
Cornaro, Caterina 118
Corniglia 66
Cortina d'Ampezzo 123
Cortona 150, 153, 281
Costa Smeralda 250, 278
Cremona 81, 84
crete 151, 155
crime 215, 258–9
Customs regulations 259

d

d'Annunzio, Gabriele 85
Deep South 212–25
  accommodation 277
  eating out 283
  essential sights 212
  social problems 16

tourist information 212
wines 214
Diamante 222
Diano Marina 72
disabled travelers 260
Dobbiaco 123
Dolomiti (Dolomites) 116, 120–3
Dolomiti Bellunesi 118
Dolomiti di Brenta 120, 123
Dolomiti di Sesto 123
domestic travel 260–1
Donizetti, Gaetano 82
Dorgali 248
driving
  accidents and breakdowns 261
  car rental 262
  documents 262
  gasoline 262
  parking 262
  regulations 262–3
  to Italy 258

e

Ega, Val d' 121
Egadi, Isole 232
Elba, Isola di 154
  Capoliveri 154
  Marciana 154
  Marina di Campo 154
  Poggio 154
  Portoferraio 154
electricity 263
embassies and consulates 263
emergency telephone numbers 263
Emilia-Romagna *see* Lombardy and Emilia-Romagna
Enna 232, 278
Eremo delle Carceri 172
Erice 232, 278, 283
etiquette 263
Etna 233
Etruscan tombs 163
Etruscan towns 186–7

f

Faenza 84
  Museo Internazionale delle Ceramiche 84
family, importance of 11
Fenis 76
Ferrara 84, 273, 279–80
Ferrari factory 91
ferry services 260
Finale Ligure 72
Florence (Firenze) 132–47
  accommodation 146, 275
  art galleries 140
  Bargello, Museo Nazionale del 140
  Battistero (Baptistery) 137
  Campanile 137
  Casa Buonarroti (Michelangelo Museum) 141
  churches 134, 137–9
  David 140
  Duomo 137
  eating out 147, 281
  essential sights 134

INDEX

INDEX

INDEX

Picture credits

The Automobile Association would like to thank the following for their assistance in the preparation of this book. J ALLAN CASH PHOTO LIBRARY 72 San Remo harbour, 77a St Bernard Tunnel, 119a Traditional houses, Bolzano, 119b Bassano del Grappa market, 124 Equestrian statue Padua, 126 Trieste. ASSOCIATED PRESS/TOPHAM 237a Funeral at Palermo. MARTIN BLACK/IMPACT PHOTOS 70 Walkers. BRIDGEMAN ART LIBRARY 26b *Napoleon crossing the Alps* by David, Jacques Louis (1748–1825) Schloss Charlottenburg, Berlin, 27b *General Garibaldi* by Barucco, F (fl 1864–6) Guildhall Art Gallery, Corporation of London, 30b Golden Etruscan bowl, 7th century BC by courtesy of the Board of Trustees of the V & A, 38b *The Melancholy of Departure* by Chirico, Giorgio de (1888–1978) Tate Gallery, London, 98b *The Tempest* by Giorgione, Giorgio (1476/8–1510) Galleria dell'Accademia, Venice, 99a *The Miracle of the Cross on San Lorenzo Bridge* by Bellini, Gentile (c 1429–1507) Galleria dell'Accademia, Venice, 136b *Venice: San Giorgio from the Dogana, Sunrise* by Turner, Joseph Mallord William (1775–1851) British Museum, London, 187 Etruscan vase showing boxers fighting c 500 BC British Museum, London, 207 Spring—maiden gathering flowers—wall painting from Stabiae (1st century AD) Archeological Museum, Naples. JAMES DAVIS 234 Messina. STEVE DAY 120, 121, 122b Dolomites. CHRIS DONAGHUE 131 San Giorgio Maggiore. E T ARCHIVE 76 Turin Shroud. MARY EVANS PICTURE LIBRARY 21a Punic Wars, 22b Assassination of Caesar, 24b Pope Gregory VII, 256b Bandits. RONALD GRANT ARCHIVE 18a *Città Aperta*, 18b *Ossessione*. HULTON DEUTSCH COLLECTION LTD 28a, 28b Mussolini, 29b Student riot. INTERNATIONAL PHOTOBANK Cover Amalfi Coast. T JEPSON 68 Parco Nazionale del Gran Paradiso. NATURE PHOTOGRAPHERS LTD 195a Grey wolf (E A Janes), 195b European brown bear (P R Sterry). REX FEATURES LTD 14b Coins, 15 Italian election. ROYAL GEOGRAPHICAL SOCIETY 25b Map. SPECTRUM COLOUR LIBRARY 67 Genoa Campanile, 74 Turin, 75a Replica of Turin Shroud, 75c Turin San Giovanni Cathedral, 122–3a Skiers Vigo di Fassa, 123 Skiers Dolomites, 127a Verona Aida, 162a,b Siena Palio, 200a,b Vesuvius, 204 Capri, 256a Sheep. THE GARDEN PICTURE LIBRARY 73a,b,c, Hanbury Gardens. THE MANSELL COLLECTION LTD 20b Phoenician merchant ships, 21b Julius Caesar, 23a Barbarians, 23b Charlemagne, 24a Henry IV, 99b Titian. TOPHAM PICTURE SOURCE 237b Coffin of policeman. ZEFA PICTURE LIBRARY (UK) LTD Spine Man in costume.

All remaining pictures are held in the Association's own library (AA PHOTO LIBRARY) with contributions from: ADRIAN BAKER 77b. PETE BENNETT 26a. JERRY EDMANSON 34a,b, 137, 141, 142, 144a, 145, 152. DARIO MITIDIERI 12b, 22c, 27a, 31b, 35, 36b, 37a,b, 39, 45a,b, 47, 48a, 52, 53, 58, 60, 61. ERIC MEACHER 13b. RICHARD NEWTON 98a, 101, 103, 104a, 106, 108. KEN PATERSON 11a,b, 16a, 30a,c, 33a,b, 135, 139, 140, 143a,b, 144b, 146, 147, 150, 151, 153, 154, 156, 157, 158, 159, 160, 161a,b, 163, 164–5, 168, 169a,b, 170, 171, 173, 174a,b, 175a, 176a,b, 177, 179b, 186a. CLIVE SAWYER 3, 4, 5a,b, 6–7a, 7b, 9, 10b, 14a, 16b,c, 17a,b, 19, 20a, 31a, 32c, 36a, 42, 46, 48b, 49b, 50a, 54, 56, 65, 70, 71, 76a,b, 80–a, 82, 83, 85, 87a,b, 88, 89, 90a,b, 96, 97, 100a,b, 104b, 105a,b, 107, 109, 110a,b, 111a,b, 112, 113, 117, 125, 127b, 128, 129, 130, 132, 134, 166, 167, 175b, 180, 184, 185, 188, 189a,b, 190, 192, 193, 194a,b, 196–7, 19, 201a,b, 202, 203, 209b, 210, 211, 215a,b, 216a,b, 217, 219a,b, 222, 223a,b, 224, 225b, 226, 228, 229, 230, 231, 232, 233, 235a,b, 236, 238, 239a,b, 240, 242a,b, 243, 245, 246, 247a,b, 248, 249a,b, 250, 251, 252, 253, 254a,b, 255, 260, 266, 270. BARRIE SMITH 25a, 29a, 33c, 132, 138, 268. ANTONY SOUTER 2, 13a, 21c, 32a,b, 55b, 66, 69, 84, 91, 92, 93a,b, 131a, 172, 178, 179a, 182a,b, 183, 186b, 187b, 191, 198, 205a,b, 207a,b, 208, 209a, 218a,b, 220, 221a,b, 225a, 271. PETER WILSON 10a, 12a, 22a, 37c, 43, 49a, 50b, 51, 55a, 57, 59.

Contributors

Designer: Design 23
Indexer: Marie Lorimer **Original Copy editor**: Audrey Horne
Revisions Editor: Brigitte Lee